Thank you for purchasing volume 30!
I once received a fan letter from a five-year-
old boy, and I keep it in a visible spot when I
work. I wonder if he's still reading the series?
Somewhere in a corner of my brain, I'm always
thinking, "Are five-year-old boys
enjoying my work?"

KOHEI HORIKOSHI

MY HERO ACADEMIA

30

SHONEN JUMP Manga Edition

STORY & ART KOHEI HORIKOSHI

TRANSLATION & ENGLISH ADAPTATION **Caleb Cook**
TOUCH-UP ART & LETTERING **John Hunt**
DESIGNER **Julian [JR] Robinson**
SHONEN JUMP SERIES EDITOR **John Bae**
GRAPHIC NOVEL EDITOR **Mike Montesa**

Printed in the U.S.A.

Published by VIZ Media, LLC
P.O. Box 77010
San Francisco, CA 94107

10 9 8 7 6 5 4 3 2 1
First printing, March 2022

MY HERO ACADEMIA vol.30

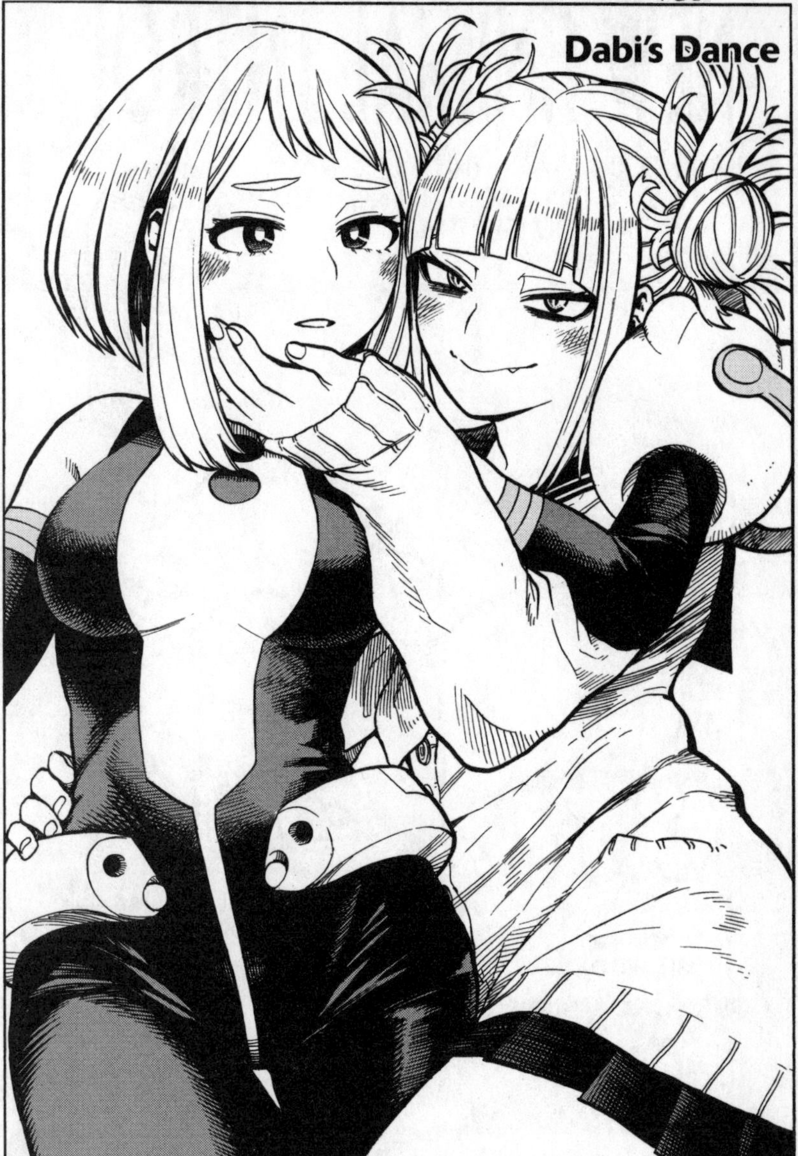

Dabi's Dance

KOHEI HORIKOSHI

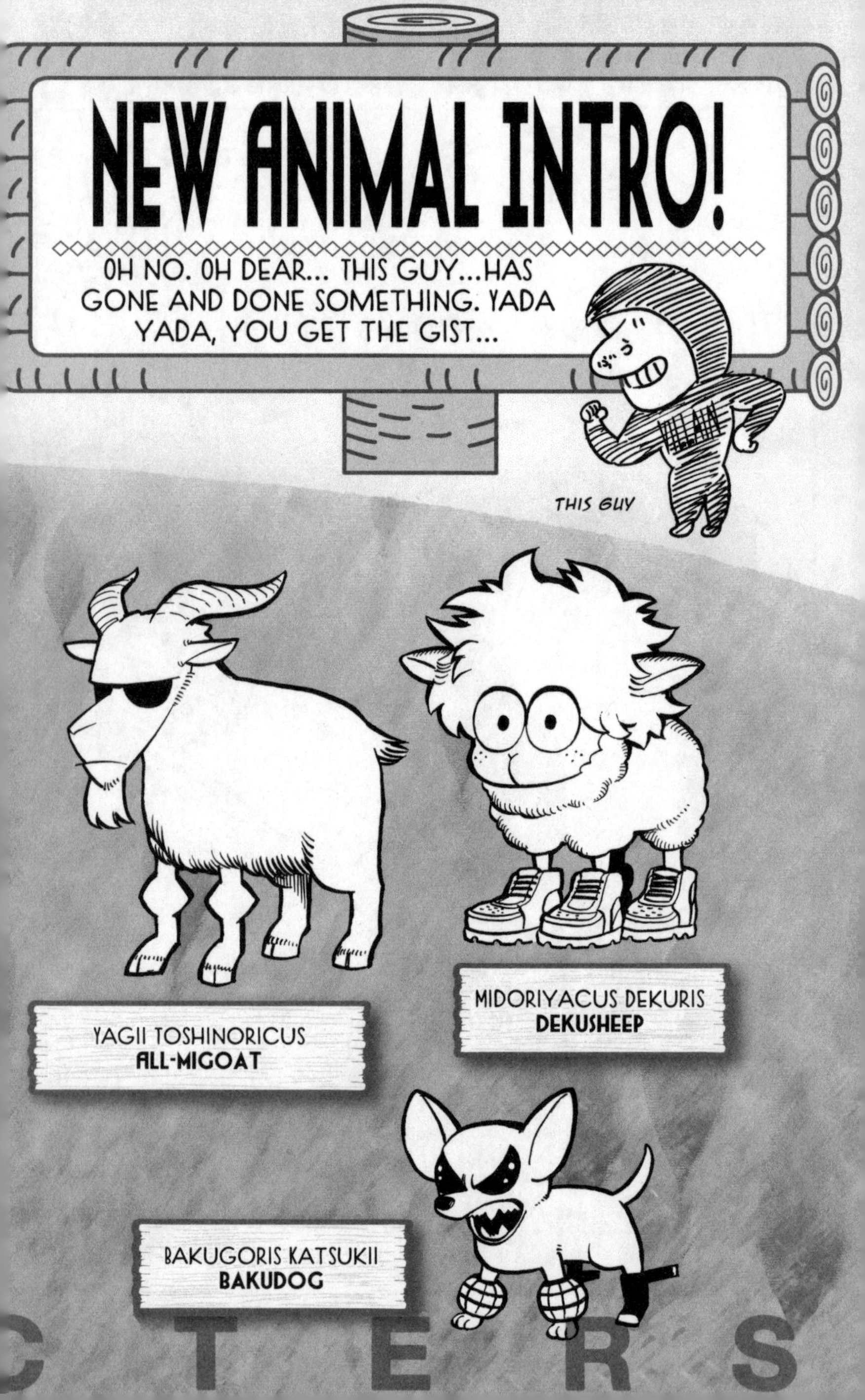
NEW ANIMAL INTRO!
OH NO. OH DEAR... THIS GUY...HAS GONE AND DONE SOMETHING. YADA YADA, YOU GET THE GIST...
VILLAIN
THIS GUY
YAGII TOSHINORICUS
ALL-MIGOAT
MIDORIYACUS DEKURIS
DEKUSHEEP
BAKUGORIS KATSUKII
BAKUDOG

STORY

One day, people began manifesting special abilities that came to be known as "Quirks," and before long, the world was full of superpowered humans. But with the advent of these exceptional individuals came an increase in crime, and governments alone were unable to deal with the situation. At the same time, others emerged to oppose the spread of evil! As if straight from the comic books, these heroes keep the peace and are even officially authorized to fight crime. Our story begins when a certain Quirkless boy and lifelong hero fan meets the world's number one hero, starting him on his path to becoming the greatest hero ever!

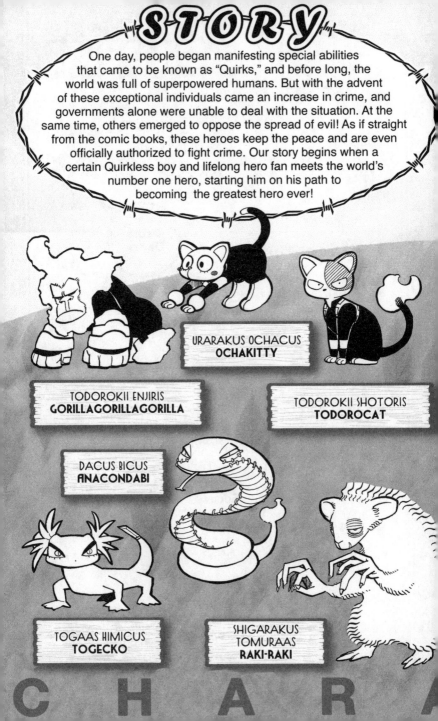

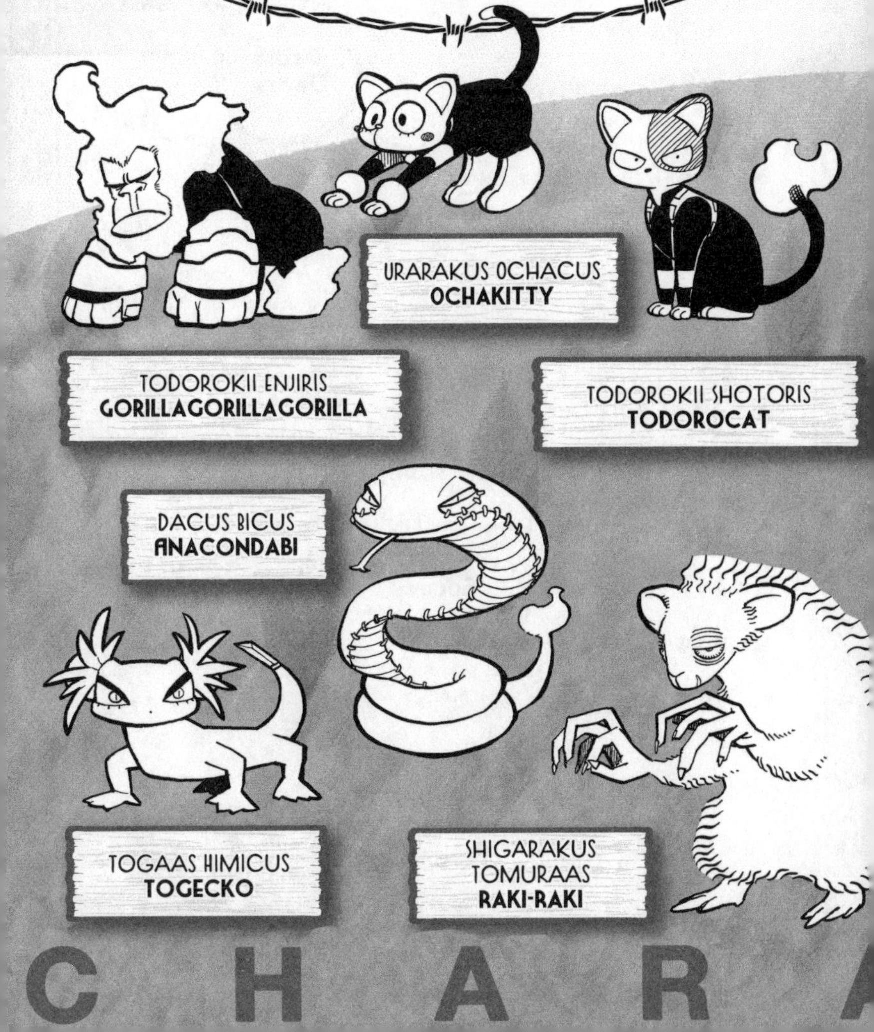
URARAKUS OCHACUS
OCHAKITTY
TODOROKII ENJIRIS
GORILLAGORILLAGORILLA
TODOROKII SHOTORIS
TODOROCAT
DACUS BICUS
ANACONDABI
TOGAAS HIMICUS
TOGECKO
SHIGARAKUS
TOMURAAS
RAKI-RAKI
C H A R A

MY HERO ACADEMIA

Vol. 30

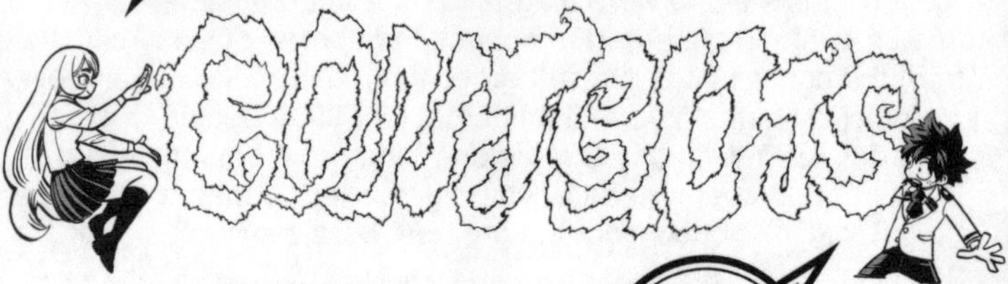
CONTENTS

Dabi's Dance

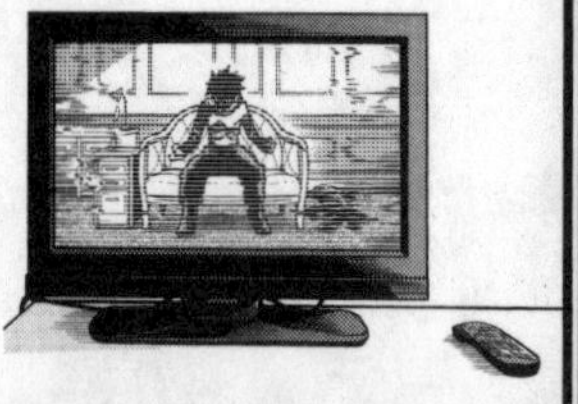

No. 286 - The Ones Within Us

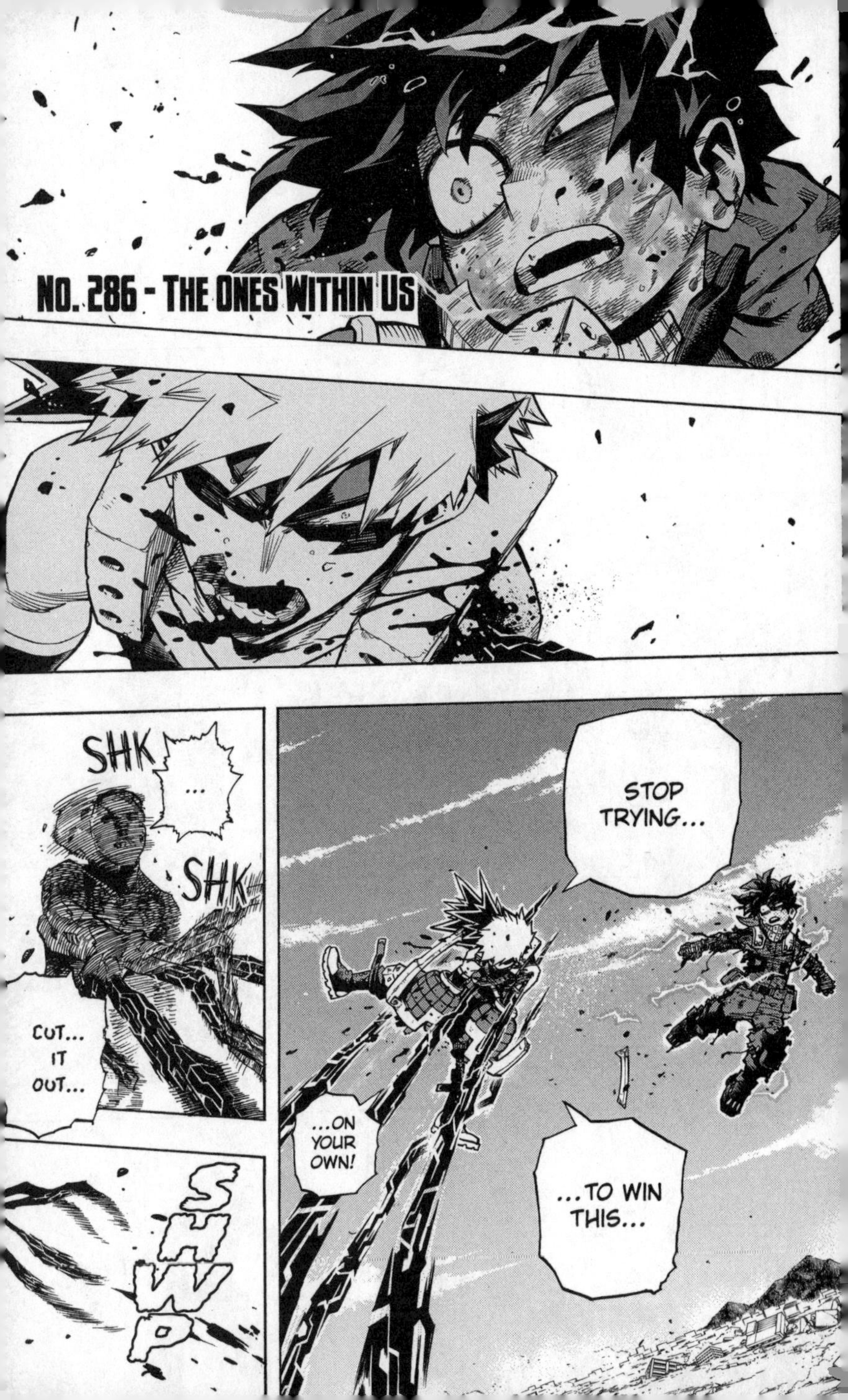

STOP TRYING...
...TO WIN THIS...
...ON YOUR OWN!
SHK
...
SHK
CUT... IT OUT...
SHWP

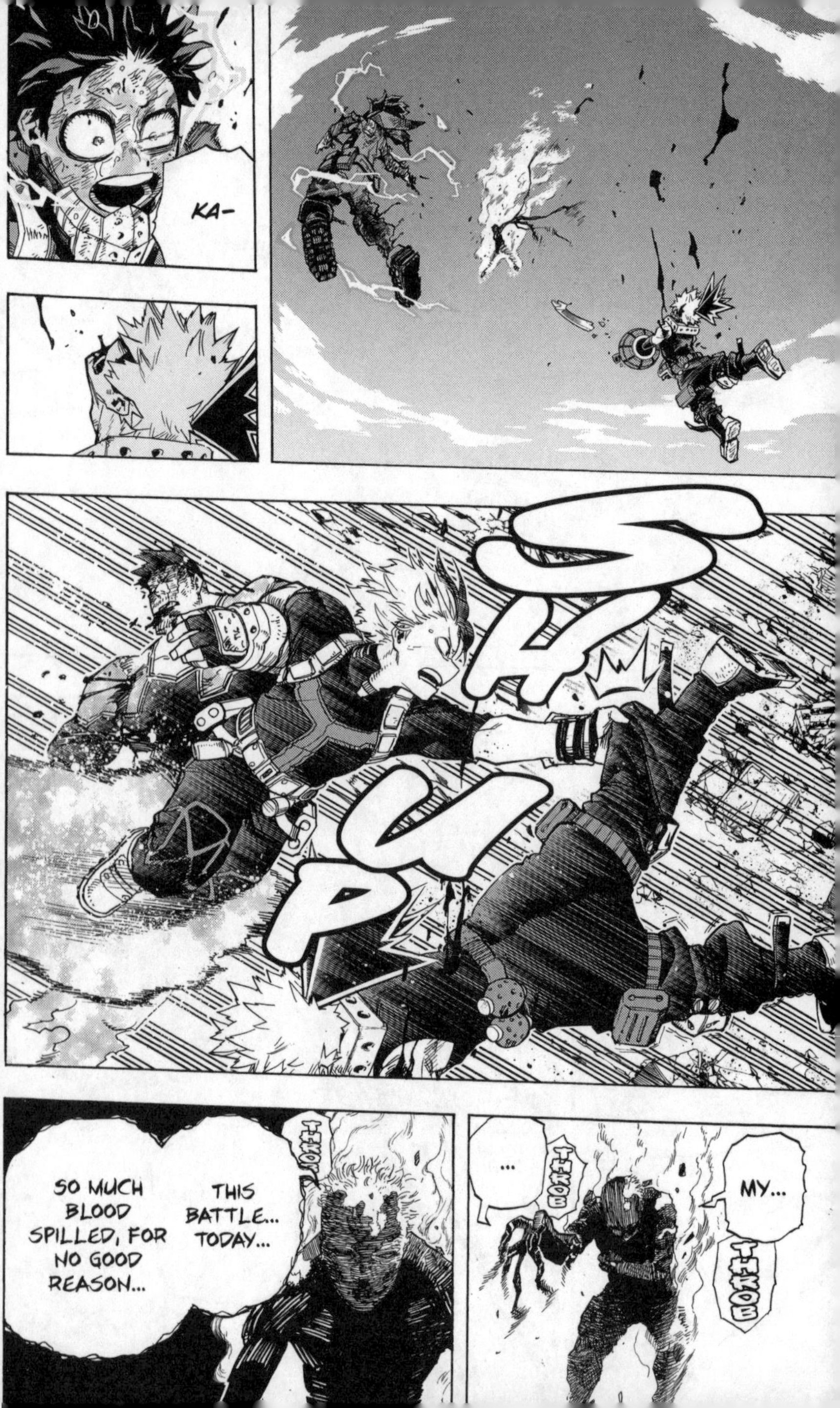
KA-
SHUP
THROB
MY...
THROB
...
THROB
THIS BATTLE... TODAY...
SO MUCH BLOOD SPILLED, FOR NO GOOD REASON...

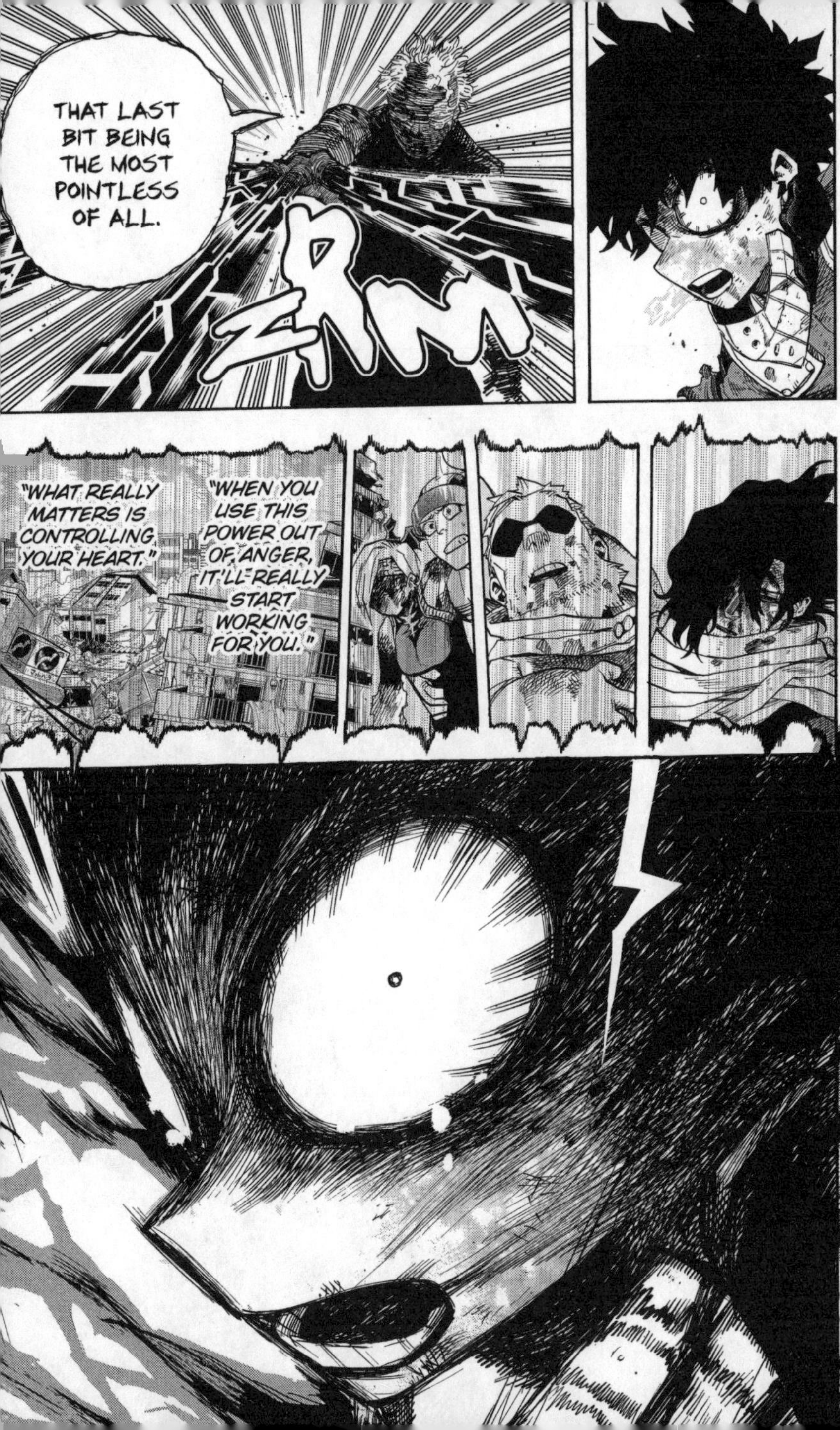
THAT LAST BIT BEING THE MOST POINTLESS OF ALL.
"WHEN YOU USE THIS POWER OUT OF ANGER, IT'LL REALLY START WORKING FOR YOU."
"WHAT REALLY MATTERS IS CONTROLLING YOUR HEART."

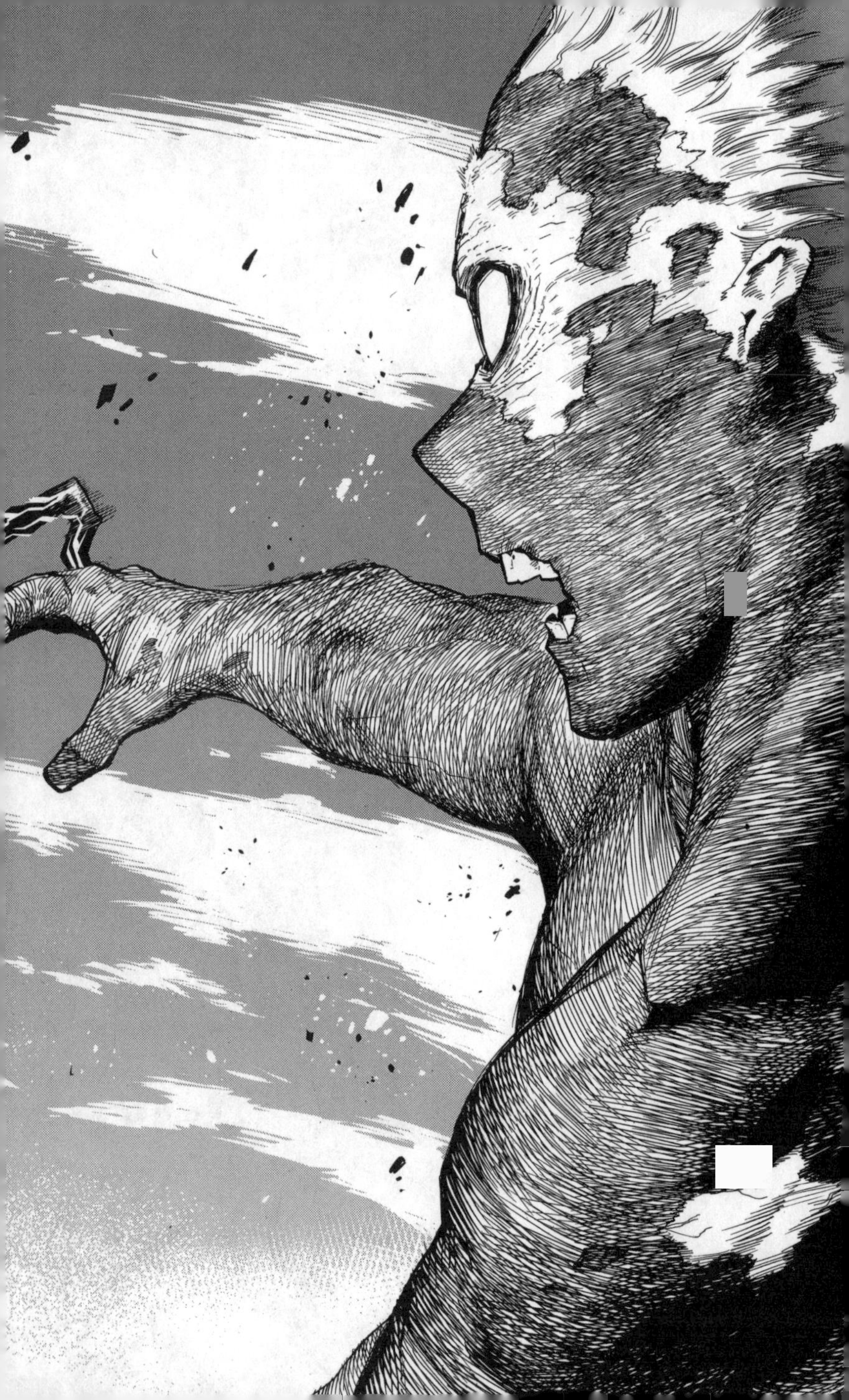

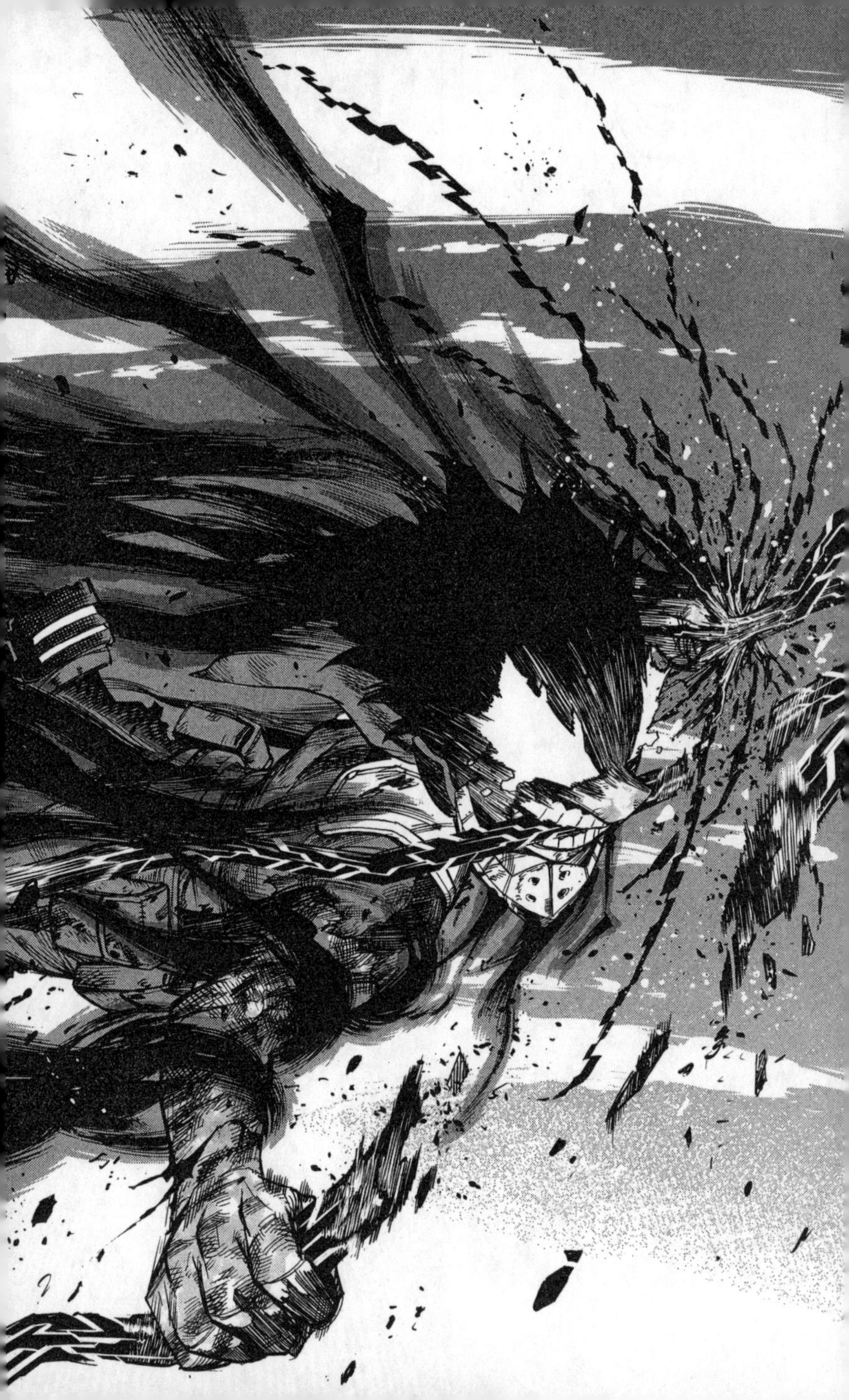

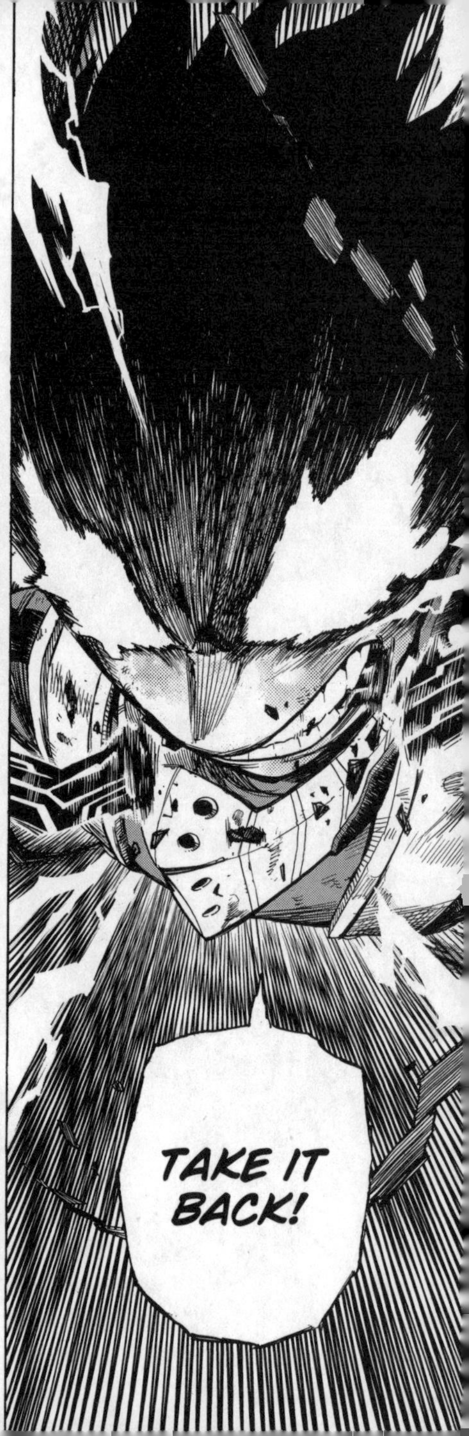
TAKE IT BACK!
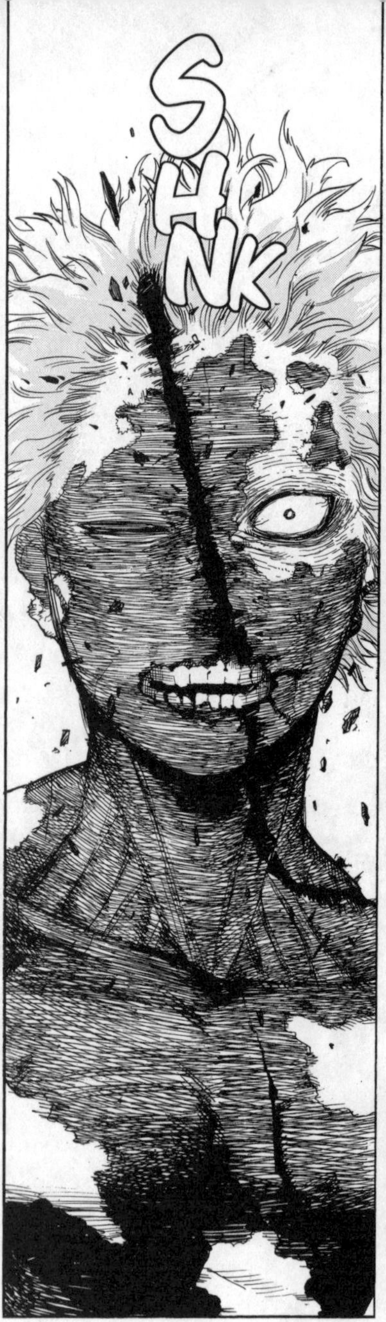
SHNK

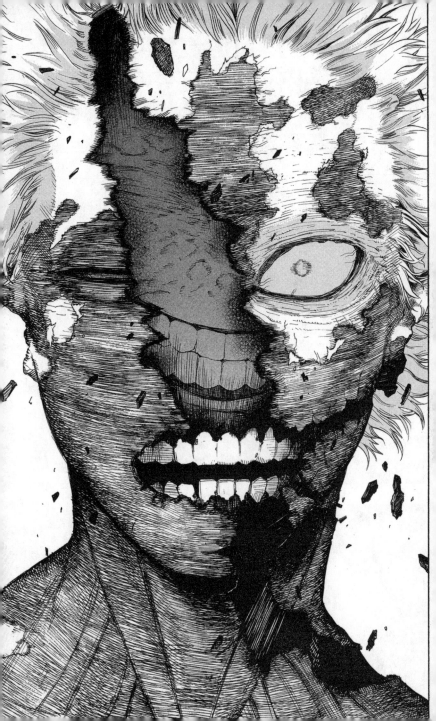

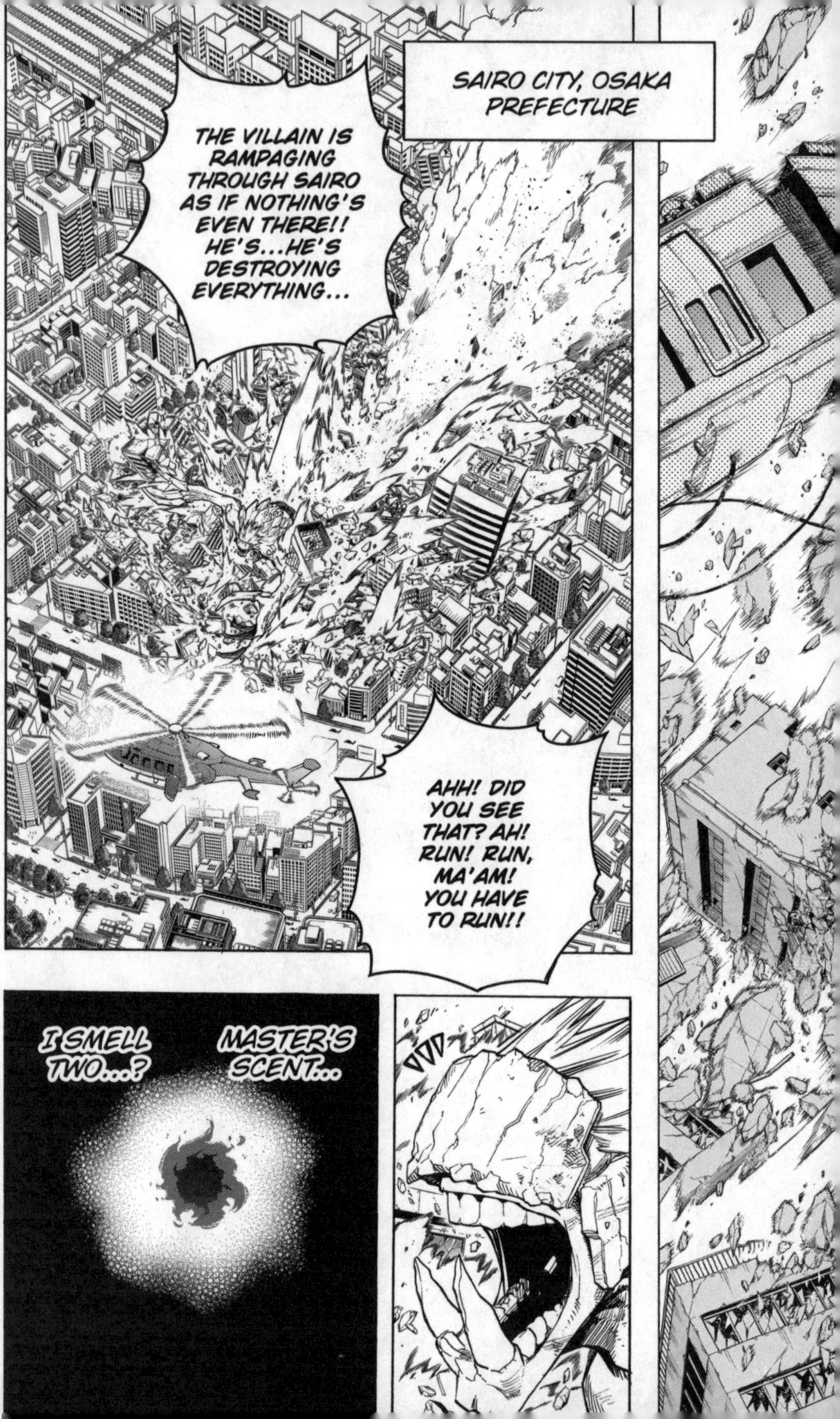
SAIRO CITY, OSAKA PREFECTURE
THE VILLAIN IS RAMPAGING THROUGH SAIRO AS IF NOTHING'S EVEN THERE!! HE'S...HE'S DESTROYING EVERYTHING...
AHH! DID YOU SEE THAT? AH! RUN! RUN, MA'AM! YOU HAVE TO RUN!!
MASTER'S SCENT...
I SMELL TWO...?

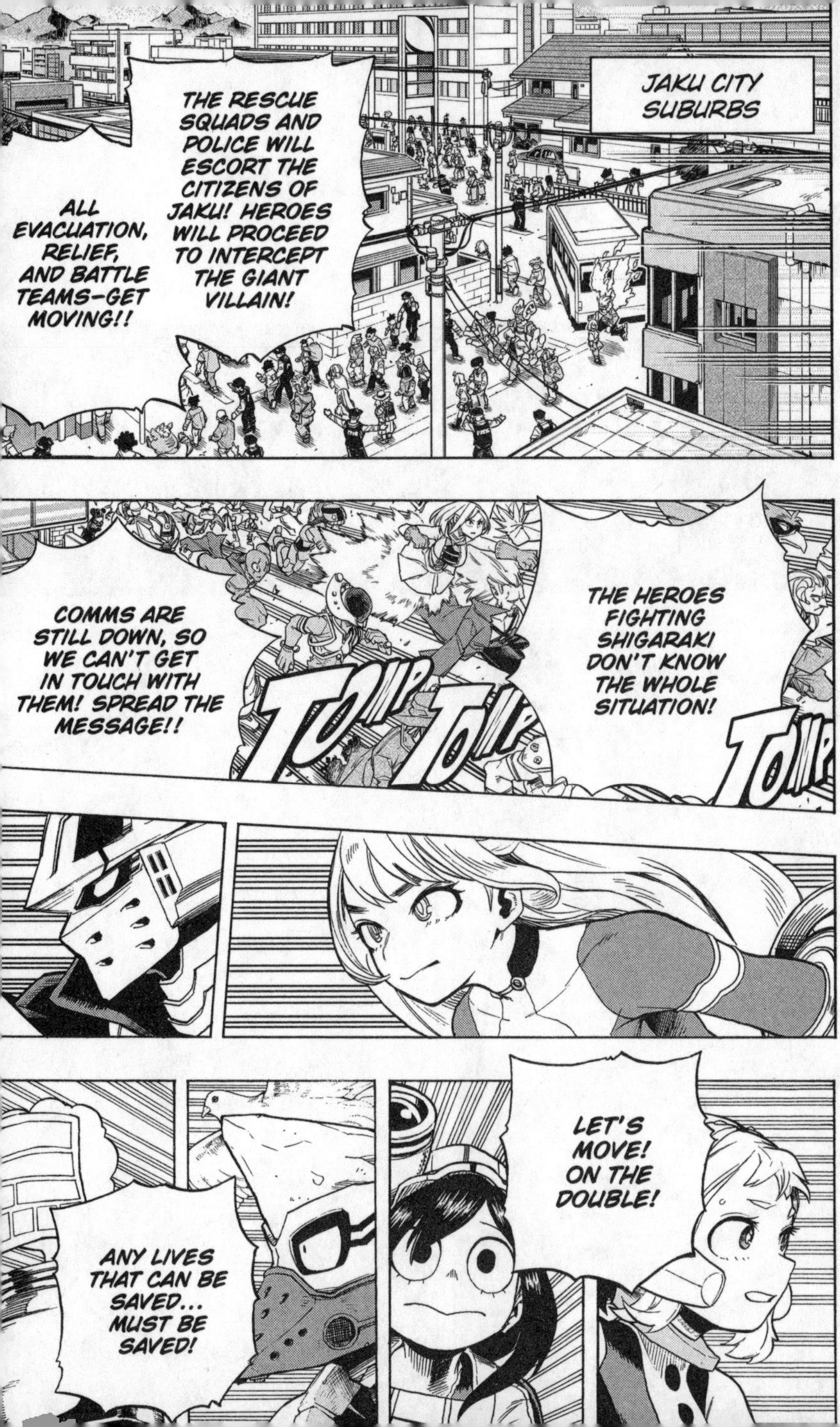
JAKU CITY SUBURBS
THE RESCUE SQUADS AND POLICE WILL ESCORT THE CITIZENS OF JAKU! HEROES WILL PROCEED TO INTERCEPT THE GIANT VILLAIN!
ALL EVACUATION, RELIEF, AND BATTLE TEAMS—GET MOVING!!
THE HEROES FIGHTING SHIGARAKI DON'T KNOW THE WHOLE SITUATION!
COMMS ARE STILL DOWN, SO WE CAN'T GET IN TOUCH WITH THEM! SPREAD THE MESSAGE!!
LET'S MOVE! ON THE DOUBLE!
ANY LIVES THAT CAN BE SAVED... MUST BE SAVED!

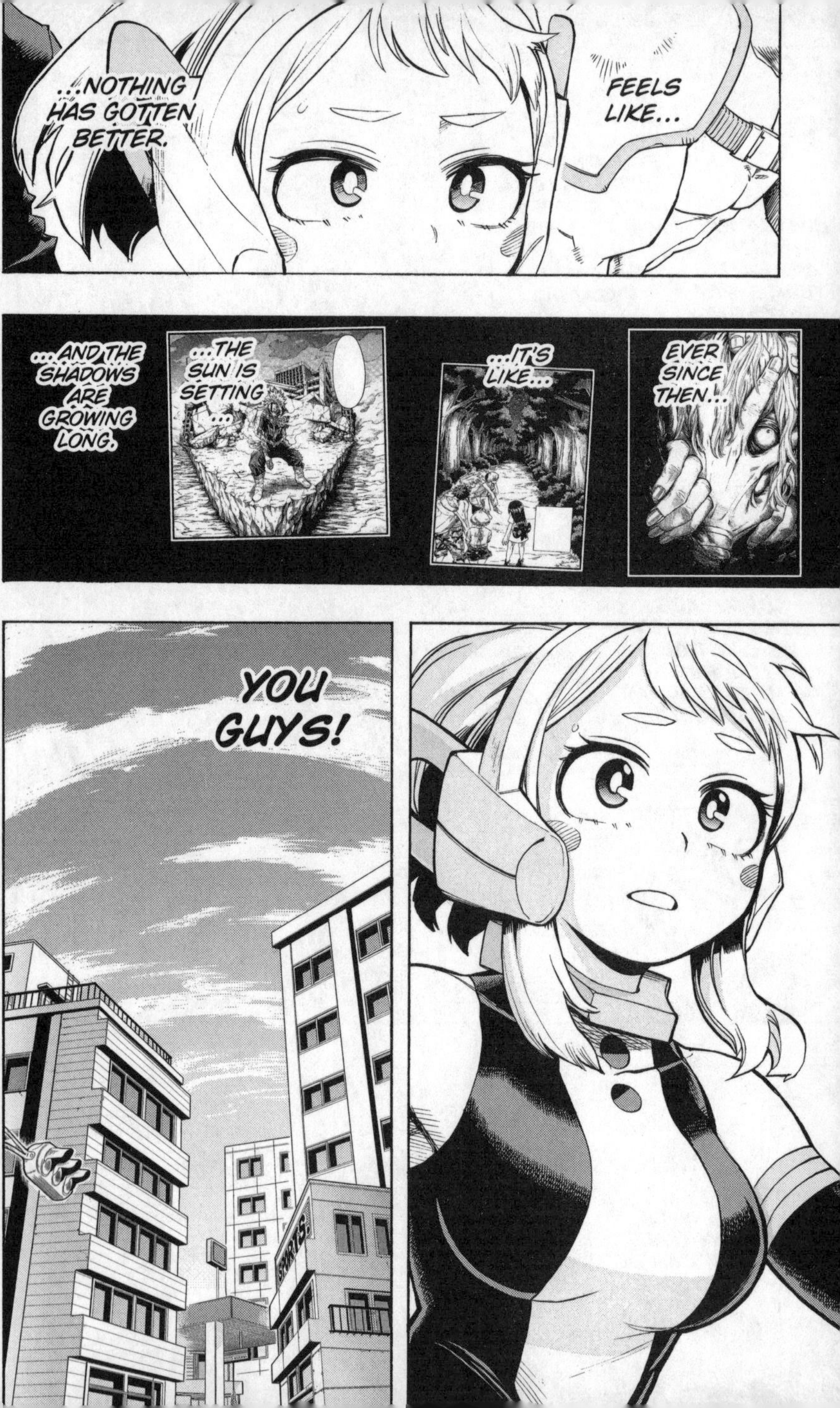
FEELS LIKE...
...NOTHING HAS GOTTEN BETTER.
EVER SINCE THEN...
...IT'S LIKE...
...THE SUN IS SETTING...
...AND THE SHADOWS ARE GROWING LONG.
YOU GUYS!
SPORTS

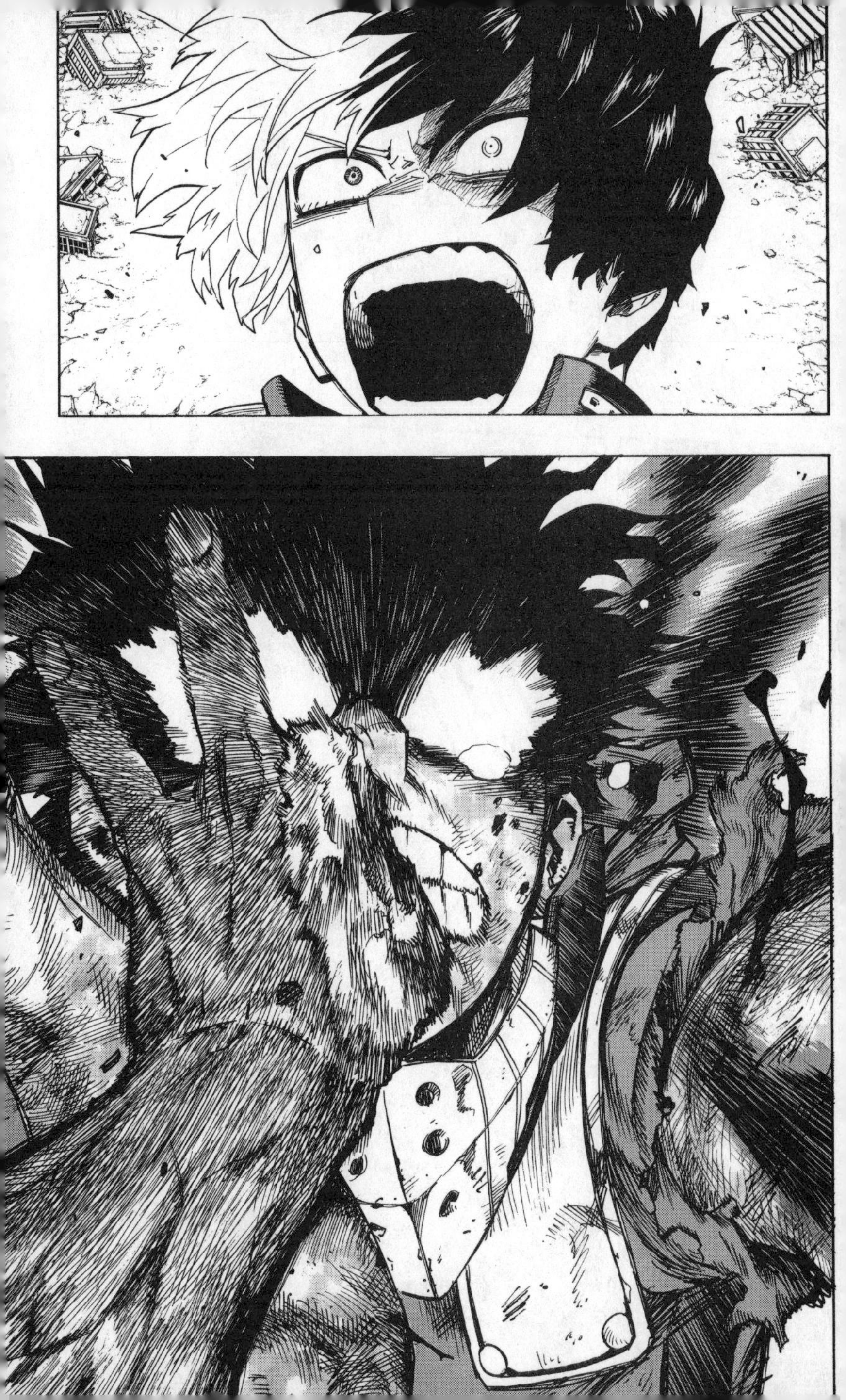

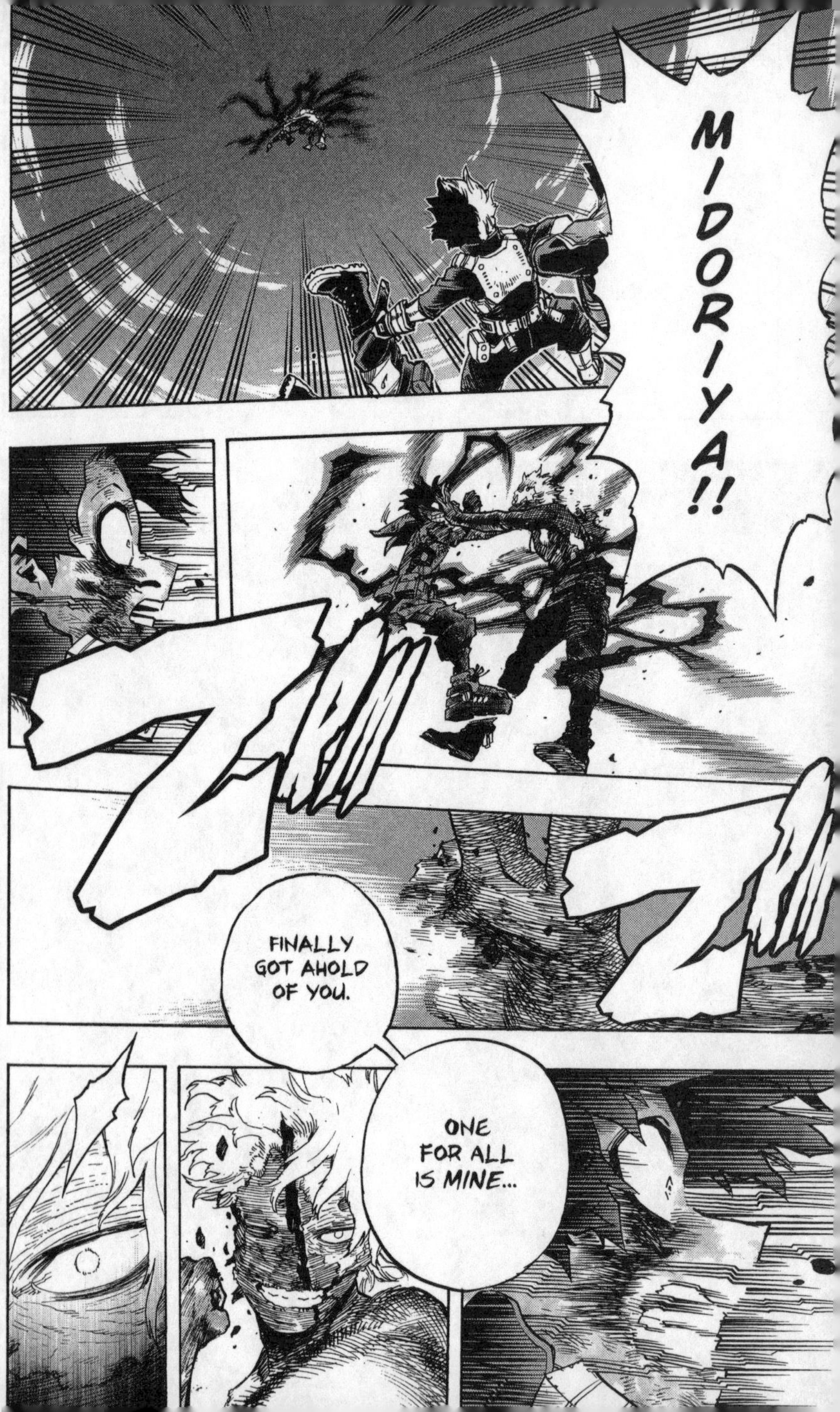
MIDORIYA!!
ZM
ZM
FINALLY GOT AHOLD OF YOU.
ONE FOR ALL IS MINE...

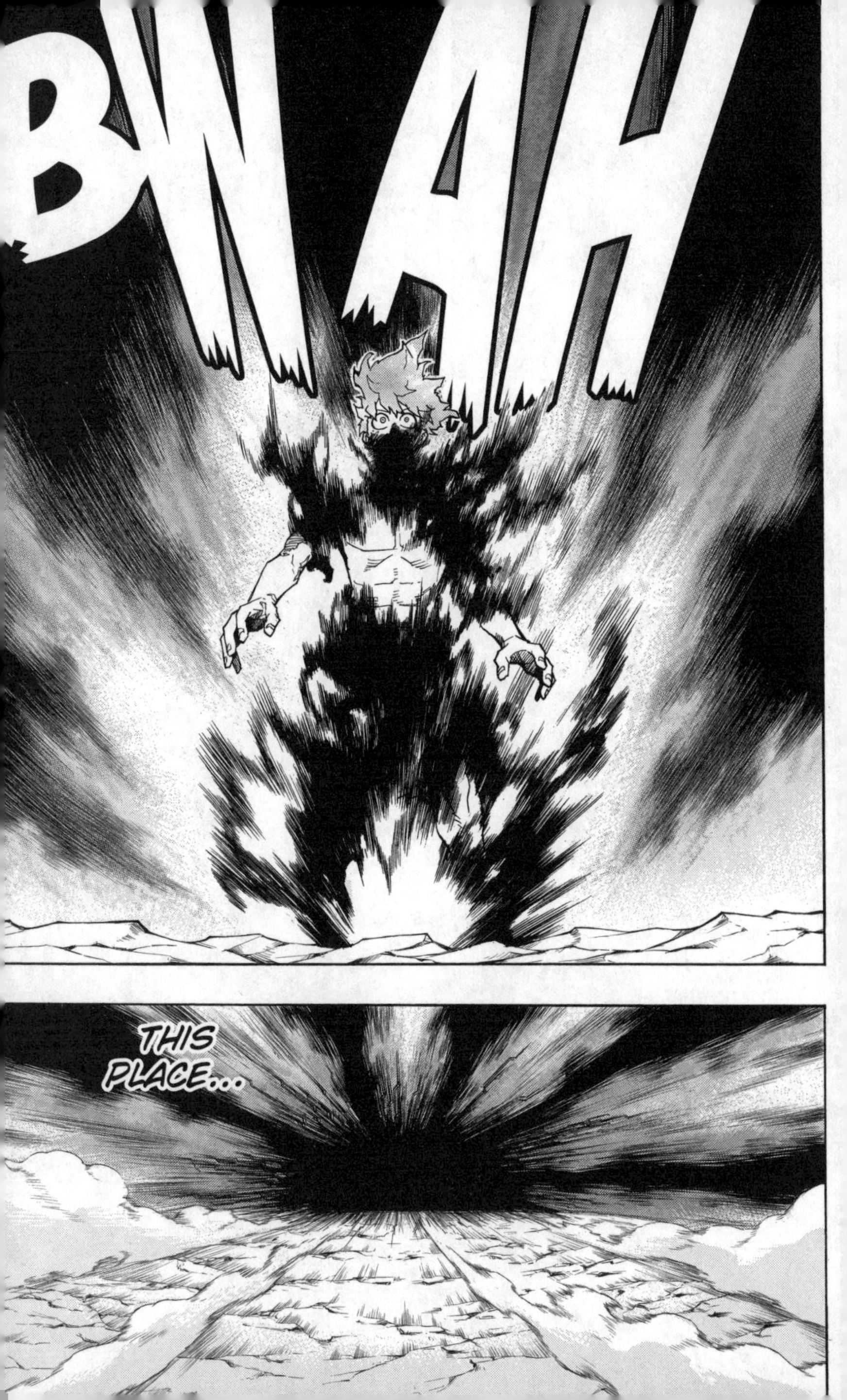
BWAH
THIS PLACE...

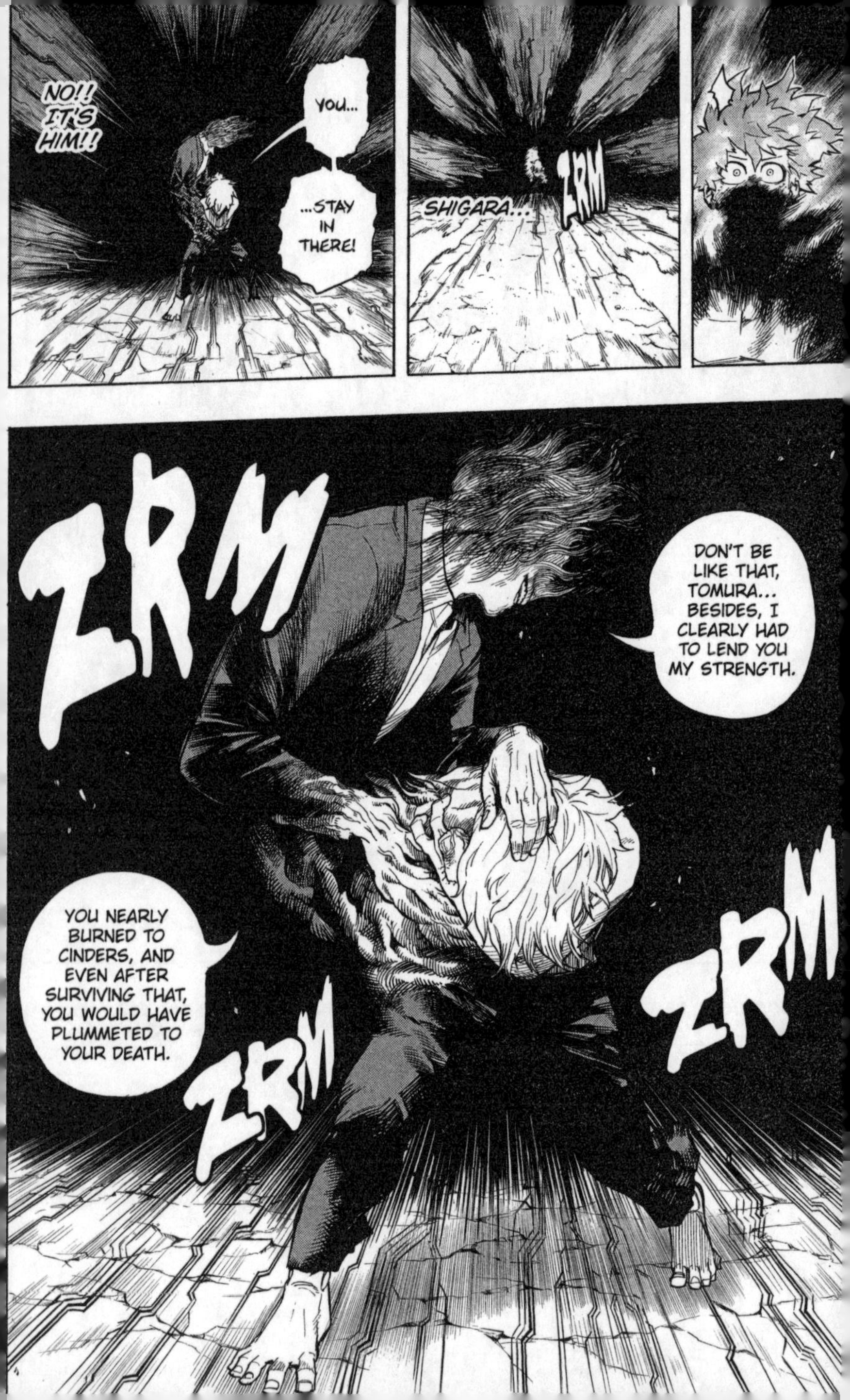
SHIGARA...
ZRM
NO!! IT'S HIM!!
YOU...
...STAY IN THERE!
ZRM
DON'T BE LIKE THAT, TOMURA... BESIDES, I CLEARLY HAD TO LEND YOU MY STRENGTH.
ZRM
YOU NEARLY BURNED TO CINDERS, AND EVEN AFTER SURVIVING THAT, YOU WOULD HAVE PLUMMETED TO YOUR DEATH.
ZRM

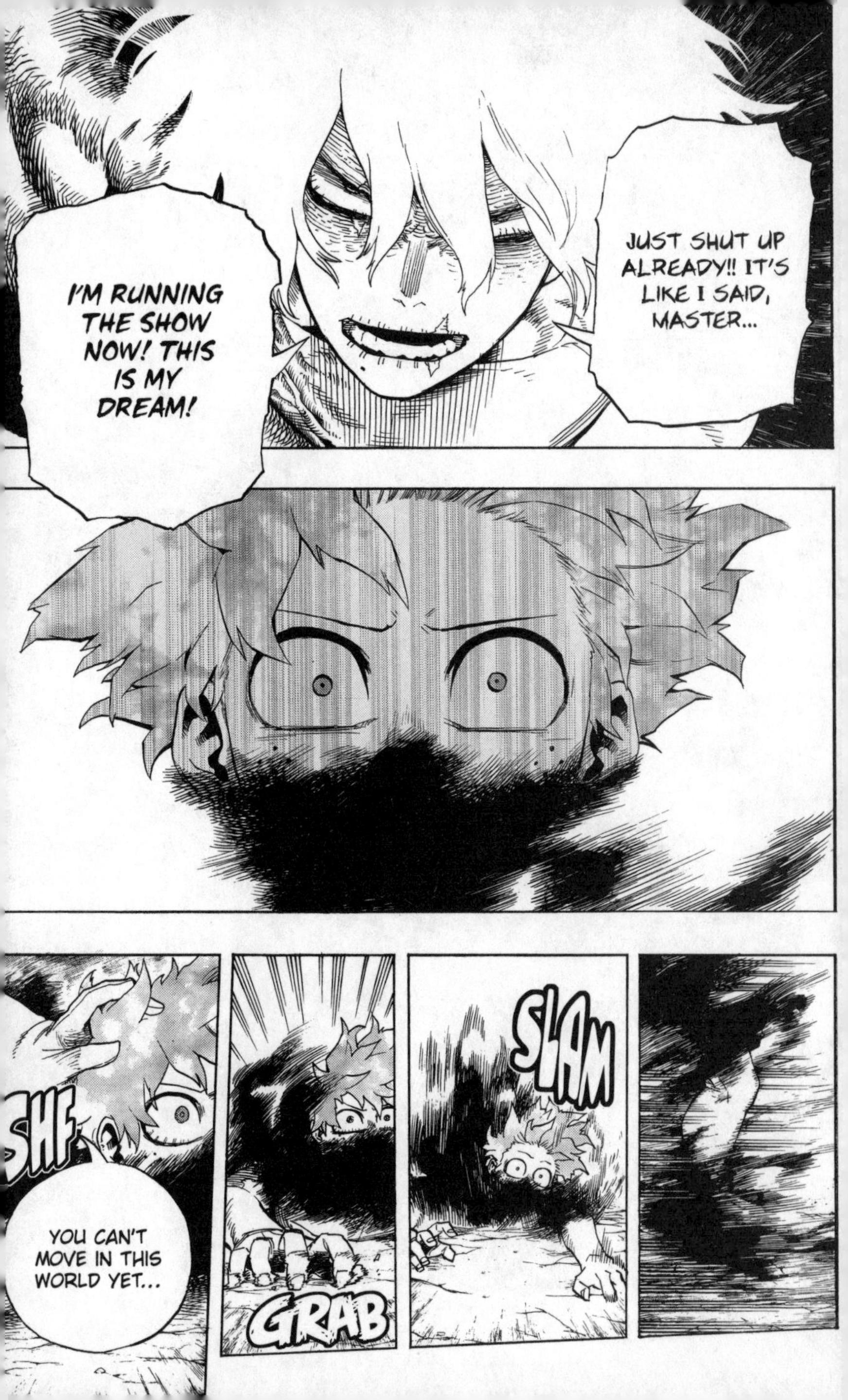
JUST SHUT UP ALREADY!! IT'S LIKE I SAID, MASTER...
I'M RUNNING THE SHOW NOW! THIS IS MY DREAM!
SLAM
GRAB
SHF
YOU CAN'T MOVE IN THIS WORLD YET...

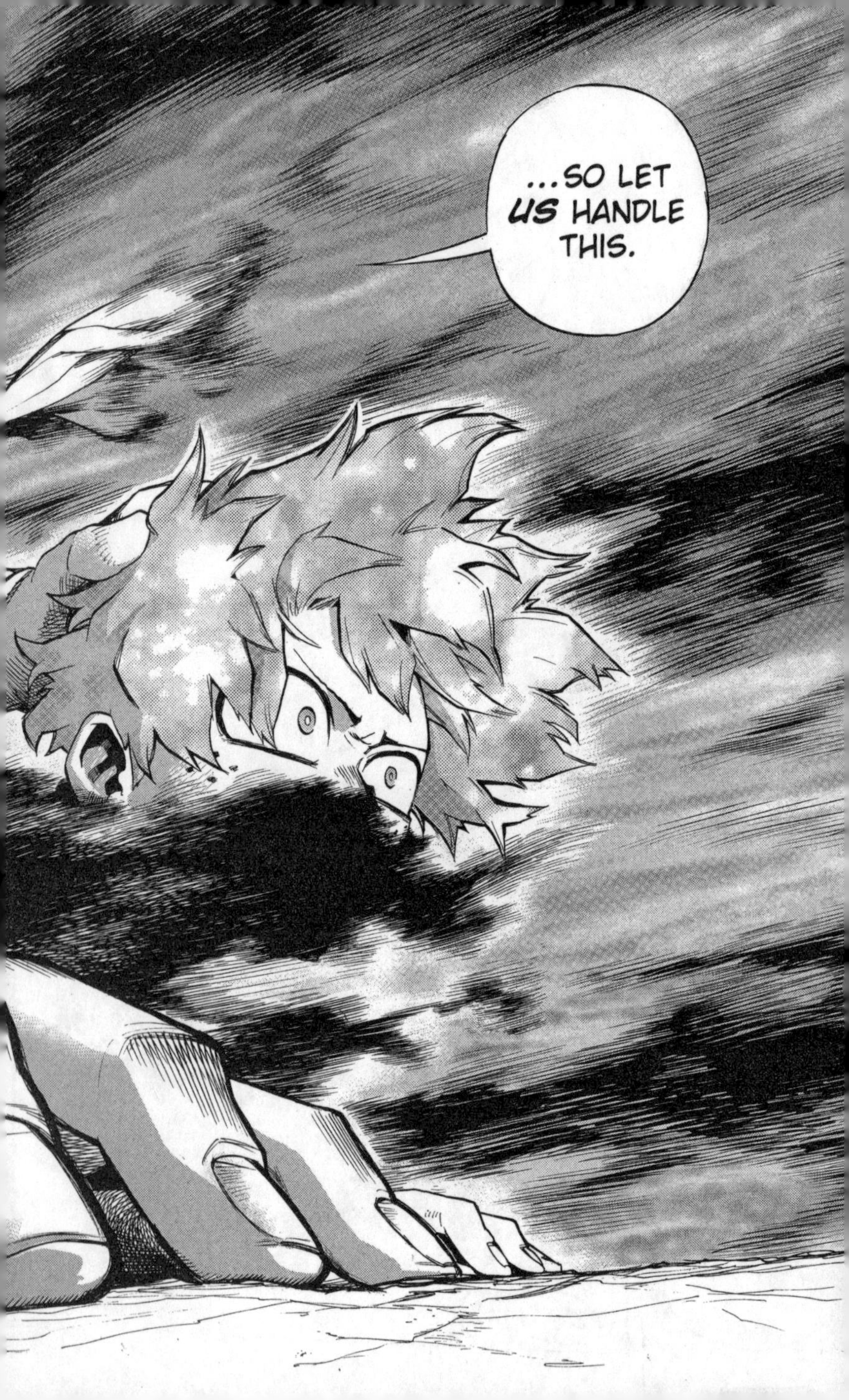
...SO LET *US* HANDLE THIS.

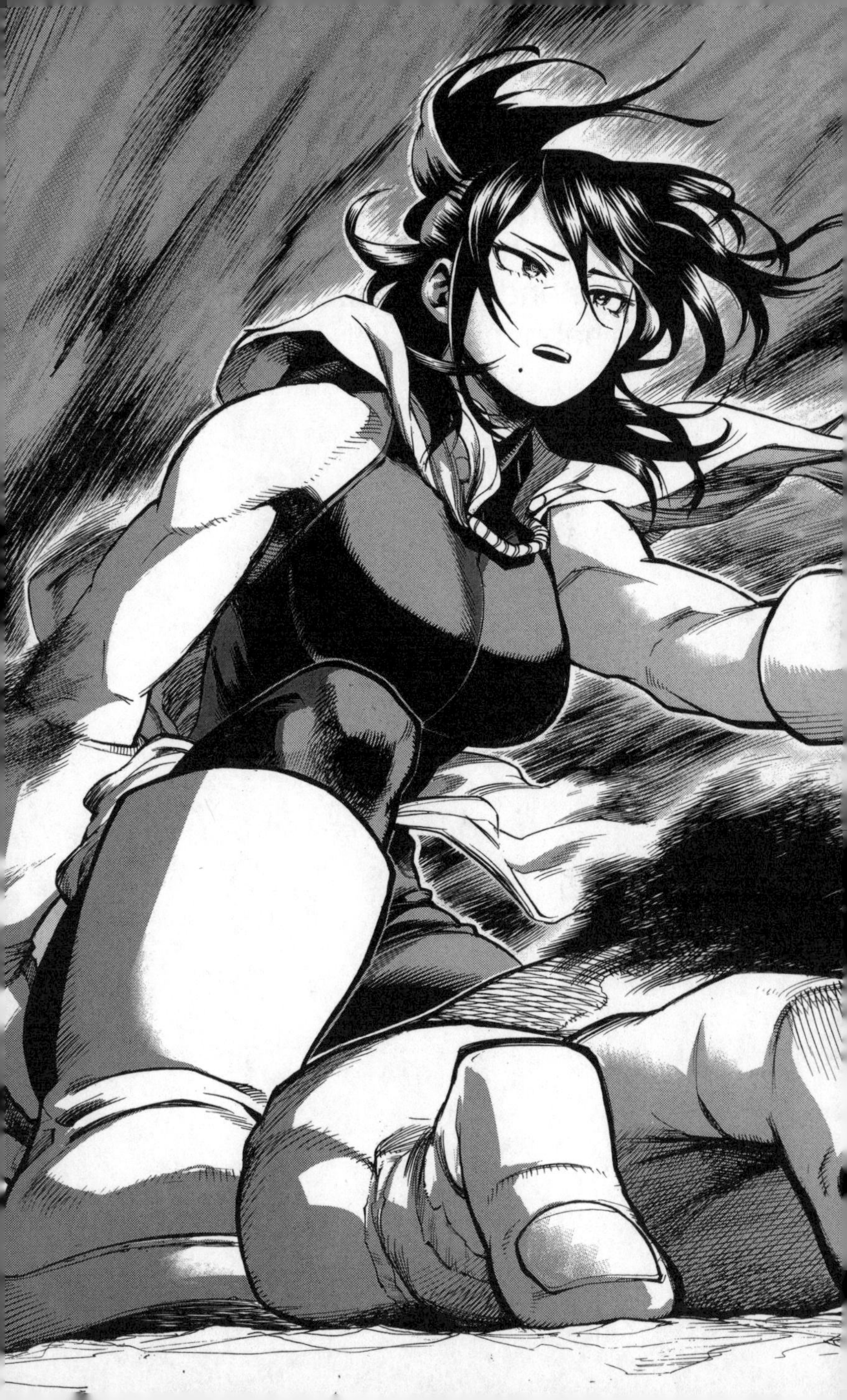

This isn't limited to just Nana Shimura, but my female characters have been looking more and more ripped. Weird how that's happening!

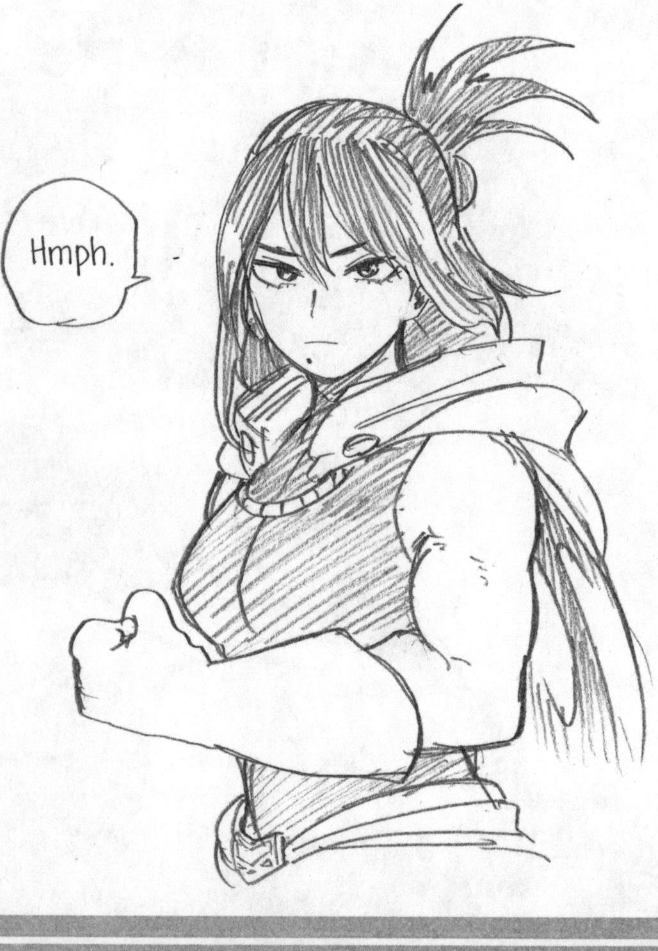
Hmph.

NO. 287 - MISTAKE

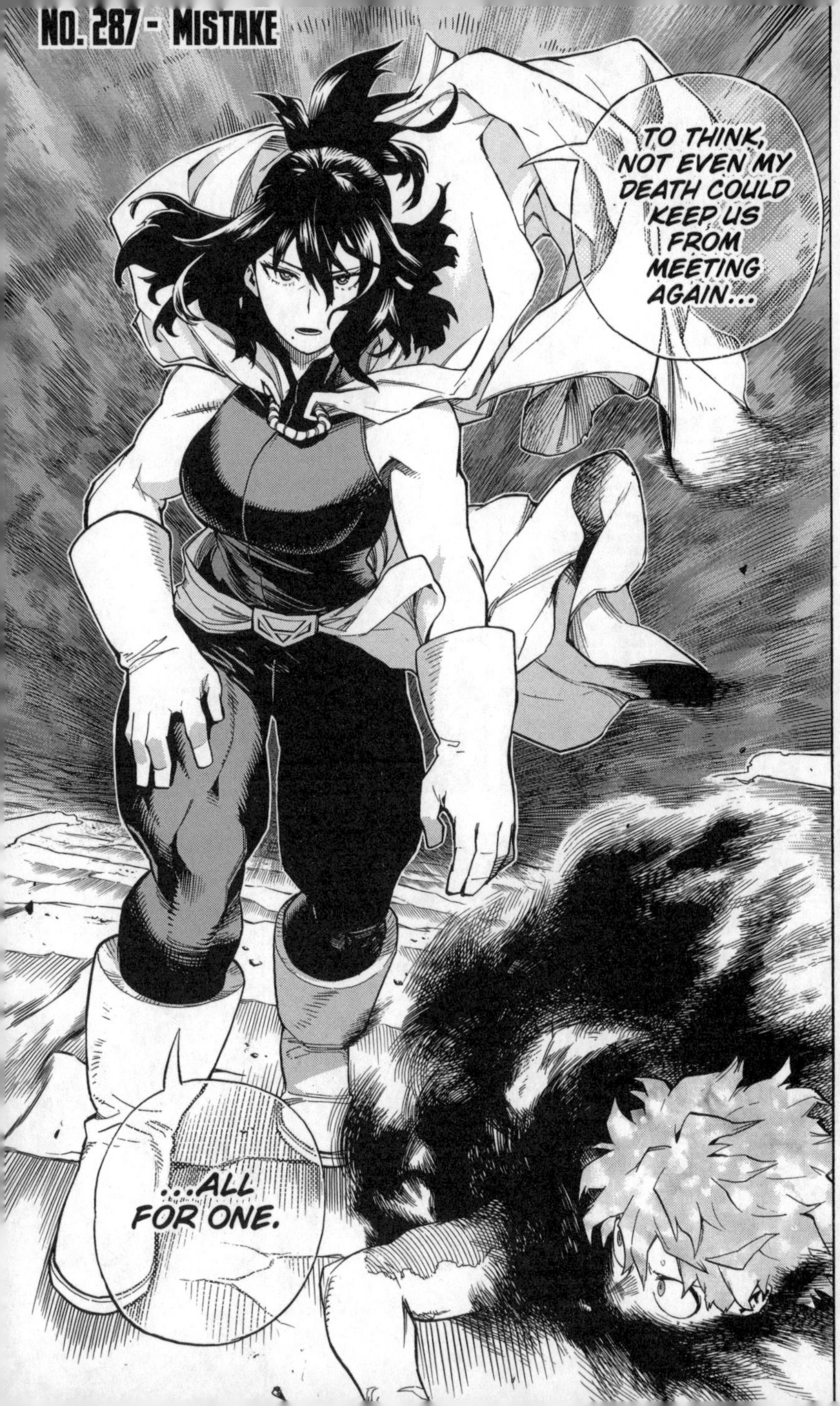
TO THINK, NOT EVEN MY DEATH COULD KEEP US FROM MEETING AGAIN...
...ALL FOR ONE.

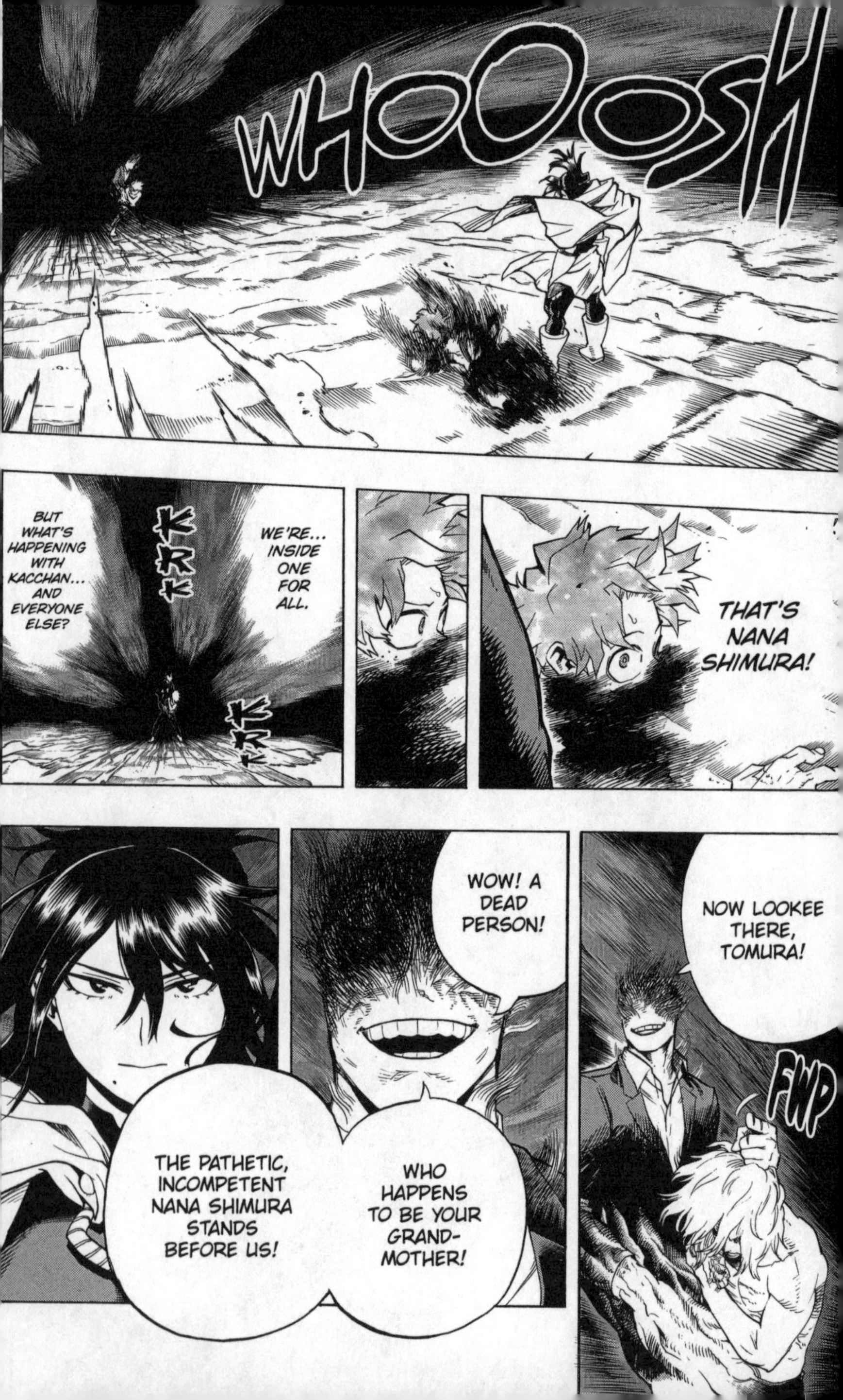
WHOOOSH
THAT'S NANA SHIMURA!
WE'RE... INSIDE ONE FOR ALL.
KRK
BUT WHAT'S HAPPENING WITH KACCHAN... AND EVERYONE ELSE?
KRK
NOW LOOKEE THERE, TOMURA!
FWP
WOW! A DEAD PERSON!
THE PATHETIC, INCOMPETENT NANA SHIMURA STANDS BEFORE US!
WHO HAPPENS TO BE YOUR GRAND-MOTHER!

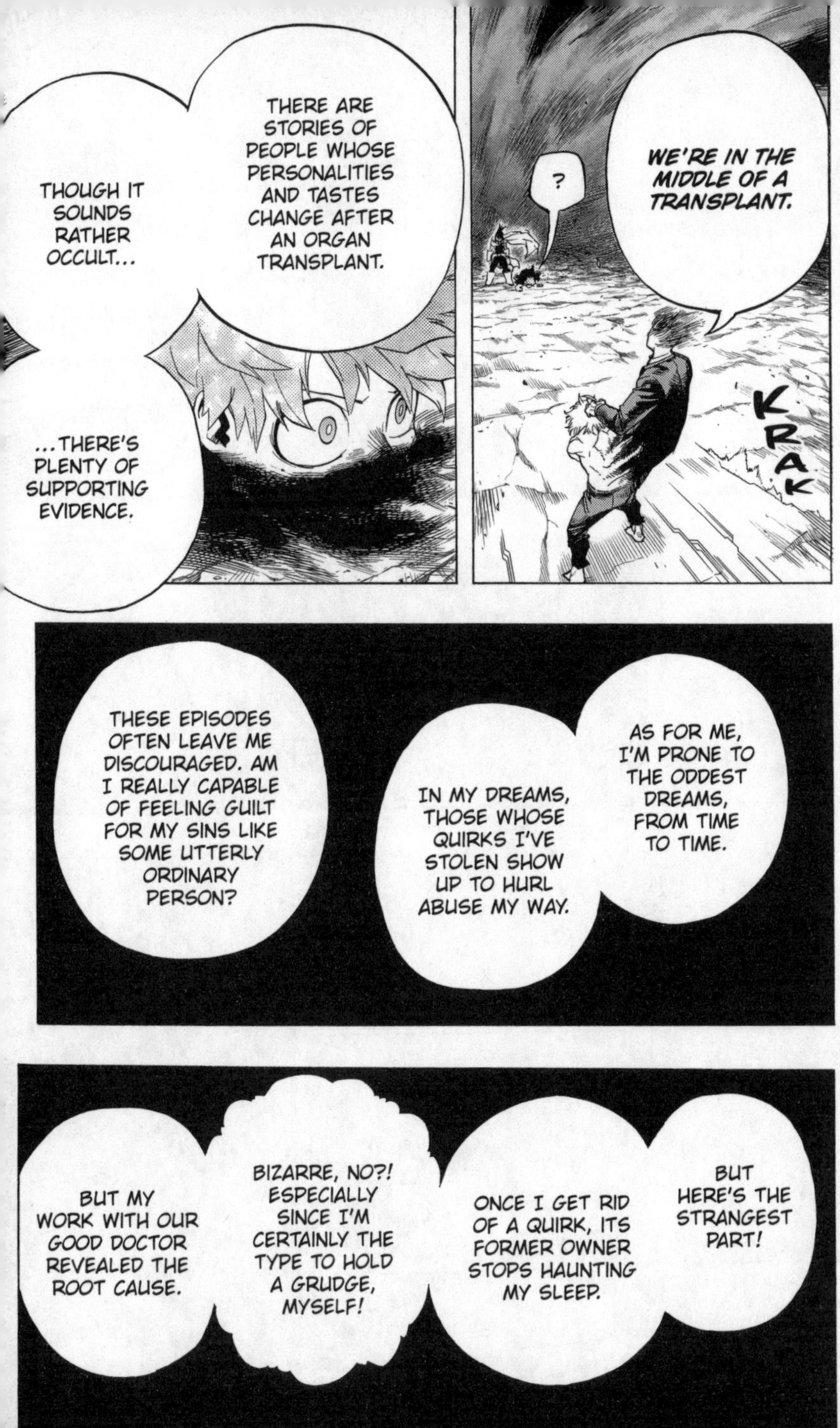
WE'RE IN THE MIDDLE OF A TRANSPLANT.
?
KRAK
THERE ARE STORIES OF PEOPLE WHOSE PERSONALITIES AND TASTES CHANGE AFTER AN ORGAN TRANSPLANT.
THOUGH IT SOUNDS RATHER OCCULT...
...THERE'S PLENTY OF SUPPORTING EVIDENCE.
AS FOR ME, I'M PRONE TO THE ODDEST DREAMS, FROM TIME TO TIME.
IN MY DREAMS, THOSE WHOSE QUIRKS I'VE STOLEN SHOW UP TO HURL ABUSE MY WAY.
THESE EPISODES OFTEN LEAVE ME DISCOURAGED. AM I REALLY CAPABLE OF FEELING GUILT FOR MY SINS LIKE SOME UTTERLY ORDINARY PERSON?
BUT HERE'S THE STRANGEST PART!
ONCE I GET RID OF A QUIRK, ITS FORMER OWNER STOPS HAUNTING MY SLEEP.
BIZARRE, NO?! ESPECIALLY SINCE I'M CERTAINLY THE TYPE TO HOLD A GRUDGE, MYSELF!
BUT MY WORK WITH OUR GOOD DOCTOR REVEALED THE ROOT CAUSE.

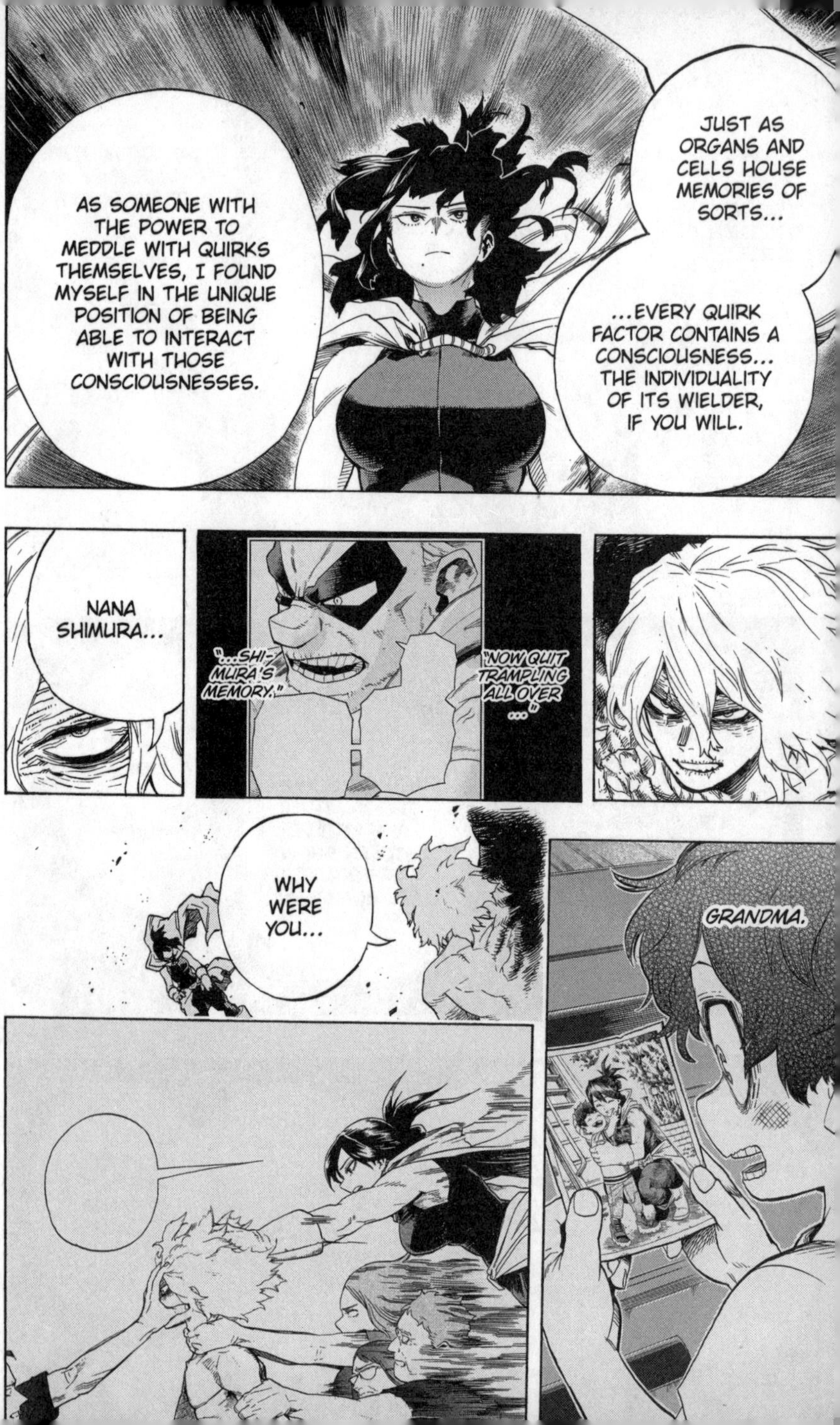
JUST AS ORGANS AND CELLS HOUSE MEMORIES OF SORTS...
...EVERY QUIRK FACTOR CONTAINS A CONSCIOUSNESS... THE INDIVIDUALITY OF ITS WIELDER, IF YOU WILL.
AS SOMEONE WITH THE POWER TO MEDDLE WITH QUIRKS THEMSELVES, I FOUND MYSELF IN THE UNIQUE POSITION OF BEING ABLE TO INTERACT WITH THOSE CONSCIOUSNESSES.
"NOW QUIT TRAMPLING ALL OVER..."
"...SHIMURA'S MEMORY."
NANA SHIMURA...
GRANDMA.
WHY WERE YOU...

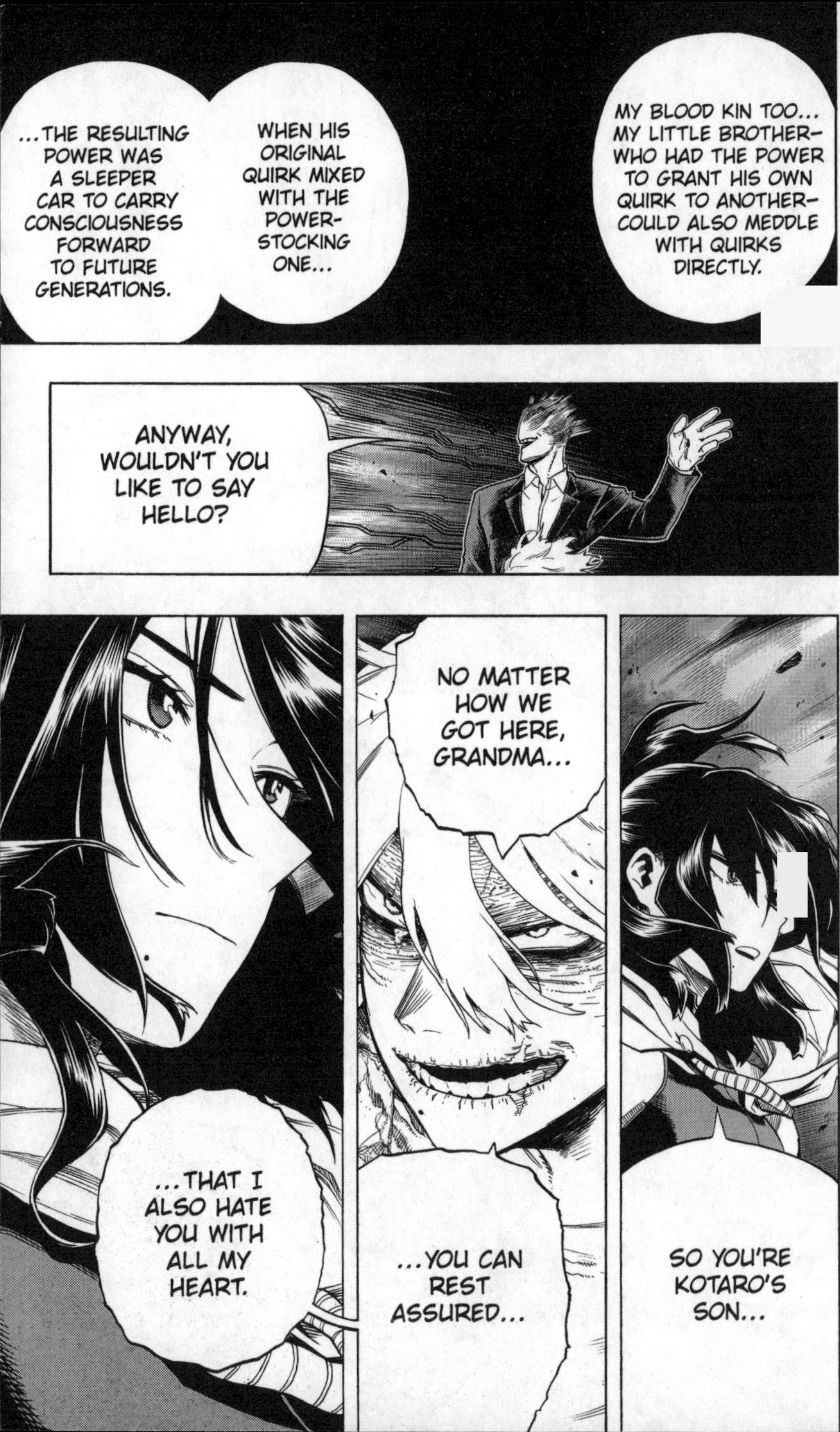
MY BLOOD KIN TOO... MY LITTLE BROTHER- WHO HAD THE POWER TO GRANT HIS OWN QUIRK TO ANOTHER- COULD ALSO MEDDLE WITH QUIRKS DIRECTLY.
WHEN HIS ORIGINAL QUIRK MIXED WITH THE POWER-STOCKING ONE...
...THE RESULTING POWER WAS A SLEEPER CAR TO CARRY CONSCIOUSNESS FORWARD TO FUTURE GENERATIONS.
ANYWAY, WOULDN'T YOU LIKE TO SAY HELLO?
SO YOU'RE KOTARO'S SON...
NO MATTER HOW WE GOT HERE, GRANDMA...
...YOU CAN REST ASSURED...
...THAT I ALSO HATE YOU WITH ALL MY HEART.

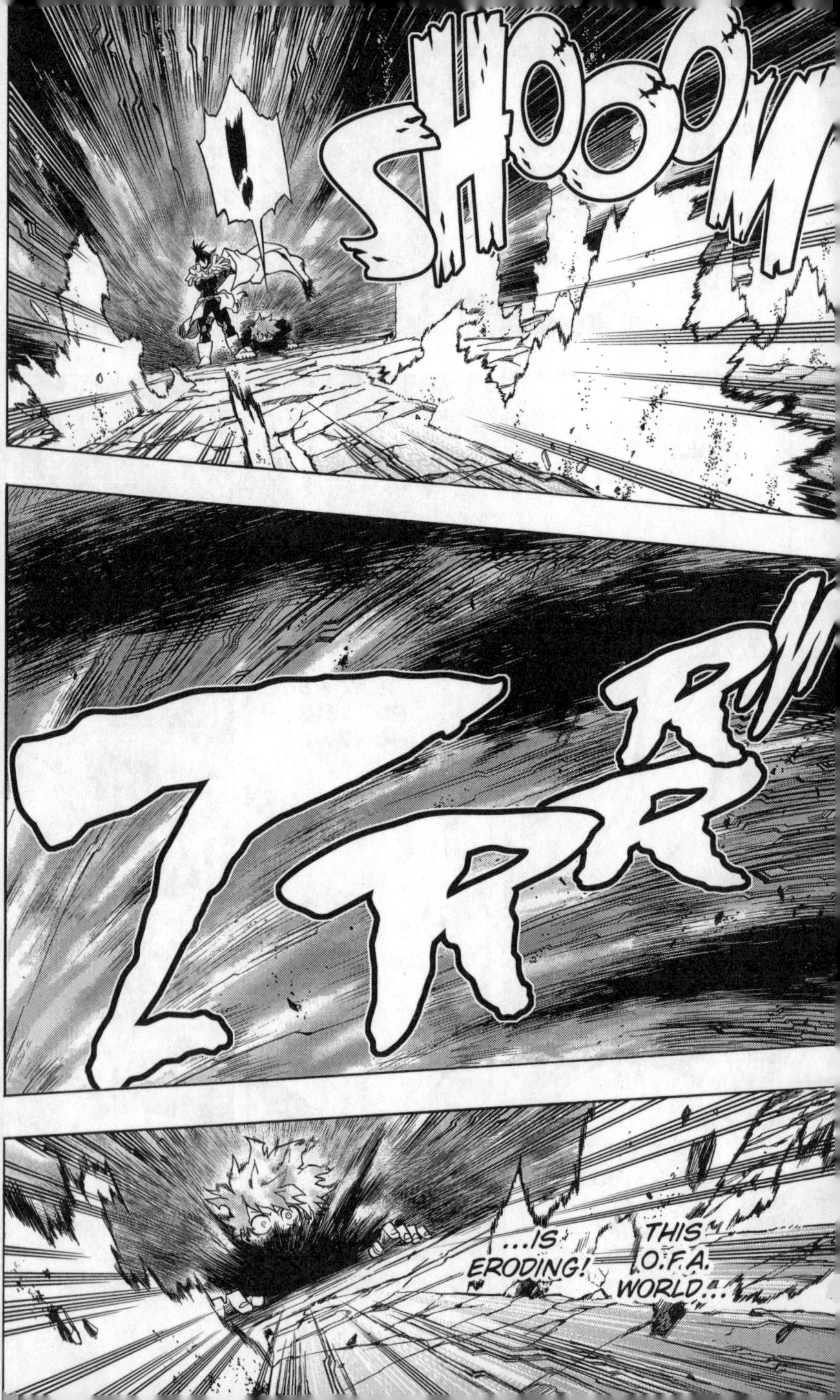
SHOOOM
THIS O.F.A. WORLD...
...IS ERODING!

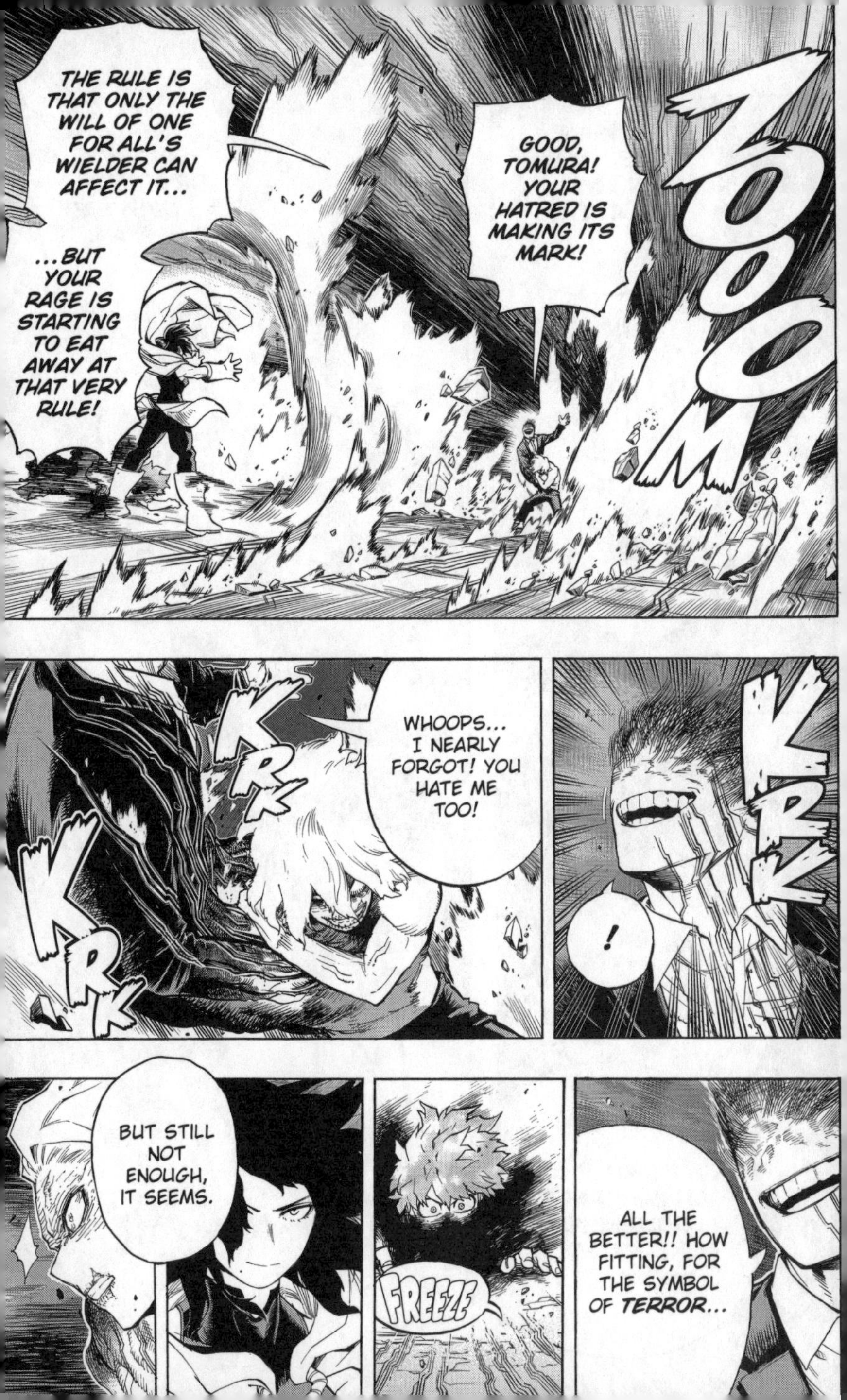
ZOOOM
GOOD, TOMURA! YOUR HATRED IS MAKING ITS MARK!
THE RULE IS THAT ONLY THE WILL OF ONE FOR ALL'S WIELDER CAN AFFECT IT...
...BUT YOUR RAGE IS STARTING TO EAT AWAY AT THAT VERY RULE!
KRK
!
WHOOPS... I NEARLY FORGOT! YOU HATE ME TOO!
KRK
KRK
ALL THE BETTER!! HOW FITTING, FOR THE SYMBOL OF TERROR...
FREEZE
BUT STILL NOT ENOUGH, IT SEEMS.

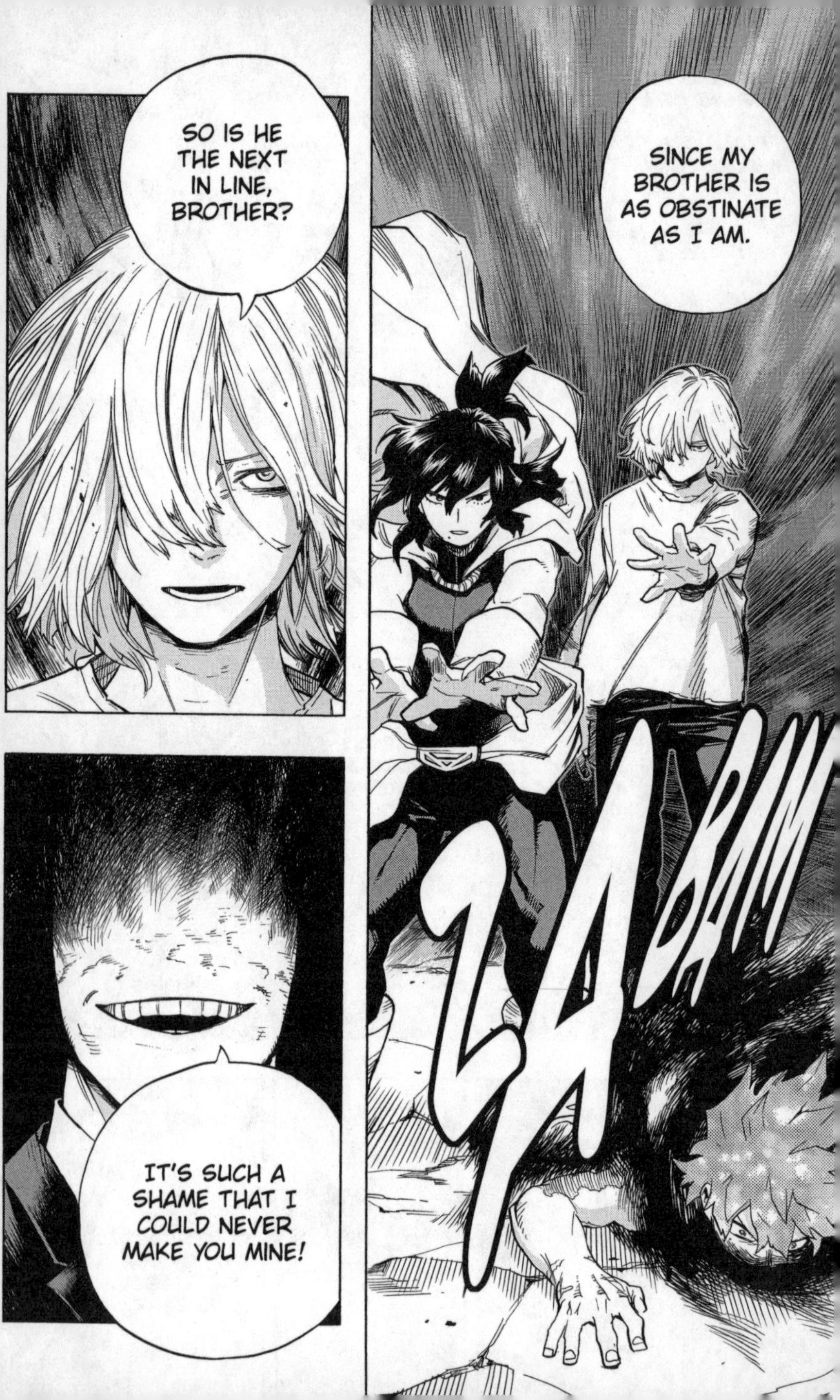
SINCE MY BROTHER IS AS OBSTINATE AS I AM.
SO IS HE THE NEXT IN LINE, BROTHER?
IT'S SUCH A SHAME THAT I COULD NEVER MAKE YOU MINE!

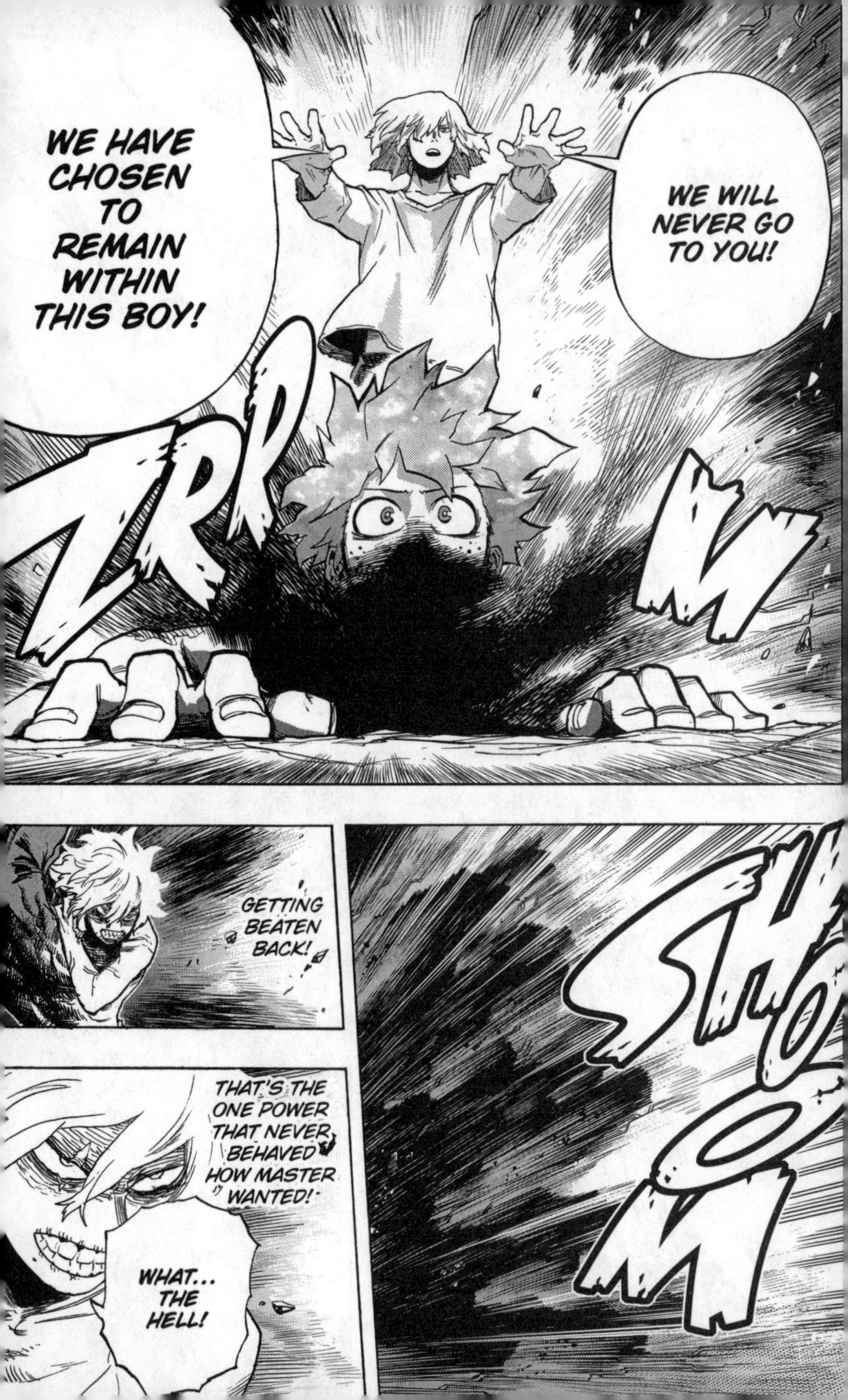
WE WILL NEVER GO TO YOU!
WE HAVE CHOSEN TO REMAIN WITHIN THIS BOY!
SHOOM
GETTING BEATEN BACK!
THAT'S THE ONE POWER THAT NEVER BEHAVED HOW MASTER WANTED!
WHAT... THE HELL!

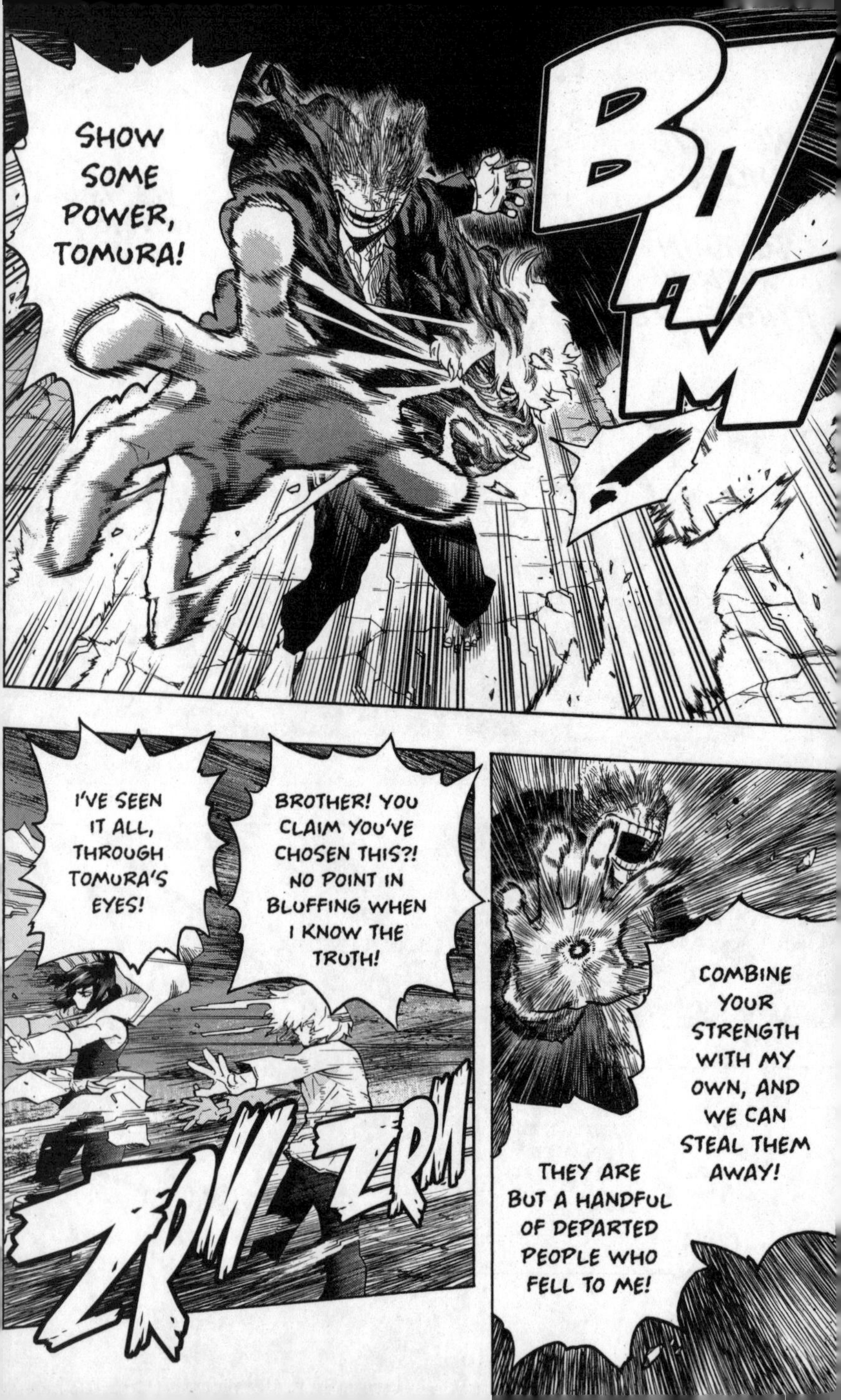
BAM!
SHOW SOME POWER, TOMURA!
COMBINE YOUR STRENGTH WITH MY OWN, AND WE CAN STEAL THEM AWAY!
THEY ARE BUT A HANDFUL OF DEPARTED PEOPLE WHO FELL TO ME!
BROTHER! YOU CLAIM YOU'VE CHOSEN THIS?! NO POINT IN BLUFFING WHEN I KNOW THE TRUTH!
I'VE SEEN IT ALL, THROUGH TOMURA'S EYES!
ZRM
ZRM

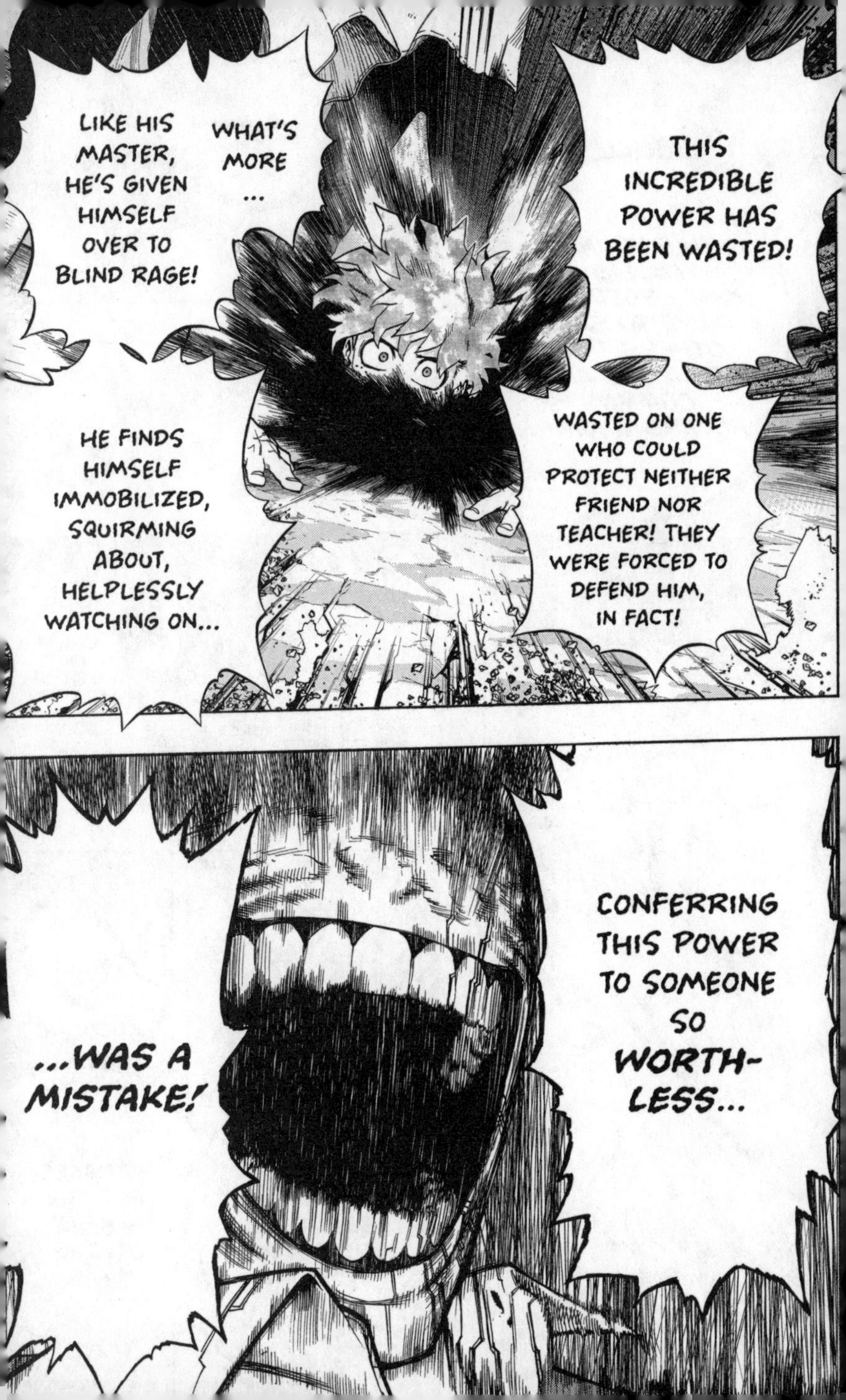
THIS INCREDIBLE POWER HAS BEEN WASTED!
WHAT'S MORE ...
LIKE HIS MASTER, HE'S GIVEN HIMSELF OVER TO BLIND RAGE!
WASTED ON ONE WHO COULD PROTECT NEITHER FRIEND NOR TEACHER! THEY WERE FORCED TO DEFEND HIM, IN FACT!
HE FINDS HIMSELF IMMOBILIZED, SQUIRMING ABOUT, HELPLESSLY WATCHING ON...
CONFERRING THIS POWER TO SOMEONE SO WORTH-LESS...
...WAS A MISTAKE!

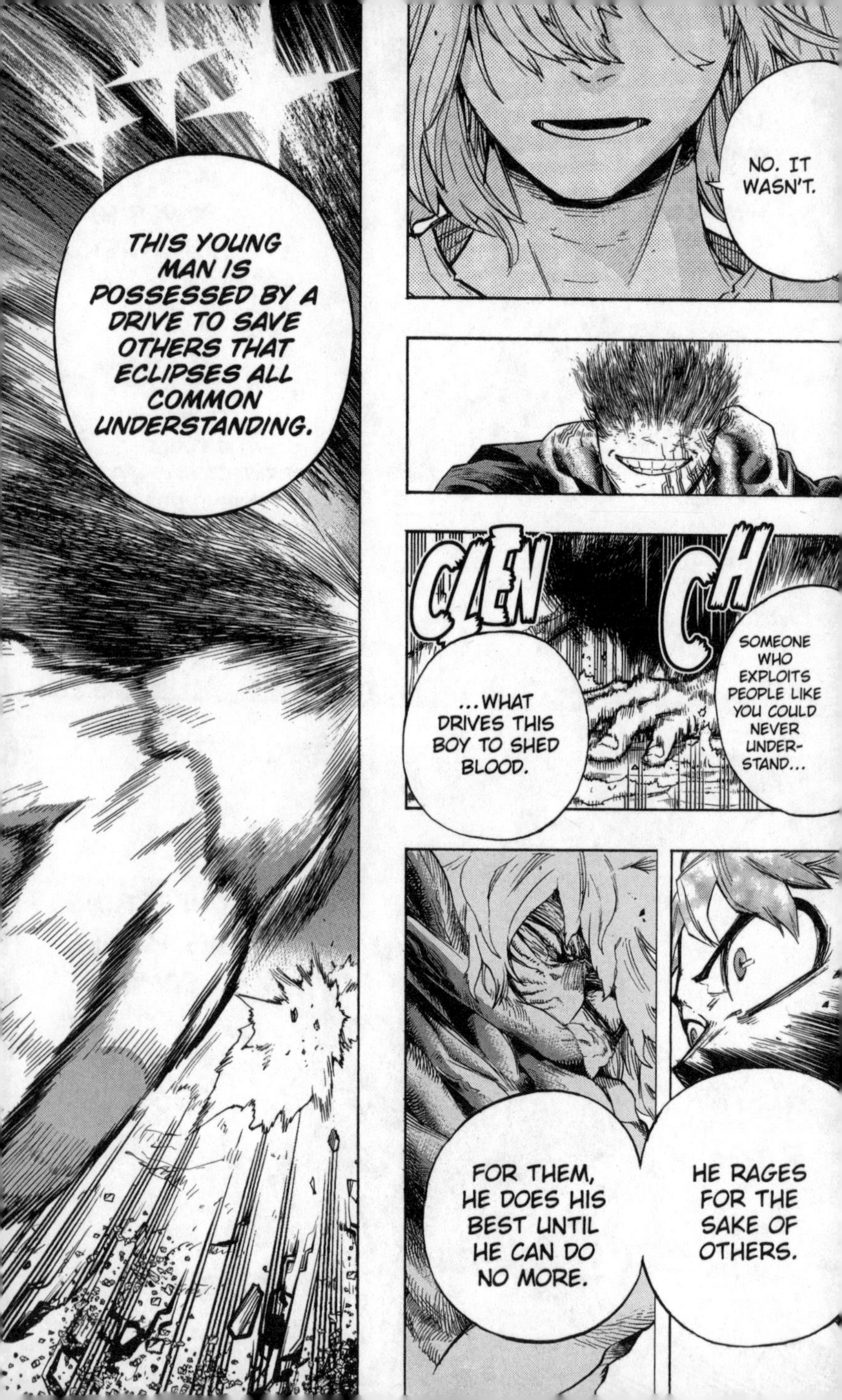
NO. IT WASN'T.
CLENCH
SOMEONE WHO EXPLOITS PEOPLE LIKE YOU COULD NEVER UNDER-STAND...
...WHAT DRIVES THIS BOY TO SHED BLOOD.
HE RAGES FOR THE SAKE OF OTHERS.
FOR THEM, HE DOES HIS BEST UNTIL HE CAN DO NO MORE.
THIS YOUNG MAN IS POSSESSED BY A DRIVE TO SAVE OTHERS THAT ECLIPSES ALL COMMON UNDERSTANDING.

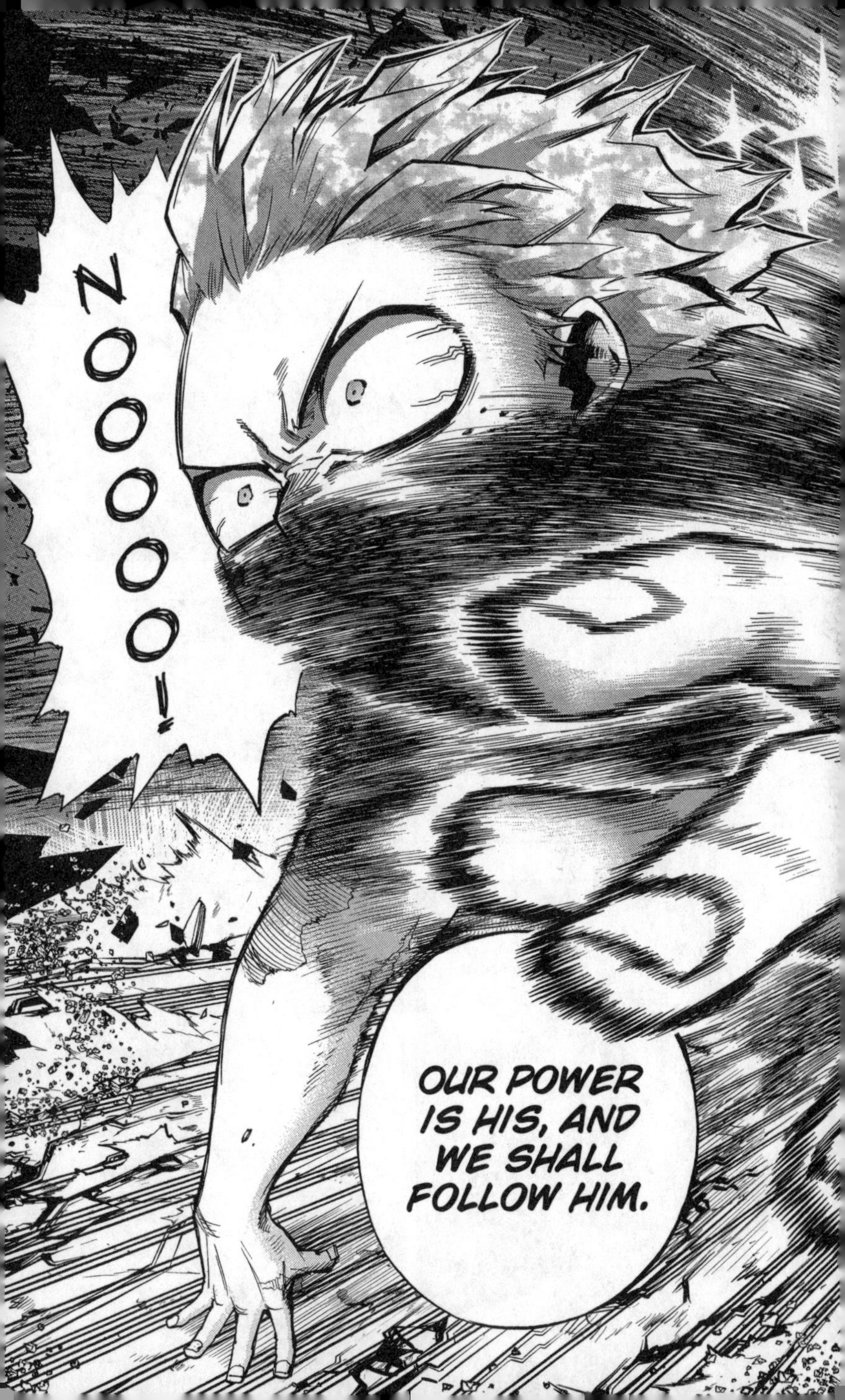
OUR POWER IS HIS, AND WE SHALL FOLLOW HIM.
NOOOOOO!!

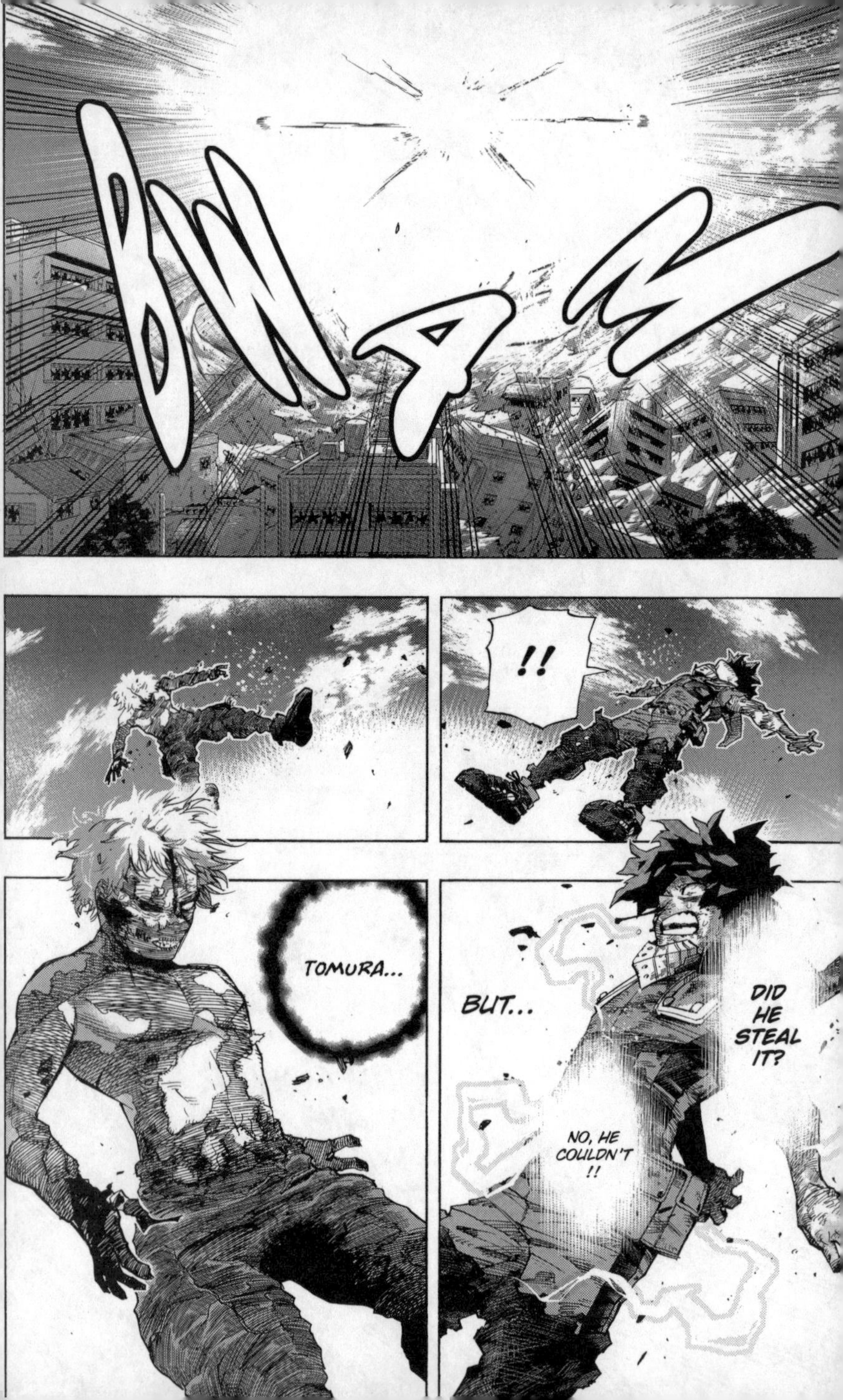
BWAM
!!
DID HE STEAL IT?
BUT...
NO, HE COULDN'T !!
TOMURA...

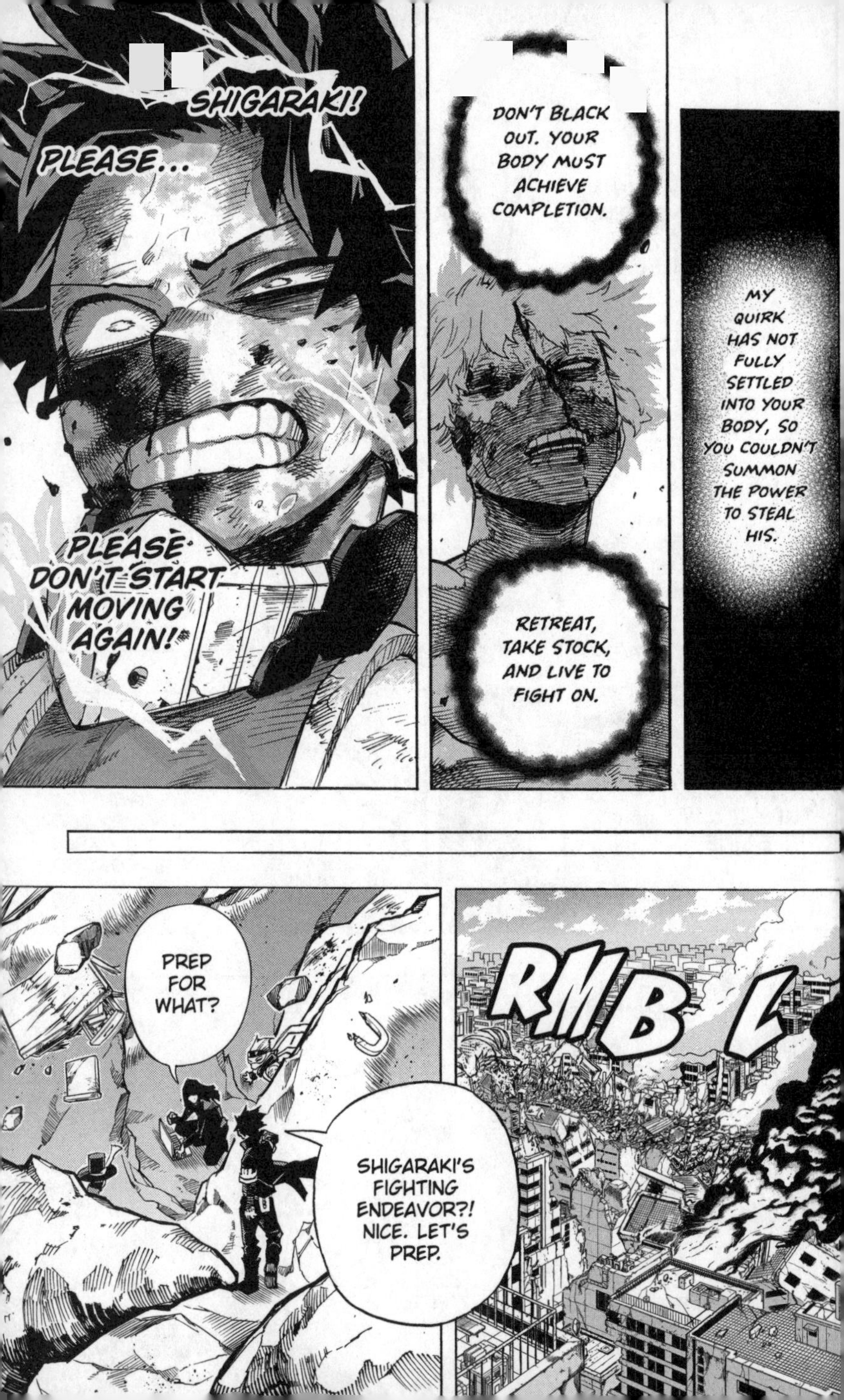
MY QUIRK HAS NOT FULLY SETTLED INTO YOUR BODY, SO YOU COULDN'T SUMMON THE POWER TO STEAL HIS.
DON'T BLACK OUT. YOUR BODY MUST ACHIEVE COMPLETION.
RETREAT, TAKE STOCK, AND LIVE TO FIGHT ON.
SHIGARAKI!
PLEASE...
PLEASE DON'T START MOVING AGAIN!
RMB L
SHIGARAKI'S FIGHTING ENDEAVOR?! NICE. LET'S PREP.
PREP FOR WHAT?

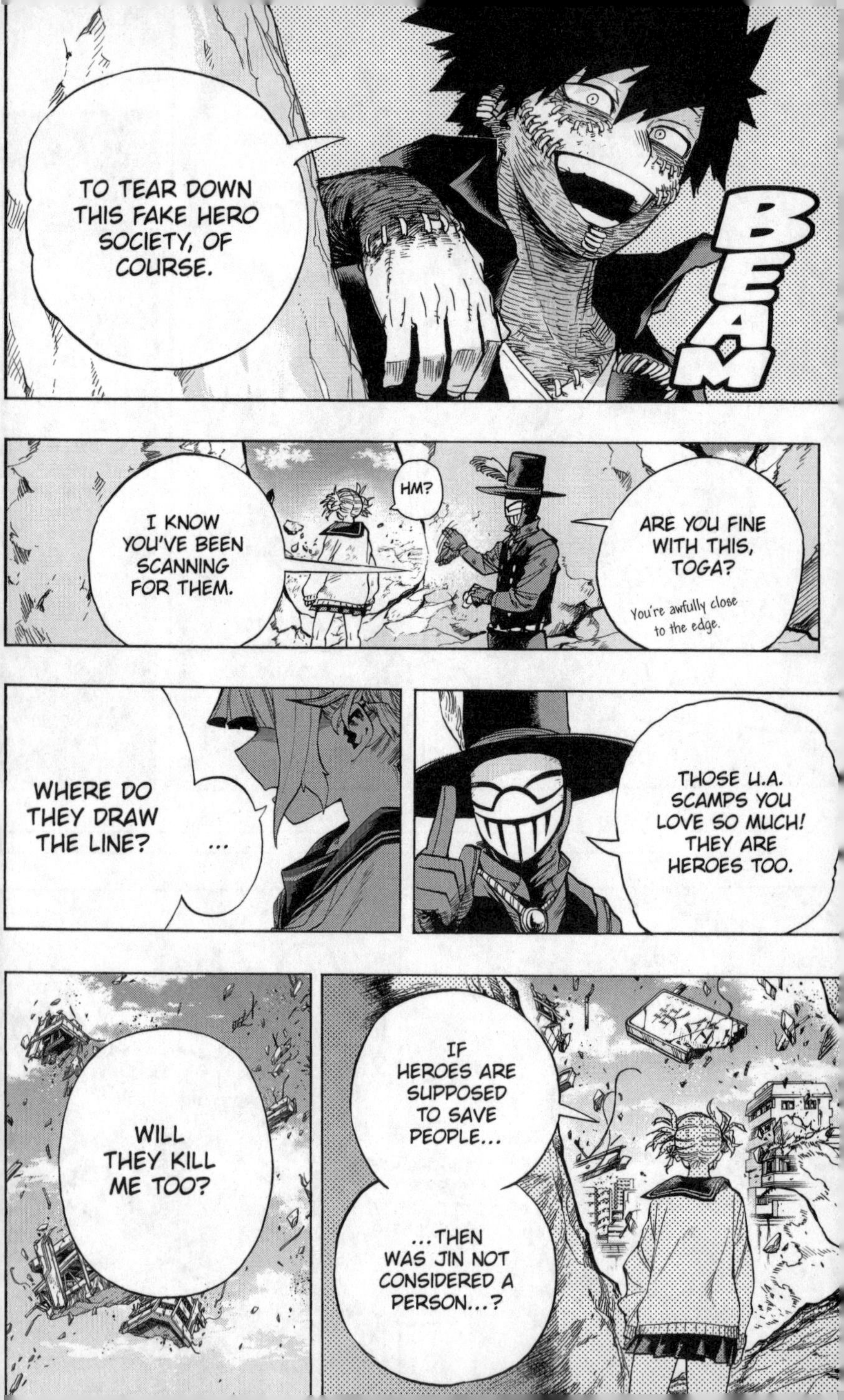
TO TEAR DOWN THIS FAKE HERO SOCIETY, OF COURSE.
BEAM
ARE YOU FINE WITH THIS, TOGA?
You're awfully close to the edge.
HM?
I KNOW YOU'VE BEEN SCANNING FOR THEM.
THOSE U.A. SCAMPS YOU LOVE SO MUCH! THEY ARE HEROES TOO.
...
WHERE DO THEY DRAW THE LINE?
IF HEROES ARE SUPPOSED TO SAVE PEOPLE...
...THEN WAS JIN NOT CONSIDERED A PERSON...?
WILL THEY KILL ME TOO?

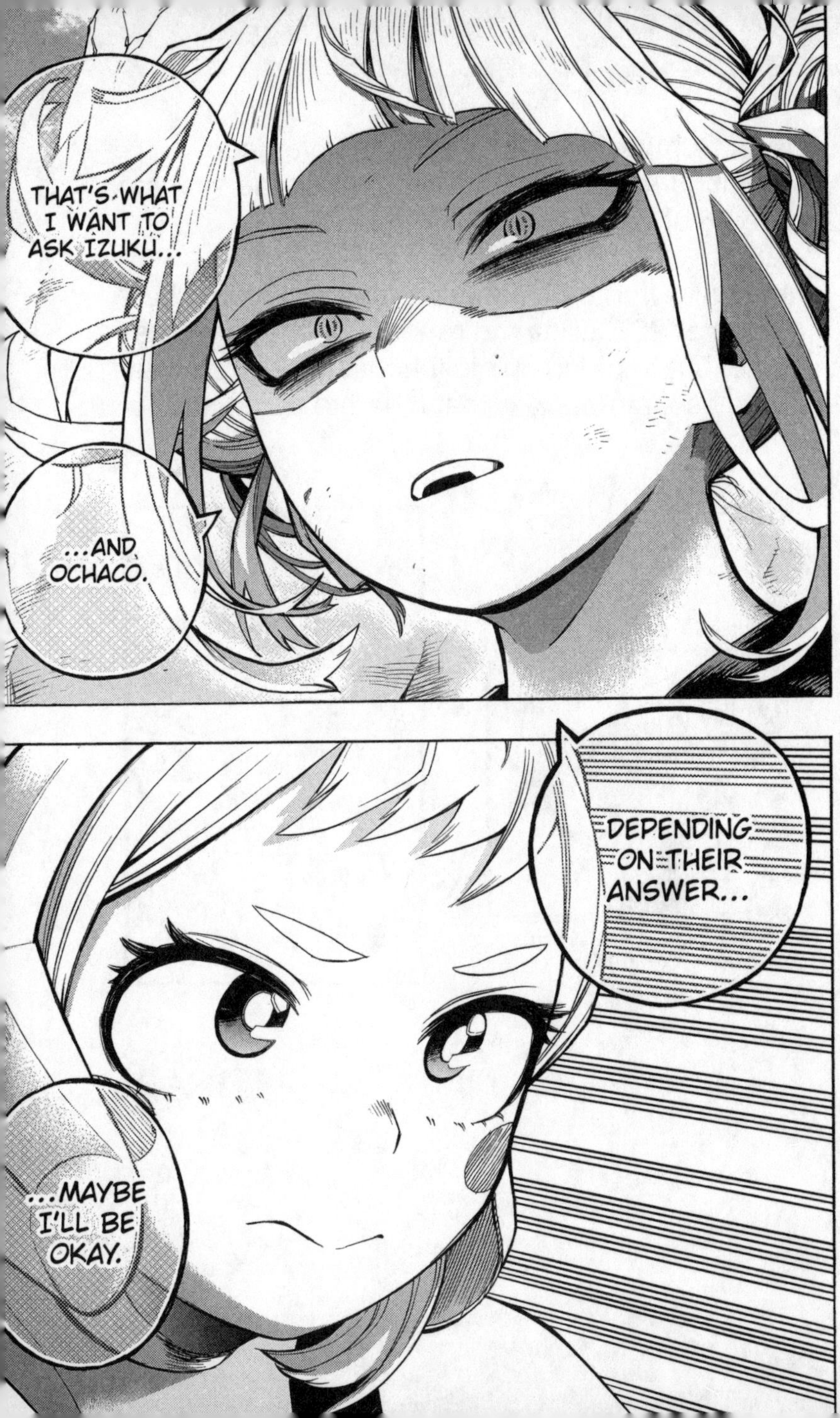
THAT'S WHAT I WANT TO ASK IZUKU...
...AND OCHACO.
DEPENDING ON THEIR ANSWER...
...MAYBE I'LL BE OKAY.

When Compress says, “I know you’ve been scanning for them,” he’s talking about the scene on page 56 of volume 29.

I originally wanted to insert a flashback panel here in chapter 287 to remind readers of that previous scene, but to be completely honest, the draft was already so jam-packed that it had to be omitted.

Volume 29, page 56

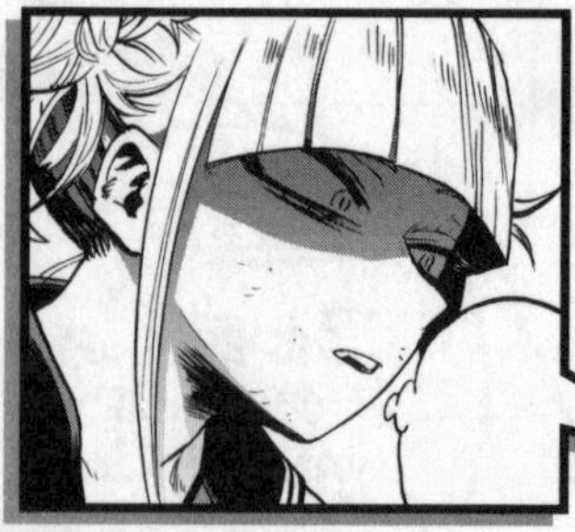

She was checking if Deku, Ochaco, or Tsuyu were down there.

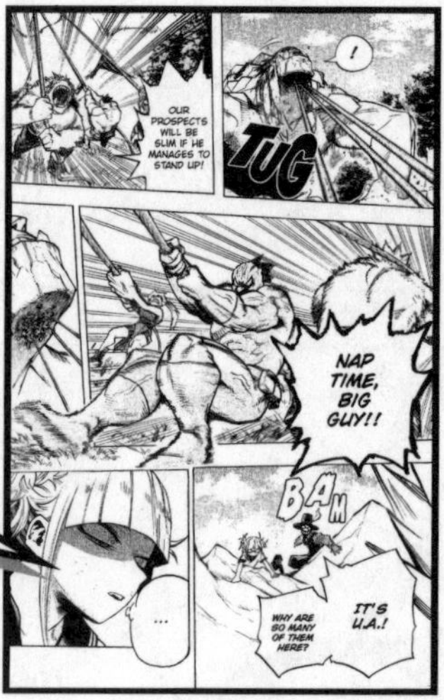
!
TUG
OUR PROSPECTS WILL BE SLIM IF HE MANAGES TO STAND UP!
NAP TIME, BIG GUY!!
BAM
IT'S U.A.!
WHY ARE SO MANY OF THEM HERE?
...

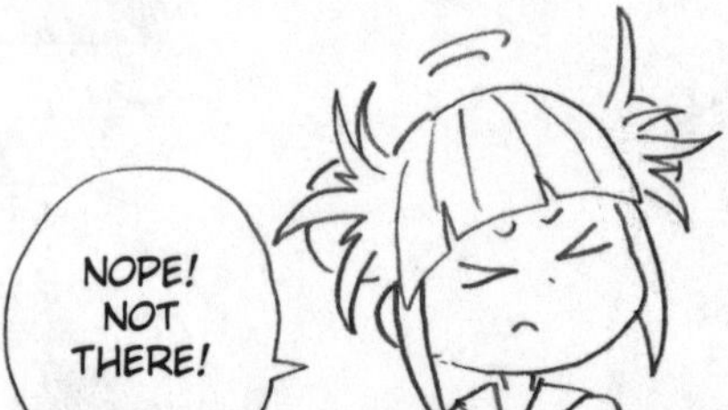
NOPE! NOT THERE!

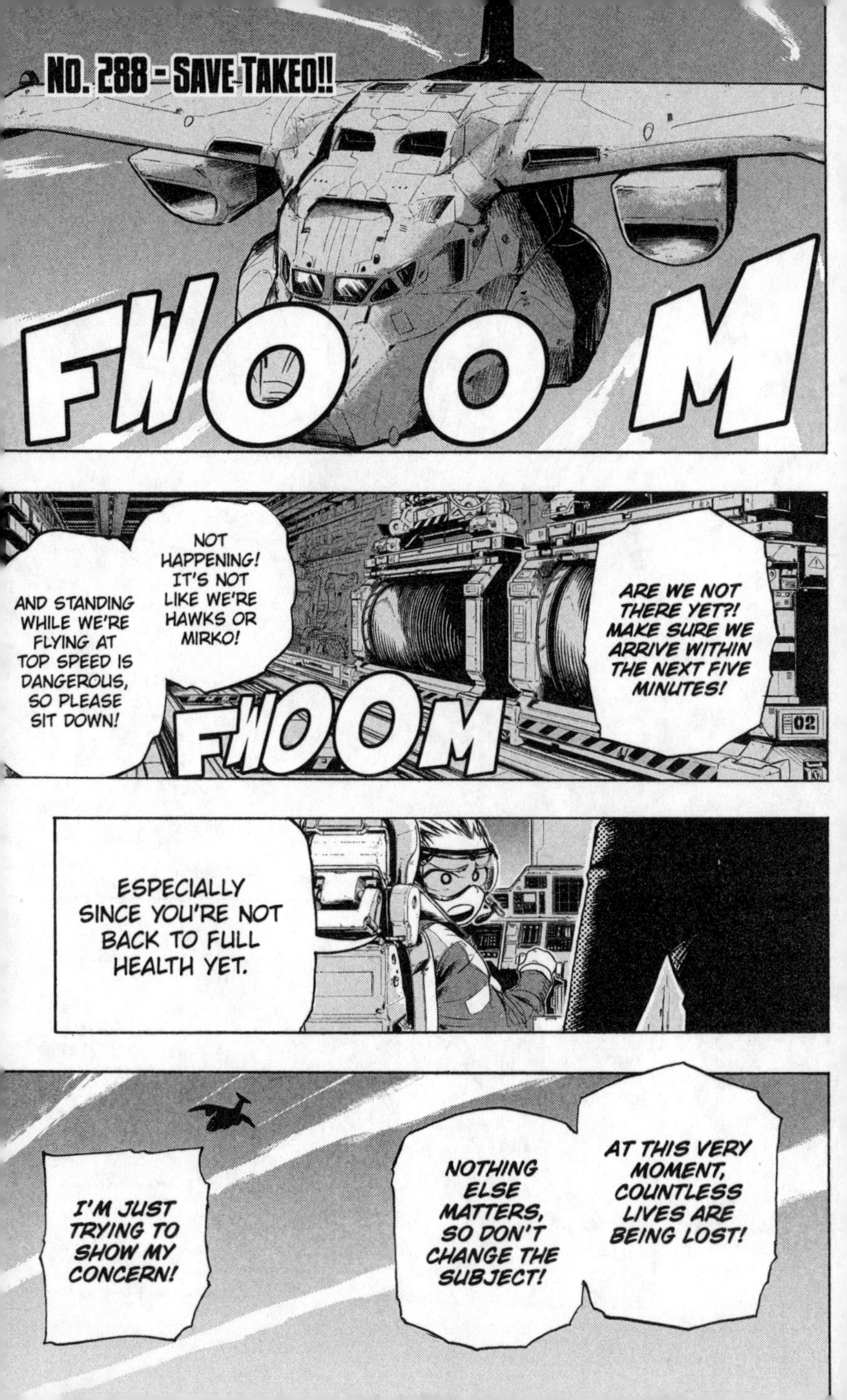
No. 288 - Save Takeo!!
FWOOM
ARE WE NOT THERE YET?! MAKE SURE WE ARRIVE WITHIN THE NEXT FIVE MINUTES!
FWOOM
NOT HAPPENING! IT'S NOT LIKE WE'RE HAWKS OR MIRKO!
AND STANDING WHILE WE'RE FLYING AT TOP SPEED IS DANGEROUS, SO PLEASE SIT DOWN!
ESPECIALLY SINCE YOU'RE NOT BACK TO FULL HEALTH YET.
AT THIS VERY MOMENT, COUNTLESS LIVES ARE BEING LOST!
NOTHING ELSE MATTERS, SO DON'T CHANGE THE SUBJECT!
I'M JUST TRYING TO SHOW MY CONCERN!

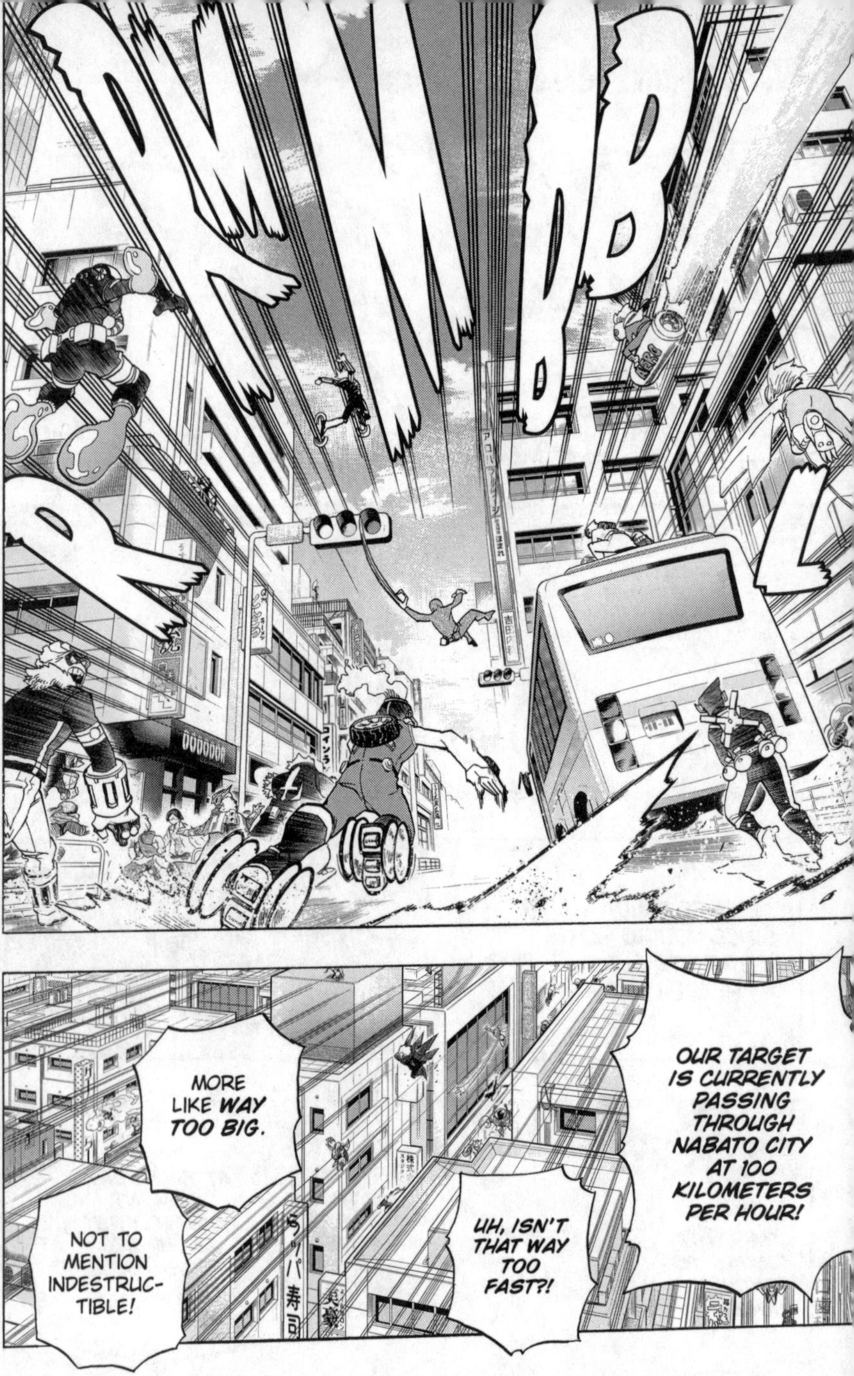
OUR TARGET IS CURRENTLY PASSING THROUGH NABATO CITY AT 100 KILOMETERS PER HOUR!
UH, ISN'T THAT WAY TOO FAST?!
MORE LIKE WAY TOO BIG.
NOT TO MENTION INDESTRUC-TIBLE!

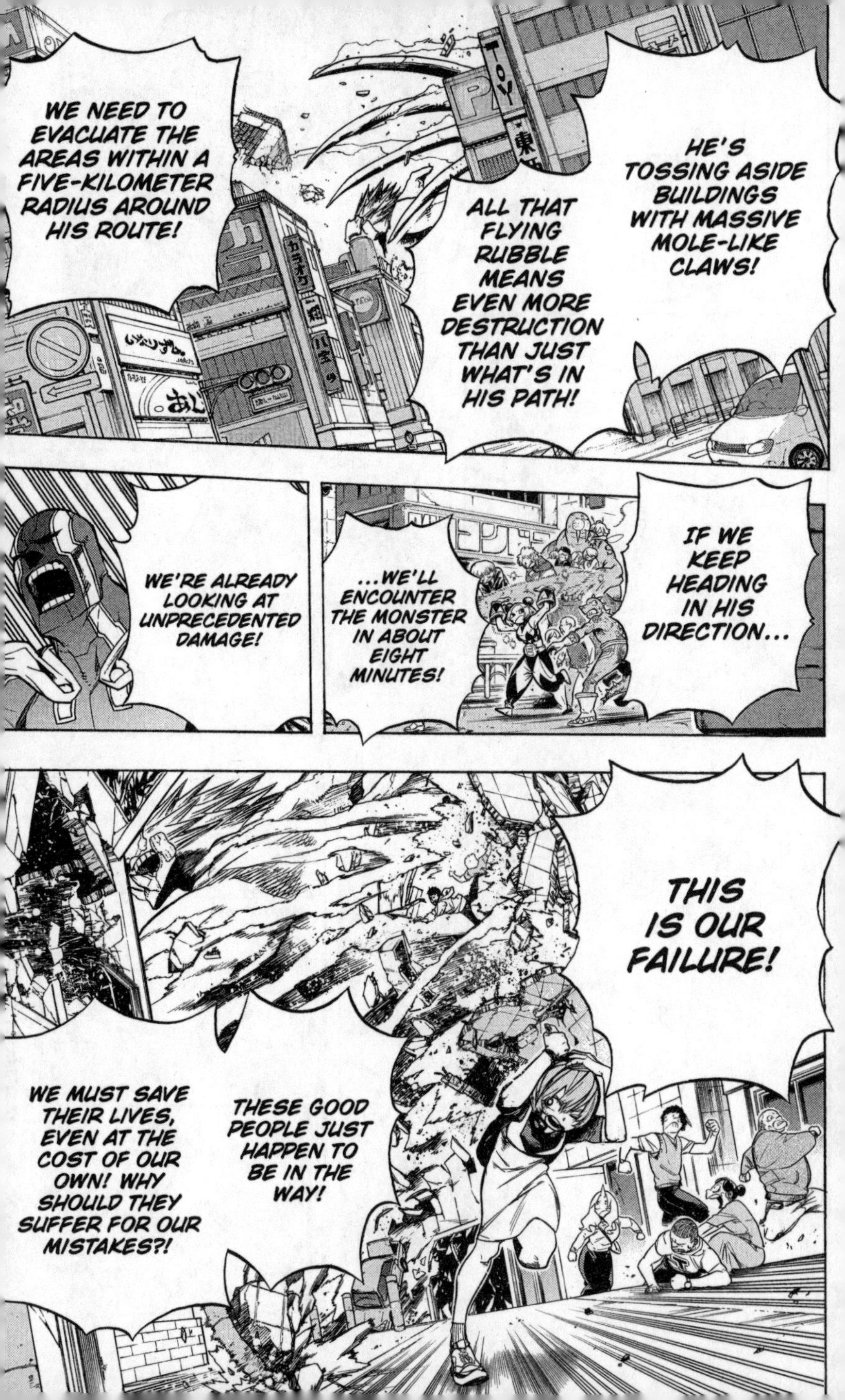
TOY
HE'S TOSSING ASIDE BUILDINGS WITH MASSIVE MOLE-LIKE CLAWS!
ALL THAT FLYING RUBBLE MEANS EVEN MORE DESTRUCTION THAN JUST WHAT'S IN HIS PATH!
WE NEED TO EVACUATE THE AREAS WITHIN A FIVE-KILOMETER RADIUS AROUND HIS ROUTE!
IF WE KEEP HEADING IN HIS DIRECTION...
...WE'LL ENCOUNTER THE MONSTER IN ABOUT EIGHT MINUTES!
WE'RE ALREADY LOOKING AT UNPRECEDENTED DAMAGE!
THIS IS OUR FAILURE!
THESE GOOD PEOPLE JUST HAPPEN TO BE IN THE WAY!
WE MUST SAVE THEIR LIVES, EVEN AT THE COST OF OUR OWN! WHY SHOULD THEY SUFFER FOR OUR MISTAKES?!

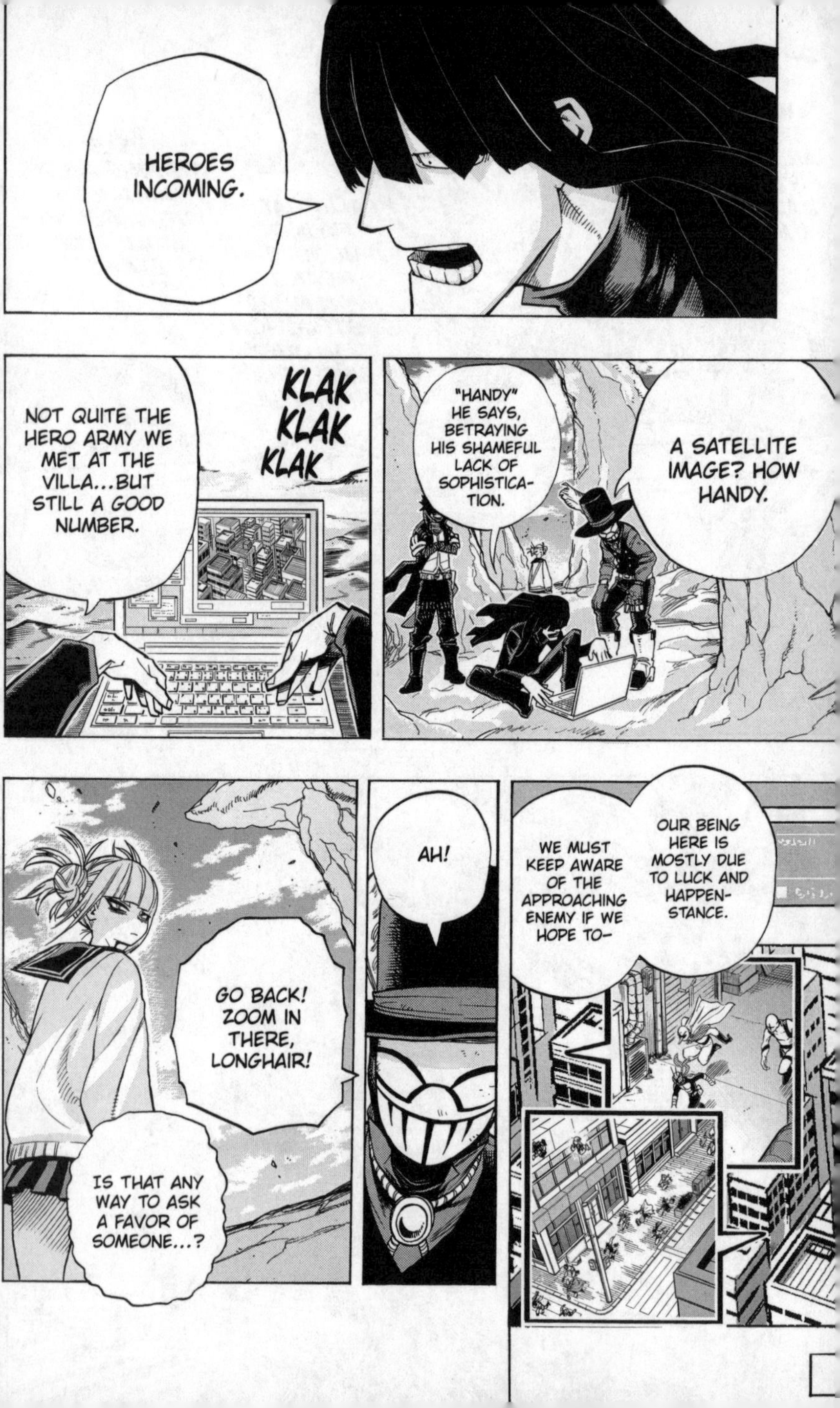
HEROES INCOMING.
A SATELLITE IMAGE? HOW HANDY.
"HANDY" HE SAYS, BETRAYING HIS SHAMEFUL LACK OF SOPHISTICA-TION.
KLAK KLAK KLAK
NOT QUITE THE HERO ARMY WE MET AT THE VILLA...BUT STILL A GOOD NUMBER.
OUR BEING HERE IS MOSTLY DUE TO LUCK AND HAPPEN-STANCE.
WE MUST KEEP AWARE OF THE APPROACHING ENEMY IF WE HOPE TO—
AH!
GO BACK! ZOOM IN THERE, LONGHAIR!
IS THAT ANY WAY TO ASK A FAVOR OF SOMEONE...?

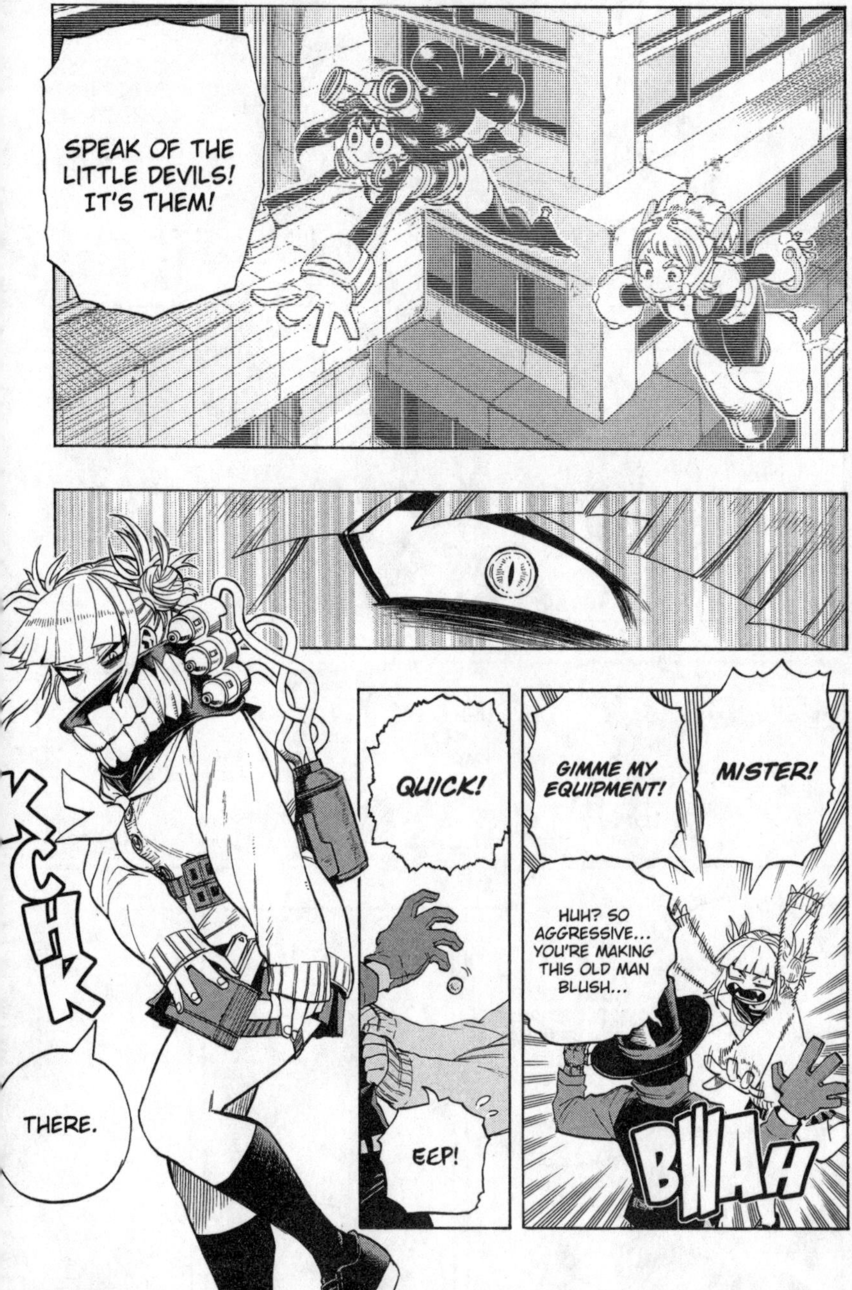
SPEAK OF THE LITTLE DEVILS! IT'S THEM!
MISTER!
GIMME MY EQUIPMENT!
HUH? SO AGGRESSIVE... YOU'RE MAKING THIS OLD MAN BLUSH...
BWAH
QUICK!
EEP!
KCHK
THERE.

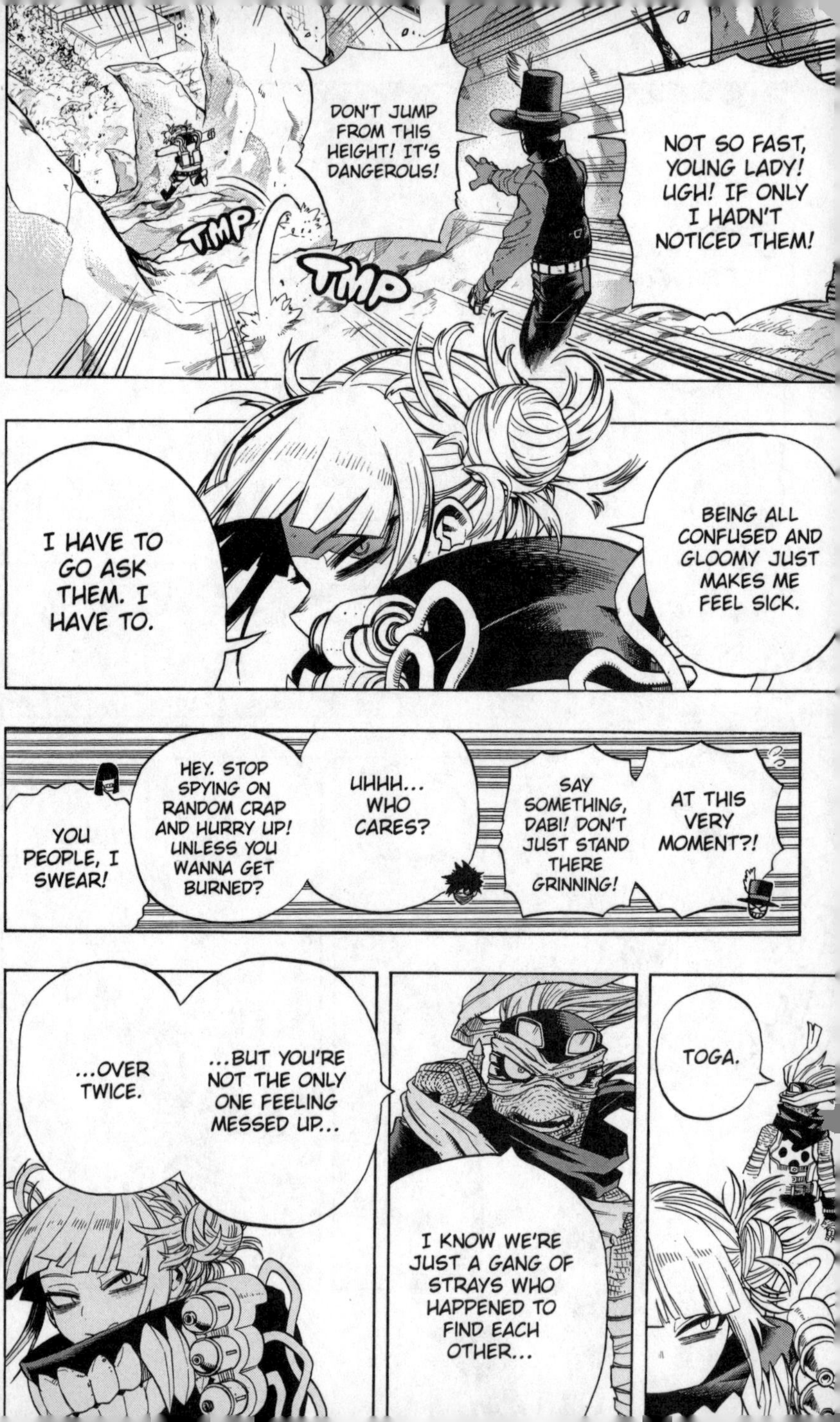
NOT SO FAST, YOUNG LADY! UGH! IF ONLY I HADN'T NOTICED THEM!
DON'T JUMP FROM THIS HEIGHT! IT'S DANGEROUS!
TMP
TMP
BEING ALL CONFUSED AND GLOOMY JUST MAKES ME FEEL SICK.
I HAVE TO GO ASK THEM. I HAVE TO.
AT THIS VERY MOMENT?!
SAY SOMETHING, DABI! DON'T JUST STAND THERE GRINNING!
UHHH... WHO CARES?
HEY. STOP SPYING ON RANDOM CRAP AND HURRY UP! UNLESS YOU WANNA GET BURNED?
YOU PEOPLE, I SWEAR!
TOGA.
I KNOW WE'RE JUST A GANG OF STRAYS WHO HAPPENED TO FIND EACH OTHER...
...BUT YOU'RE NOT THE ONLY ONE FEELING MESSED UP...
...OVER TWICE.

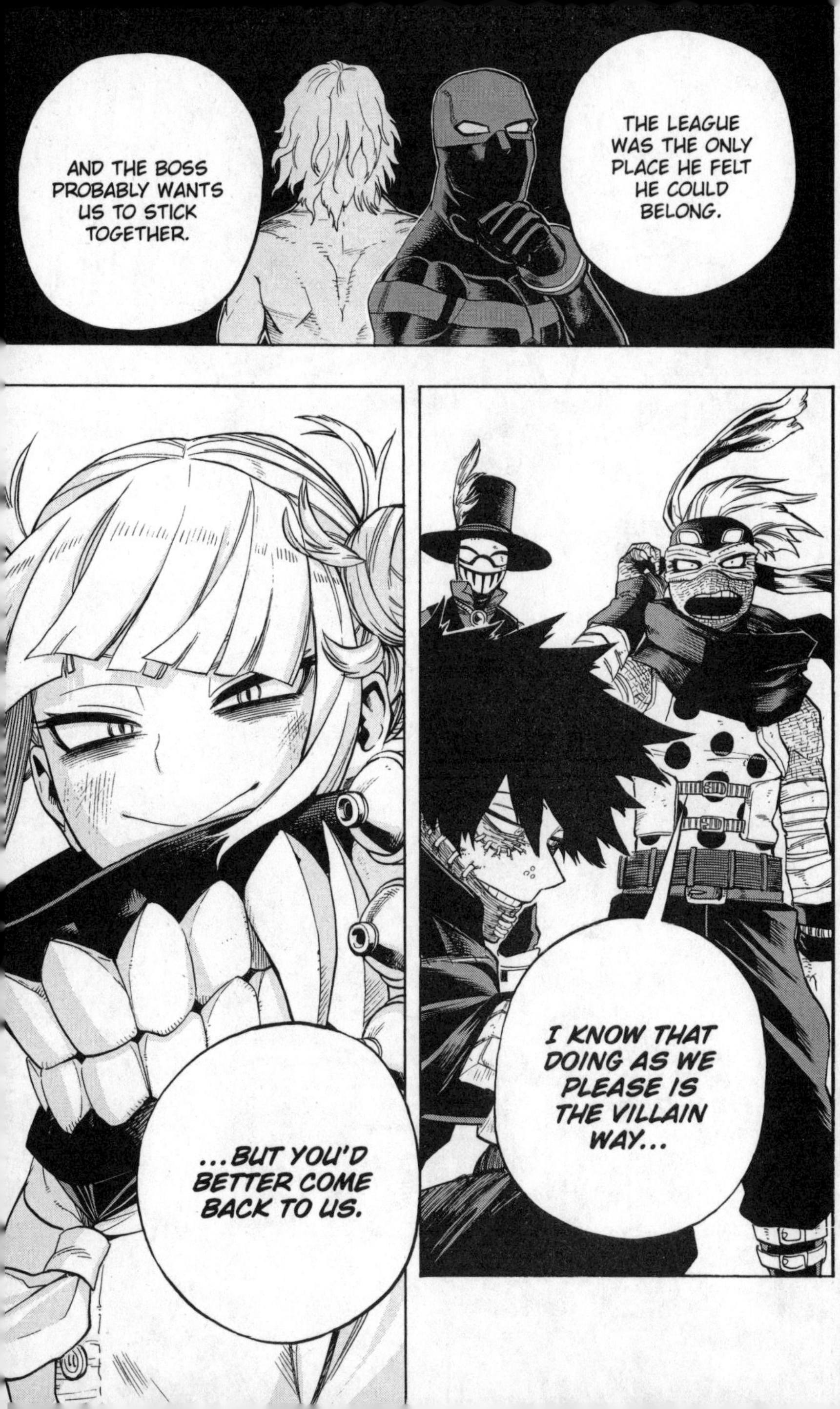
THE LEAGUE WAS THE ONLY PLACE HE FELT HE COULD BELONG.
AND THE BOSS PROBABLY WANTS US TO STICK TOGETHER.
I KNOW THAT DOING AS WE PLEASE IS THE VILLAIN WAY...
...BUT YOU'D BETTER COME BACK TO US.

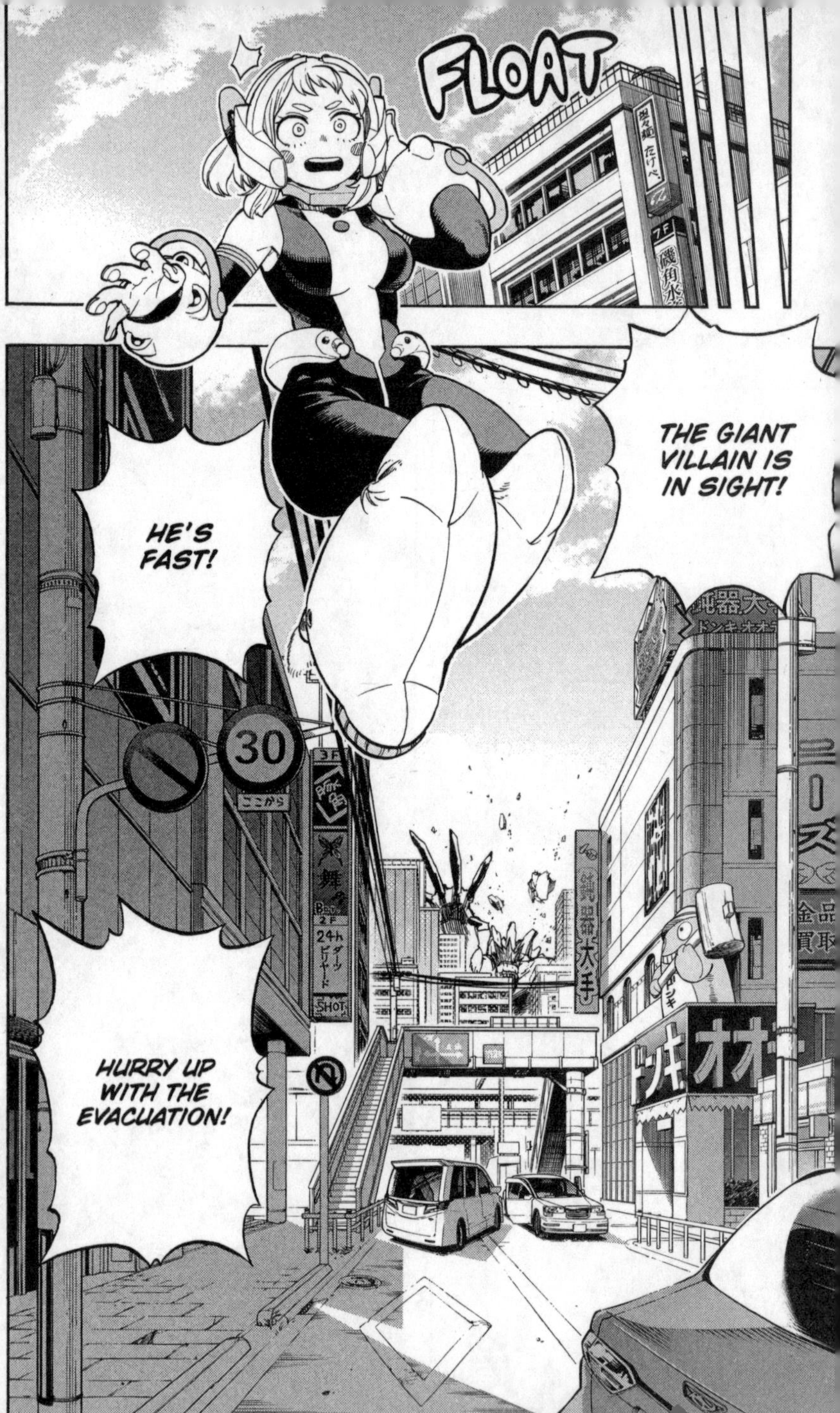
FLOAT
THE GIANT VILLAIN IS IN SIGHT!
HE'S FAST!
HURRY UP WITH THE EVACUATION!
30

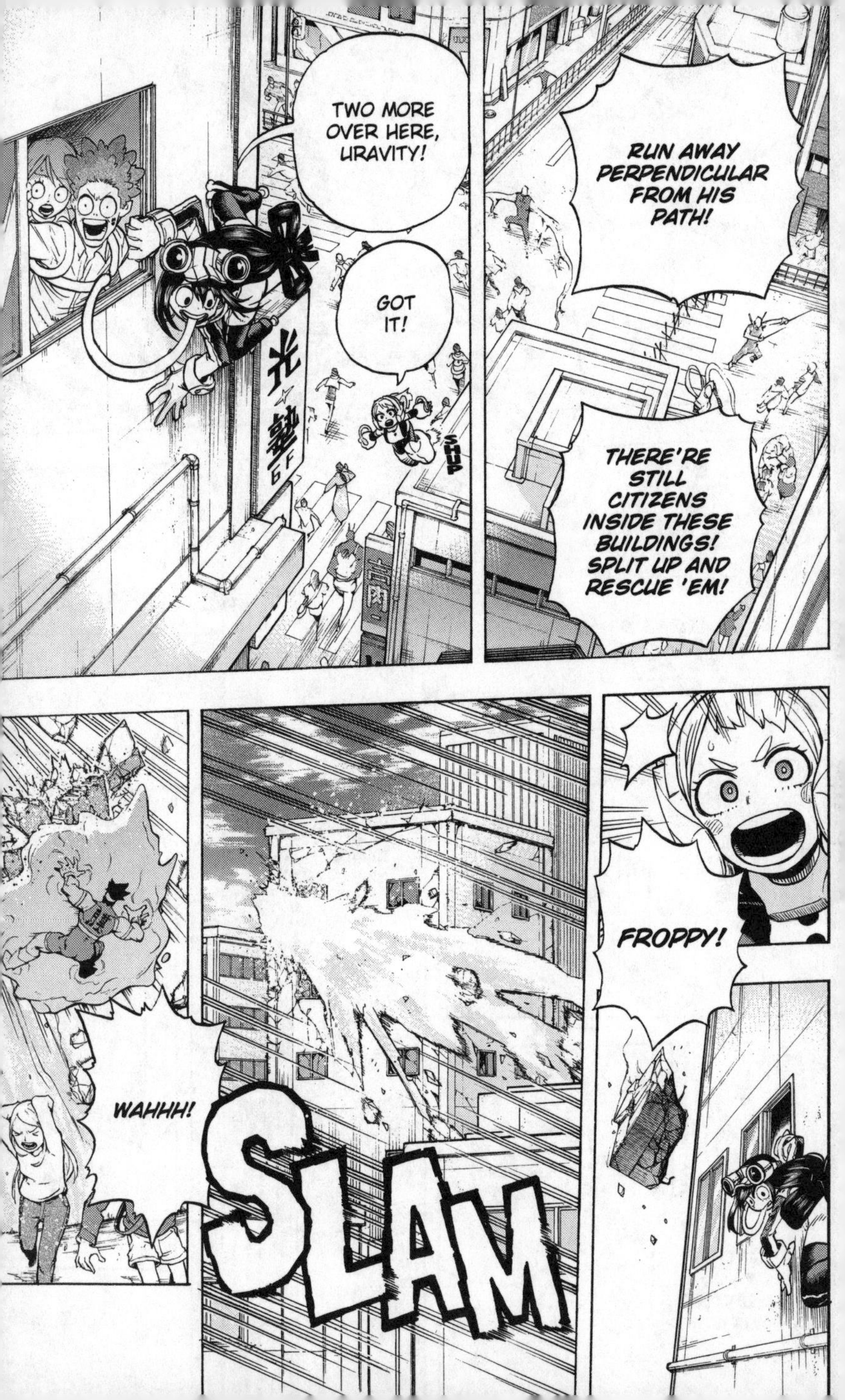
RUN AWAY PERPENDICULAR FROM HIS PATH!
THERE'RE STILL CITIZENS INSIDE THESE BUILDINGS! SPLIT UP AND RESCUE 'EM!
TWO MORE OVER HERE, URAVITY!
GOT IT!
SHUP
FROPPY!
SLAM
WAHHH!

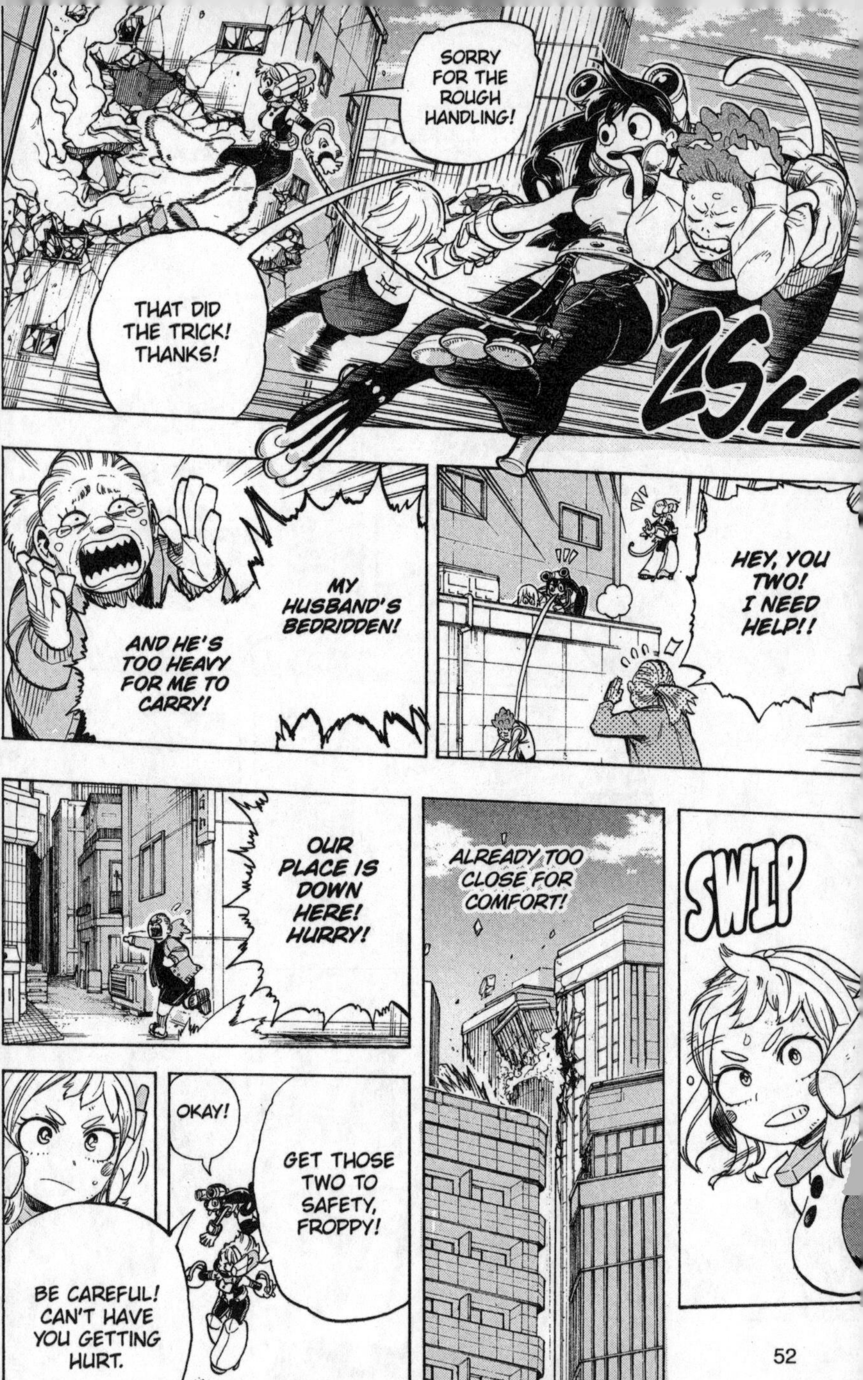
SORRY FOR THE ROUGH HANDLING!
ZSH
THAT DID THE TRICK! THANKS!
HEY, YOU TWO! I NEED HELP!!
MY HUSBAND'S BEDRIDDEN!
AND HE'S TOO HEAVY FOR ME TO CARRY!
SWIP
ALREADY TOO CLOSE FOR COMFORT!
OUR PLACE IS DOWN HERE! HURRY!
GET THOSE TWO TO SAFETY, FROPPY!
OKAY!
BE CAREFUL! CAN'T HAVE YOU GETTING HURT.

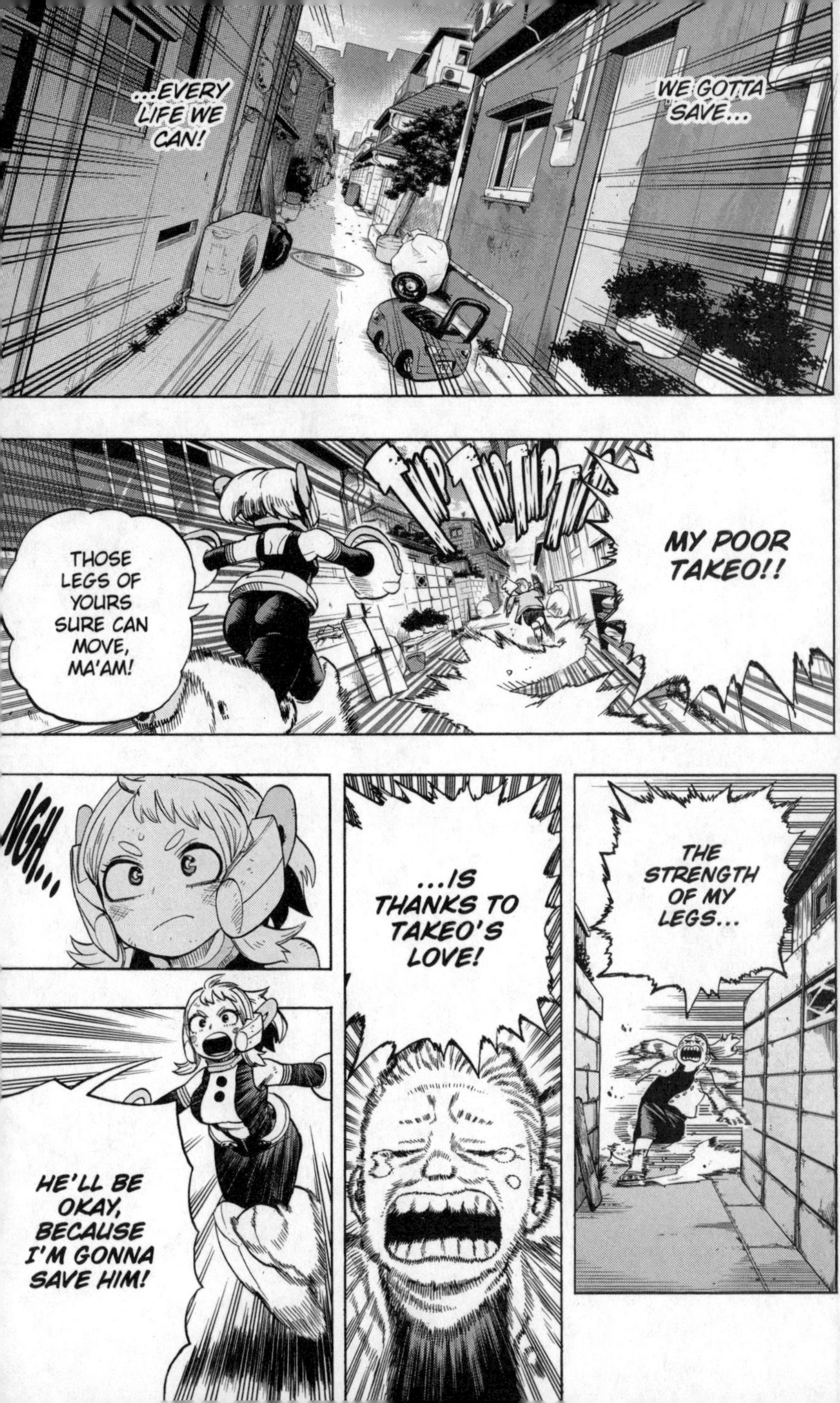

WE GOTTA SAVE...
...EVERY LIFE WE CAN!
MY POOR TAKEO!!
THOSE LEGS OF YOURS SURE CAN MOVE, MA'AM!
THE STRENGTH OF MY LEGS...
...IS THANKS TO TAKEO'S LOVE!
NGH...
HE'LL BE OKAY, BECAUSE I'M GONNA SAVE HIM!

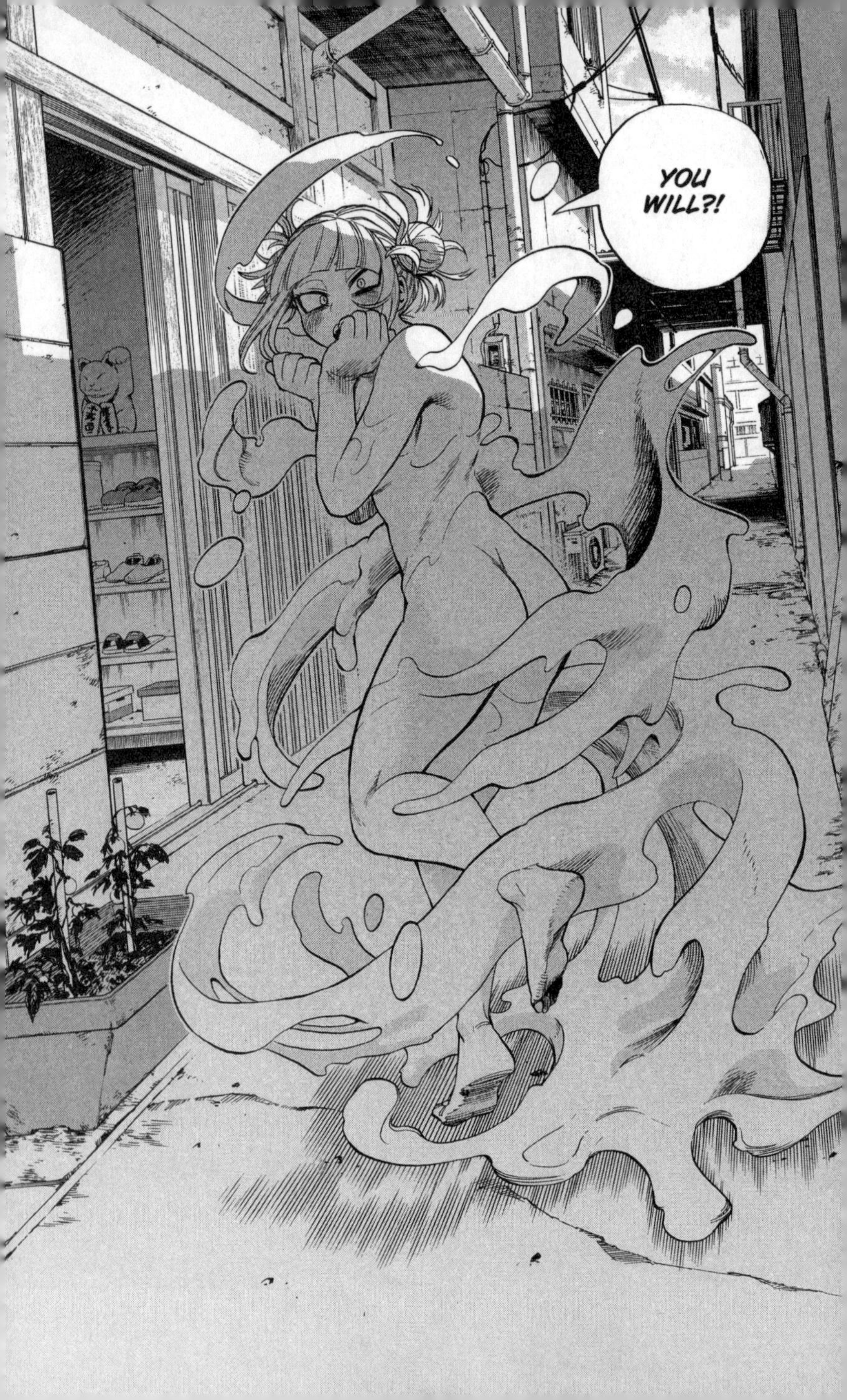
YOU WILL?!

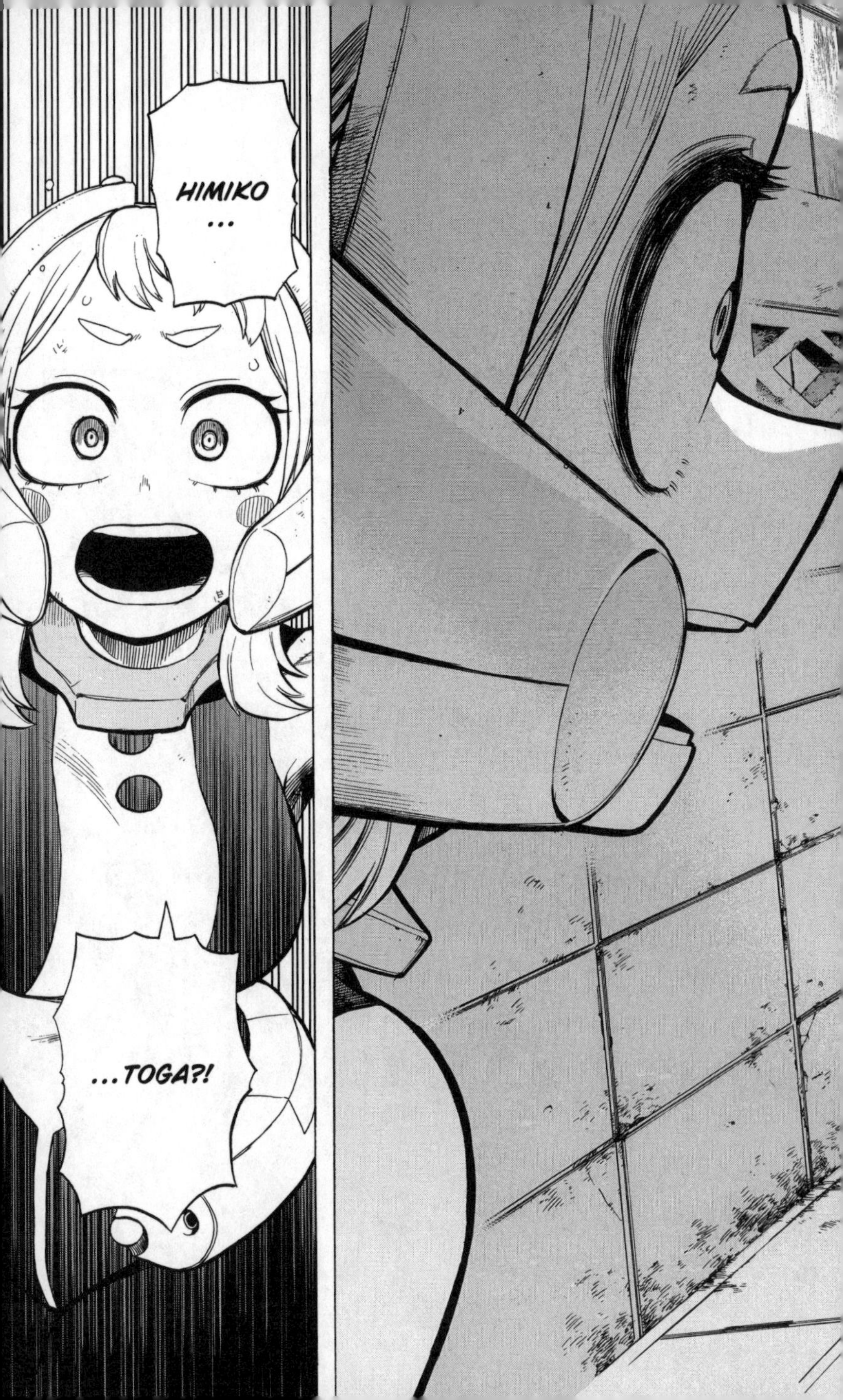
HIMIKO
...
...TOGA?!

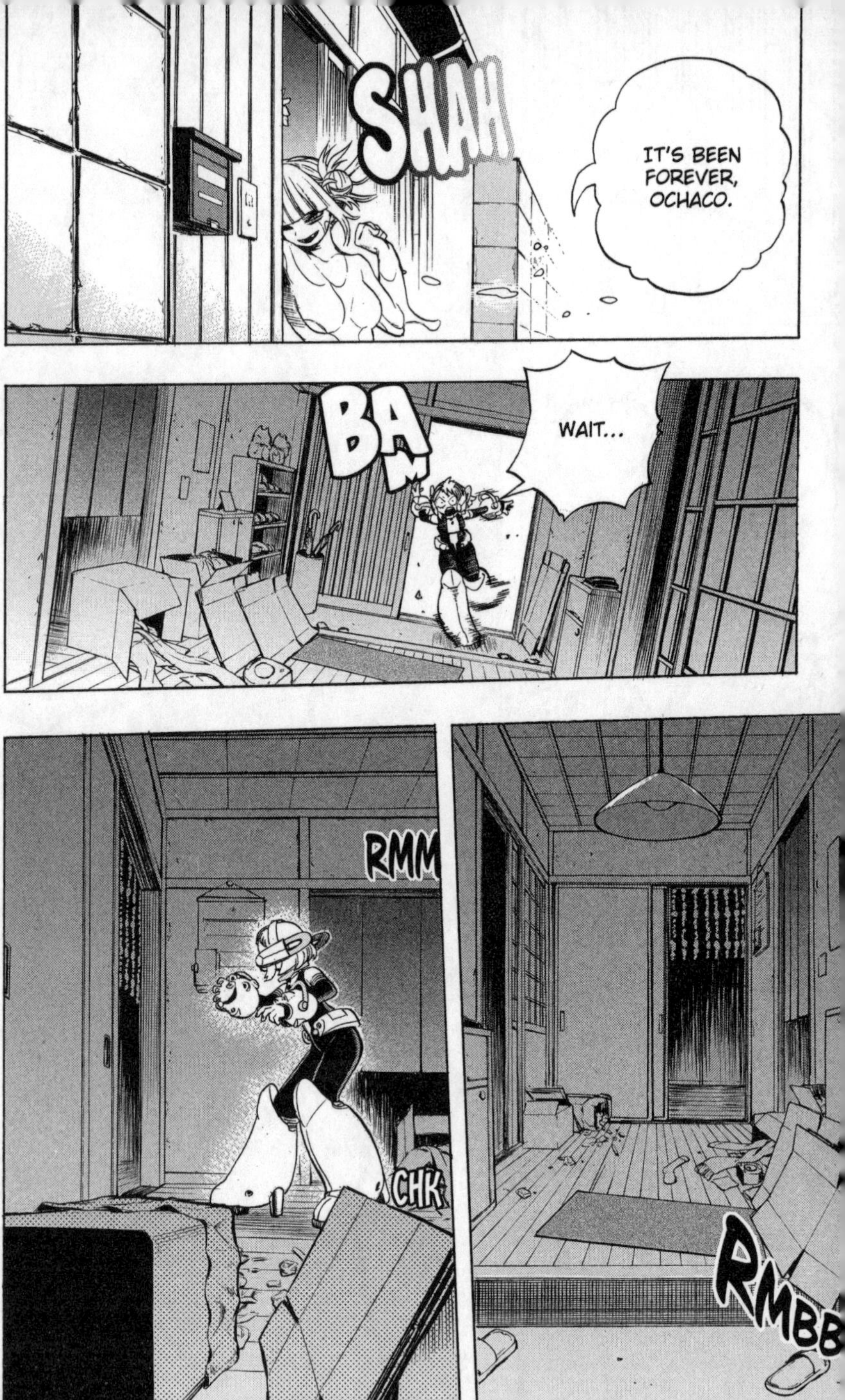
IT'S BEEN FOREVER, OCHACO.
SHAH
WAIT...
BAM
RMBB
RMM
CHK

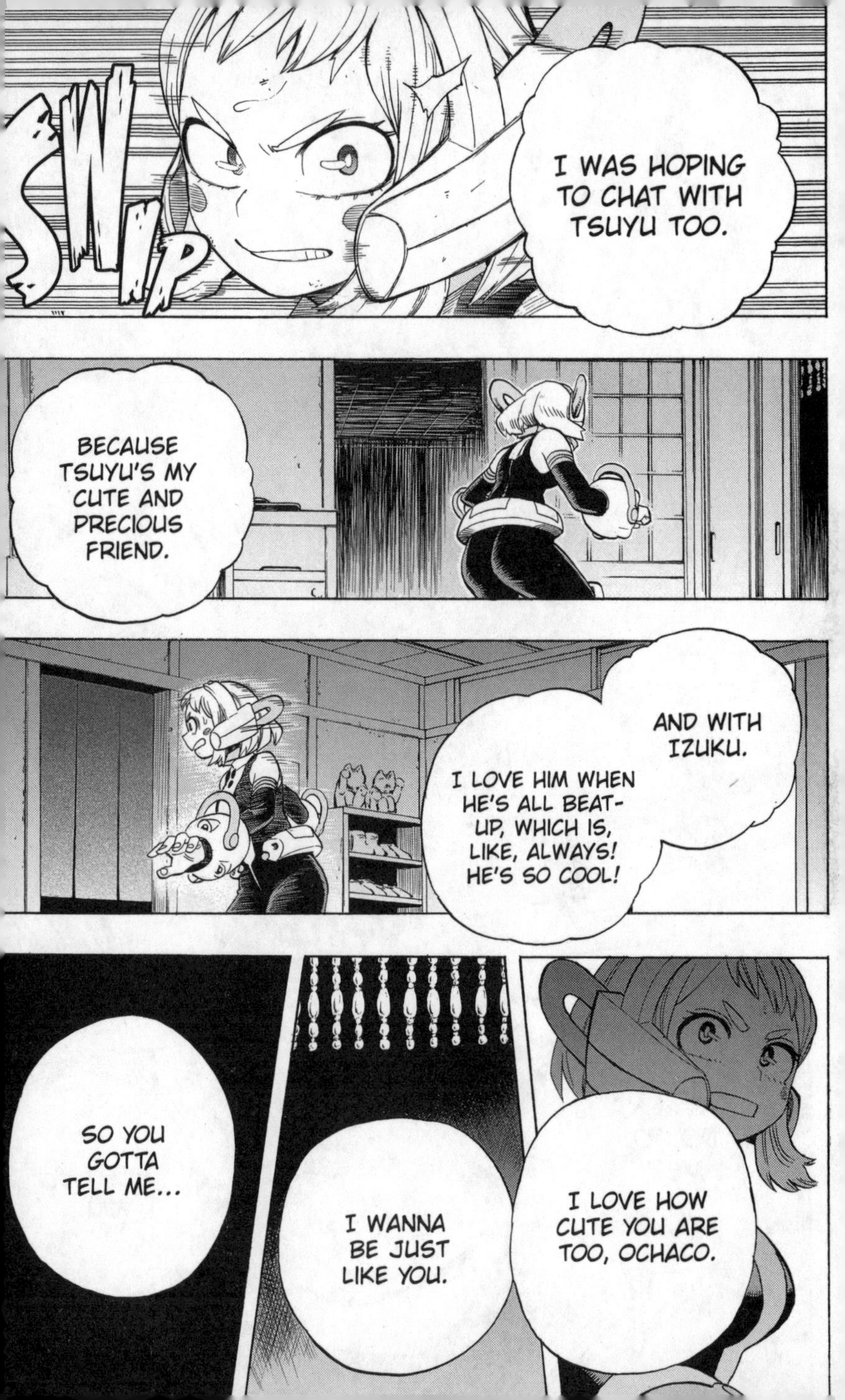
I WAS HOPING TO CHAT WITH TSUYU TOO.
SWIP
BECAUSE TSUYU'S MY CUTE AND PRECIOUS FRIEND.
AND WITH IZUKU.
I LOVE HIM WHEN HE'S ALL BEAT-UP, WHICH IS, LIKE, ALWAYS! HE'S SO COOL!
I LOVE HOW CUTE YOU ARE TOO, OCHACO.
I WANNA BE JUST LIKE YOU.
SO YOU GOTTA TELL ME...

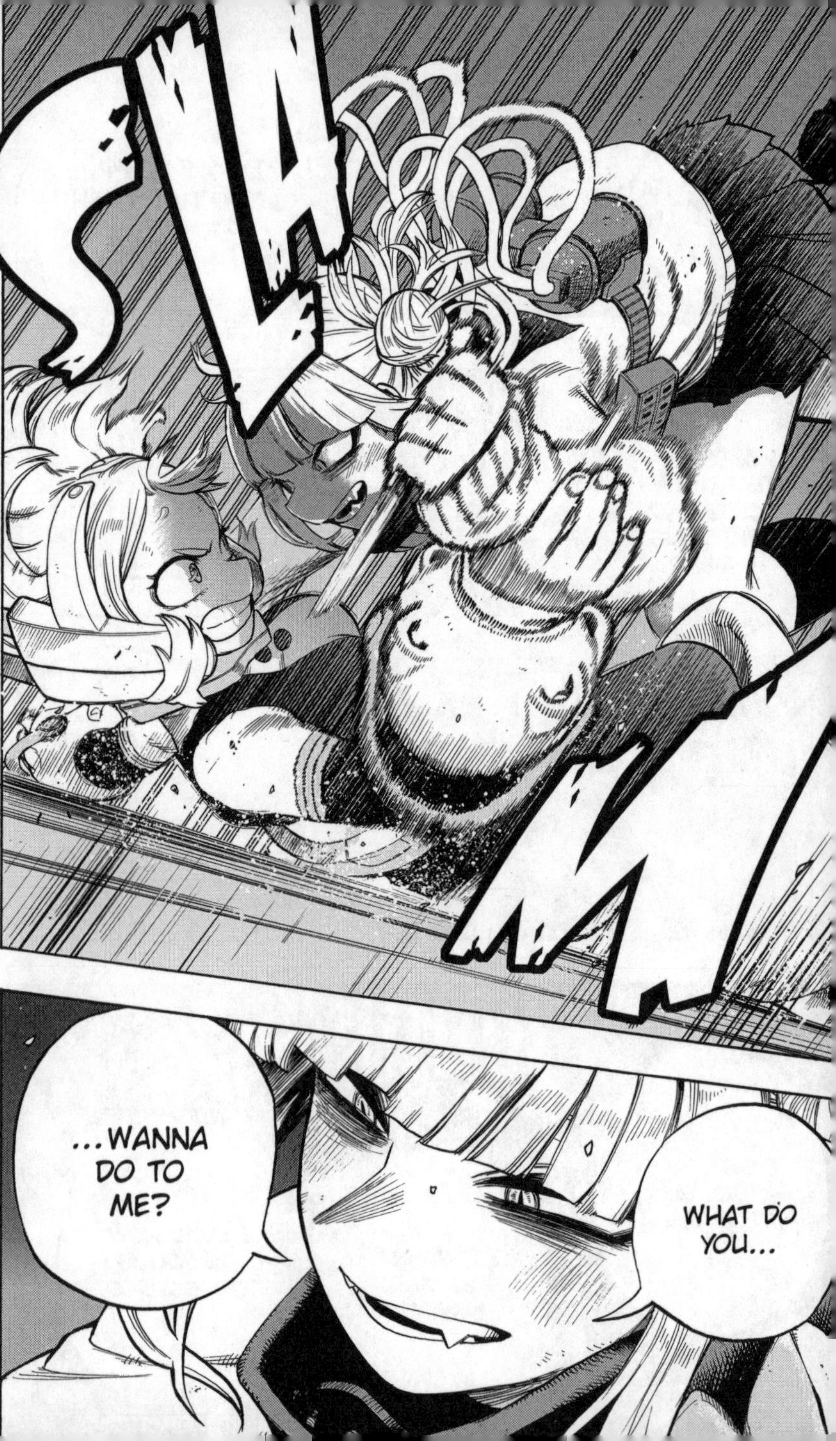
SLAM
WHAT DO YOU...
...WANNA DO TO ME?

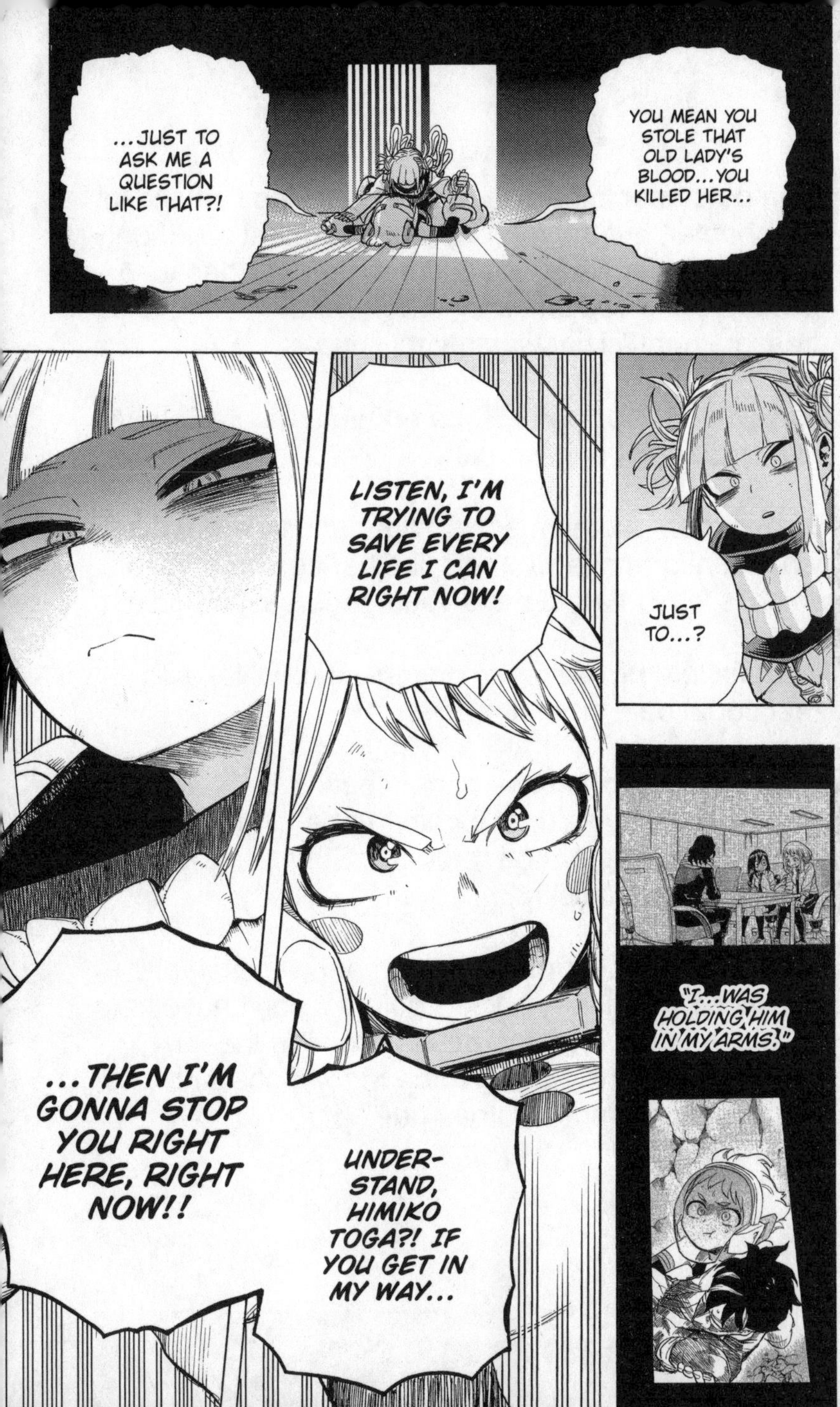
YOU MEAN YOU STOLE THAT OLD LADY'S BLOOD...YOU KILLED HER...
...JUST TO ASK ME A QUESTION LIKE THAT?!
JUST TO...?
"I...WAS HOLDING HIM IN MY ARMS."
LISTEN, I'M TRYING TO SAVE EVERY LIFE I CAN RIGHT NOW!
UNDER-STAND, HIMIKO TOGA?! IF YOU GET IN MY WAY...
...THEN I'M GONNA STOP YOU RIGHT HERE, RIGHT NOW!!

Toga puts her clothes on before attacking Ochaco in this chapter, but at first, I was thinking that she'd only bother with her weapons and equipment—because obviously she couldn't spend her sweet time getting dressed, right? That was my thinking.

However, in this scene, Toga appears before Ochaco as a budding young woman.

Both of them are high school age, and to Toga, that school uniform she wears is like her costume. All of which is why I had to have Toga get dressed again.

It's definitely *not* because editorial said, "Naked? That could be a bit of a problem."

It's obviously *not* like we had a spirited back-and-forth where they said, "It's going to be tough dealing with that, artwise," and I retorted, "But how would she get dressed so quickly?"

And it's assuredly *not* the case that I was instantly convinced when they said, "Look, we don't have time for this, and the involved action scene in the next chapter is seriously going to be tricky if she's naked, so just put her damn clothes on!"

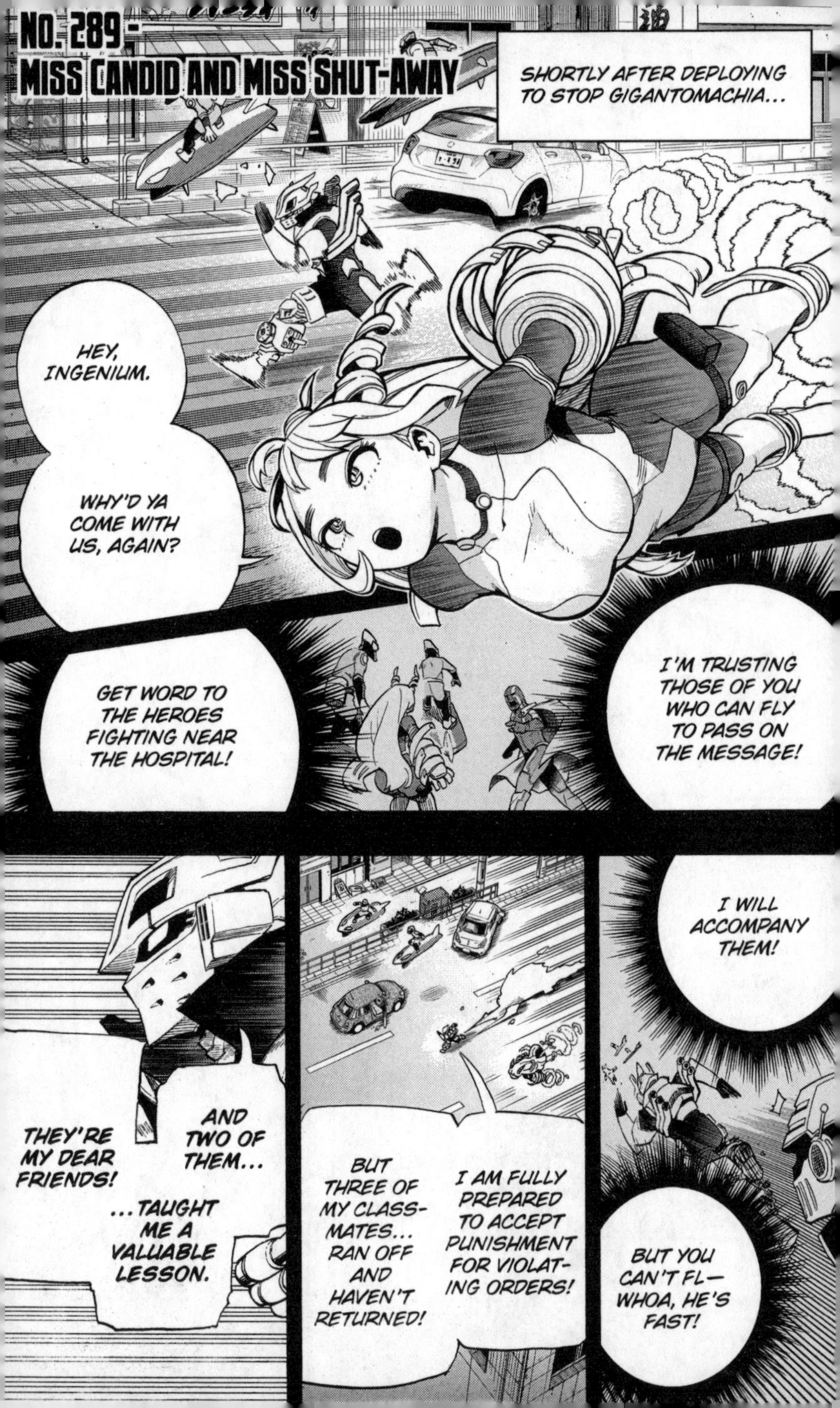
SHORTLY AFTER DEPLOYING TO STOP GIGANTOMACHIA...
NO. 289 - MISS CANDID AND MISS SHUT-AWAY
HEY, INGENIUM.
WHY'D YA COME WITH US, AGAIN?
I'M TRUSTING THOSE OF YOU WHO CAN FLY TO PASS ON THE MESSAGE!
GET WORD TO THE HEROES FIGHTING NEAR THE HOSPITAL!
I WILL ACCOMPANY THEM!
BUT YOU CAN'T FL— WHOA, HE'S FAST!
BUT THREE OF MY CLASSMATES... RAN OFF AND HAVEN'T RETURNED!
I AM FULLY PREPARED TO ACCEPT PUNISHMENT FOR VIOLATING ORDERS!
AND TWO OF THEM...
THEY'RE MY DEAR FRIENDS!
...TAUGHT ME A VALUABLE LESSON.

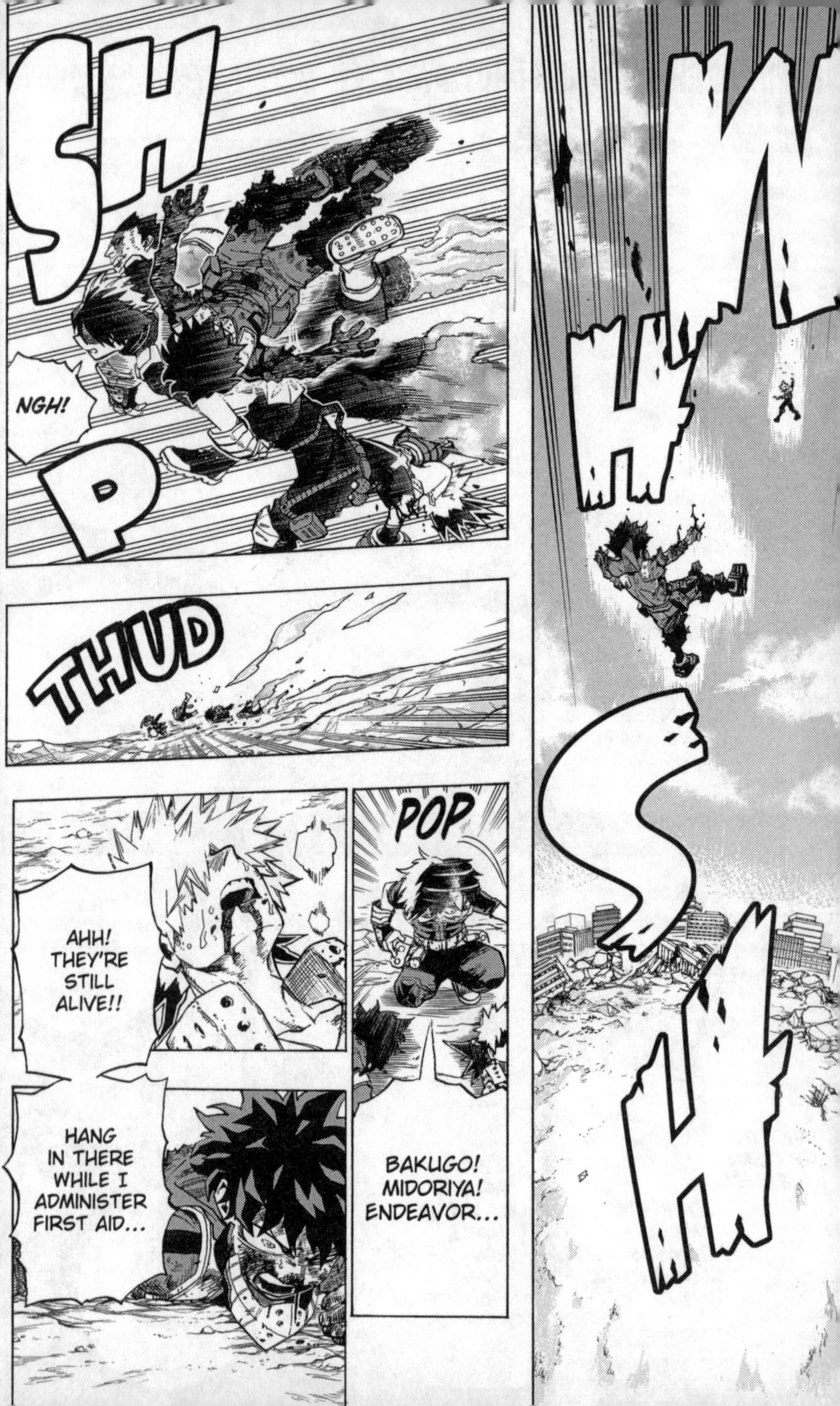
NGH!
THUD
POP
BAKUGO! MIDORIYA! ENDEAVOR...
AHH! THEY'RE STILL ALIVE!!
HANG IN THERE WHILE I ADMINISTER FIRST AID...

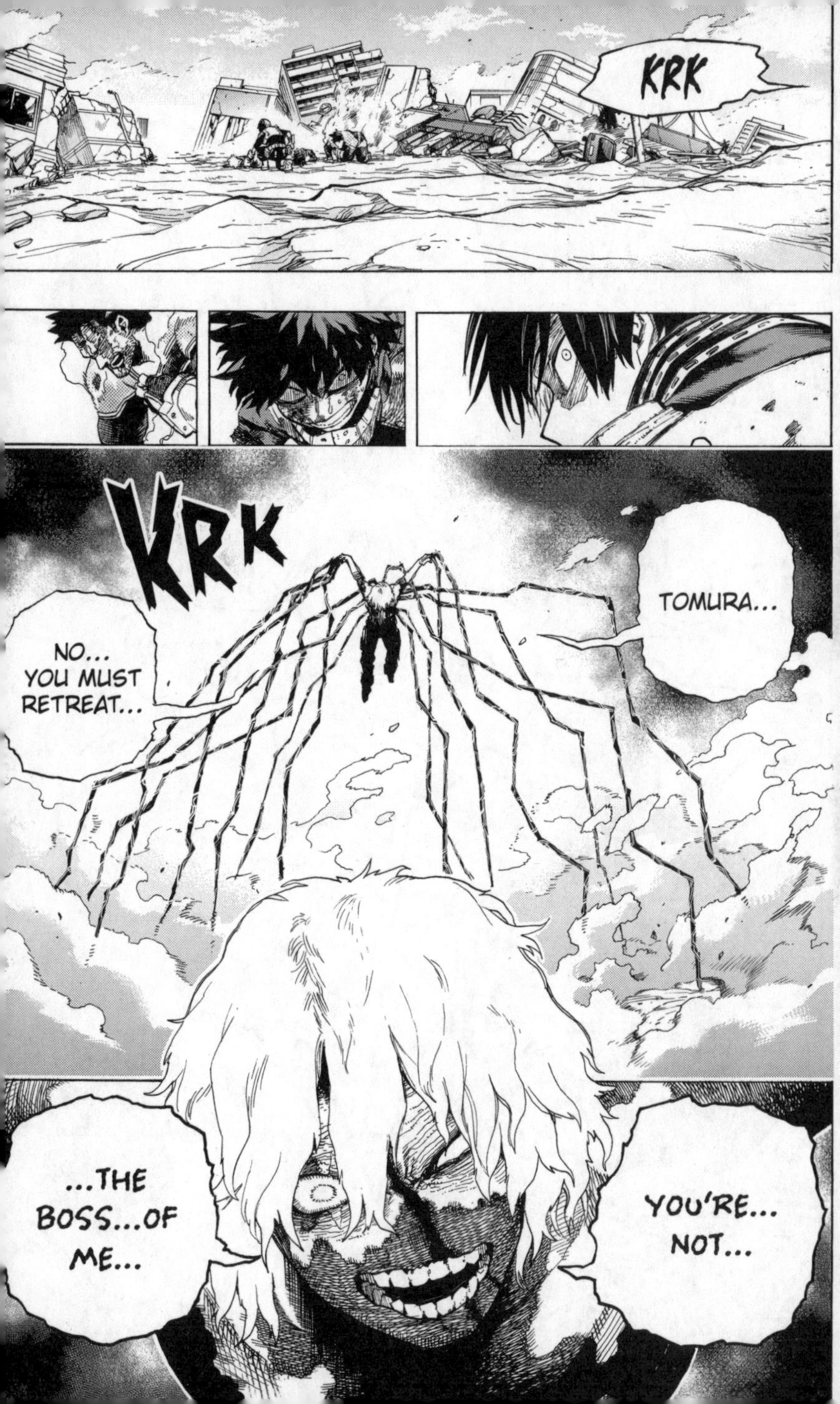
KRK
TOMURA...
KRK
NO... YOU MUST RETREAT...
YOU'RE... NOT...
...THE BOSS...OF ME...

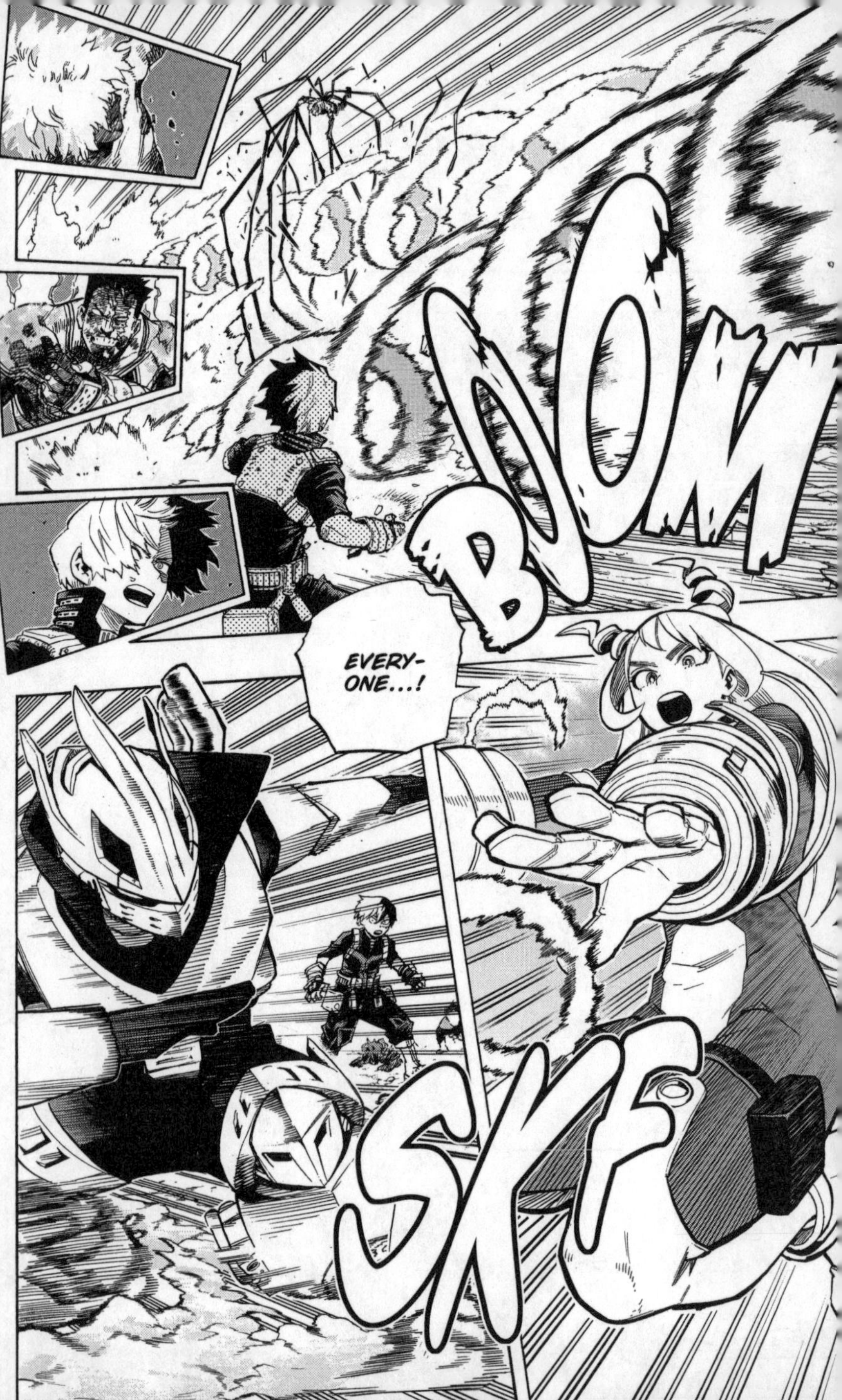
BOOM
EVERY-
ONE...!
SKF

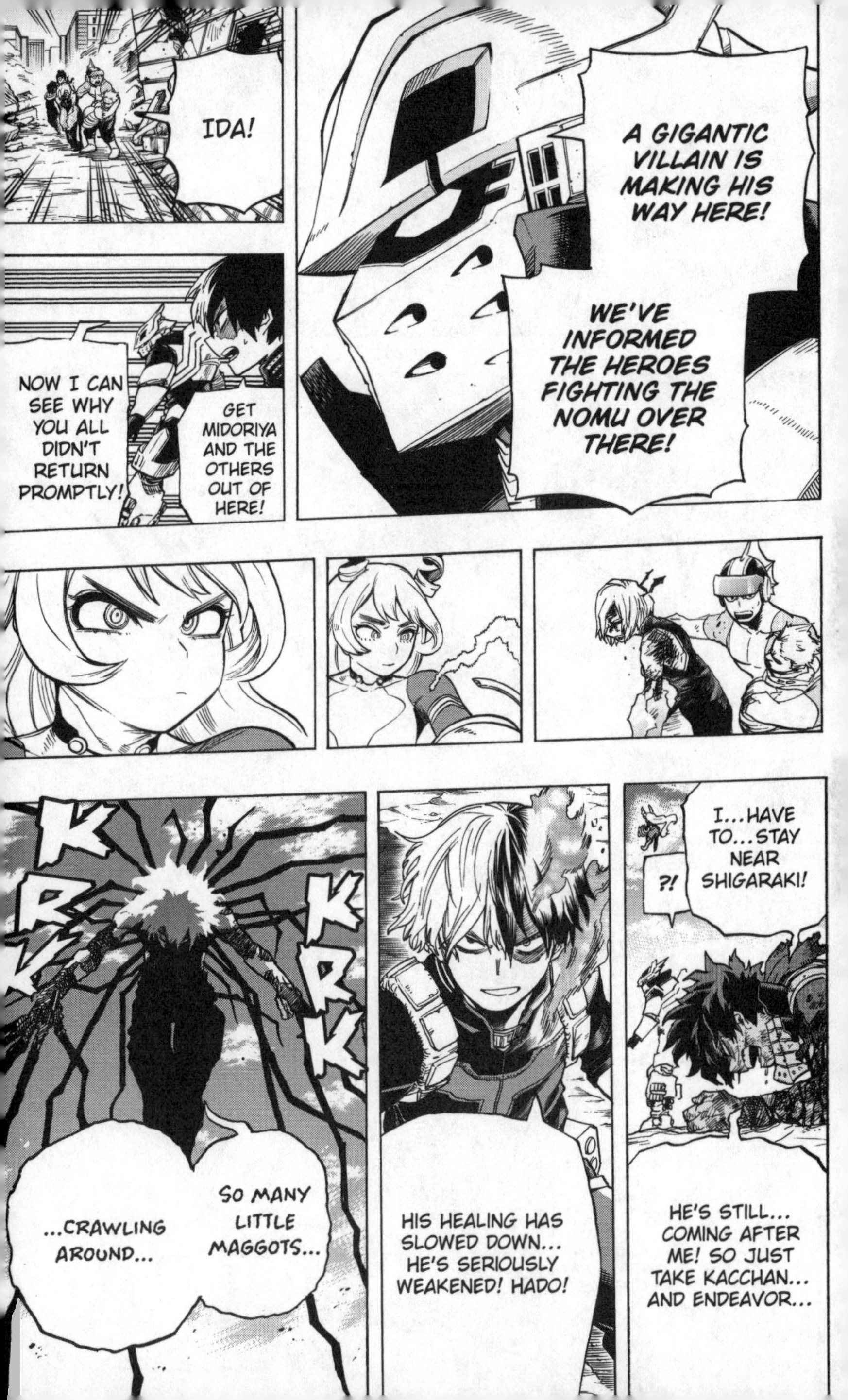
A GIGANTIC VILLAIN IS MAKING HIS WAY HERE!
WE'VE INFORMED THE HEROES FIGHTING THE NOMU OVER THERE!
IDA!
GET MIDORIYA AND THE OTHERS OUT OF HERE!
NOW I CAN SEE WHY YOU ALL DIDN'T RETURN PROMPTLY!
I...HAVE TO...STAY NEAR SHIGARAKI!
?!
HE'S STILL... COMING AFTER ME! SO JUST TAKE KACCHAN... AND ENDEAVOR...
HIS HEALING HAS SLOWED DOWN... HE'S SERIOUSLY WEAKENED! HADO!
KRK
KRK
SO MANY LITTLE MAGGOTS...
...CRAWLING AROUND...

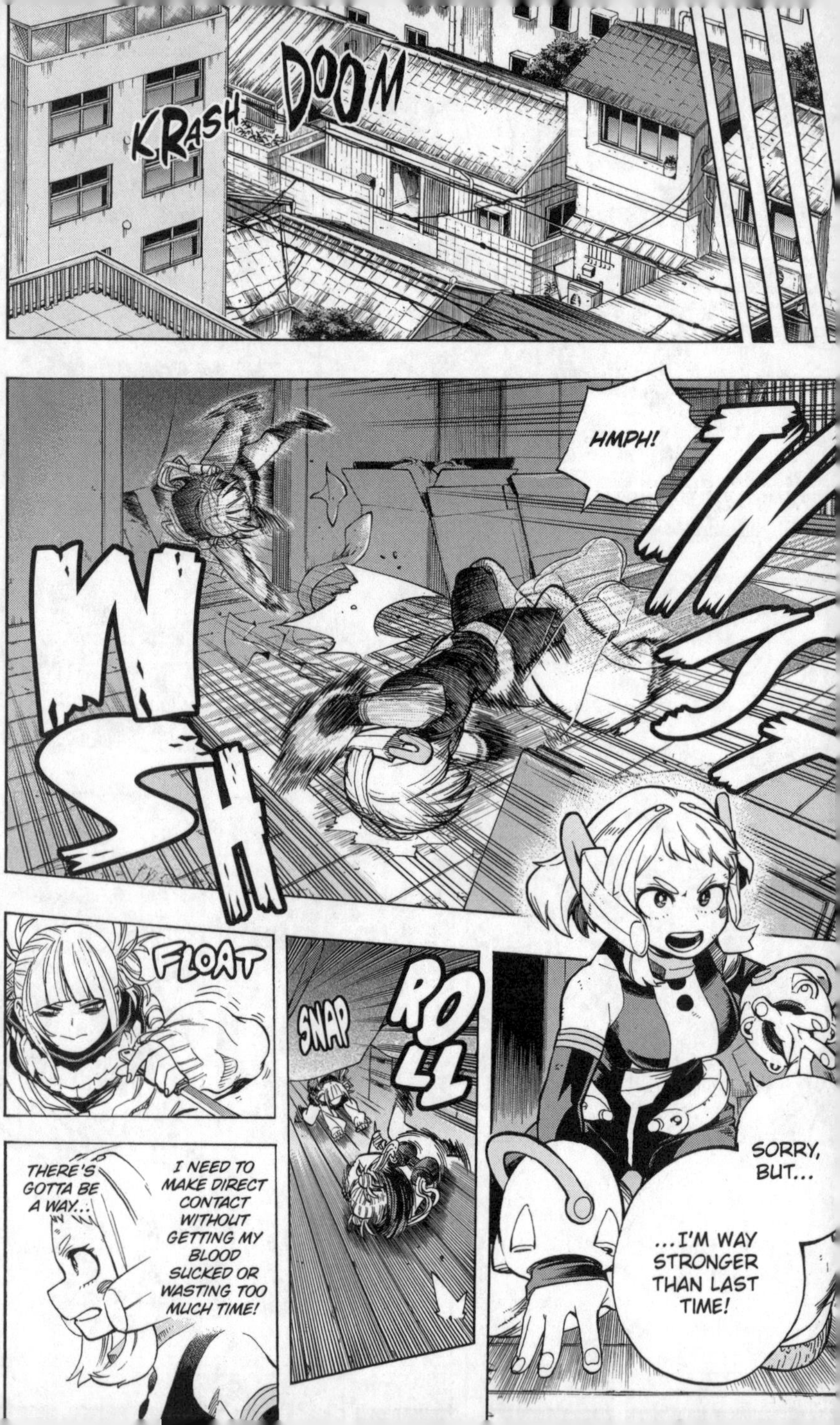
DOOM
KRASH
HMPH!
SORRY, BUT...
...I'M WAY STRONGER THAN LAST TIME!
ROLL
SNAP
FLOAT
I NEED TO MAKE DIRECT CONTACT WITHOUT GETTING MY BLOOD SUCKED OR WASTING TOO MUCH TIME!
THERE'S GOTTA BE A WAY...

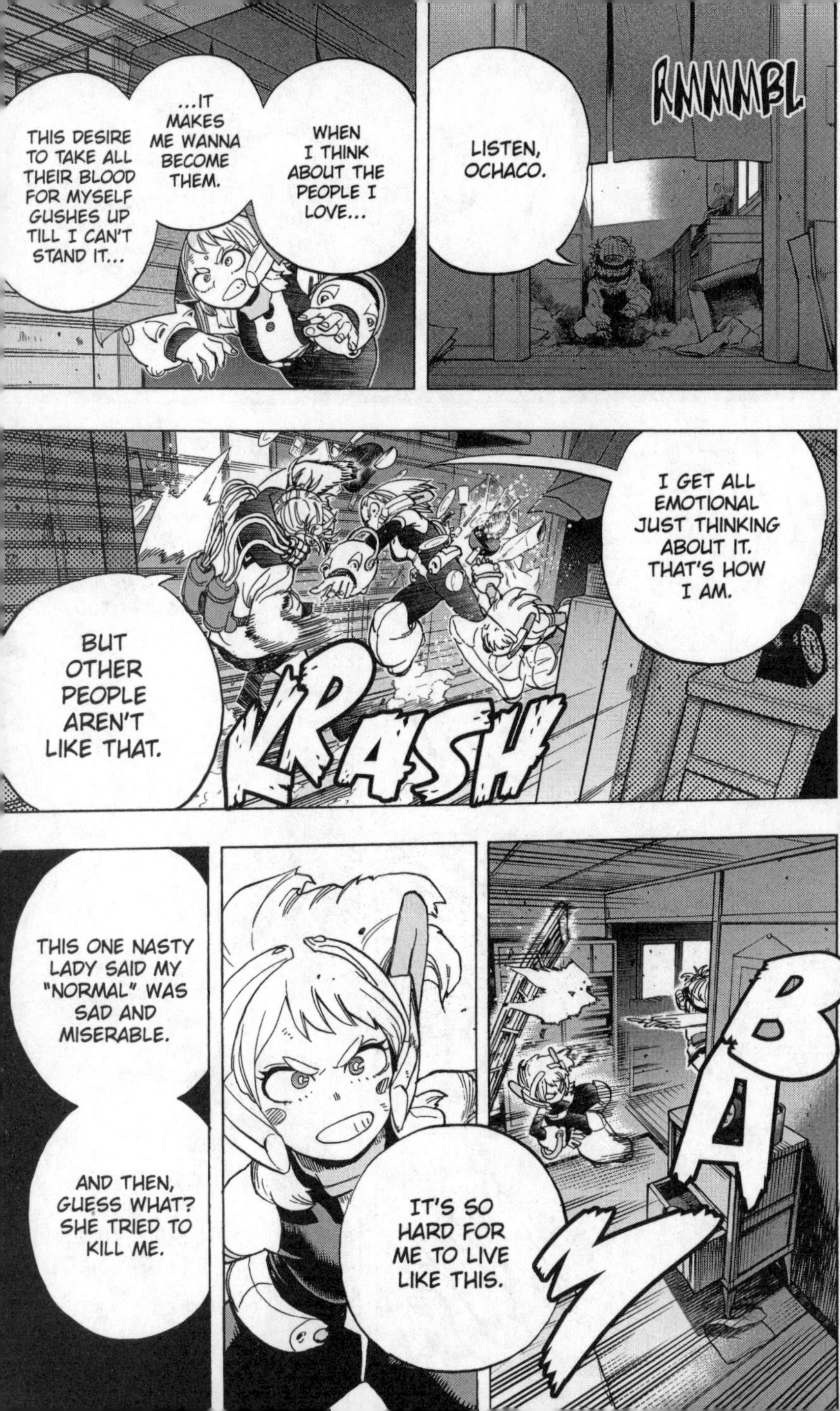
RMMMBL
LISTEN, OCHACO.
WHEN I THINK ABOUT THE PEOPLE I LOVE...
...IT MAKES ME WANNA BECOME THEM.
THIS DESIRE TO TAKE ALL THEIR BLOOD FOR MYSELF GUSHES UP TILL I CAN'T STAND IT...
I GET ALL EMOTIONAL JUST THINKING ABOUT IT. THAT'S HOW I AM.
KRASH
BUT OTHER PEOPLE AREN'T LIKE THAT.
BA
IT'S SO HARD FOR ME TO LIVE LIKE THIS.
THIS ONE NASTY LADY SAID MY "NORMAL" WAS SAD AND MISERABLE.
AND THEN, GUESS WHAT? SHE TRIED TO KILL ME.

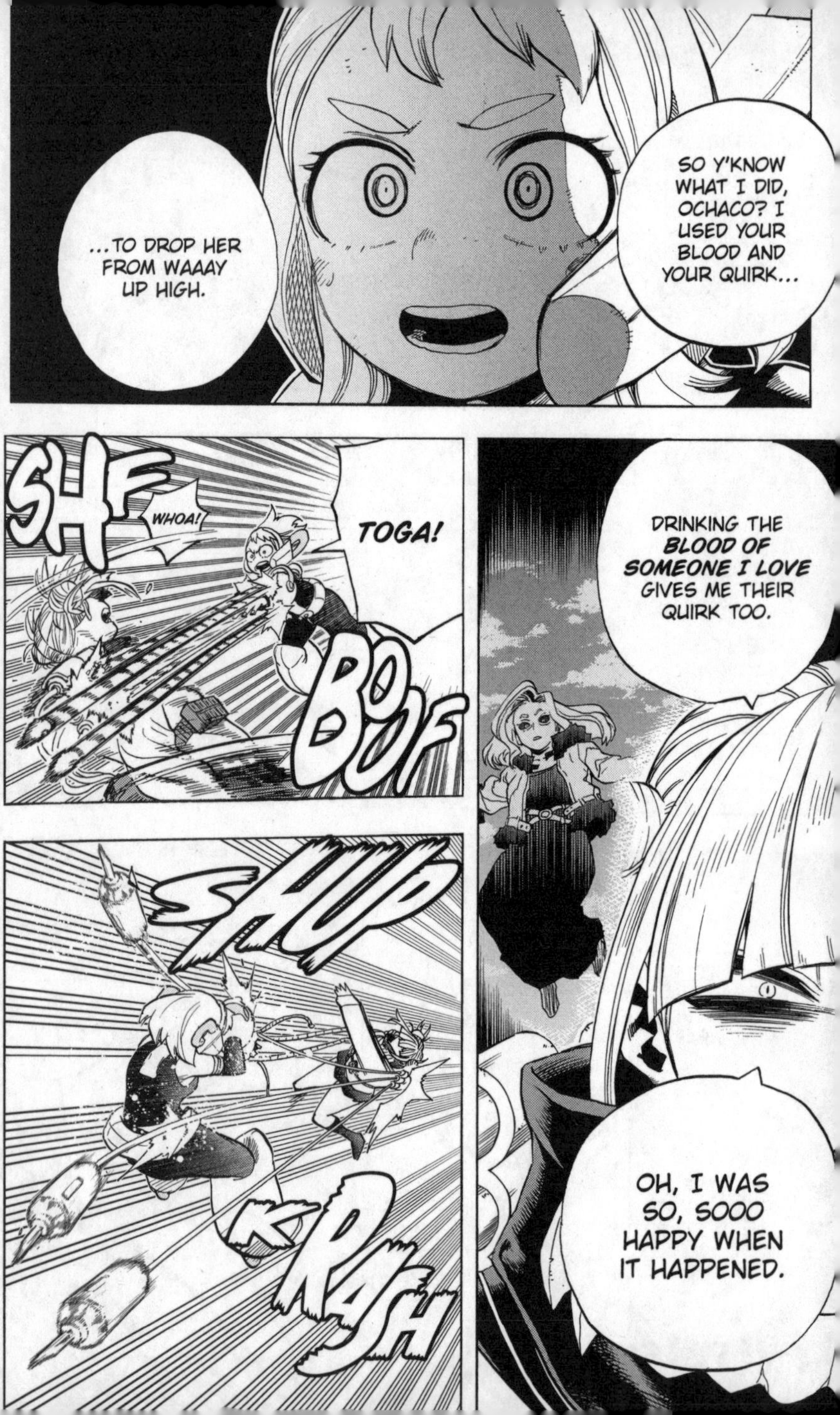
SO Y'KNOW WHAT I DID, OCHACO? I USED YOUR BLOOD AND YOUR QUIRK...
...TO DROP HER FROM WAAAY UP HIGH.
DRINKING THE *BLOOD OF SOMEONE I LOVE* GIVES ME THEIR QUIRK TOO.
OH, I WAS SO, SOOO HAPPY WHEN IT HAPPENED.
TOGA!
SHF
WHOA!
BOOF
SHUP
KRASH

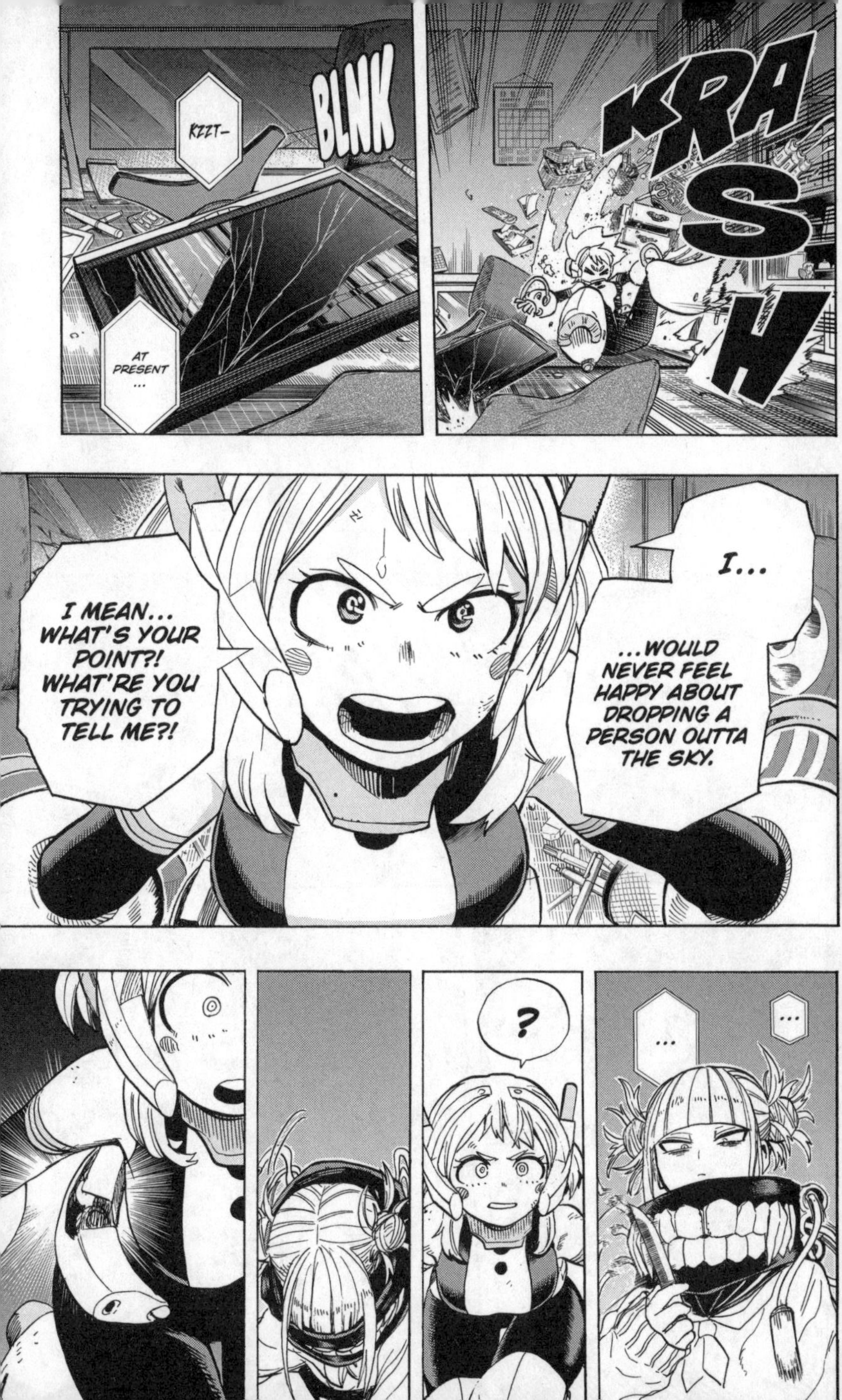
KRASH
BLNK
KZZT-
AT PRESENT ...
I...
...WOULD NEVER FEEL HAPPY ABOUT DROPPING A PERSON OUTTA THE SKY.
I MEAN... WHAT'S YOUR POINT?! WHAT'RE YOU TRYING TO TELL ME?!
...
...
?

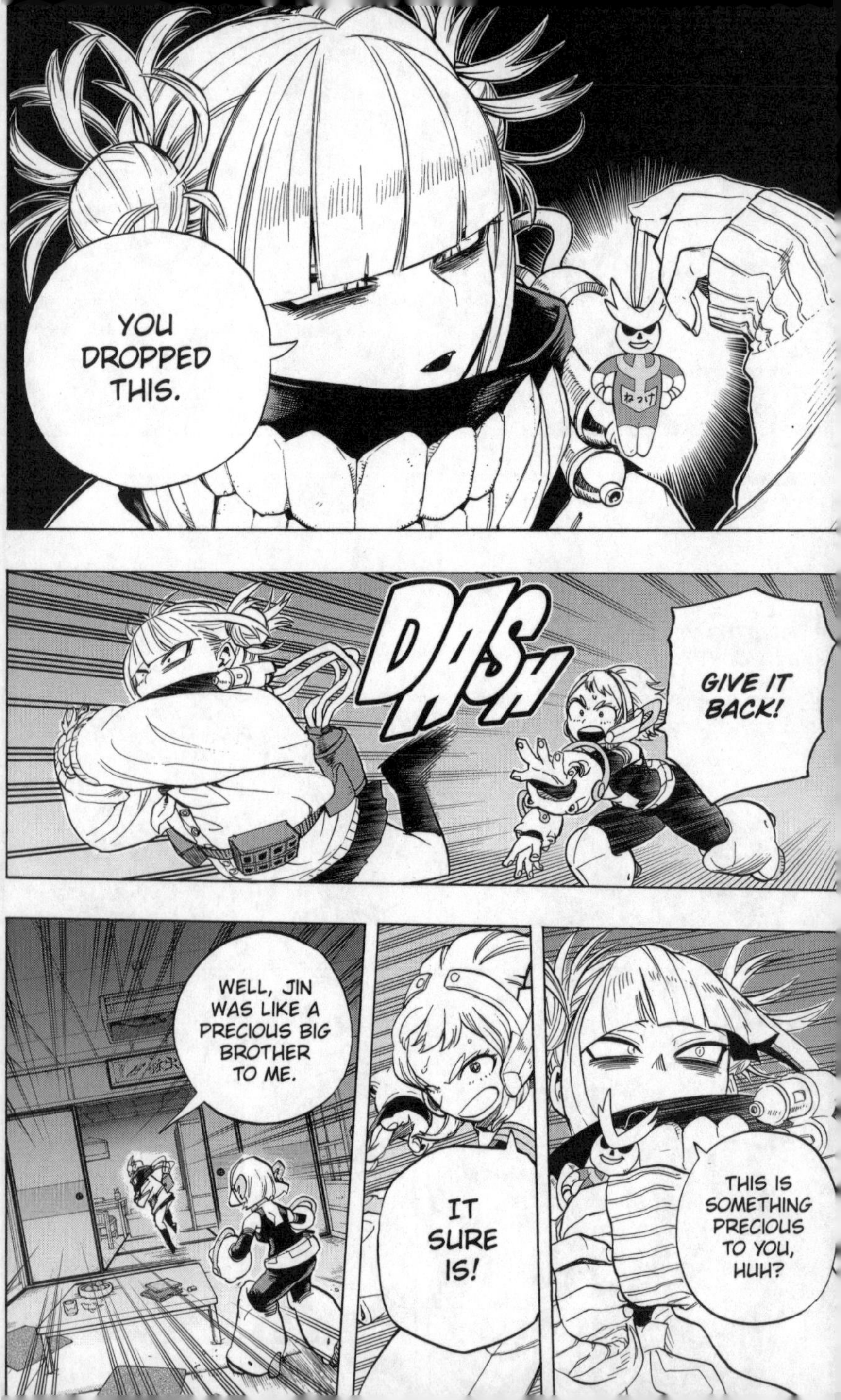
YOU DROPPED THIS.
GIVE IT BACK!
DASH
THIS IS SOMETHING PRECIOUS TO YOU, HUH?
IT SURE IS!
WELL, JIN WAS LIKE A PRECIOUS BIG BROTHER TO ME.

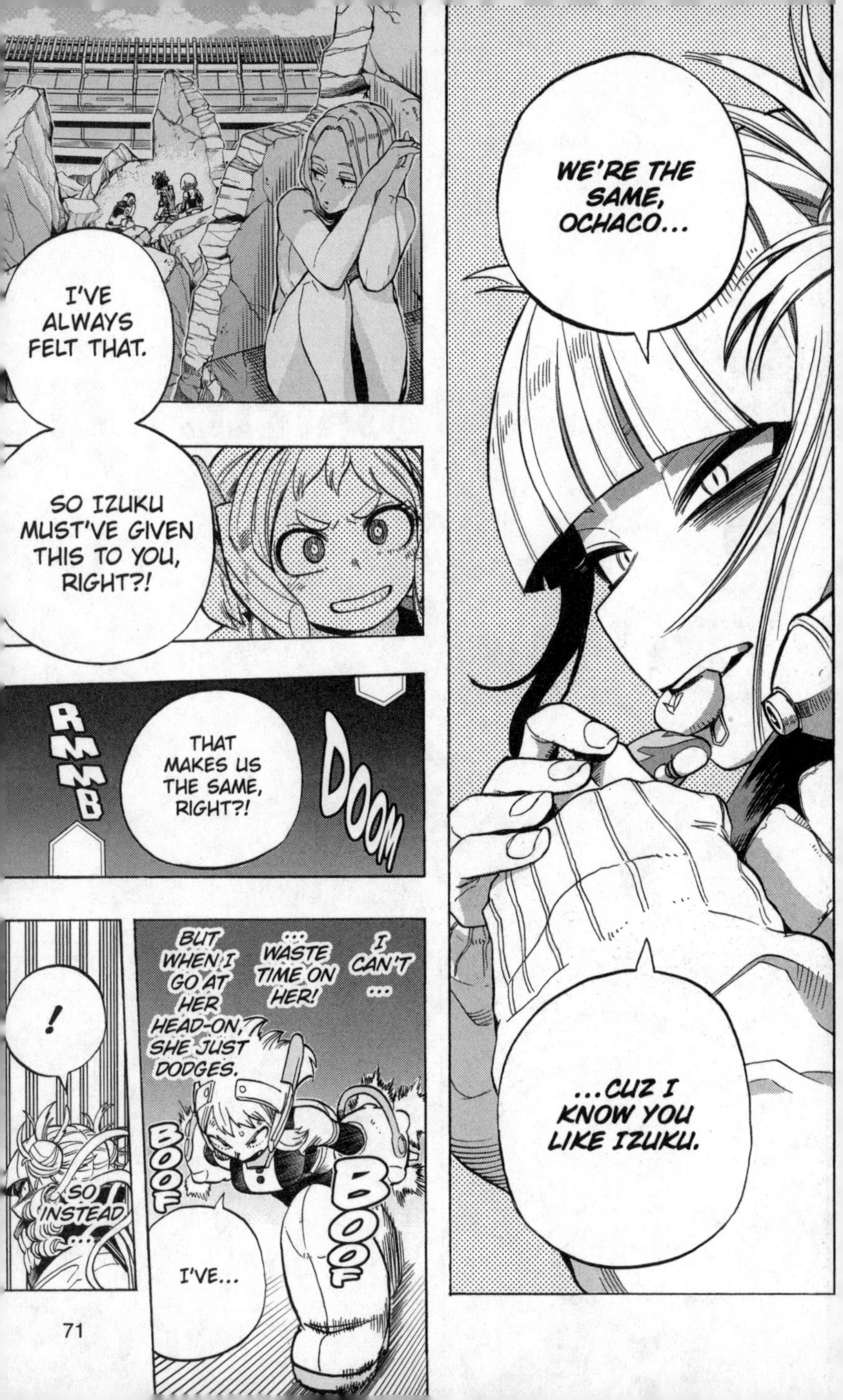
WE'RE THE SAME, OCHACO...
...CUZ I KNOW YOU LIKE IZUKU.
I'VE ALWAYS FELT THAT.
SO IZUKU MUST'VE GIVEN THIS TO YOU, RIGHT?!
DOOM
THAT MAKES US THE SAME, RIGHT?!
RMMB
I CAN'T...
...WASTE TIME ON HER!
BUT WHEN I GO AT HER HEAD-ON, SHE JUST DODGES.
BOOF
BOOF
I'VE...
!
SO INSTEAD...

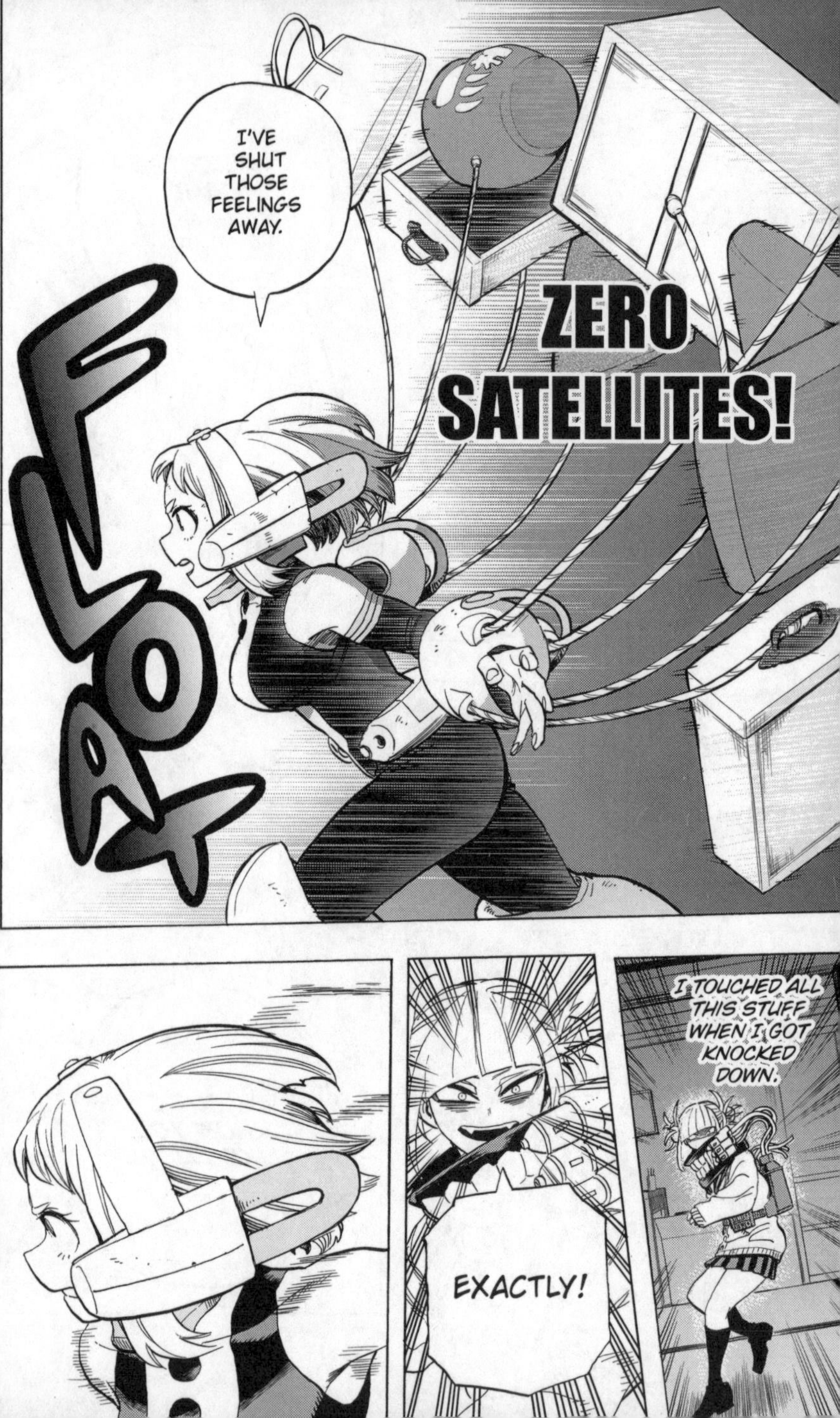
I'VE SHUT THOSE FEELINGS AWAY.
ZERO SATELLITES!
I TOUCHED ALL THIS STUFF WHEN I GOT KNOCKED DOWN.
EXACTLY!

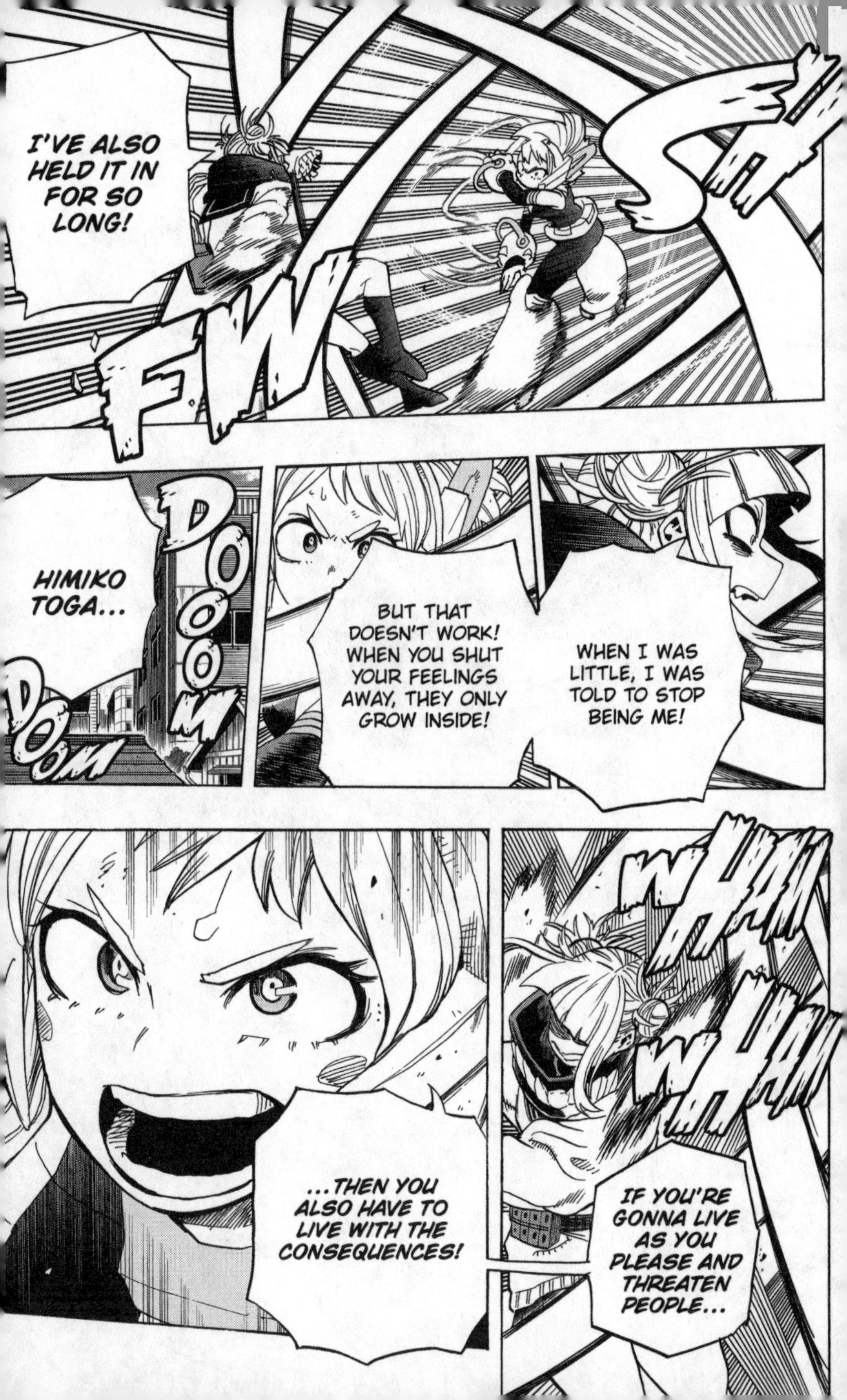
SHA
I'VE ALSO HELD IT IN FOR SO LONG!
FWM
WHEN I WAS LITTLE, I WAS TOLD TO STOP BEING ME!
BUT THAT DOESN'T WORK! WHEN YOU SHUT YOUR FEELINGS AWAY, THEY ONLY GROW INSIDE!
DOOOM
HIMIKO TOGA...
DOOM
WHA
WHA
IF YOU'RE GONNA LIVE AS YOU PLEASE AND THREATEN PEOPLE...
...THEN YOU ALSO HAVE TO LIVE WITH THE CONSEQUENCES!

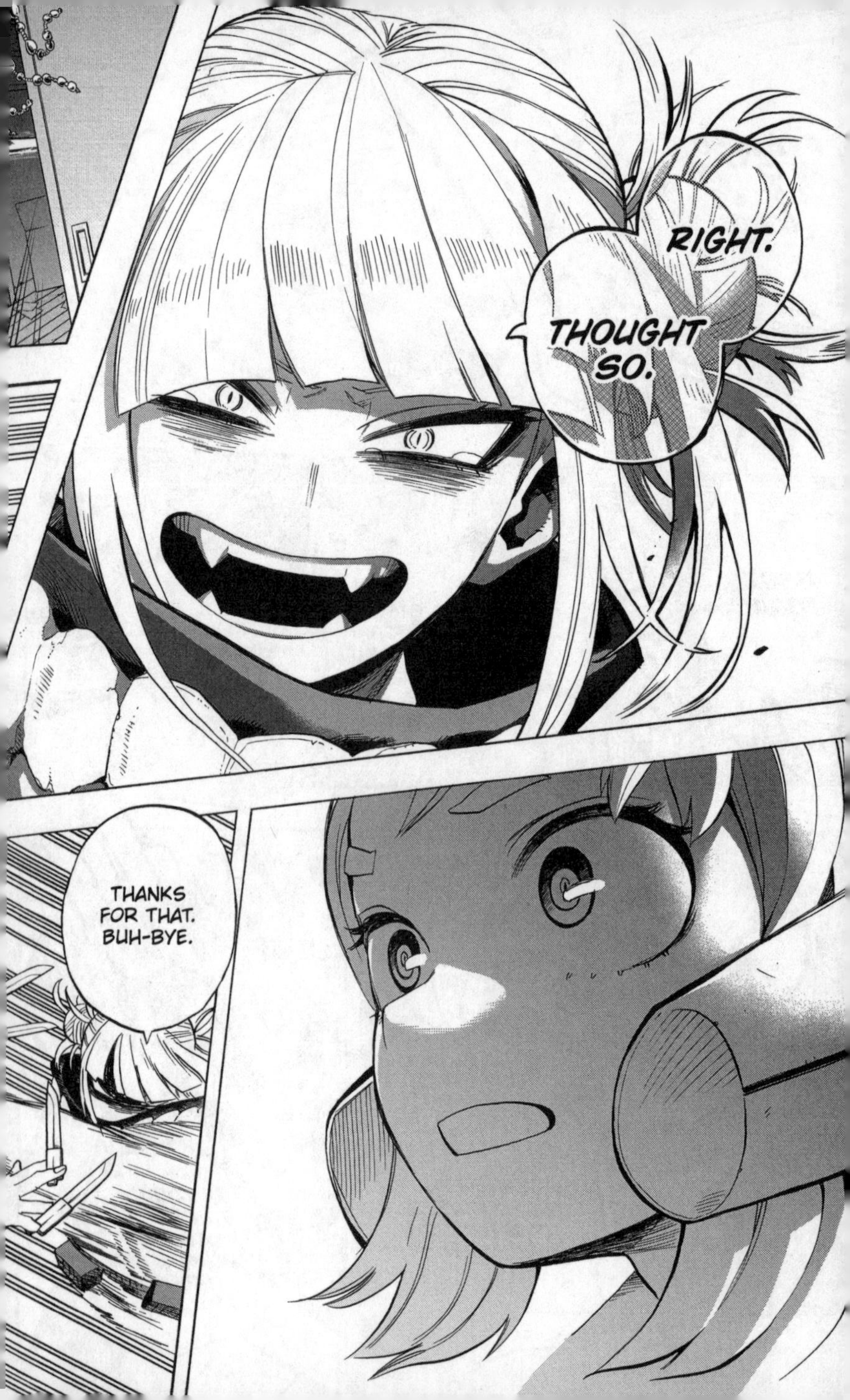
RIGHT.
THOUGHT SO.
THANKS FOR THAT. BUH-BYE.

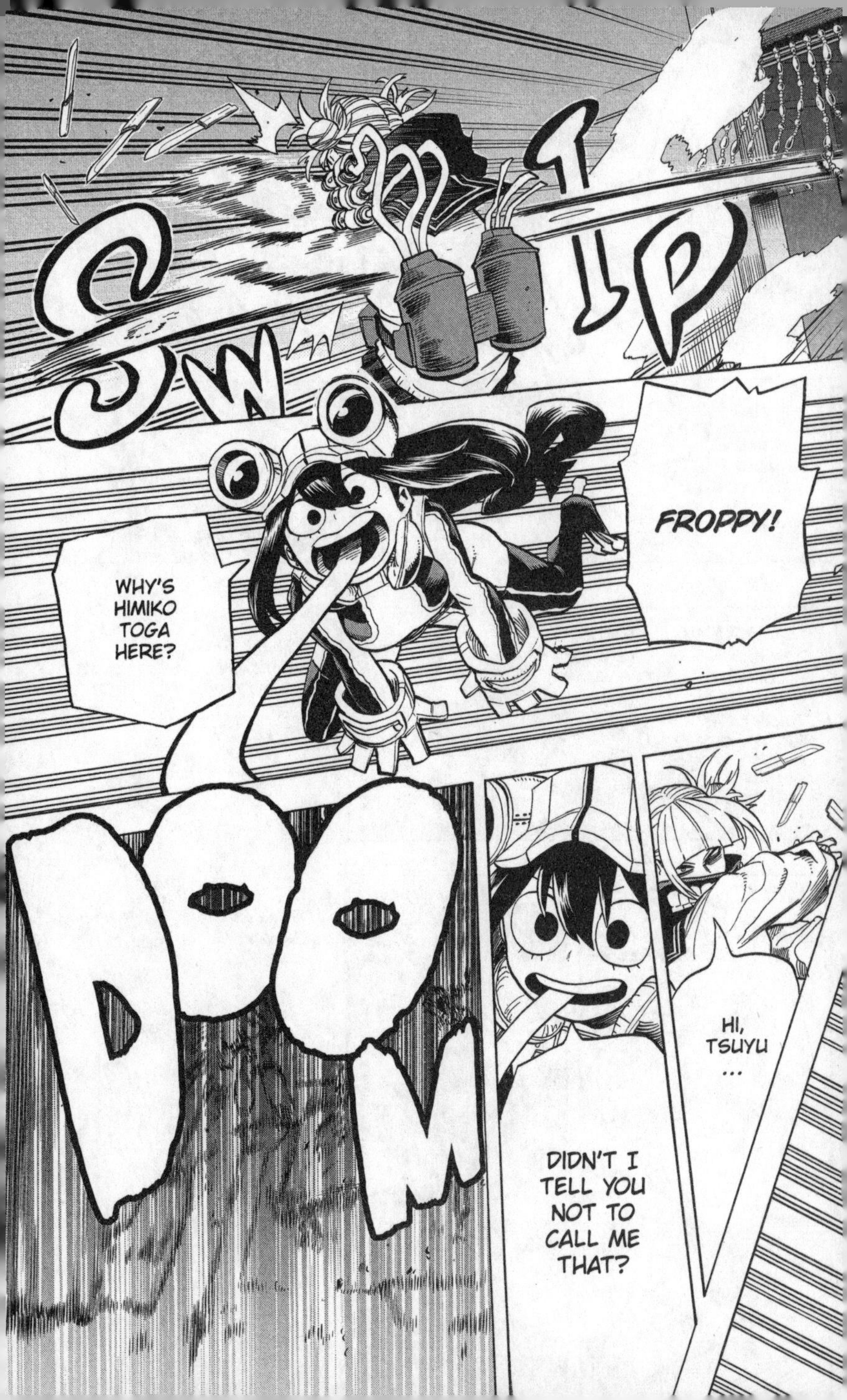
SWIP
FROPPY!
WHY'S HIMIKO TOGA HERE?
HI, TSUYU...
DIDN'T I TELL YOU NOT TO CALL ME THAT?
DOOM

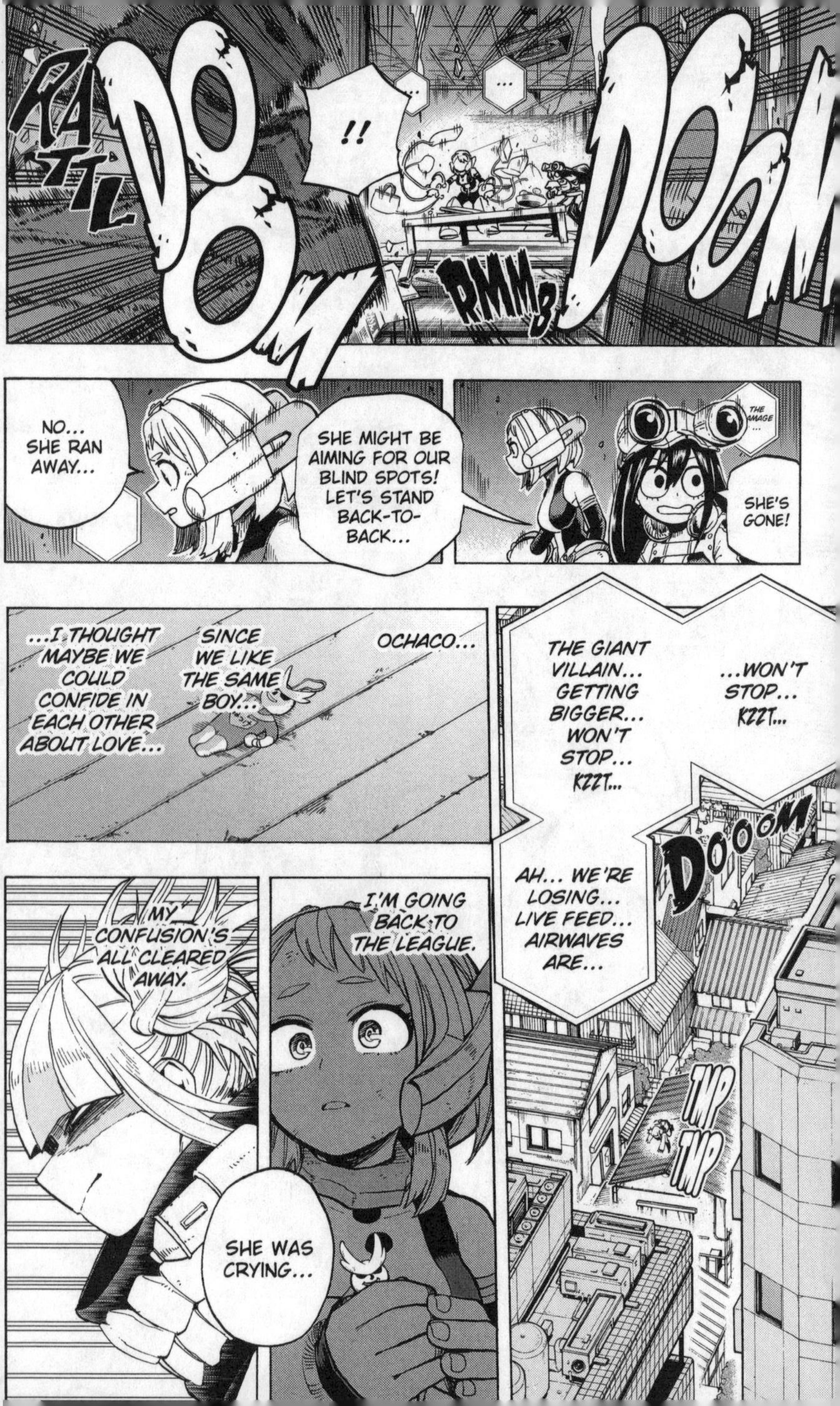
DOOM
...
...
!!
RMMB
RATTL
DOOM
THE AMAGE...
SHE'S GONE!
SHE MIGHT BE AIMING FOR OUR BLIND SPOTS! LET'S STAND BACK-TO-BACK...
NO... SHE RAN AWAY...
...WON'T STOP... KZZT...
THE GIANT VILLAIN... GETTING BIGGER... WON'T STOP... KZZT...
DOOOM
AH... WE'RE LOSING... LIVE FEED... AIRWAVES ARE...
TMP TMP
OCHACO...
SINCE WE LIKE THE SAME BOY...
...I THOUGHT MAYBE WE COULD CONFIDE IN EACH OTHER ABOUT LOVE...
I'M GOING BACK TO THE LEAGUE.
SHE WAS CRYING...
MY CONFUSION'S ALL CLEARED AWAY.

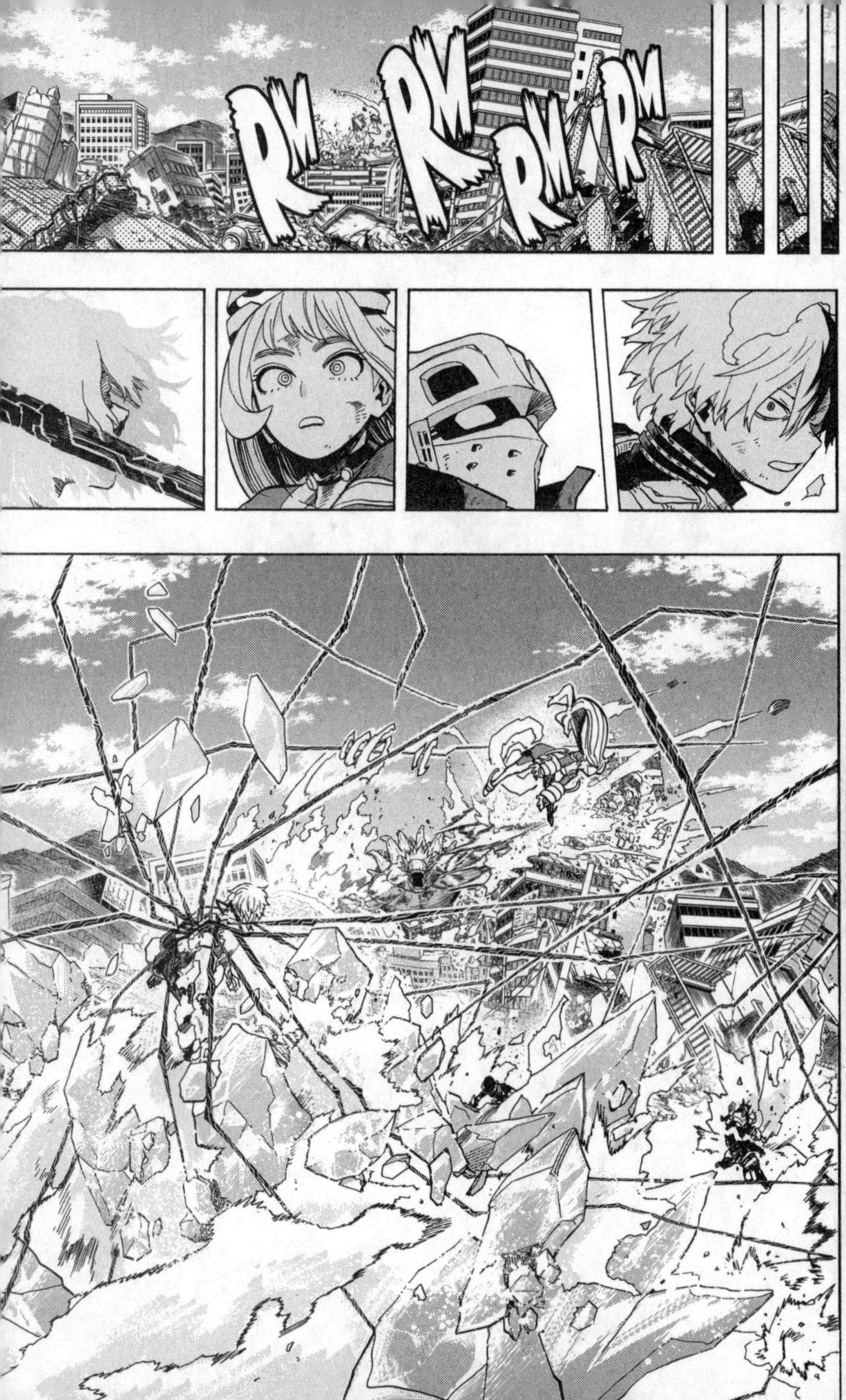
RM RM RM RM

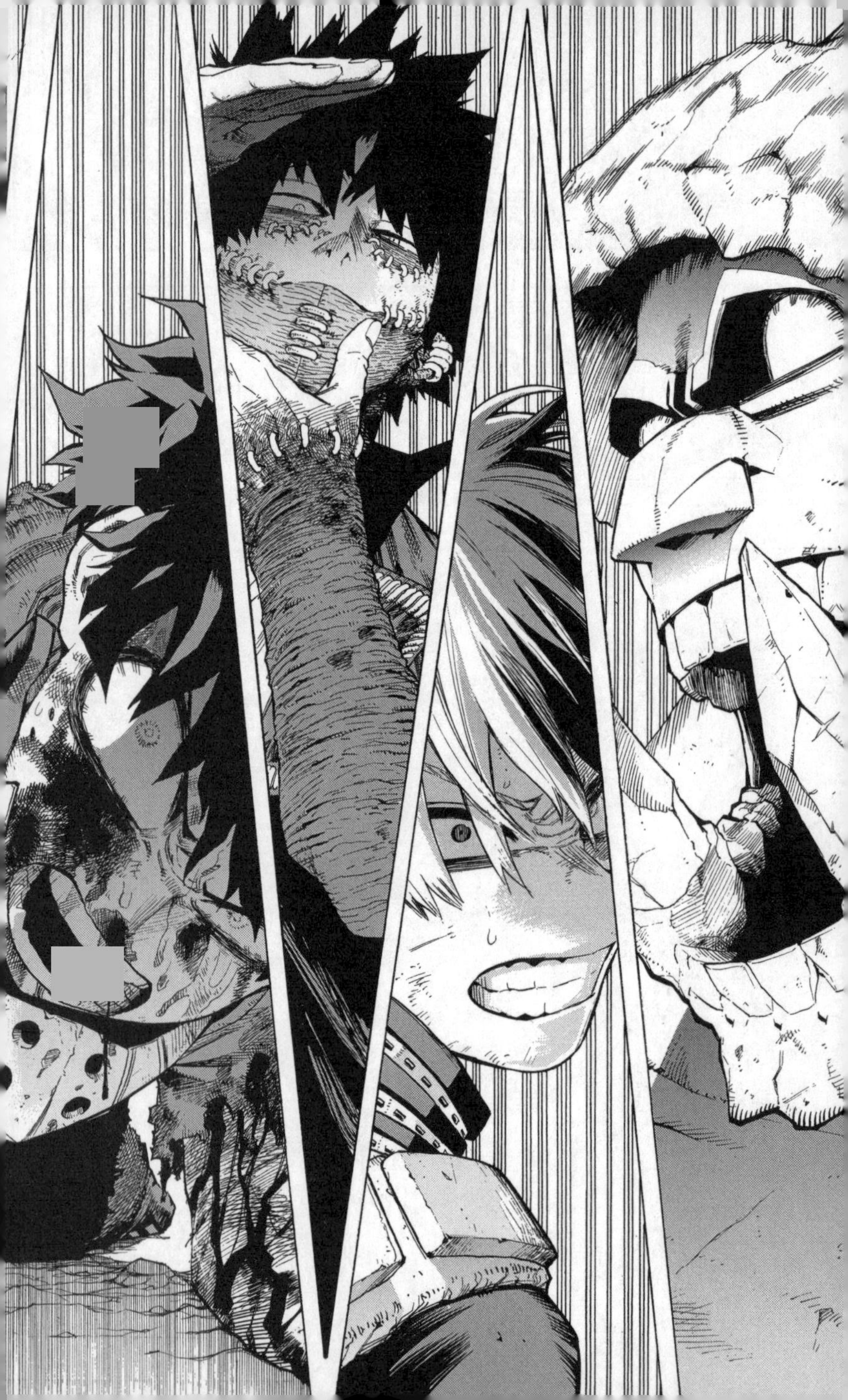

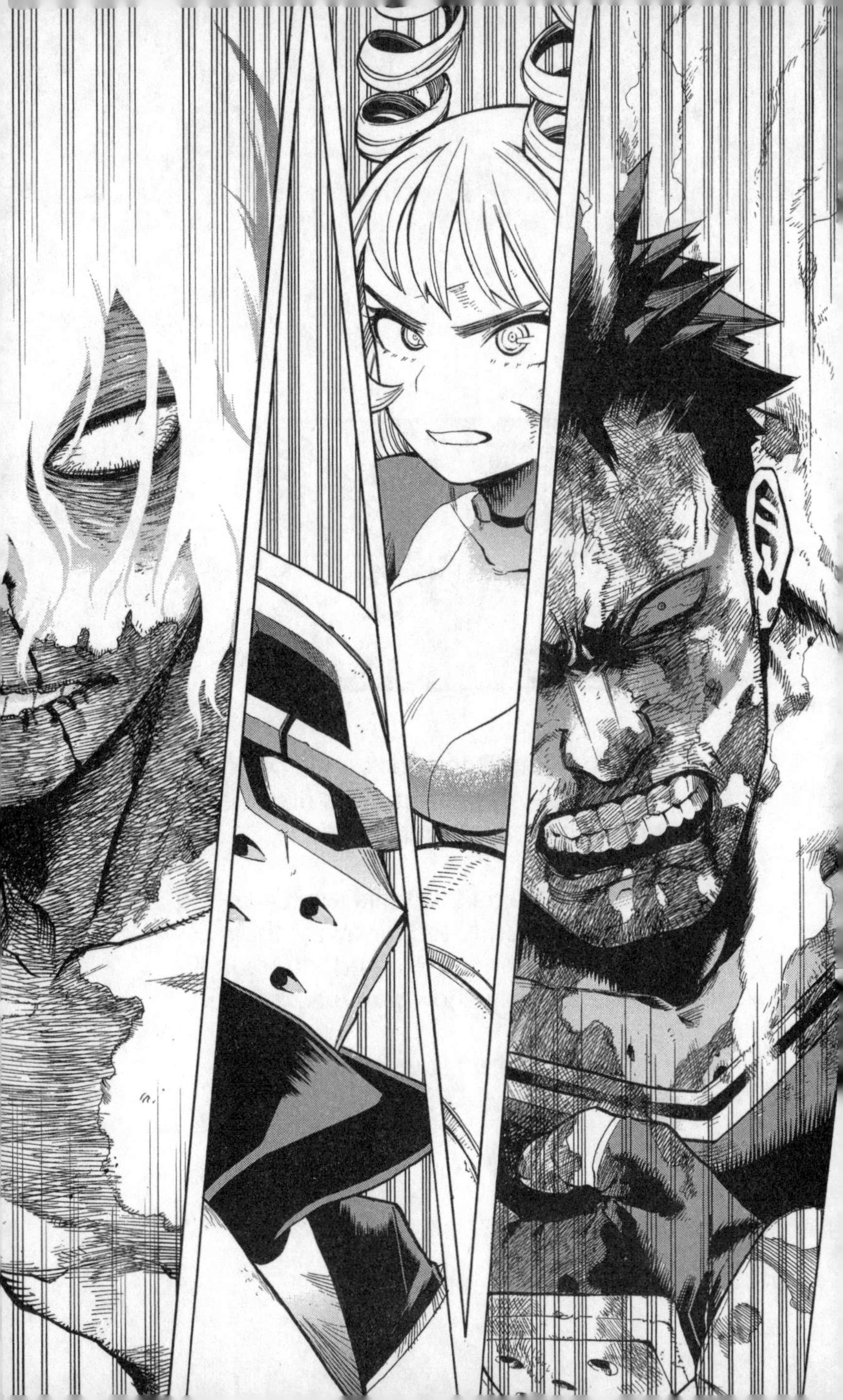

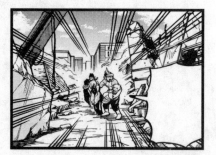

Here, Manual and Rock Lock have prioritized saving their heavily injured allies (like Aizawa) by getting them off the battlefield.

They would've helped Katsuki and Deku too, but they were already too far away, they couldn't have carried them, and Ida (plus the others) had already shown up, as backup.

Sorry if that wasn't obvious!!

NO. 290 - DABI'S DANCE

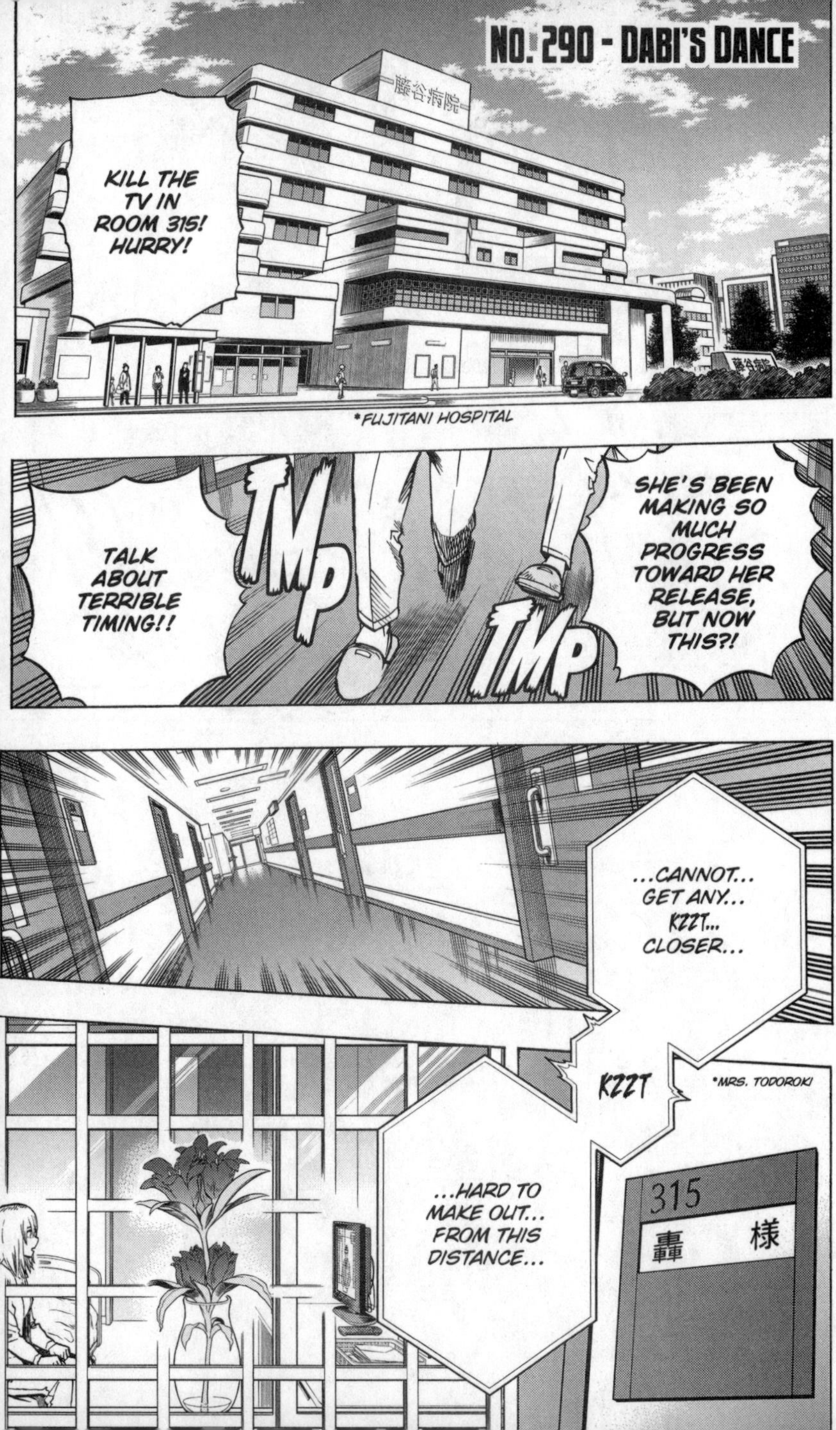

藤谷病院
KILL THE TV IN ROOM 315! HURRY!
藤谷病院
*FUJITANI HOSPITAL
SHE'S BEEN MAKING SO MUCH PROGRESS TOWARD HER RELEASE, BUT NOW THIS?!
TMP
TMP
TALK ABOUT TERRIBLE TIMING!!
...CANNOT... GET ANY... KZZT... CLOSER...
KZZT
*MRS. TODOROKI
315
轟 様
...HARD TO MAKE OUT... FROM THIS DISTANCE...

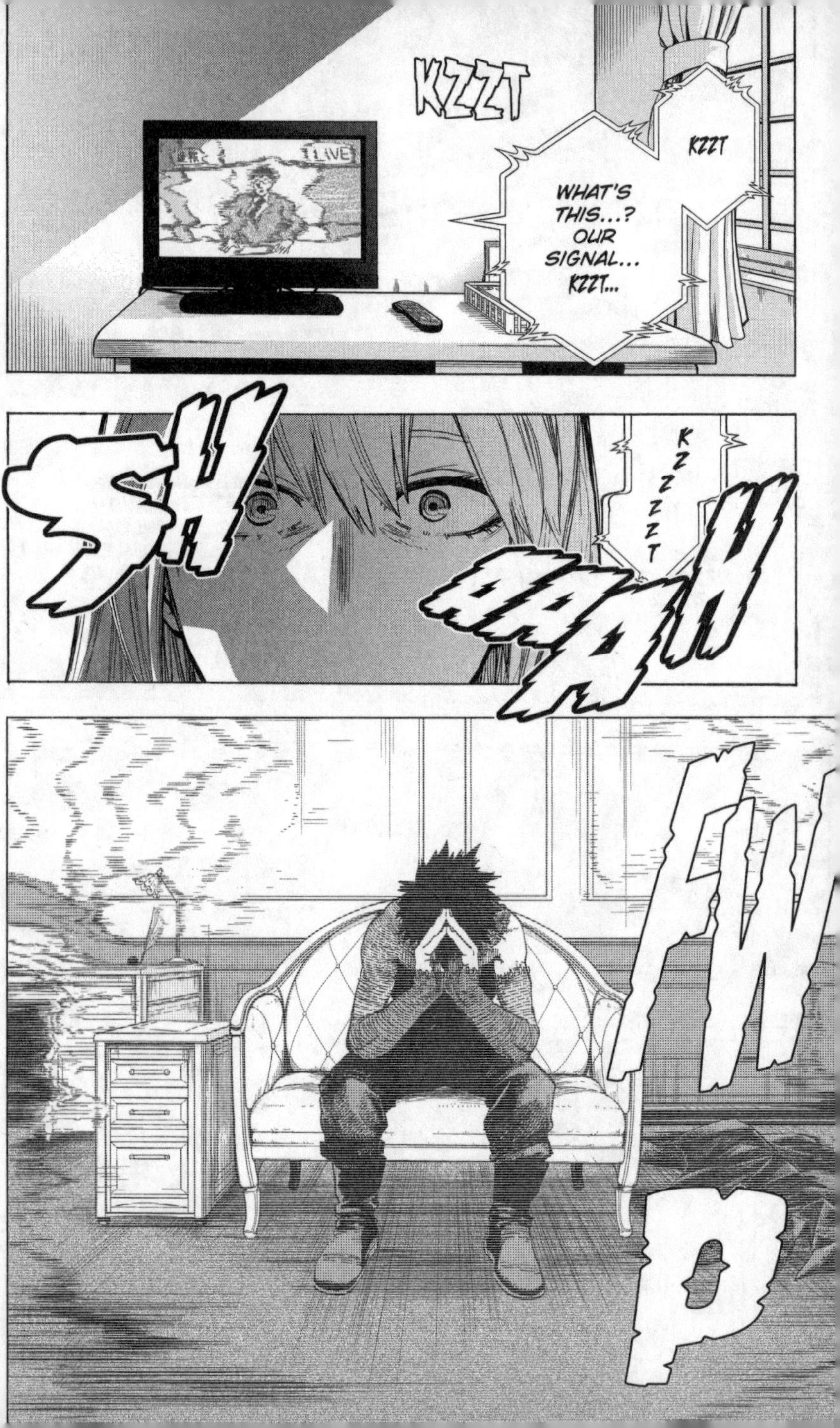
KZZT
KZZT
WHAT'S THIS...? OUR SIGNAL... KZZT...
KZZZZZT
SHAAAH
FWP

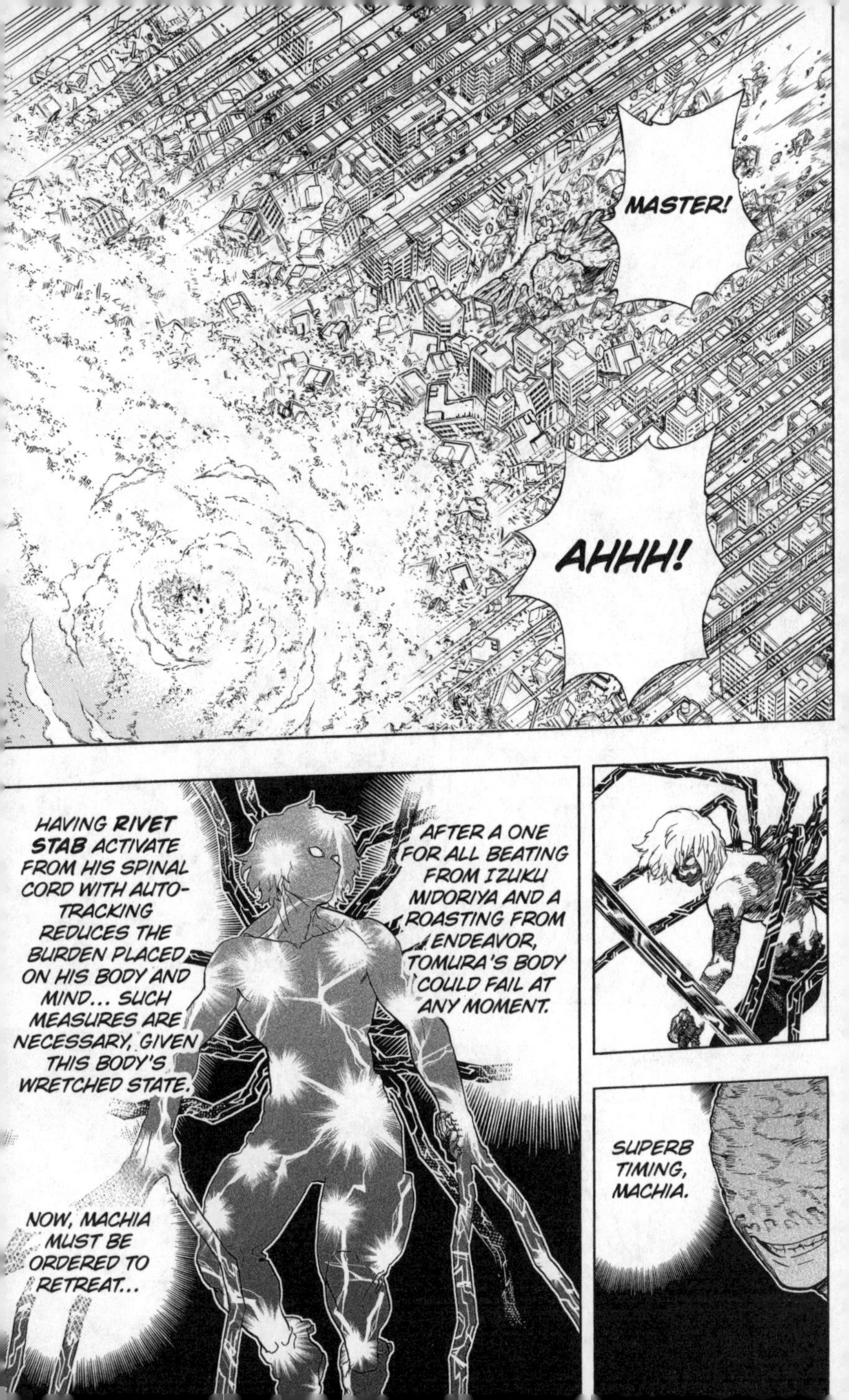
MASTER!
AHHH!
SUPERB TIMING, MACHIA.
AFTER A ONE FOR ALL BEATING FROM IZUKU MIDORIYA AND A ROASTING FROM ENDEAVOR, TOMURA'S BODY COULD FAIL AT ANY MOMENT.
HAVING RIVET STAB ACTIVATE FROM HIS SPINAL CORD WITH AUTO-TRACKING REDUCES THE BURDEN PLACED ON HIS BODY AND MIND... SUCH MEASURES ARE NECESSARY, GIVEN THIS BODY'S WRETCHED STATE.
NOW, MACHIA MUST BE ORDERED TO RETREAT...

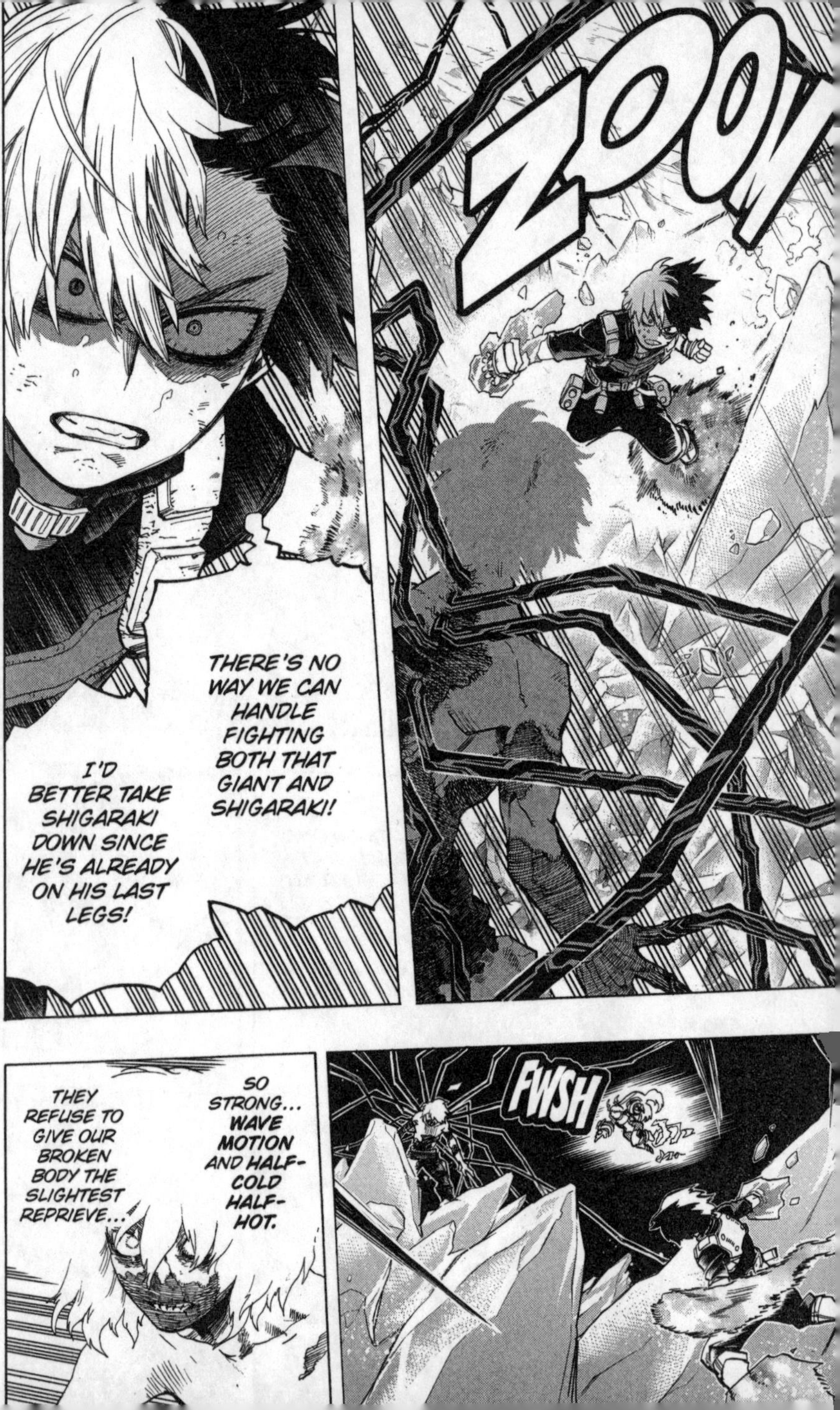
ZOOM
THERE'S NO WAY WE CAN HANDLE FIGHTING BOTH THAT GIANT AND SHIGARAKI!
I'D BETTER TAKE SHIGARAKI DOWN SINCE HE'S ALREADY ON HIS LAST LEGS!
FWSH
SO STRONG... WAVE MOTION AND HALF-COLD HALF-HOT.
THEY REFUSE TO GIVE OUR BROKEN BODY THE SLIGHTEST REPRIEVE...

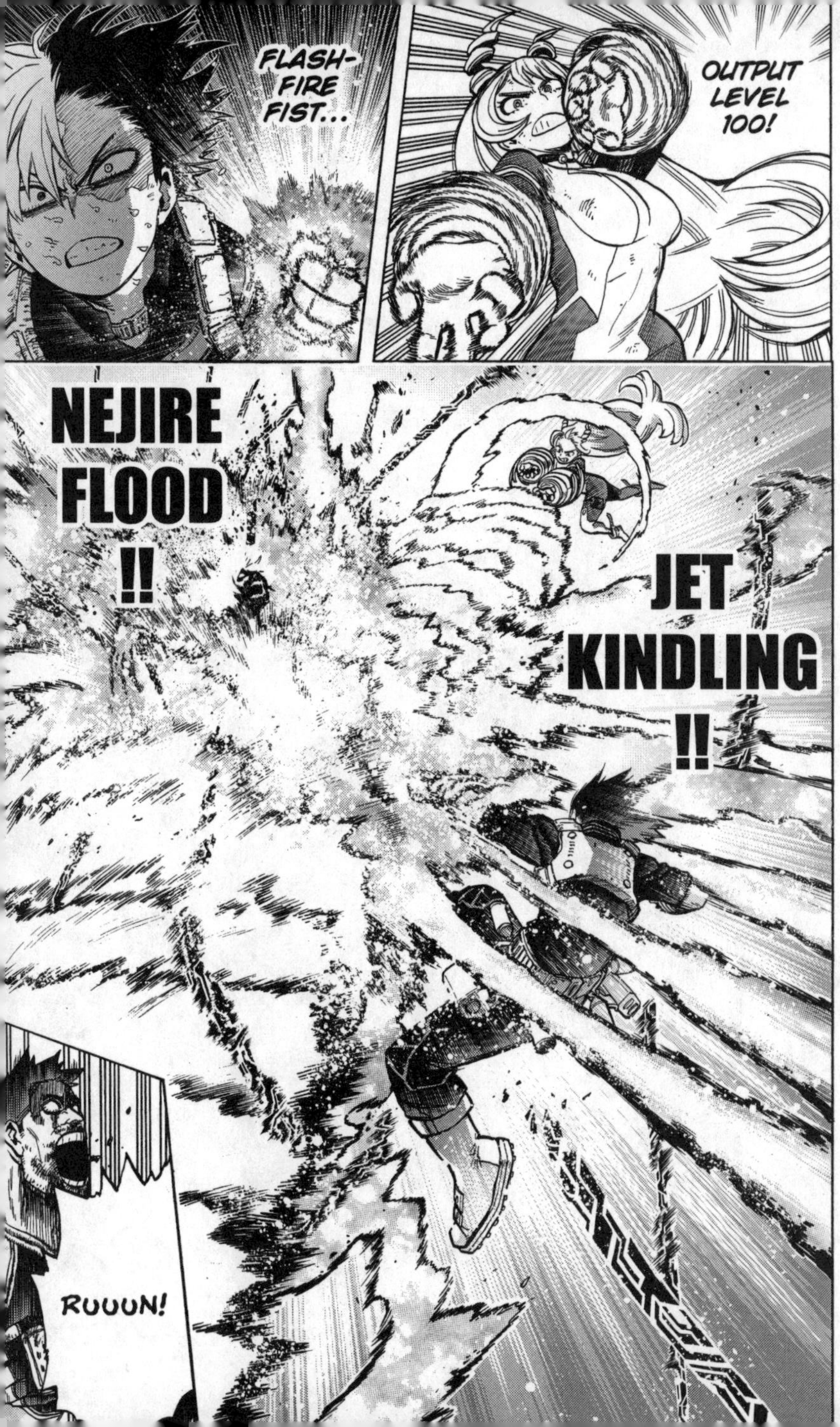
OUTPUT LEVEL 100!
FLASH-FIRE FIST...
NEJIRE FLOOD !!
JET KINDLING !!
RUUUN!

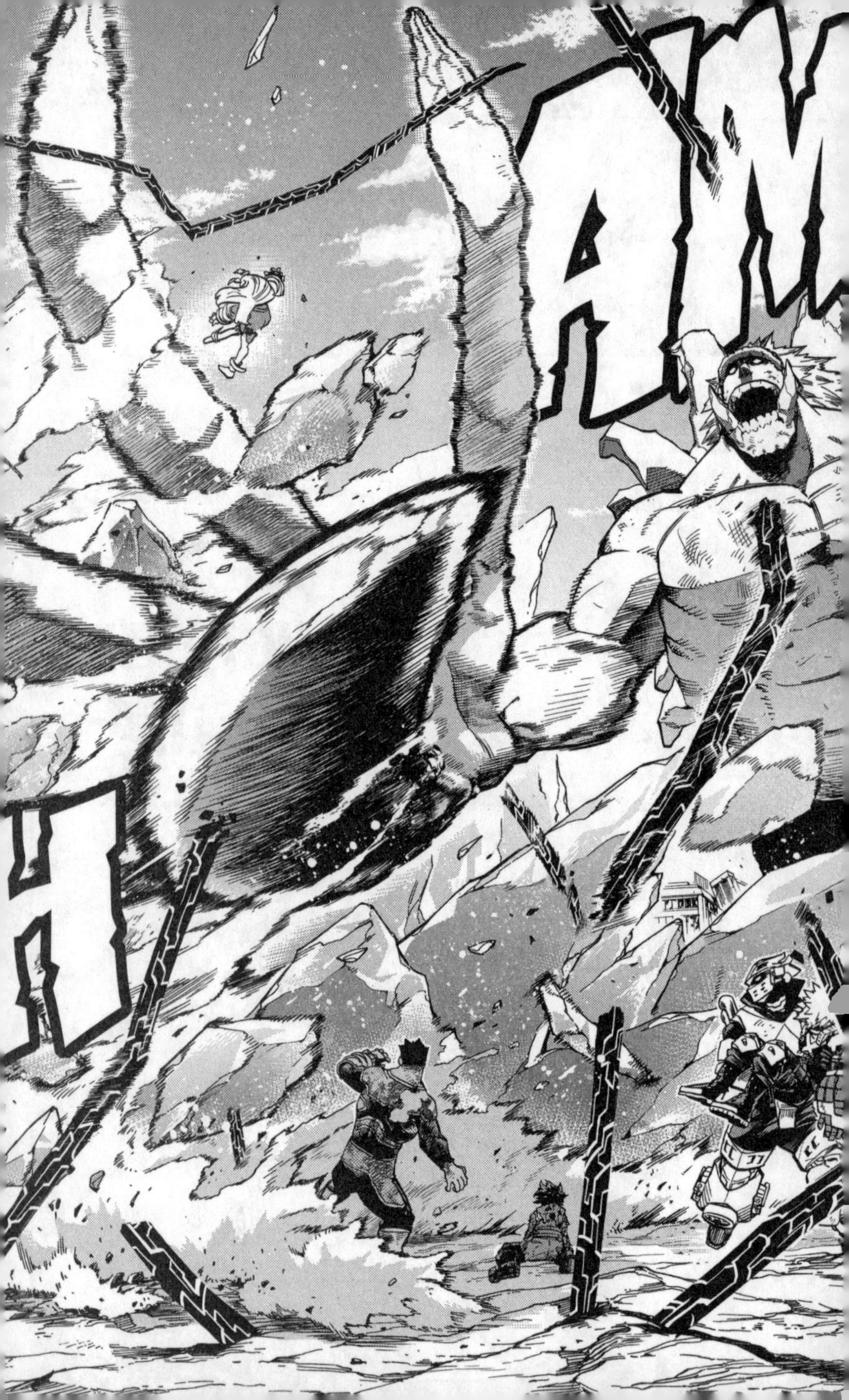

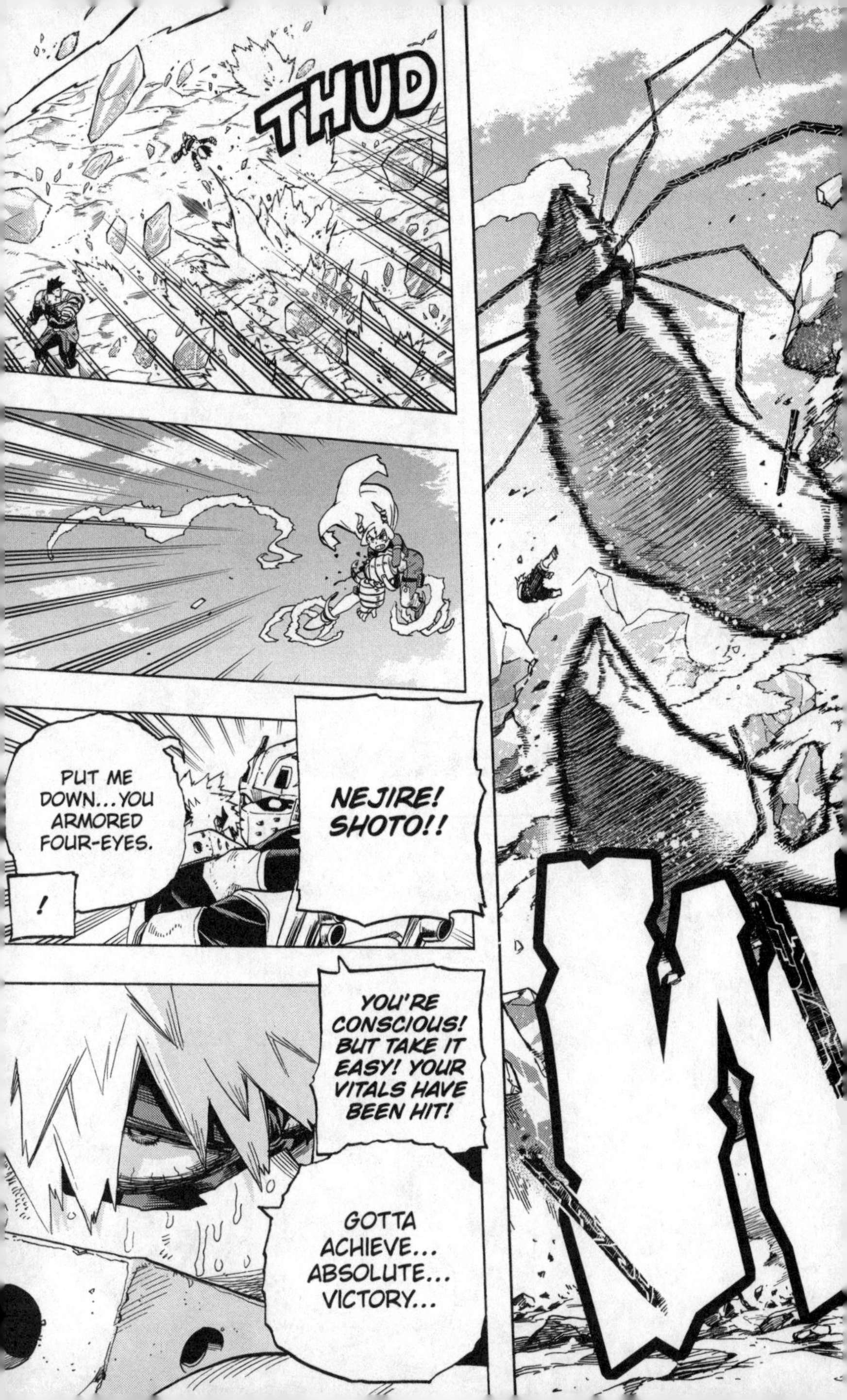
THUD
NEJIRE! SHOTO!!
PUT ME DOWN...YOU ARMORED FOUR-EYES.
!
YOU'RE CONSCIOUS! BUT TAKE IT EASY! YOUR VITALS HAVE BEEN HIT!
GOTTA ACHIEVE... ABSOLUTE... VICTORY...

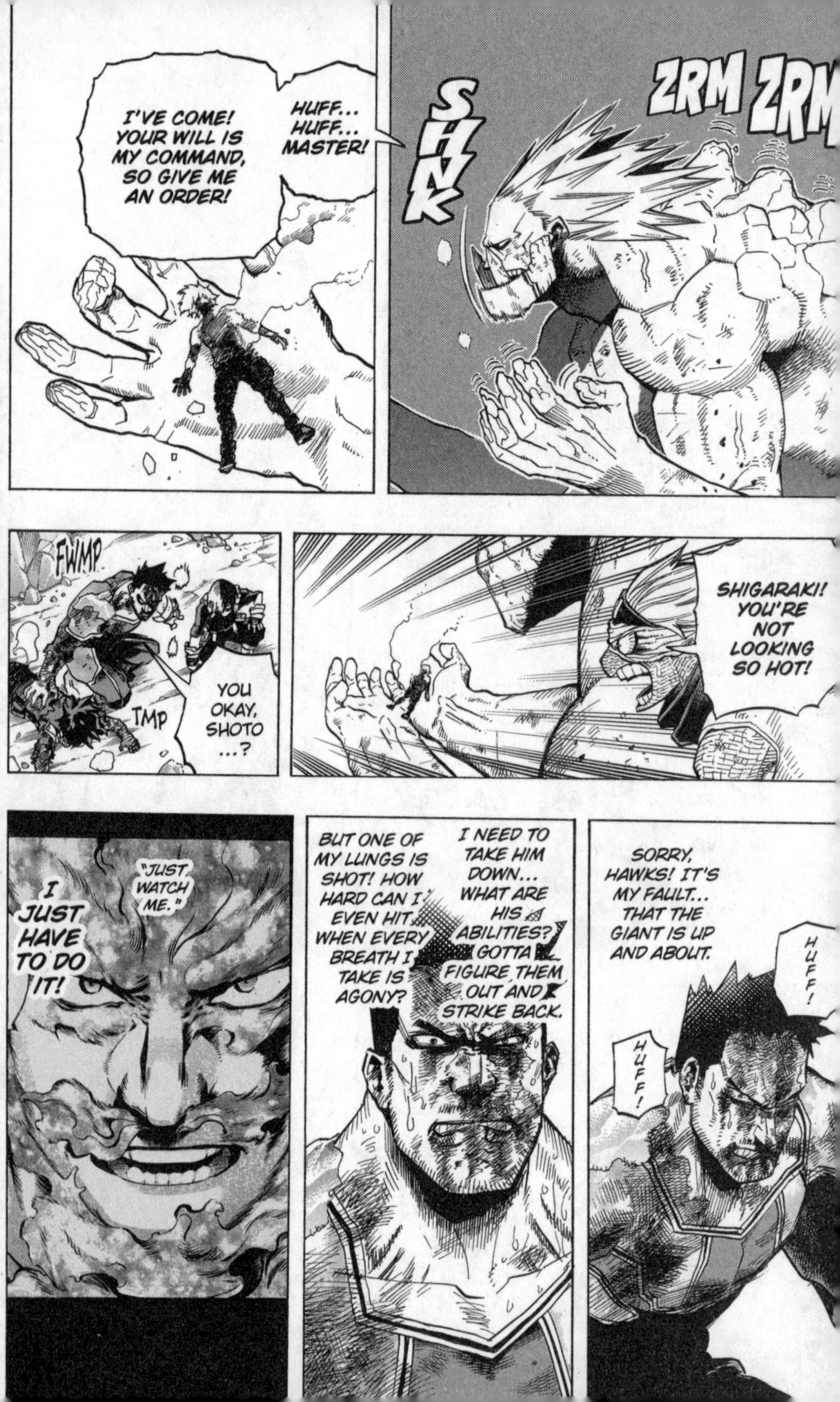
SHNK
ZRM ZRM
HUFF... HUFF... MASTER!
I'VE COME! YOUR WILL IS MY COMMAND, SO GIVE ME AN ORDER!
SHIGARAKI! YOU'RE NOT LOOKING SO HOT!
FWMP
TMP
YOU OKAY, SHOTO ...?
SORRY, HAWKS! IT'S MY FAULT... THAT THE GIANT IS UP AND ABOUT.
HUFF!
HUFF!
I NEED TO TAKE HIM DOWN... WHAT ARE HIS ABILITIES? GOTTA FIGURE THEM OUT AND STRIKE BACK.
BUT ONE OF MY LUNGS IS SHOT! HOW HARD CAN I EVEN HIT WHEN EVERY BREATH I TAKE IS AGONY?
"JUST WATCH ME."
I JUST HAVE TO DO IT!

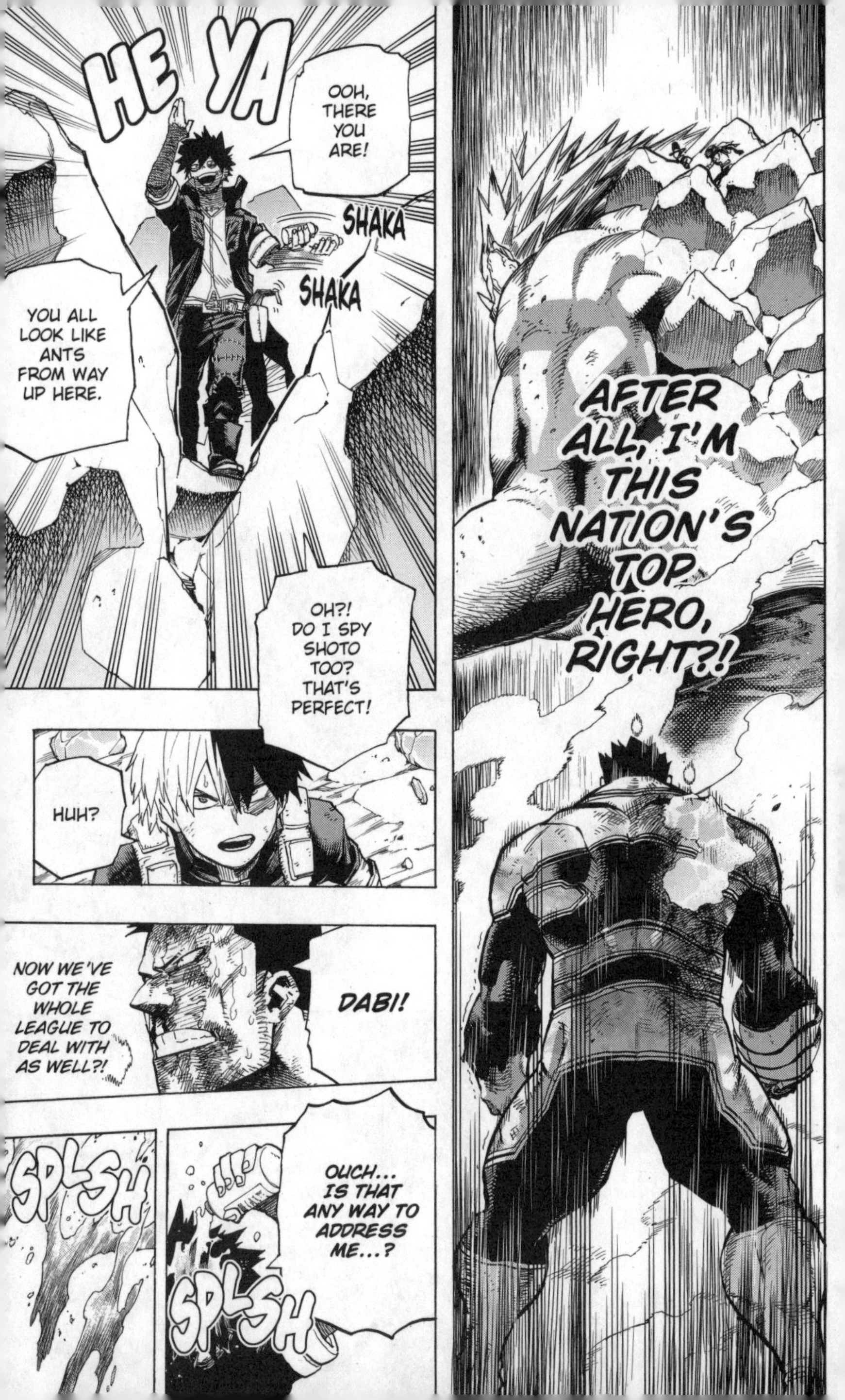
AFTER ALL, I'M THIS NATION'S TOP HERO, RIGHT?!
HE YA
OOH, THERE YOU ARE!
SHAKA
SHAKA
YOU ALL LOOK LIKE ANTS FROM WAY UP HERE.
OH?! DO I SPY SHOTO TOO? THAT'S PERFECT!
HUH?
DABI!
NOW WE'VE GOT THE WHOLE LEAGUE TO DEAL WITH AS WELL?!
OUCH... IS THAT ANY WAY TO ADDRESS ME...?
SPLSH
SPLSH

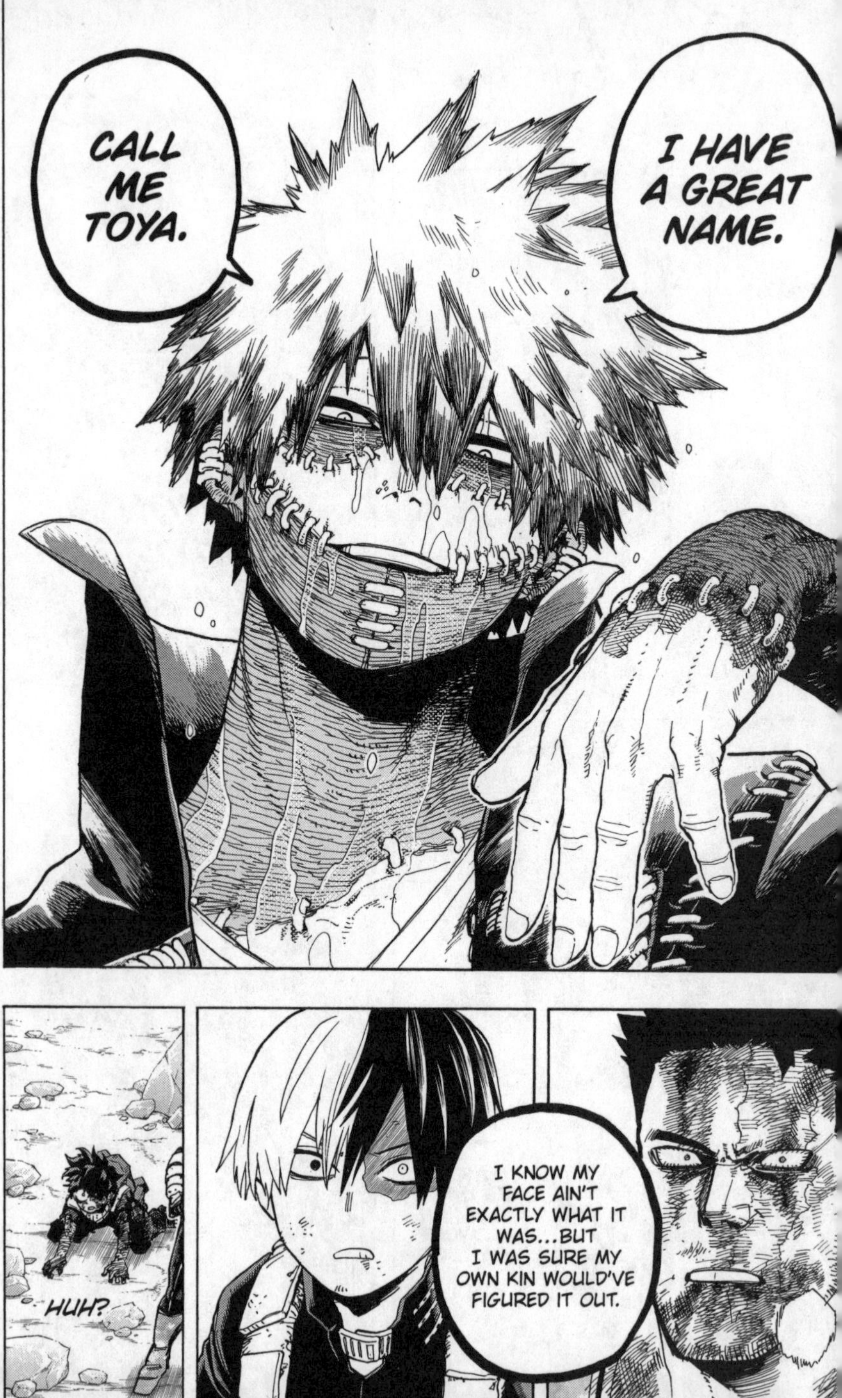
I HAVE A GREAT NAME.
CALL ME TOYA.
I KNOW MY FACE AIN'T EXACTLY WHAT IT WAS...BUT I WAS SURE MY OWN KIN WOULD'VE FIGURED IT OUT.
HUH?

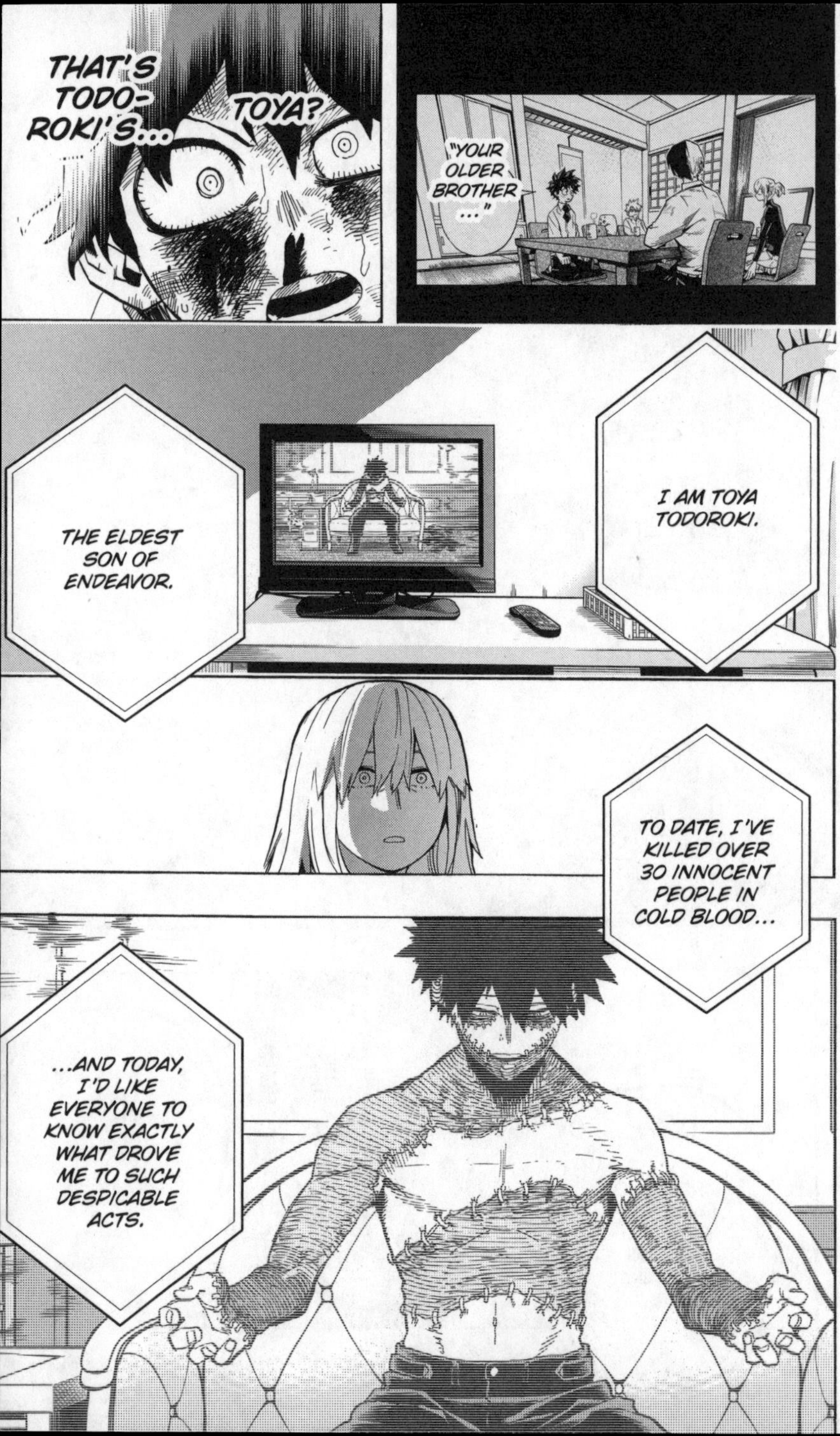
"YOUR OLDER BROTHER ..."
THAT'S TODO-ROKI'S...
TOYA?
I AM TOYA TODOROKI.
THE ELDEST SON OF ENDEAVOR.
TO DATE, I'VE KILLED OVER 30 INNOCENT PEOPLE IN COLD BLOOD...
...AND TODAY, I'D LIKE EVERYONE TO KNOW EXACTLY WHAT DROVE ME TO SUCH DESPICABLE ACTS.

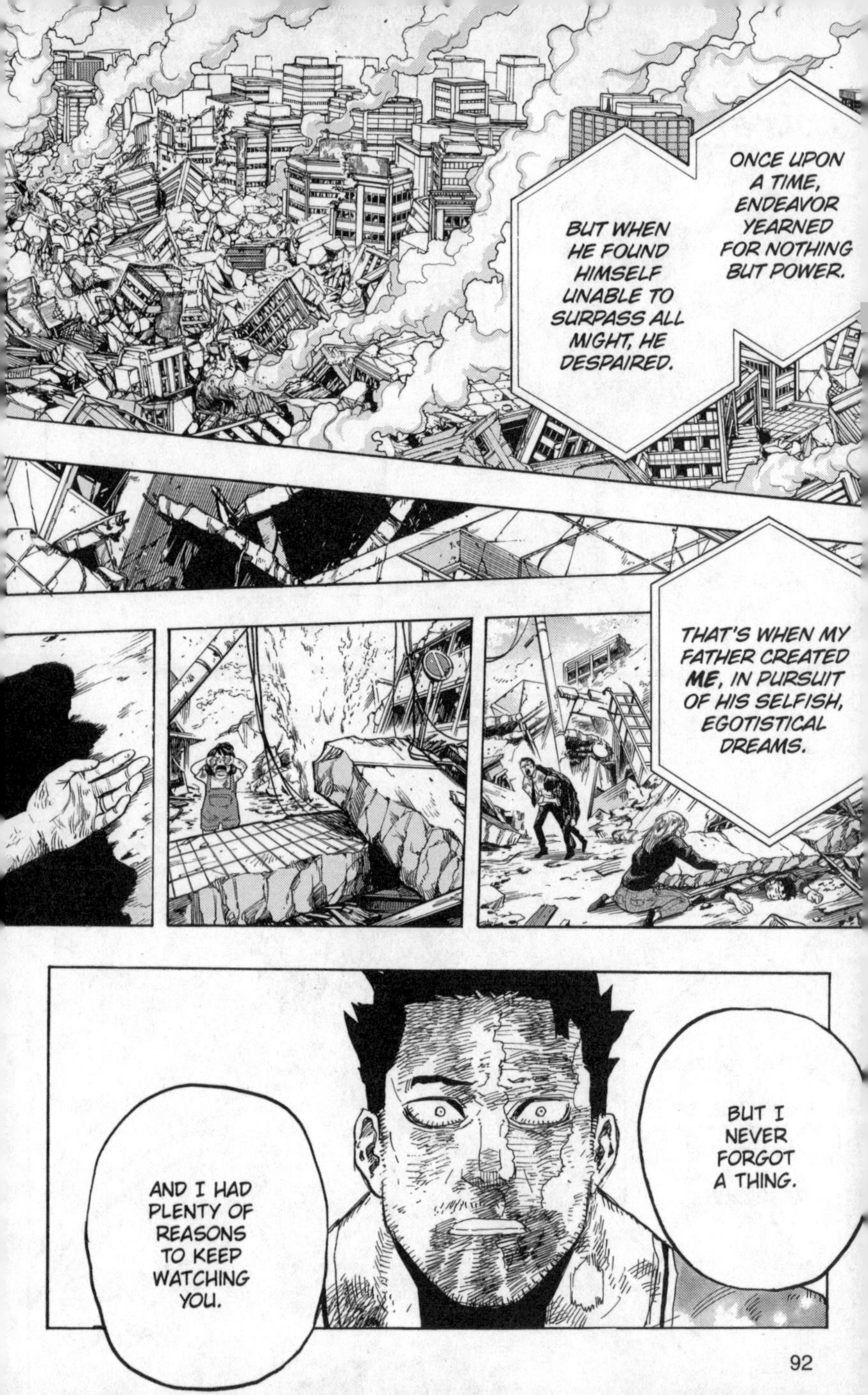
ONCE UPON A TIME, ENDEAVOR YEARNED FOR NOTHING BUT POWER.
BUT WHEN HE FOUND HIMSELF UNABLE TO SURPASS ALL MIGHT, HE DESPAIRED.
THAT'S WHEN MY FATHER CREATED **ME**, IN PURSUIT OF HIS SELFISH, EGOTISTICAL DREAMS.
BUT I NEVER FORGOT A THING.
AND I HAD PLENTY OF REASONS TO KEEP WATCHING YOU.

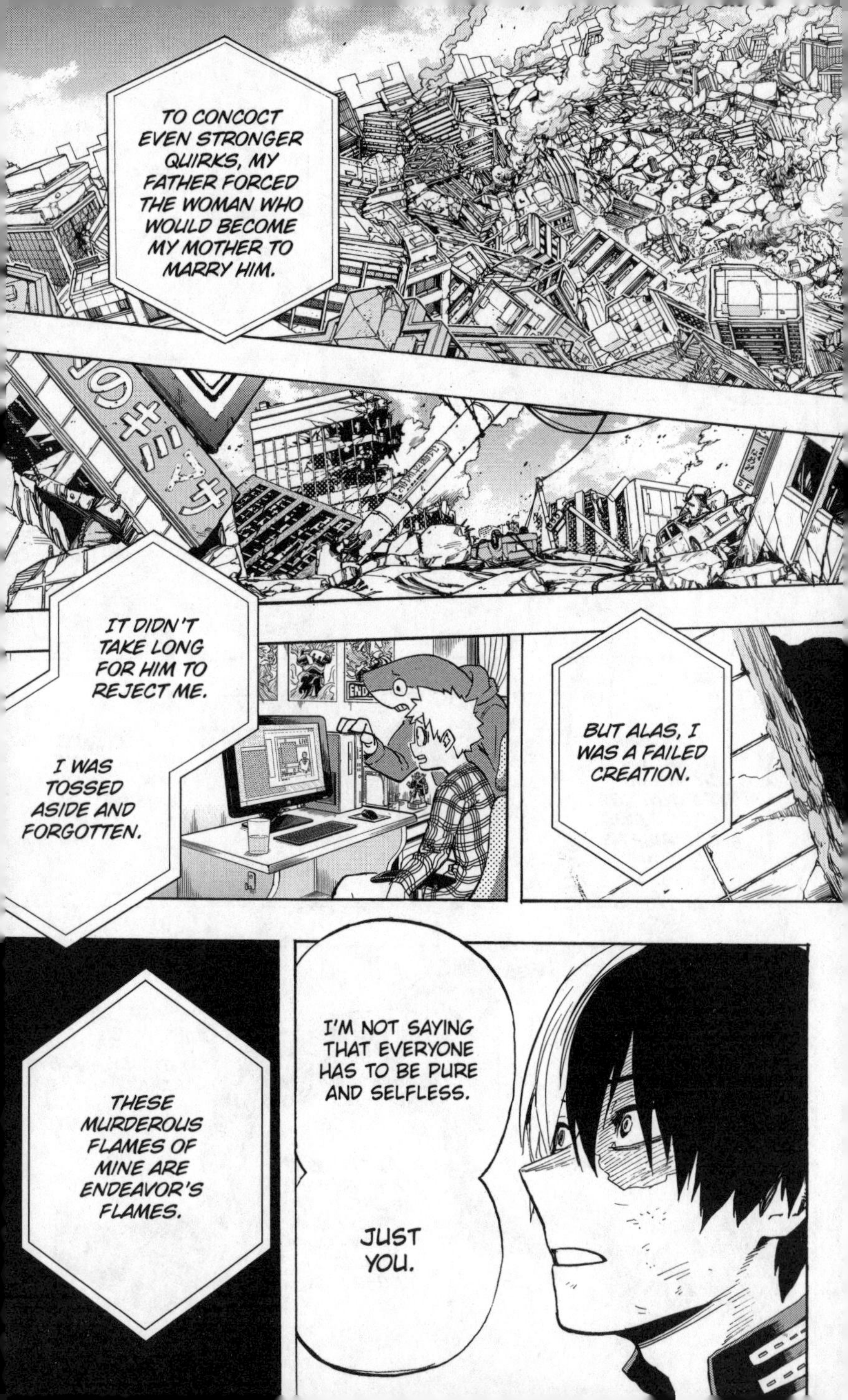
TO CONCOCT EVEN STRONGER QUIRKS, MY FATHER FORCED THE WOMAN WHO WOULD BECOME MY MOTHER TO MARRY HIM.
BUT ALAS, I WAS A FAILED CREATION.
IT DIDN'T TAKE LONG FOR HIM TO REJECT ME.
I WAS TOSSED ASIDE AND FORGOTTEN.
I'M NOT SAYING THAT EVERYONE HAS TO BE PURE AND SELFLESS.
JUST YOU.
THESE MURDEROUS FLAMES OF MINE ARE ENDEAVOR'S FLAMES.

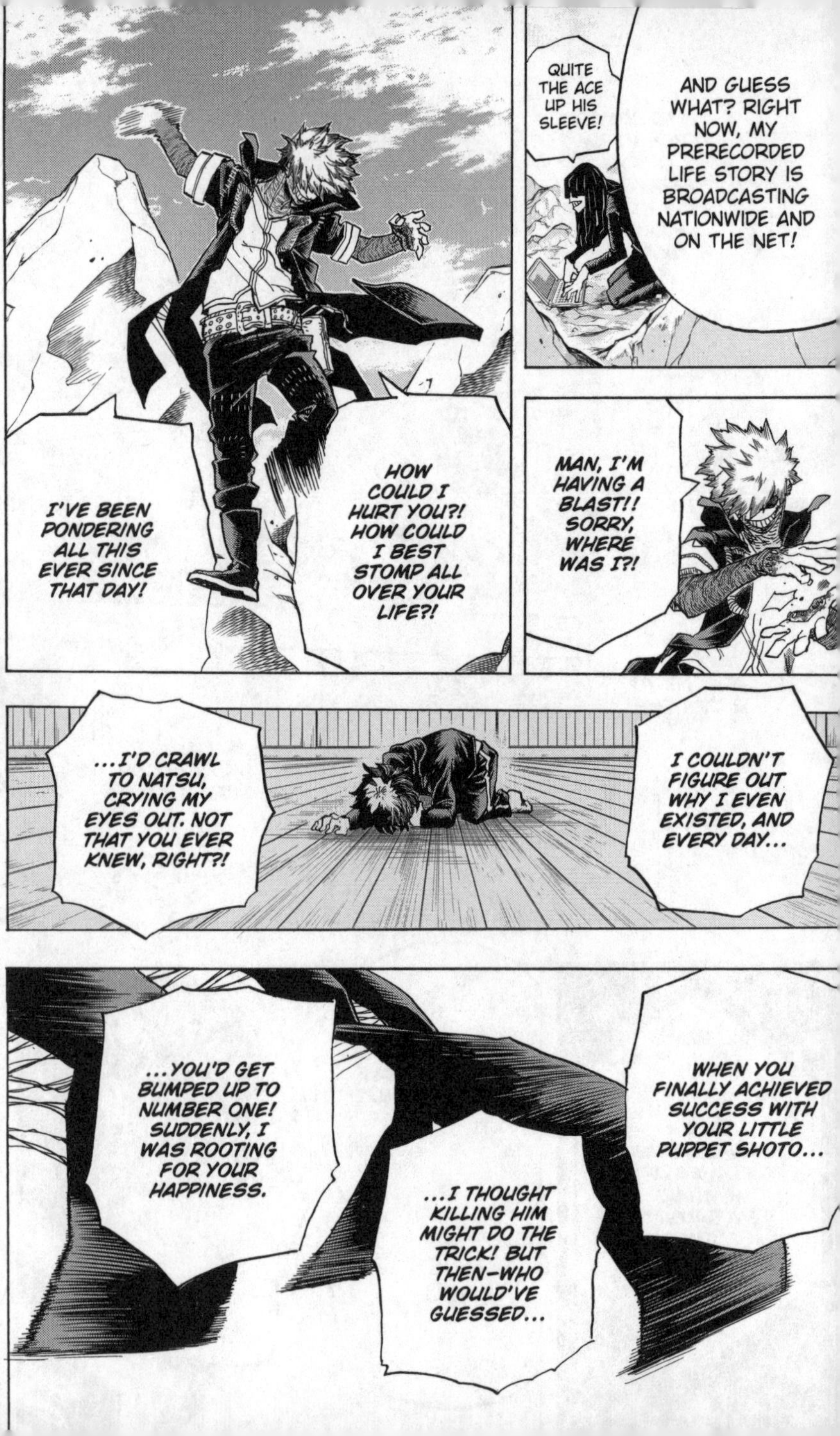
AND GUESS WHAT? RIGHT NOW, MY PRERECORDED LIFE STORY IS BROADCASTING NATIONWIDE AND ON THE NET!
QUITE THE ACE UP HIS SLEEVE!
MAN, I'M HAVING A BLAST!! SORRY, WHERE WAS I?!
HOW COULD I HURT YOU?! HOW COULD I BEST STOMP ALL OVER YOUR LIFE?!
I'VE BEEN PONDERING ALL THIS EVER SINCE THAT DAY!
I COULDN'T FIGURE OUT WHY I EVEN EXISTED, AND EVERY DAY...
...I'D CRAWL TO NATSU, CRYING MY EYES OUT. NOT THAT YOU EVER KNEW, RIGHT?!
WHEN YOU FINALLY ACHIEVED SUCCESS WITH YOUR LITTLE PUPPET SHOTO...
...I THOUGHT KILLING HIM MIGHT DO THE TRICK! BUT THEN—WHO WOULD'VE GUESSED...
...YOU'D GET BUMPED UP TO NUMBER ONE! SUDDENLY, I WAS ROOTING FOR YOUR HAPPINESS.

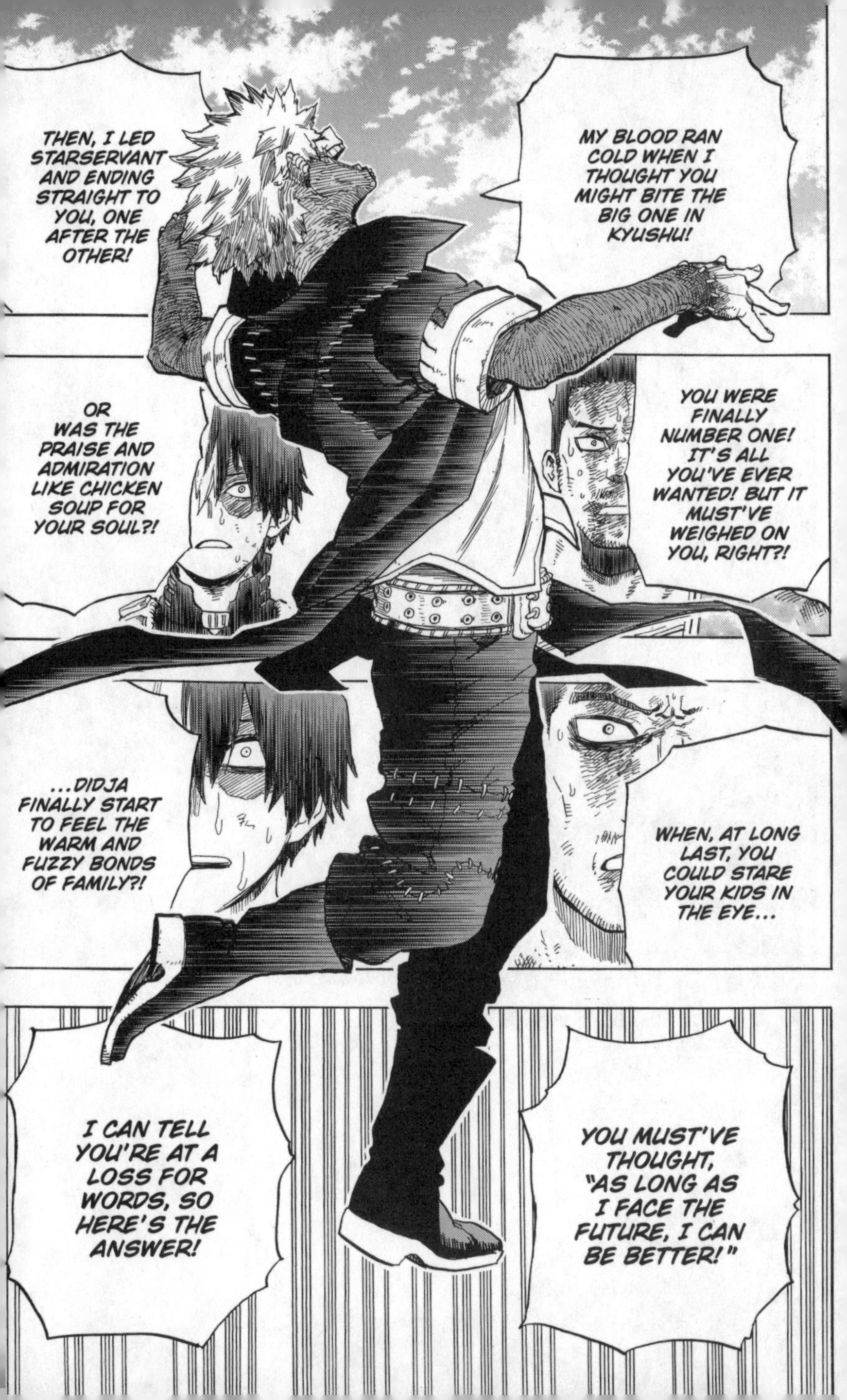
MY BLOOD RAN COLD WHEN I THOUGHT YOU MIGHT BITE THE BIG ONE IN KYUSHU!
THEN, I LED STARSERVANT AND ENDING STRAIGHT TO YOU, ONE AFTER THE OTHER!
YOU WERE FINALLY NUMBER ONE! IT'S ALL YOU'VE EVER WANTED! BUT IT MUST'VE WEIGHED ON YOU, RIGHT?!
OR WAS THE PRAISE AND ADMIRATION LIKE CHICKEN SOUP FOR YOUR SOUL?!
WHEN, AT LONG LAST, YOU COULD STARE YOUR KIDS IN THE EYE...
...DIDJA FINALLY START TO FEEL THE WARM AND FUZZY BONDS OF FAMILY?!
YOU MUST'VE THOUGHT, "AS LONG AS I FACE THE FUTURE, I CAN BE BETTER!"
I CAN TELL YOU'RE AT A LOSS FOR WORDS, SO HERE'S THE ANSWER!

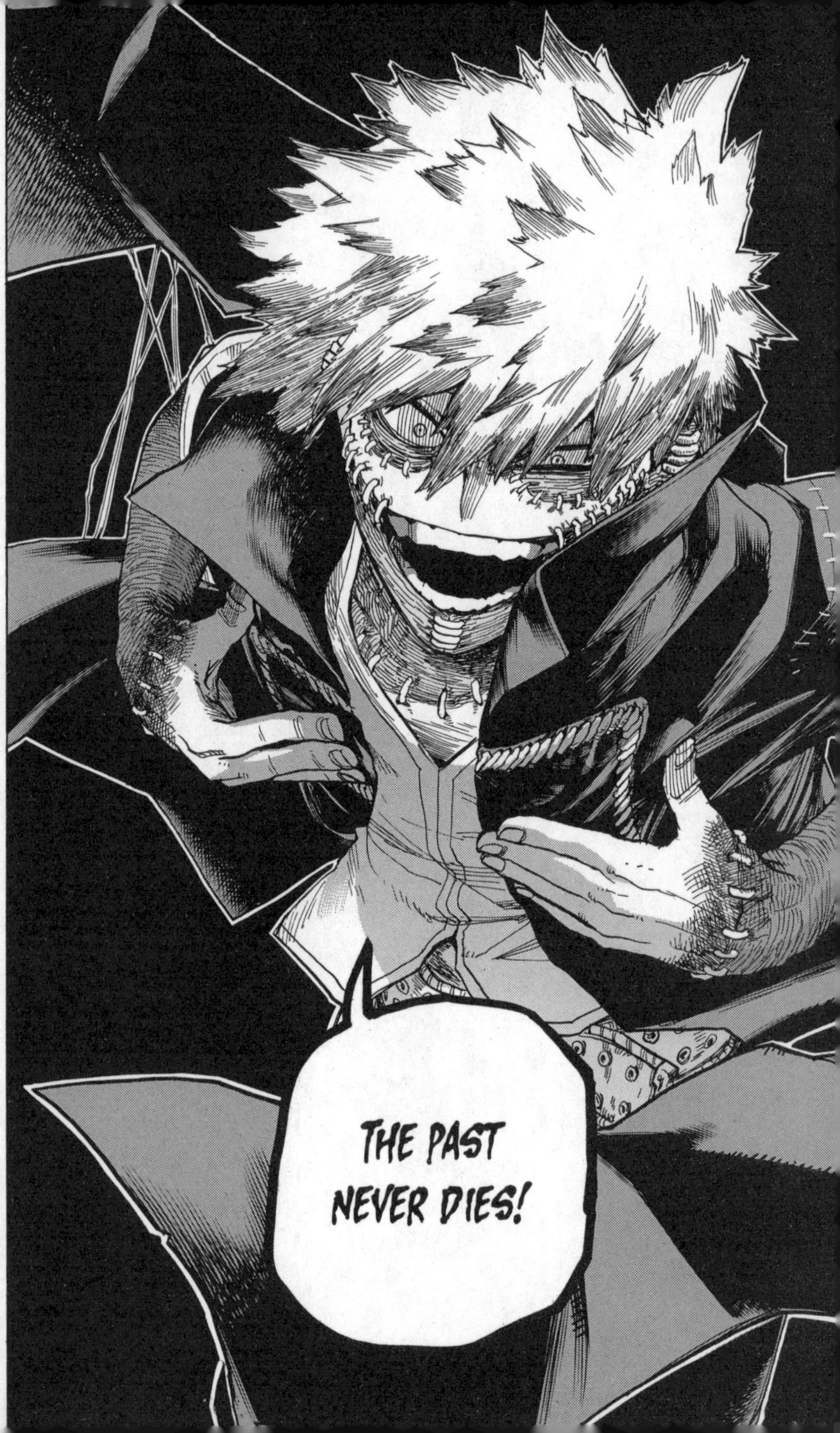
THE PAST NEVER DIES!

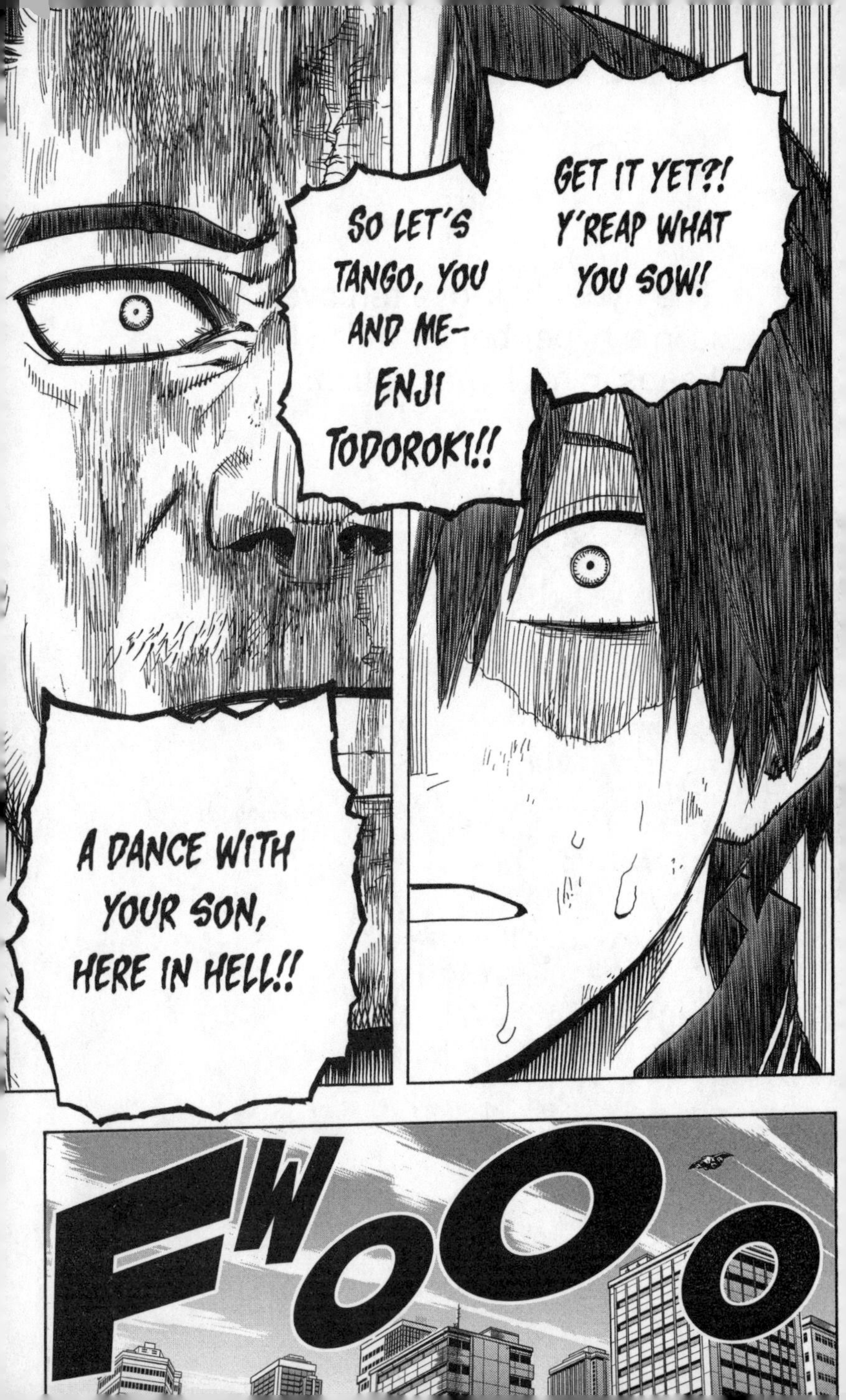
GET IT YET?! Y'REAP WHAT YOU SOW!
SO LET'S TANGO, YOU AND ME-- ENJI TODOROKI!!
A DANCE WITH YOUR SON, HERE IN HELL!!
FWOOO

The hyper hair-dye remover is in a hyper bottle, which he keeps in his hyper pouch.

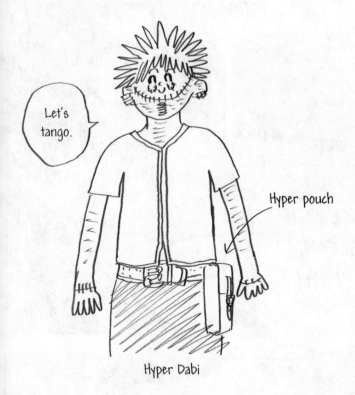

Hyper Dabi

No. 291 - Thanks for Going Strong

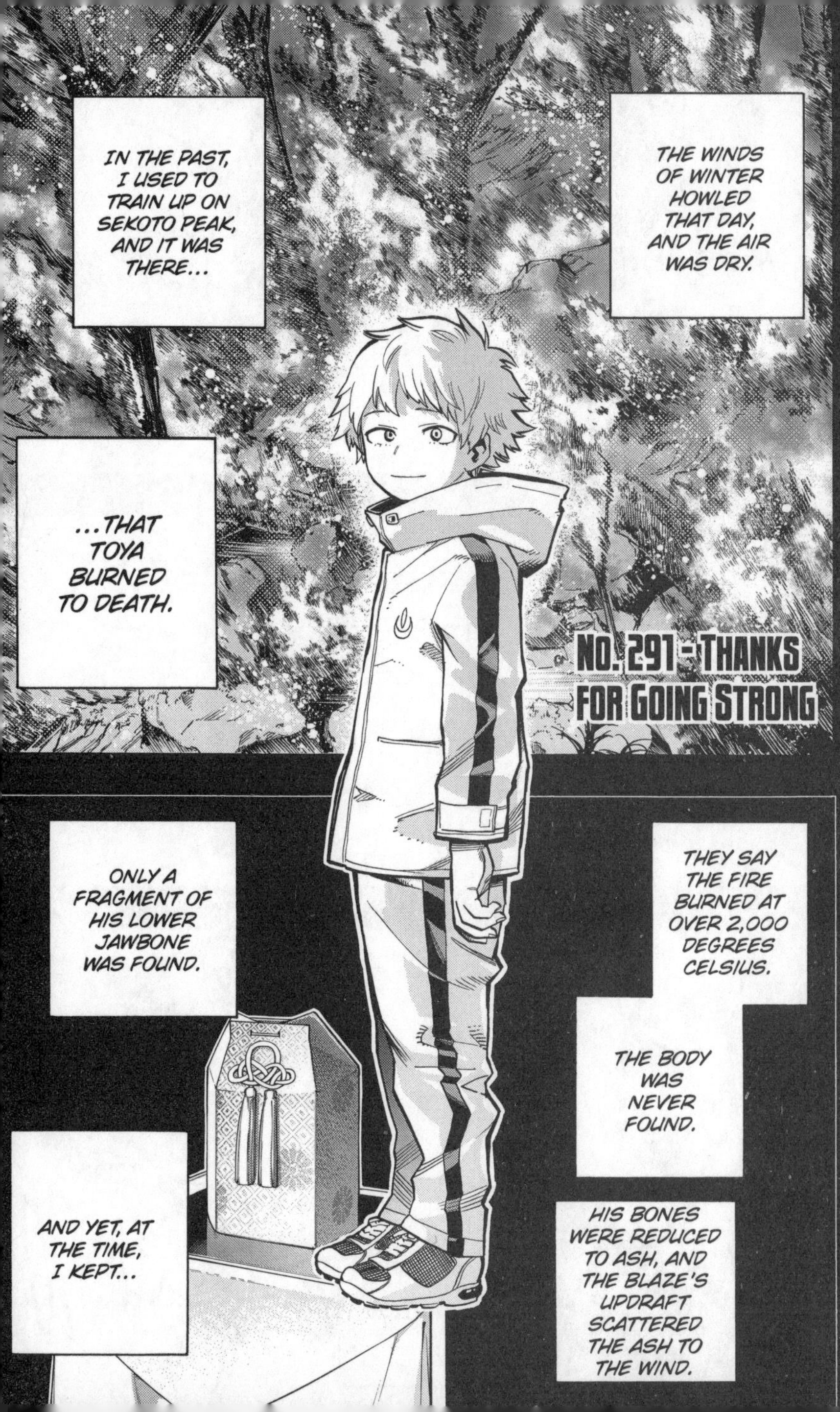
THE WINDS OF WINTER HOWLED THAT DAY, AND THE AIR WAS DRY.
IN THE PAST, I USED TO TRAIN UP ON SEKOTO PEAK, AND IT WAS THERE...
...THAT TOYA BURNED TO DEATH.
THEY SAY THE FIRE BURNED AT OVER 2,000 DEGREES CELSIUS.
THE BODY WAS NEVER FOUND.
HIS BONES WERE REDUCED TO ASH, AND THE BLAZE'S UPDRAFT SCATTERED THE ASH TO THE WIND.
ONLY A FRAGMENT OF HIS LOWER JAWBONE WAS FOUND.
AND YET, AT THE TIME, I KEPT...

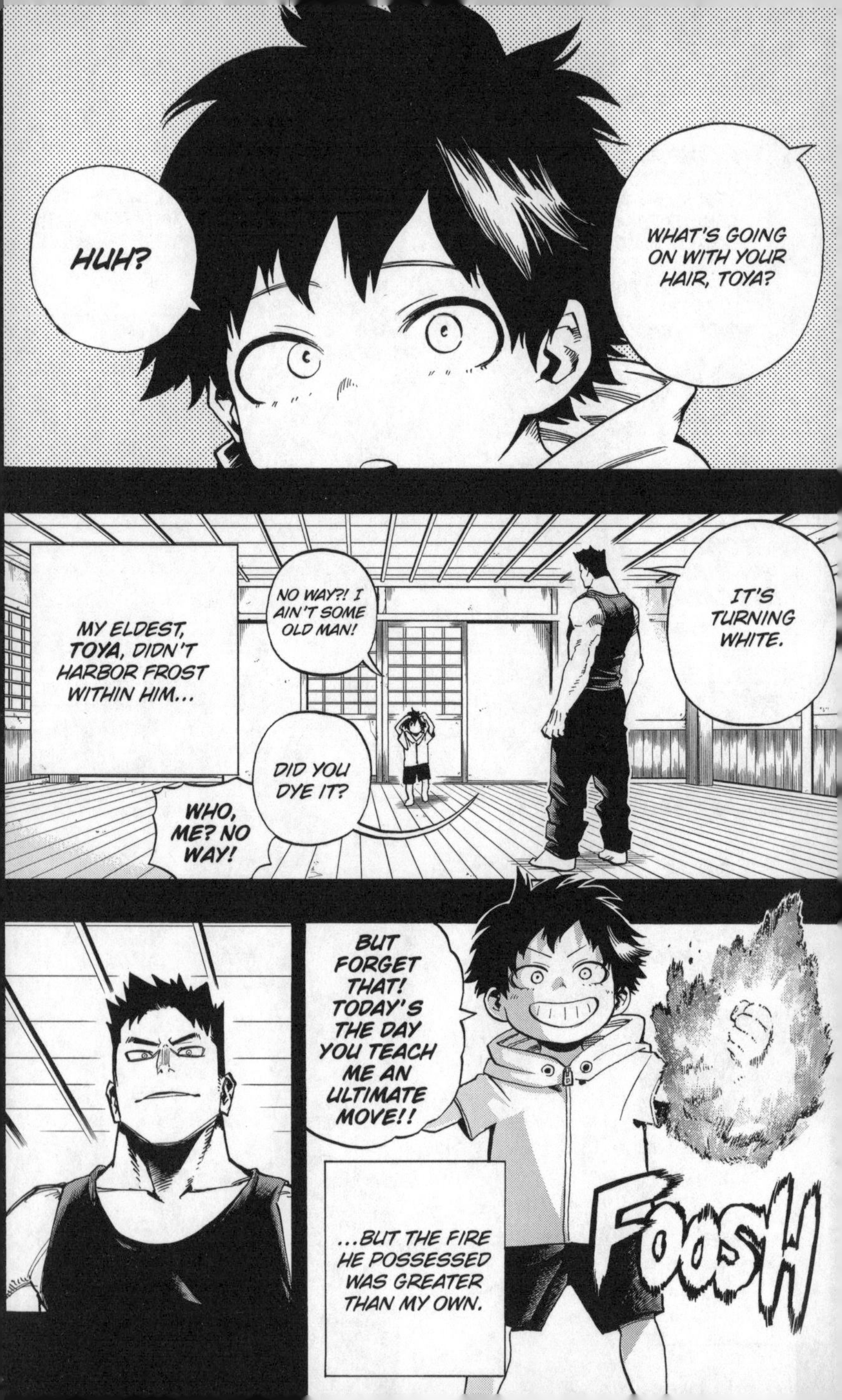
WHAT'S GOING ON WITH YOUR HAIR, TOYA?
HUH?
IT'S TURNING WHITE.
NO WAY?! I AIN'T SOME OLD MAN!
MY ELDEST, TOYA, DIDN'T HARBOR FROST WITHIN HIM...
DID YOU DYE IT?
WHO, ME? NO WAY!
BUT FORGET THAT! TODAY'S THE DAY YOU TEACH ME AN ULTIMATE MOVE!!
FOOSH
...BUT THE FIRE HE POSSESSED WAS GREATER THAN MY OWN.

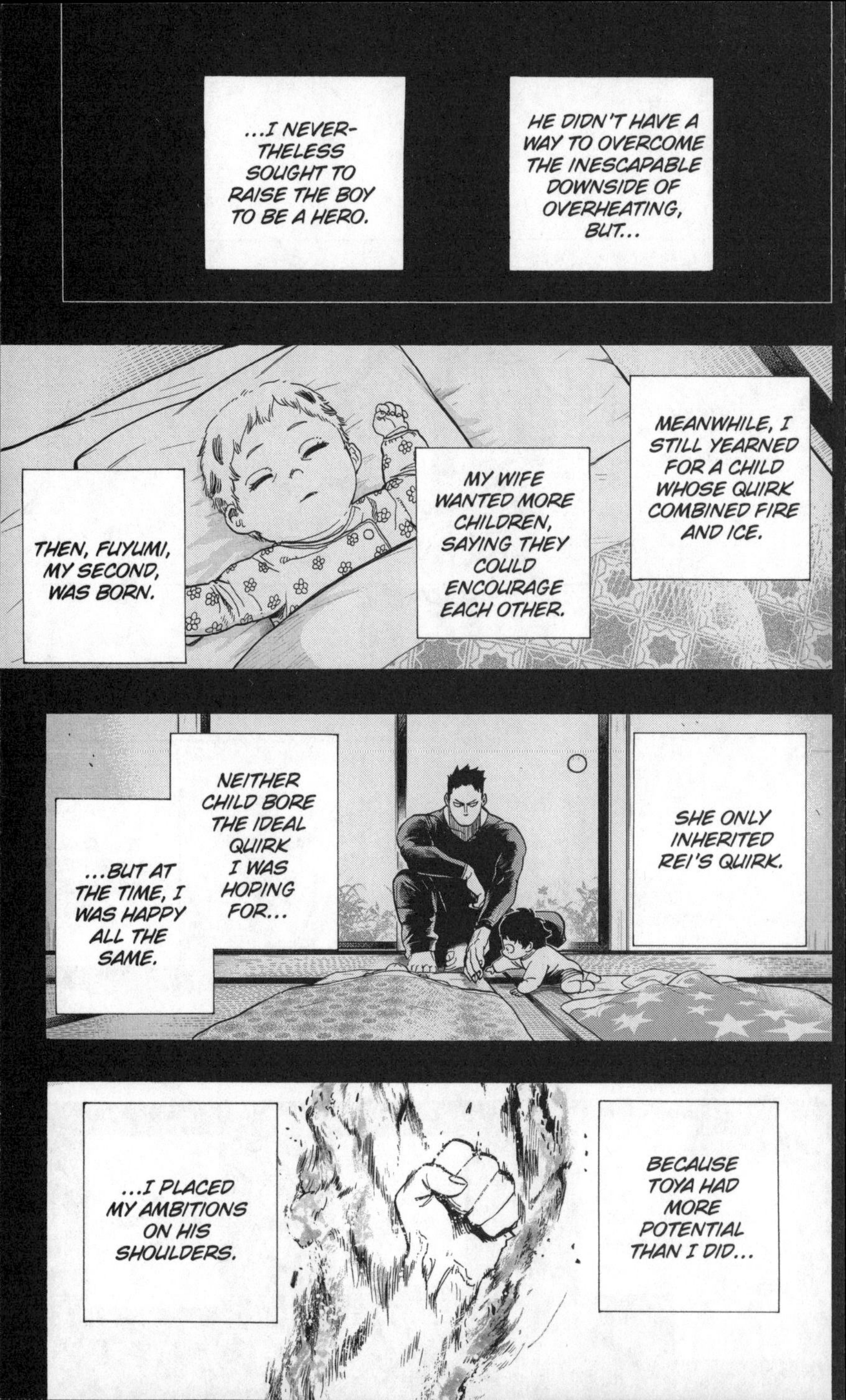
HE DIDN'T HAVE A WAY TO OVERCOME THE INESCAPABLE DOWNSIDE OF OVERHEATING, BUT...
...I NEVER-THELESS SOUGHT TO RAISE THE BOY TO BE A HERO.
MEANWHILE, I STILL YEARNED FOR A CHILD WHOSE QUIRK COMBINED FIRE AND ICE.
MY WIFE WANTED MORE CHILDREN, SAYING THEY COULD ENCOURAGE EACH OTHER.
THEN, FUYUMI, MY SECOND, WAS BORN.
SHE ONLY INHERITED REI'S QUIRK.
NEITHER CHILD BORE THE IDEAL QUIRK I WAS HOPING FOR...
...BUT AT THE TIME, I WAS HAPPY ALL THE SAME.
BECAUSE TOYA HAD MORE POTENTIAL THAN I DID...
...I PLACED MY AMBITIONS ON HIS SHOULDERS.

OW!
I THOUGHT IT COULD BE YOU.
YOU COULD HAVE BEEN THE ONE...
...TO REACH MY ETERNAL GOAL.
MY FRUSTRA-TION...
MY ENVY...
THE UGLINESS IN MY HEART...
YOU COULD HAVE BEEN THE ONE...

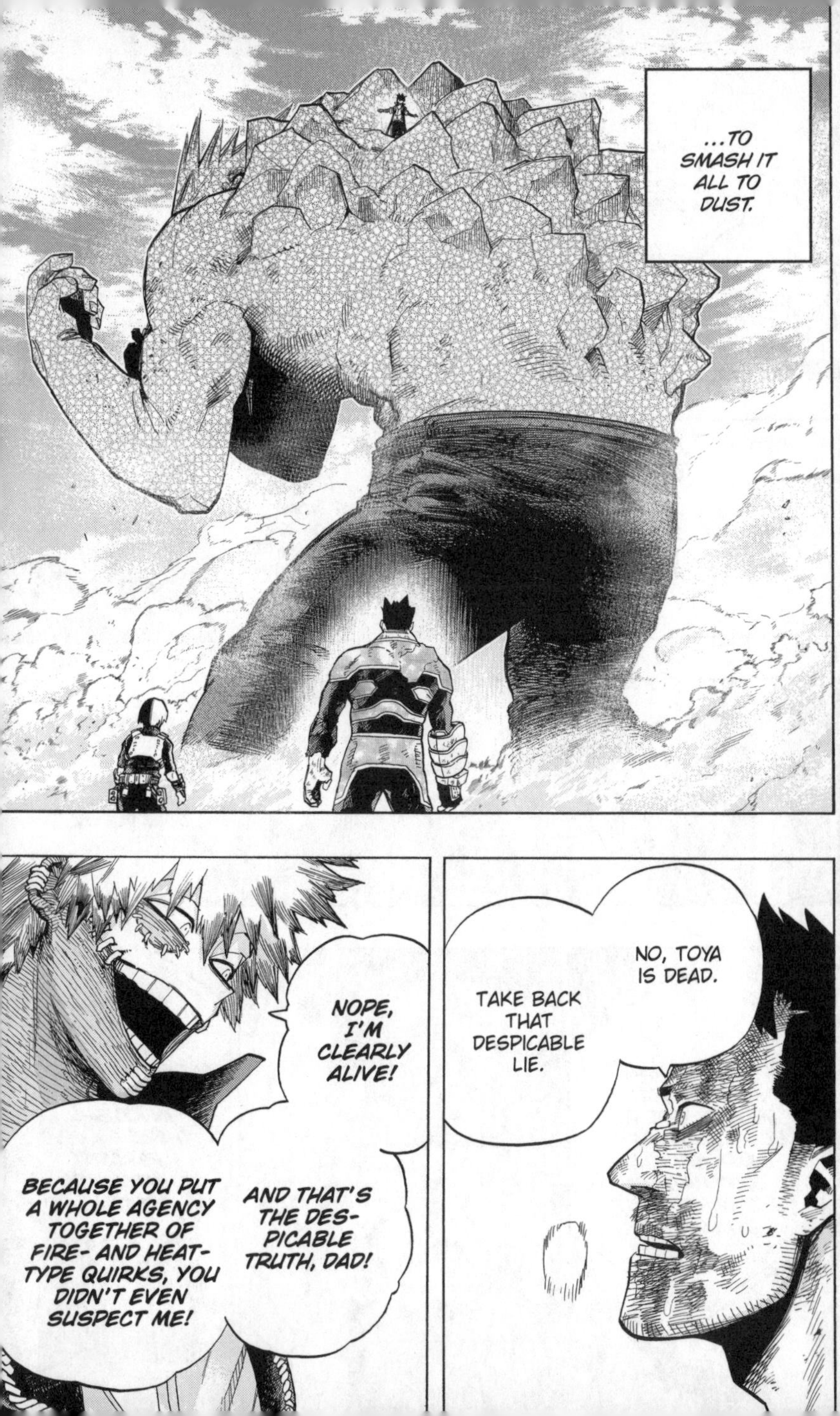
...TO SMASH IT ALL TO DUST.
NO, TOYA IS DEAD.
TAKE BACK THAT DESPICABLE LIE.
NOPE, I'M CLEARLY ALIVE!
AND THAT'S THE DES-PICABLE TRUTH, DAD!
BECAUSE YOU PUT A WHOLE AGENCY TOGETHER OF FIRE- AND HEAT-TYPE QUIRKS, YOU DIDN'T EVEN SUSPECT ME!

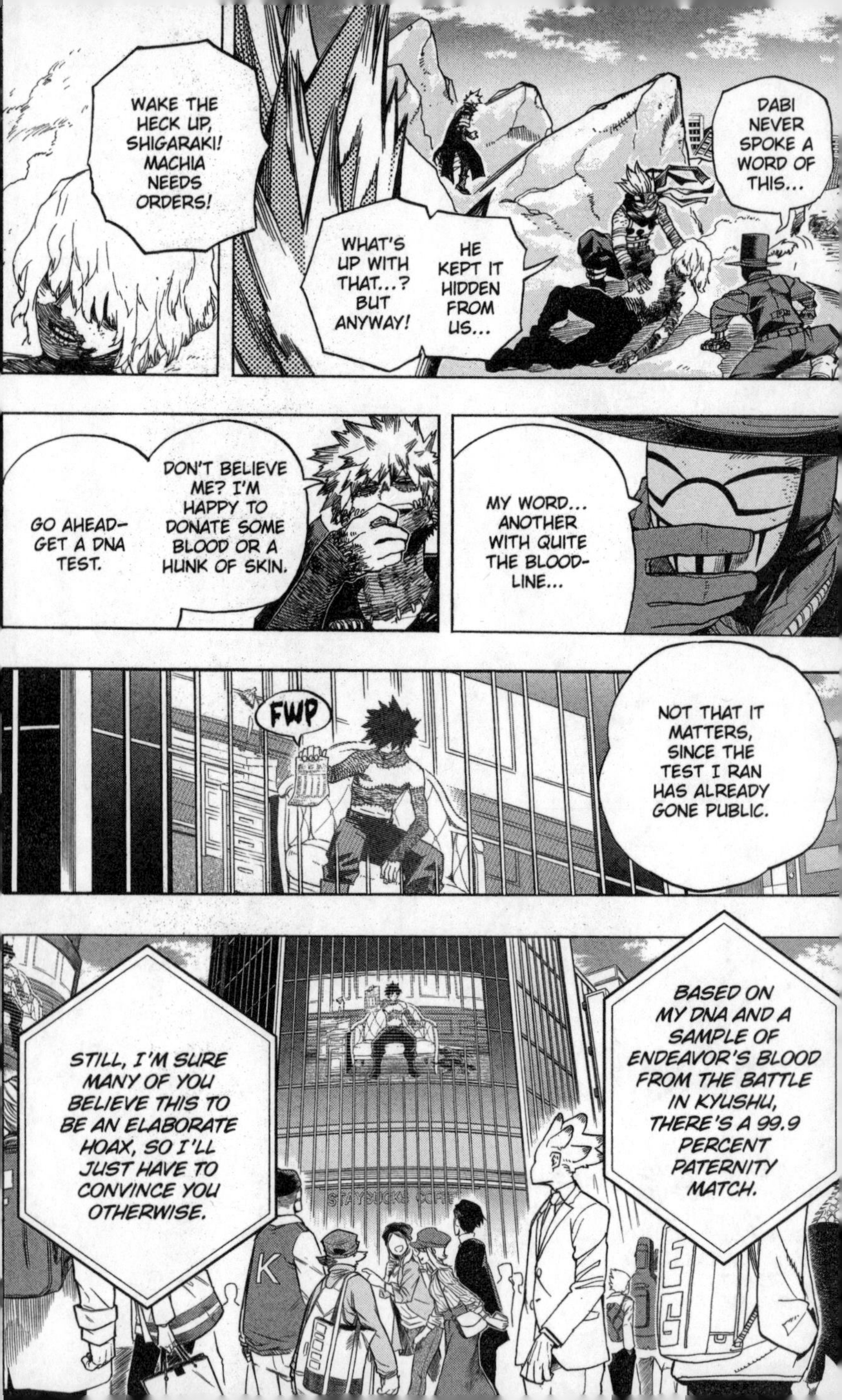
DABI NEVER SPOKE A WORD OF THIS...
HE KEPT IT HIDDEN FROM US...
WHAT'S UP WITH THAT...? BUT ANYWAY!
WAKE THE HECK UP, SHIGARAKI! MACHIA NEEDS ORDERS!
MY WORD... ANOTHER WITH QUITE THE BLOOD-LINE...
DON'T BELIEVE ME? I'M HAPPY TO DONATE SOME BLOOD OR A HUNK OF SKIN.
GO AHEAD- GET A DNA TEST.
NOT THAT IT MATTERS, SINCE THE TEST I RAN HAS ALREADY GONE PUBLIC.
FWP
BASED ON MY DNA AND A SAMPLE OF ENDEAVOR'S BLOOD FROM THE BATTLE IN KYUSHU, THERE'S A 99.9 PERCENT PATERNITY MATCH.
STILL, I'M SURE MANY OF YOU BELIEVE THIS TO BE AN ELABORATE HOAX, SO I'LL JUST HAVE TO CONVINCE YOU OTHERWISE.

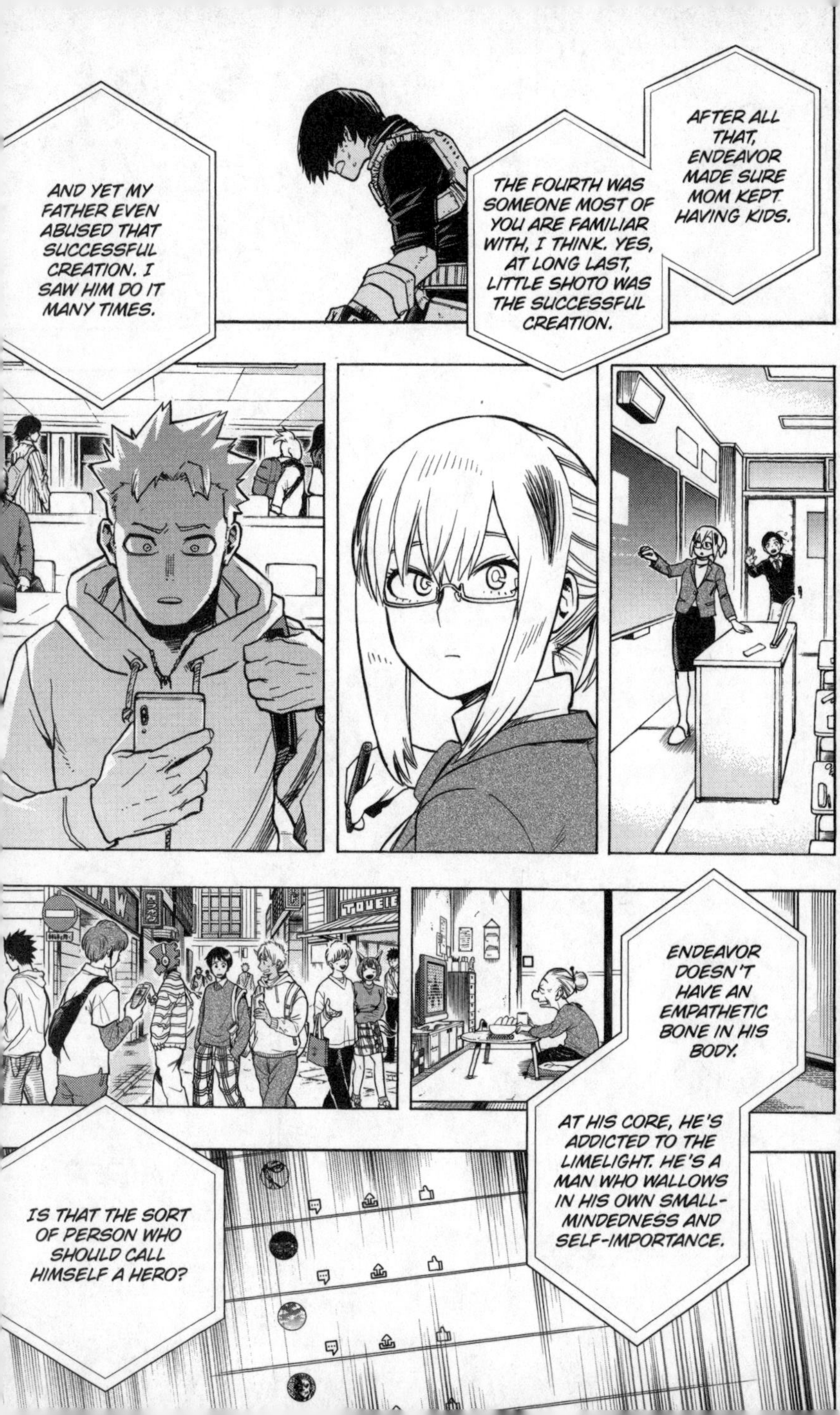
AFTER ALL THAT, ENDEAVOR MADE SURE MOM KEPT HAVING KIDS.
THE FOURTH WAS SOMEONE MOST OF YOU ARE FAMILIAR WITH, I THINK. YES, AT LONG LAST, LITTLE SHOTO WAS THE SUCCESSFUL CREATION.
AND YET MY FATHER EVEN ABUSED THAT SUCCESSFUL CREATION. I SAW HIM DO IT MANY TIMES.
ENDEAVOR DOESN'T HAVE AN EMPATHETIC BONE IN HIS BODY.
AT HIS CORE, HE'S ADDICTED TO THE LIMELIGHT. HE'S A MAN WHO WALLOWS IN HIS OWN SMALL-MINDEDNESS AND SELF-IMPORTANCE.
IS THAT THE SORT OF PERSON WHO SHOULD CALL HIMSELF A HERO?

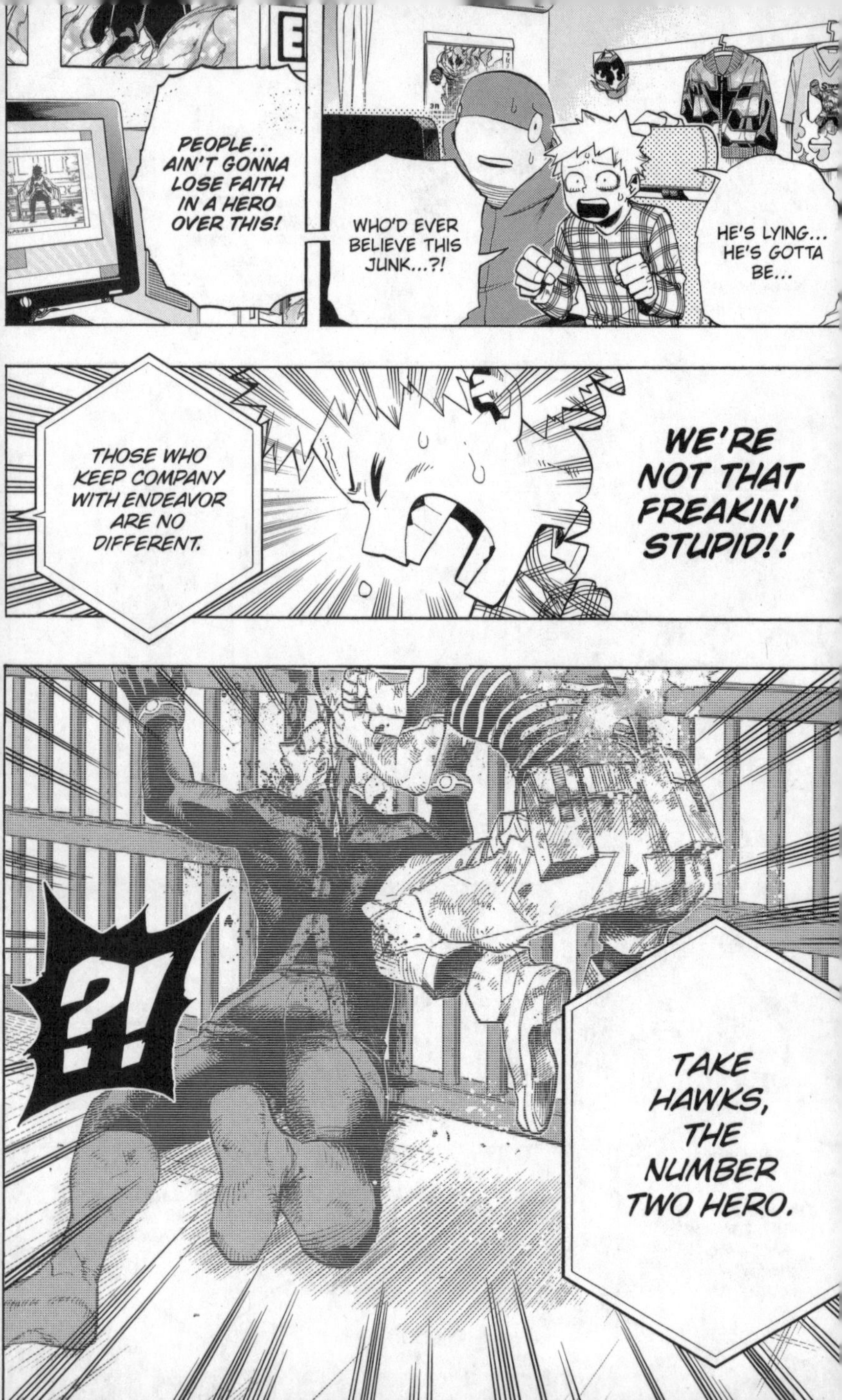
HE'S LYING... HE'S GOTTA BE...
WHO'D EVER BELIEVE THIS JUNK...?!
PEOPLE... AIN'T GONNA LOSE FAITH IN A HERO OVER THIS!
WE'RE NOT THAT FREAKIN' STUPID!!
THOSE WHO KEEP COMPANY WITH ENDEAVOR ARE NO DIFFERENT.
TAKE HAWKS, THE NUMBER TWO HERO.
?!

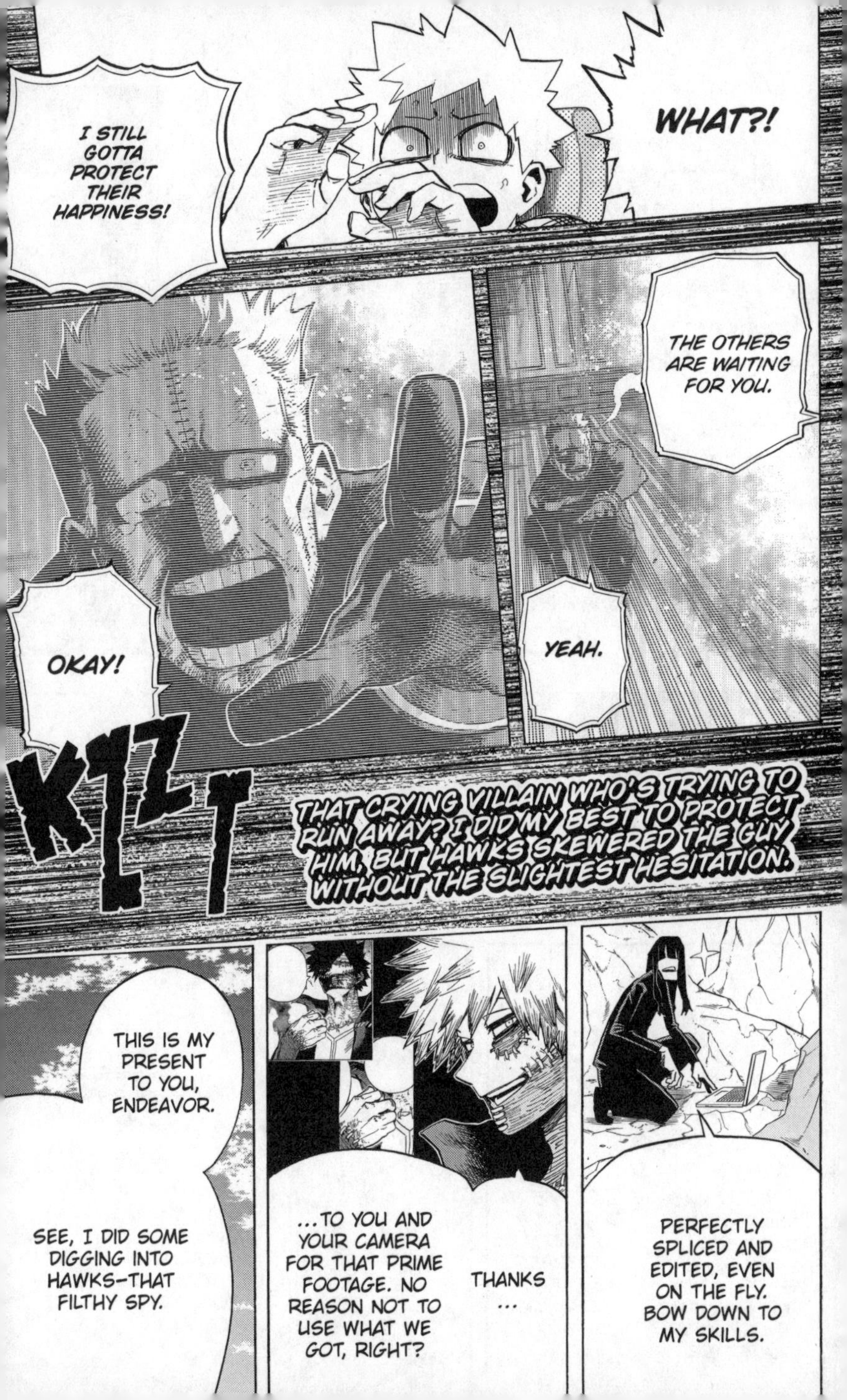
WHAT?!
I STILL GOTTA PROTECT THEIR HAPPINESS!
THE OTHERS ARE WAITING FOR YOU.
YEAH.
OKAY!
KZZZT
THAT CRYING VILLAIN WHO'S TRYING TO RUN AWAY? I DID MY BEST TO PROTECT HIM, BUT HAWKS SKEWERED THE GUY WITHOUT THE SLIGHTEST HESITATION.
PERFECTLY SPLICED AND EDITED, EVEN ON THE FLY. BOW DOWN TO MY SKILLS.
THANKS ...
...TO YOU AND YOUR CAMERA FOR THAT PRIME FOOTAGE. NO REASON NOT TO USE WHAT WE GOT, RIGHT?
THIS IS MY PRESENT TO YOU, ENDEAVOR.
SEE, I DID SOME DIGGING INTO HAWKS—THAT FILTHY SPY.

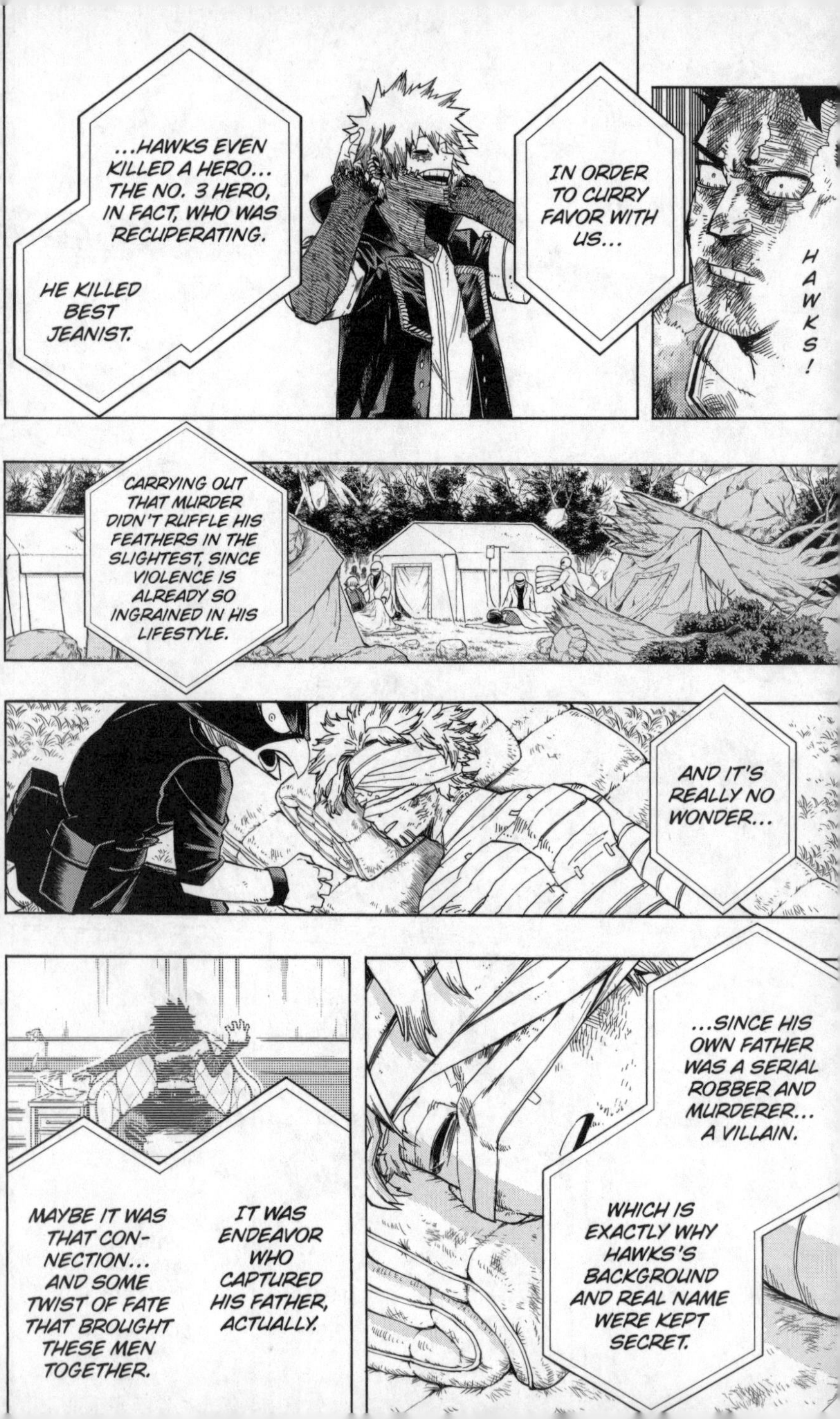
HAWKS!
IN ORDER TO CURRY FAVOR WITH US...
...HAWKS EVEN KILLED A HERO... THE NO. 3 HERO, IN FACT, WHO WAS RECUPERATING.
HE KILLED BEST JEANIST.
CARRYING OUT THAT MURDER DIDN'T RUFFLE HIS FEATHERS IN THE SLIGHTEST, SINCE VIOLENCE IS ALREADY SO INGRAINED IN HIS LIFESTYLE.
AND IT'S REALLY NO WONDER...
...SINCE HIS OWN FATHER WAS A SERIAL ROBBER AND MURDERER... A VILLAIN.
WHICH IS EXACTLY WHY HAWKS'S BACKGROUND AND REAL NAME WERE KEPT SECRET.
IT WAS ENDEAVOR WHO CAPTURED HIS FATHER, ACTUALLY.
MAYBE IT WAS THAT CONNECTION... AND SOME TWIST OF FATE THAT BROUGHT THESE MEN TOGETHER.

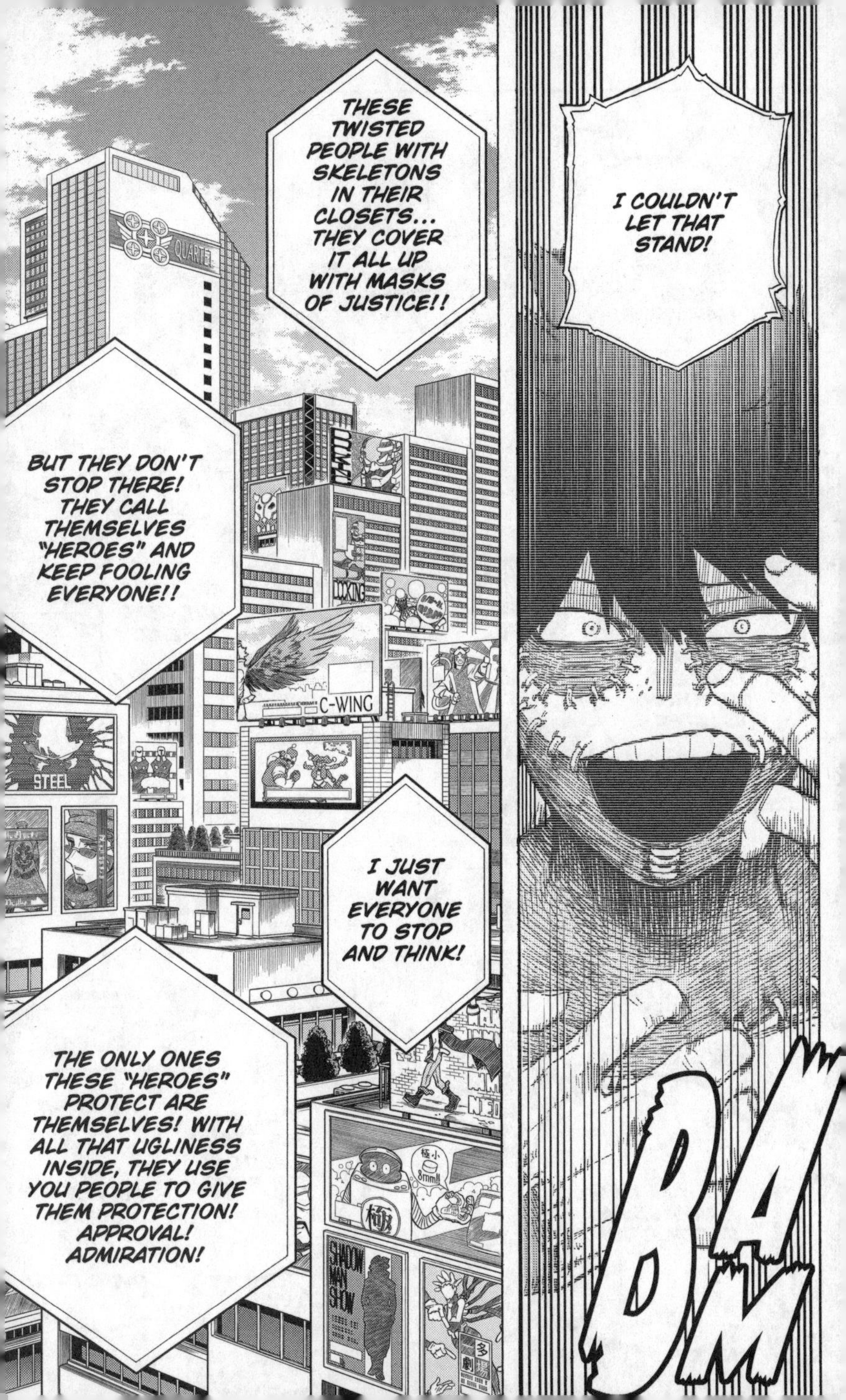
I COULDN'T LET THAT STAND!
BA
THESE TWISTED PEOPLE WITH SKELETONS IN THEIR CLOSETS... THEY COVER IT ALL UP WITH MASKS OF JUSTICE!!
QUARTET
BUT THEY DON'T STOP THERE! THEY CALL THEMSELVES "HEROES" AND KEEP FOOLING EVERYONE!!
C-WING
STEEL
I JUST WANT EVERYONE TO STOP AND THINK!
THE ONLY ONES THESE "HEROES" PROTECT ARE THEMSELVES! WITH ALL THAT UGLINESS INSIDE, THEY USE YOU PEOPLE TO GIVE THEM PROTECTION! APPROVAL! ADMIRATION!
SHADOW MAN SHOW

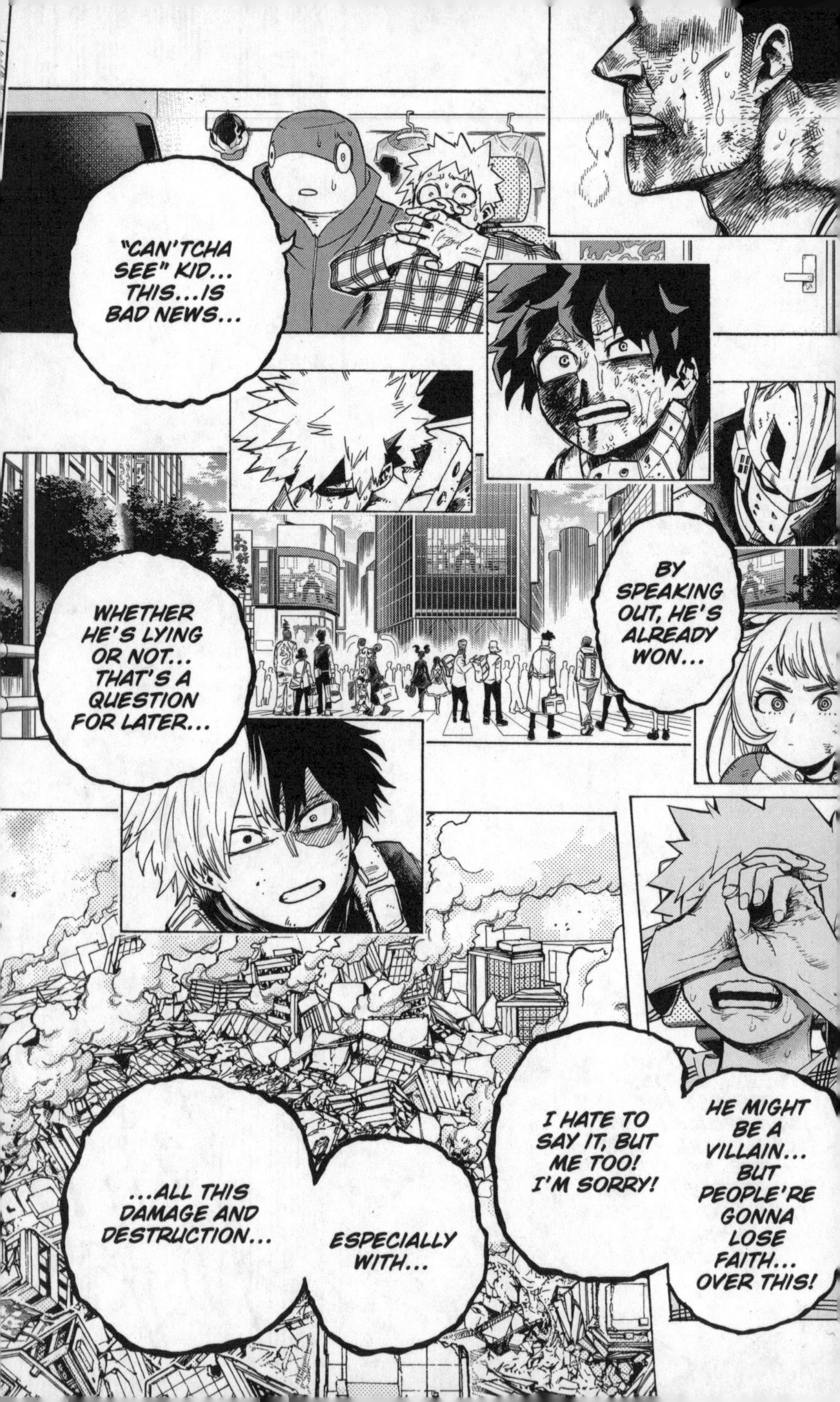
"CAN'TCHA SEE" KID... THIS...IS BAD NEWS...
BY SPEAKING OUT, HE'S ALREADY WON...
WHETHER HE'S LYING OR NOT... THAT'S A QUESTION FOR LATER...
HE MIGHT BE A VILLAIN... BUT PEOPLE'RE GONNA LOSE FAITH... OVER THIS!
I HATE TO SAY IT, BUT ME TOO! I'M SORRY!
ESPECIALLY WITH...
...ALL THIS DAMAGE AND DESTRUCTION...

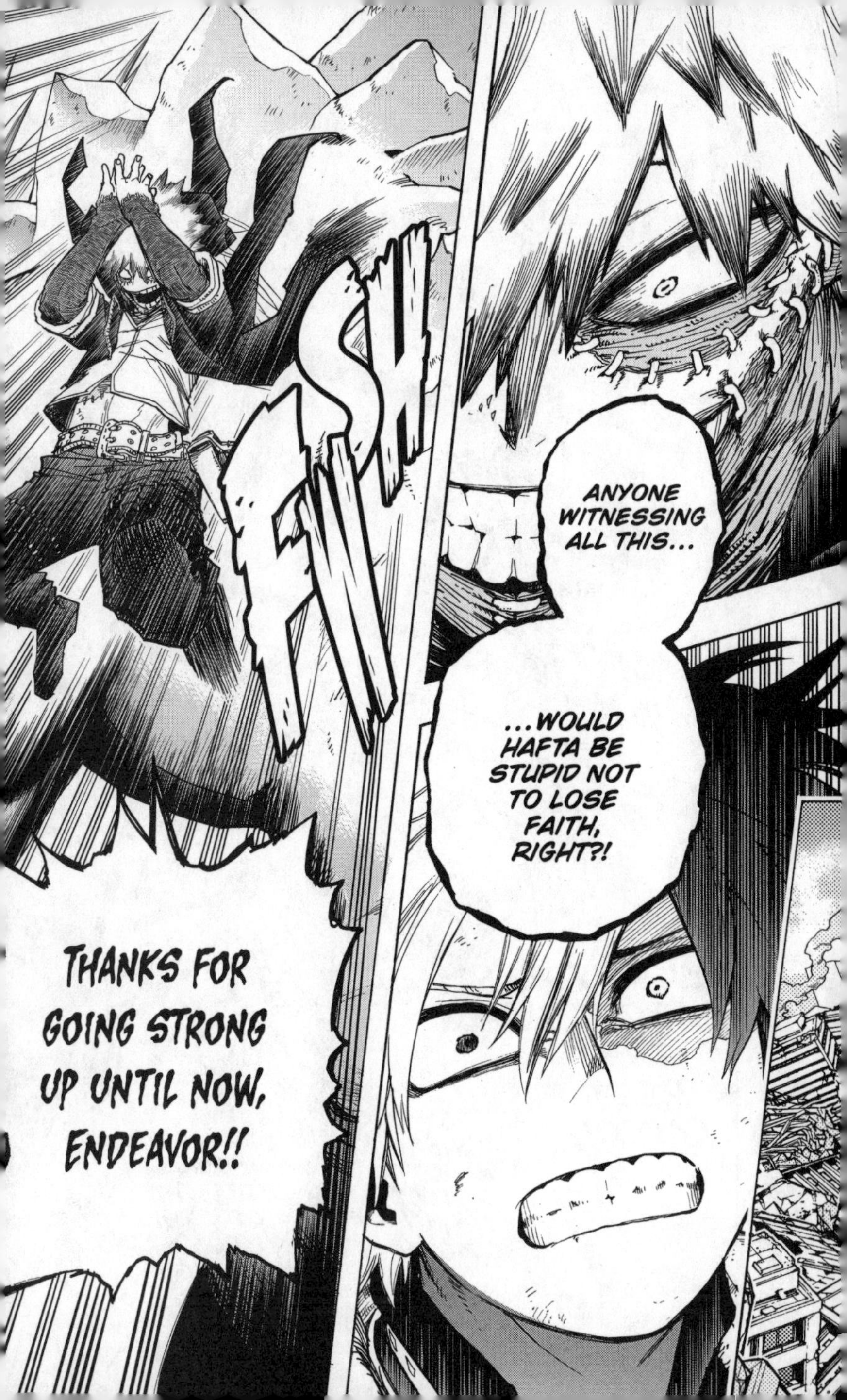
ANYONE WITNESSING ALL THIS...
...WOULD HAFTA BE STUPID NOT TO LOSE FAITH, RIGHT?!
THANKS FOR GOING STRONG UP UNTIL NOW, ENDEAVOR!!

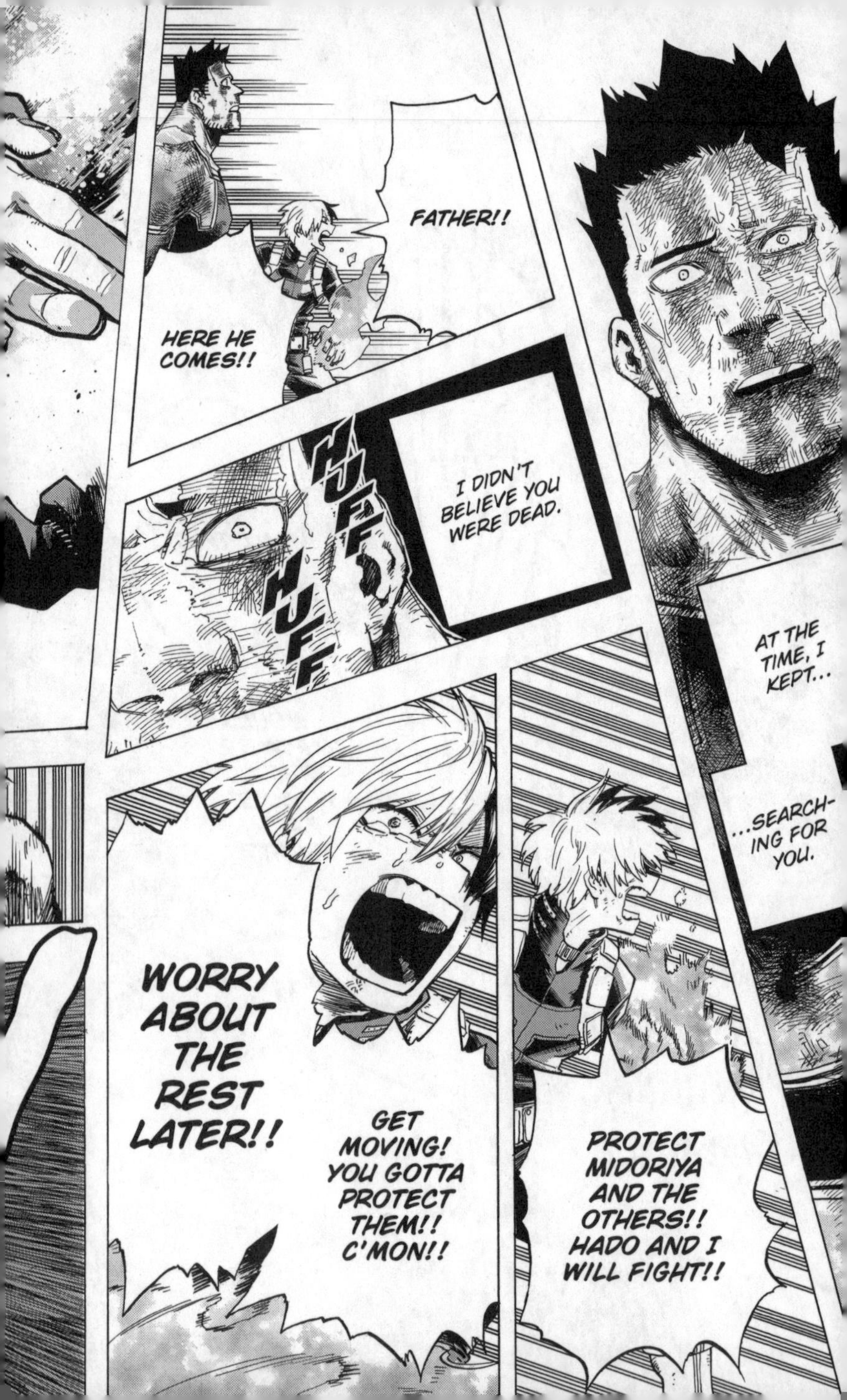
FATHER!!
HERE HE COMES!!
I DIDN'T BELIEVE YOU WERE DEAD.
HUFF
HUFF
AT THE TIME, I KEPT...
...SEARCHING FOR YOU.
PROTECT MIDORIYA AND THE OTHERS!! HADO AND I WILL FIGHT!!
WORRY ABOUT THE REST LATER!!
GET MOVING! YOU GOTTA PROTECT THEM!! C'MON!!

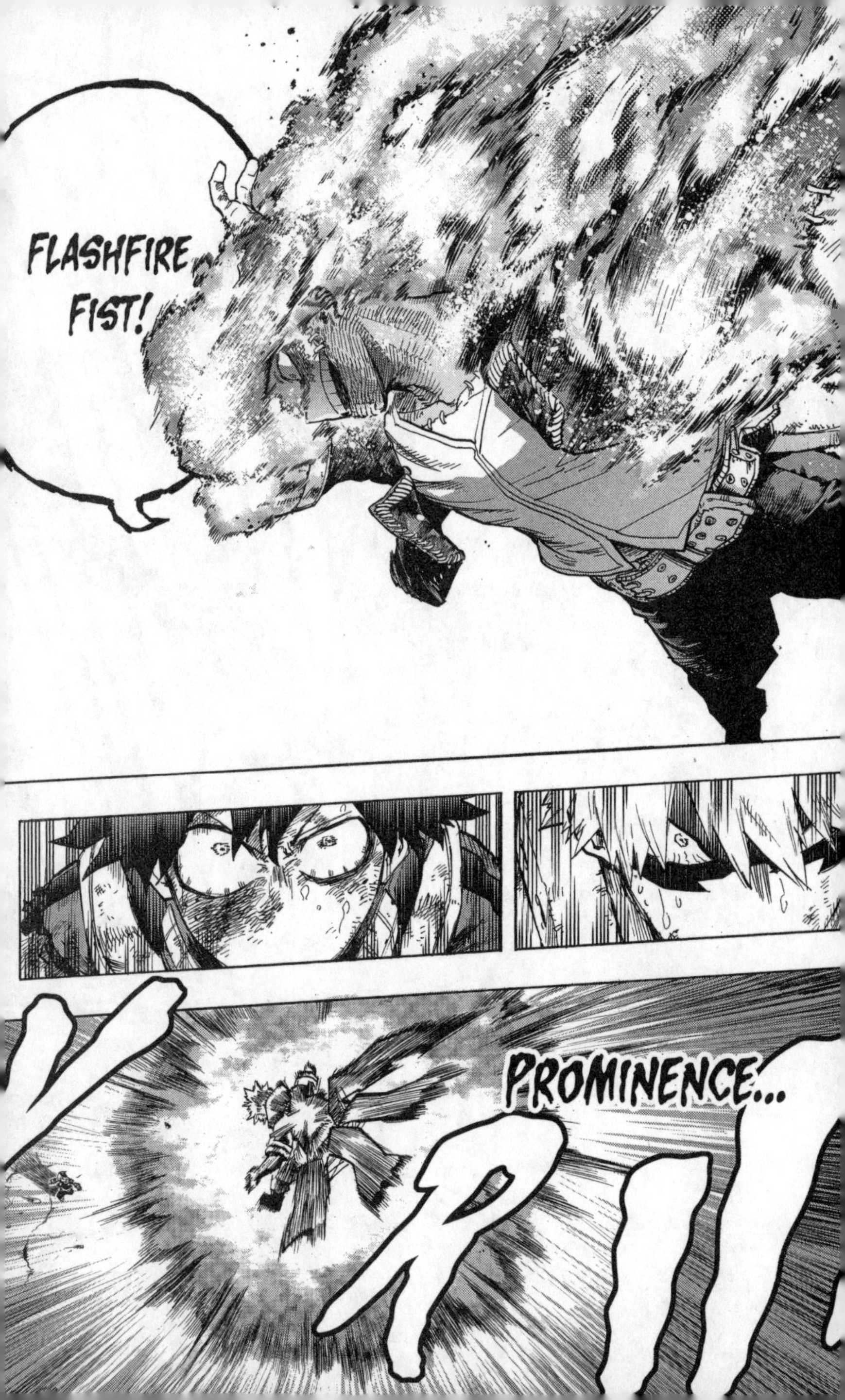
FLASHFIRE FIST!
PROMINENCE...

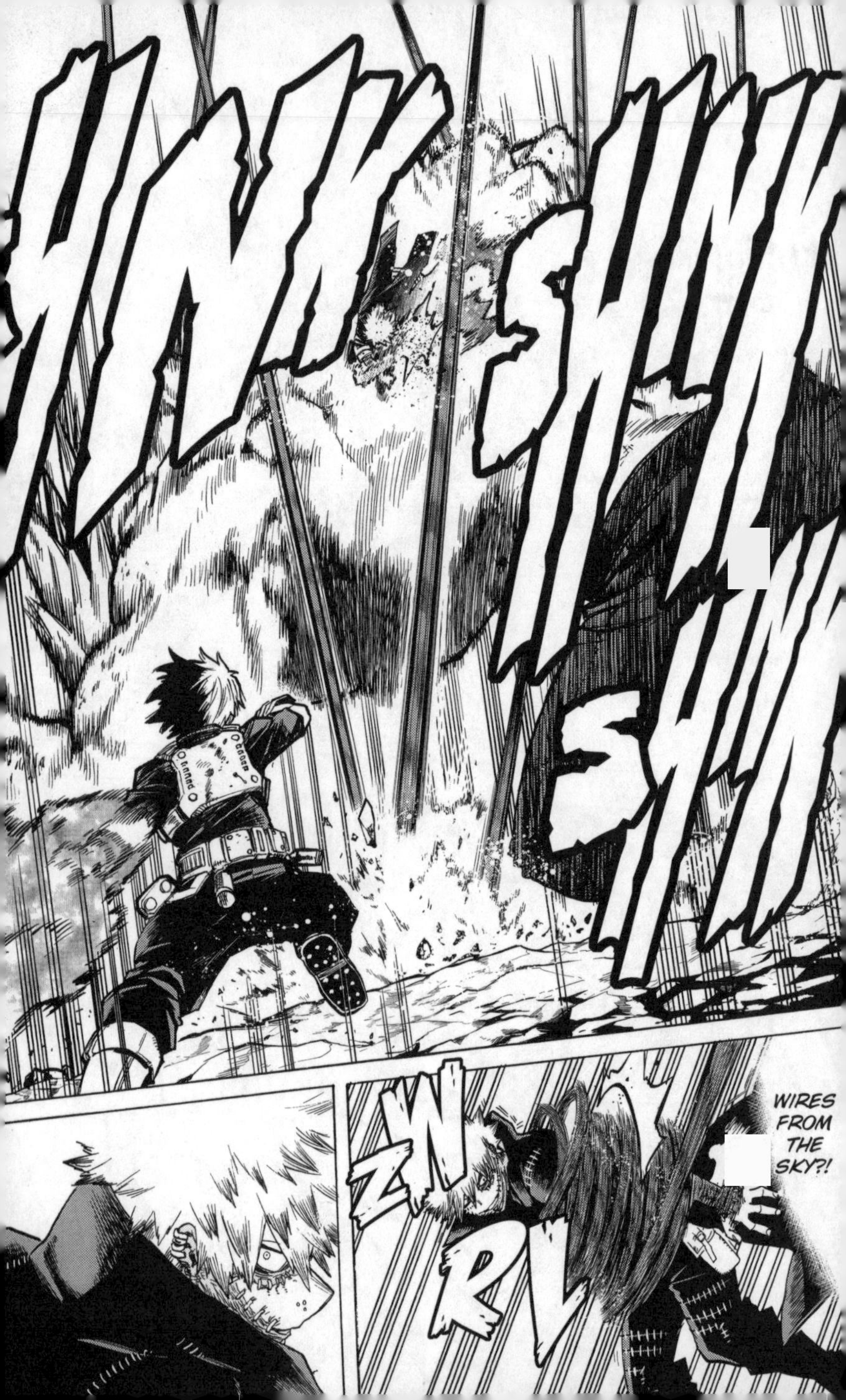
WIRES FROM THE SKY?!

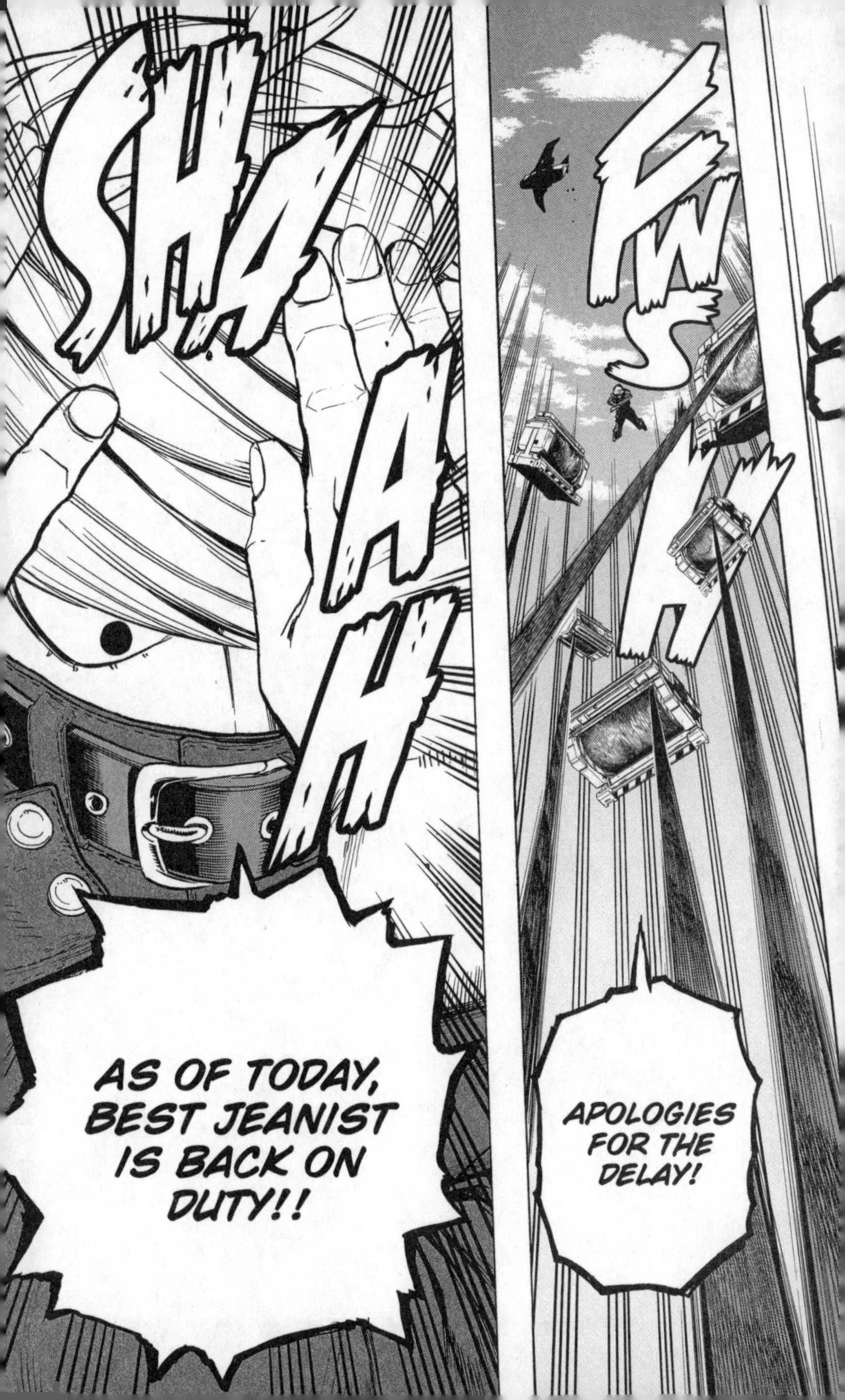
FWSH
APOLOGIES FOR THE DELAY!
SHAAH
AS OF TODAY, BEST JEANIST IS BACK ON DUTY!!

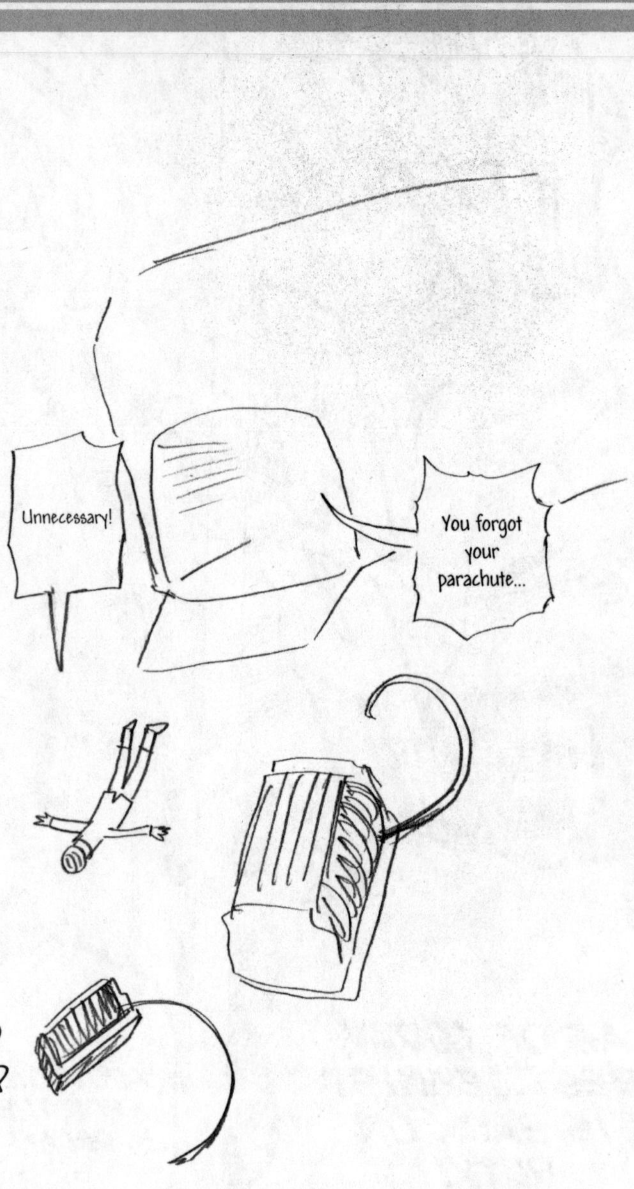
You forgot your parachute...
Unnecessary!
FWOOP

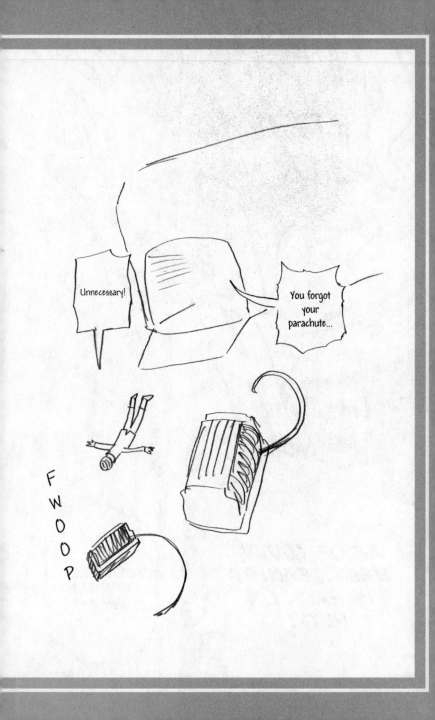

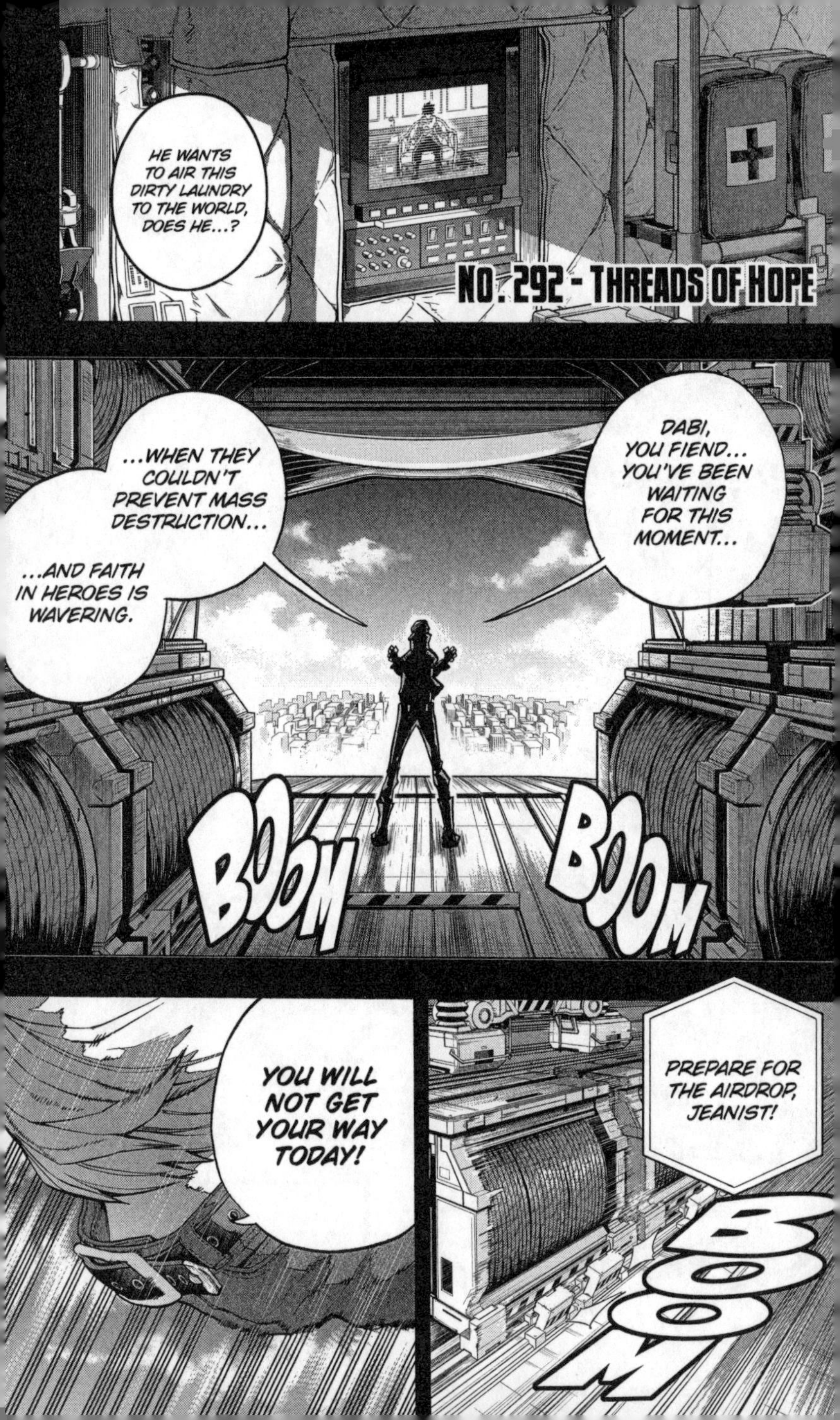
HE WANTS TO AIR THIS DIRTY LAUNDRY TO THE WORLD, DOES HE...?
No. 292 - Threads of Hope
DABI, YOU FIEND... YOU'VE BEEN WAITING FOR THIS MOMENT...
...WHEN THEY COULDN'T PREVENT MASS DESTRUCTION...
...AND FAITH IN HEROES IS WAVERING.
BOOM
BOOM
PREPARE FOR THE AIRDROP, JEANIST!
BOOM
YOU WILL NOT GET YOUR WAY TODAY!

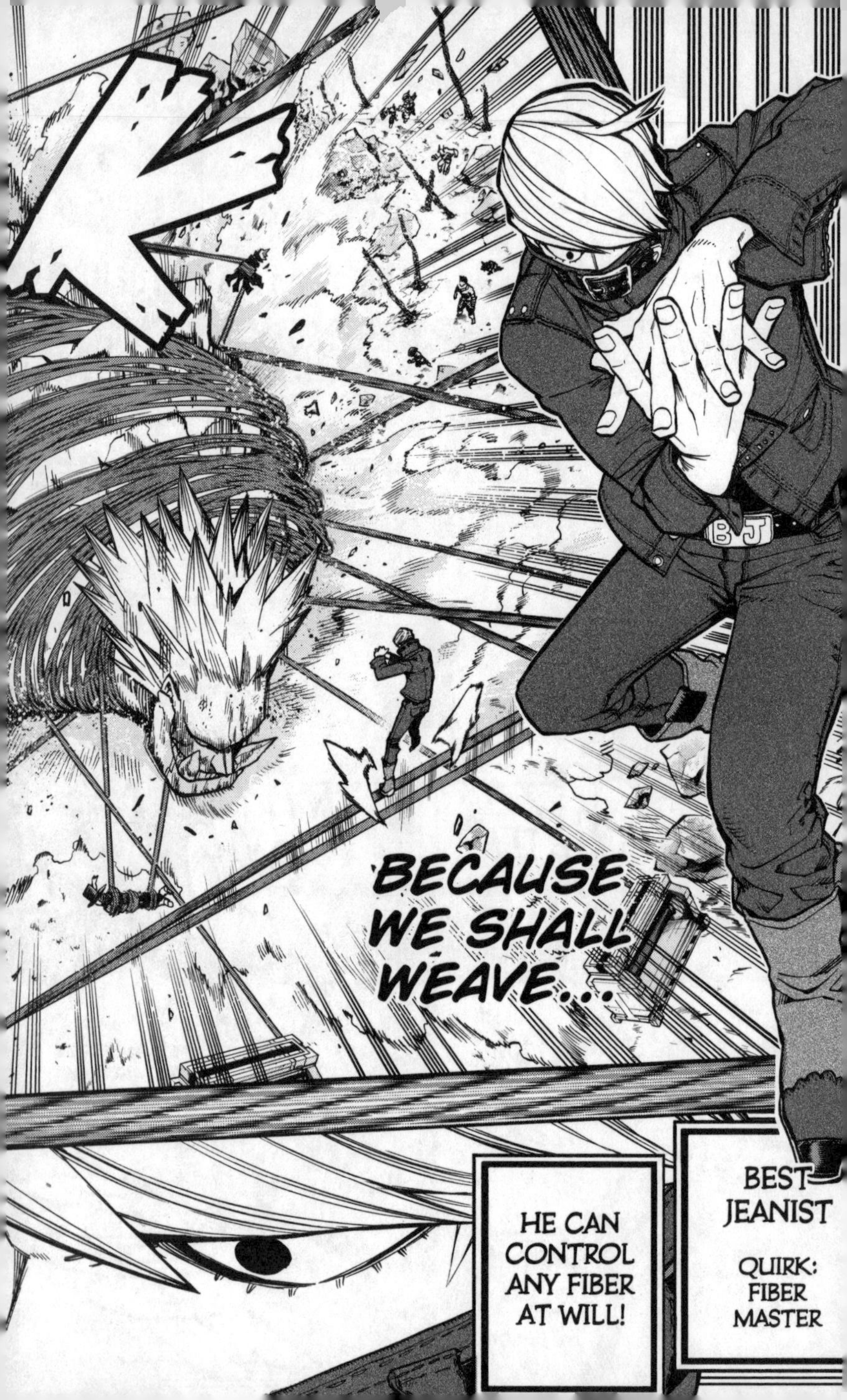
BECAUSE WE SHALL WEAVE...
BEST JEANIST
QUIRK: FIBER MASTER
HE CAN CONTROL ANY FIBER AT WILL!

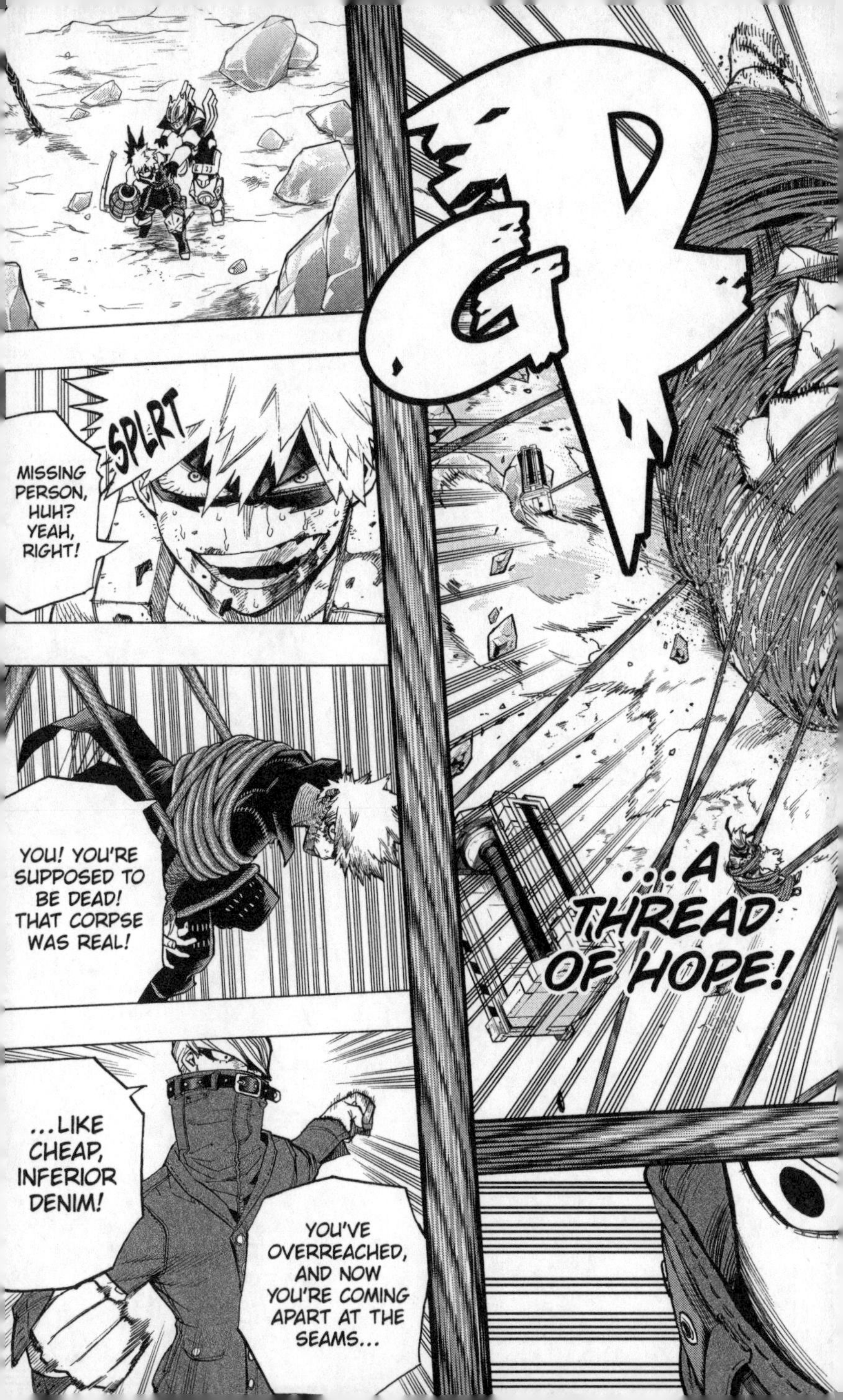

...A THREAD OF HOPE!
SPLRT
MISSING PERSON, HUH? YEAH, RIGHT!
YOU! YOU'RE SUPPOSED TO BE DEAD! THAT CORPSE WAS REAL!
YOU'VE OVERREACHED, AND NOW YOU'RE COMING APART AT THE SEAMS...
...LIKE CHEAP, INFERIOR DENIM!

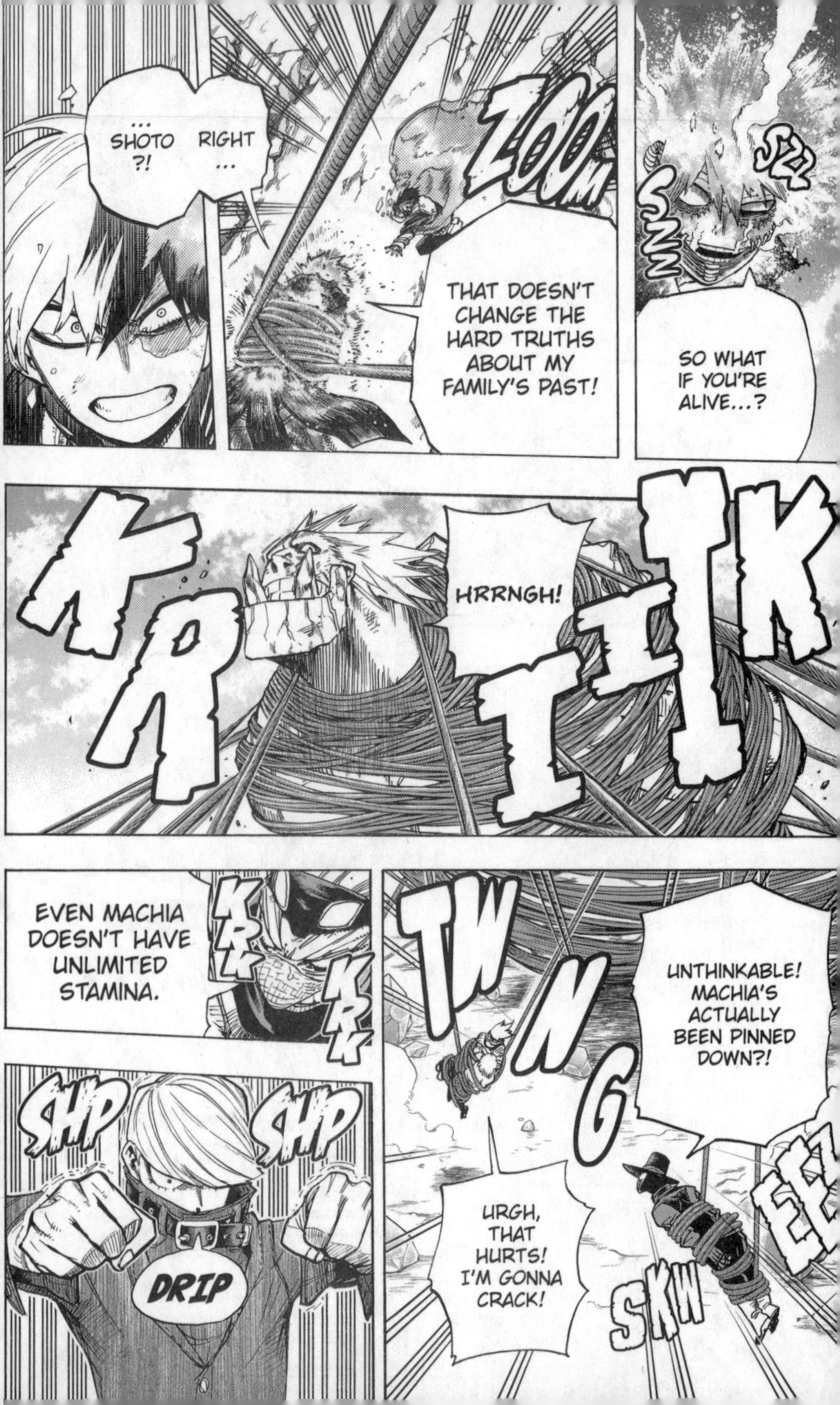
SZZ
SO WHAT IF YOU'RE ALIVE...?
ZOOM
THAT DOESN'T CHANGE THE HARD TRUTHS ABOUT MY FAMILY'S PAST!
...SHOTO?! RIGHT...
KRIIK
HRRNGH!
TWNG
UNTHINKABLE! MACHIA'S ACTUALLY BEEN PINNED DOWN?!
URGH, THAT HURTS! I'M GONNA CRACK!
SKW
EVEN MACHIA DOESN'T HAVE UNLIMITED STAMINA.
KRK
KRK
SHP
SHP
DRIP

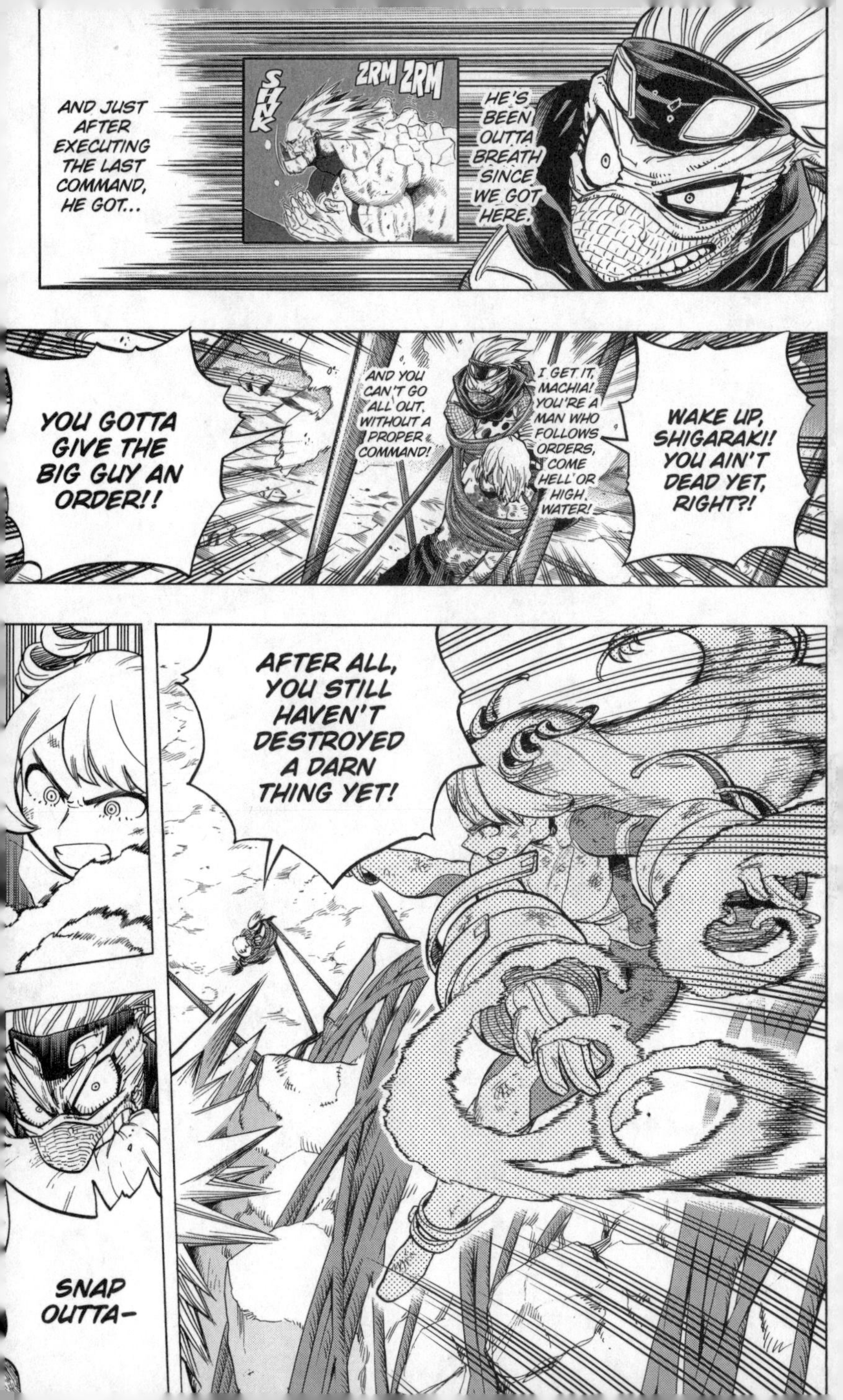
HE'S BEEN OUTTA BREATH SINCE WE GOT HERE.
ZRM ZRM
SHNK
AND JUST AFTER EXECUTING THE LAST COMMAND, HE GOT...
WAKE UP, SHIGARAKI! YOU AIN'T DEAD YET, RIGHT?!
I GET IT, MACHIA! YOU'RE A MAN WHO FOLLOWS ORDERS, COME HELL OR HIGH WATER!
AND YOU CAN'T GO ALL OUT WITHOUT A PROPER COMMAND!
YOU GOTTA GIVE THE BIG GUY AN ORDER!!
AFTER ALL, YOU STILL HAVEN'T DESTROYED A DARN THING YET!
SNAP OUTTA-

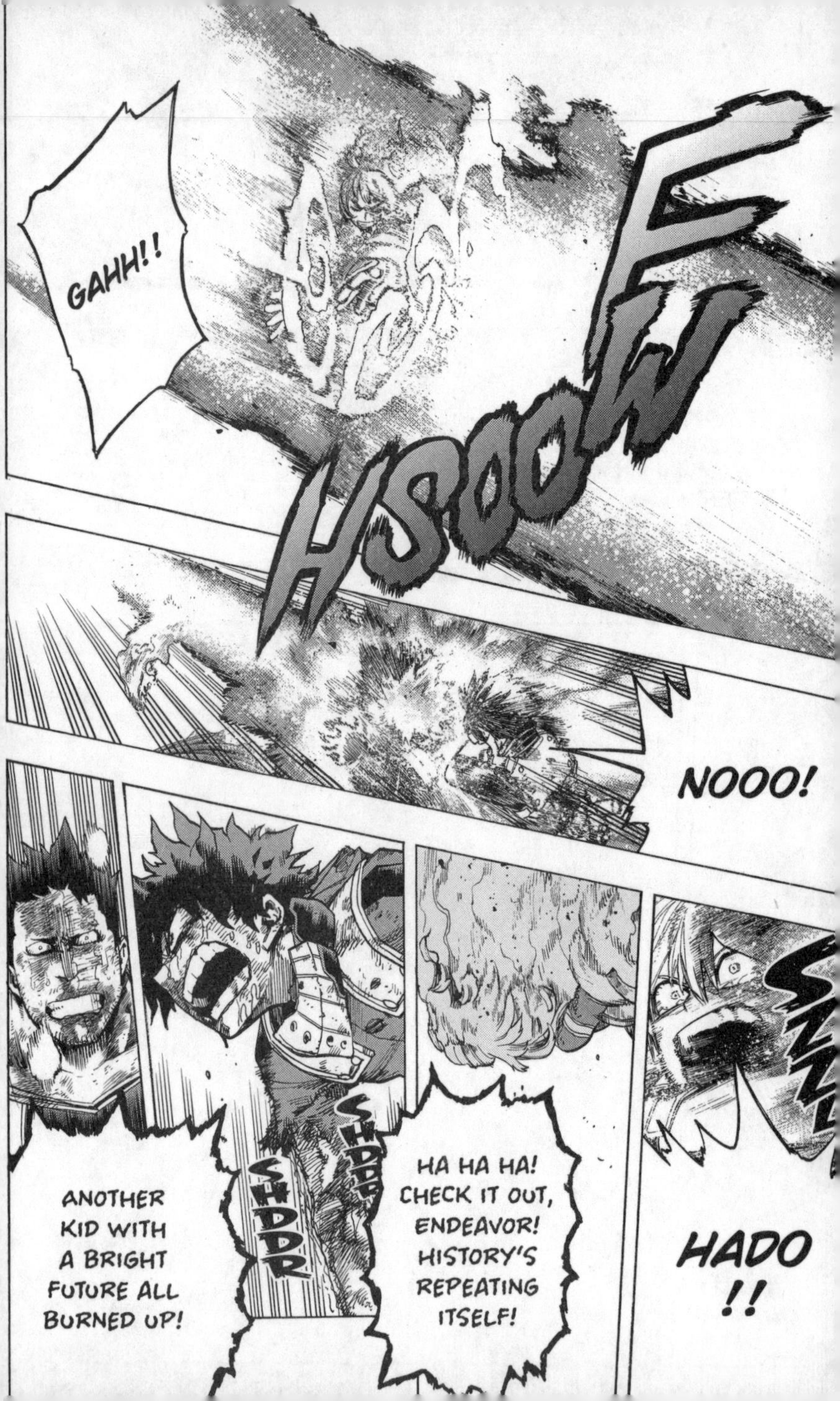

GAHH!!
HSOOW
NOOO!
HADO !!
HA HA HA! CHECK IT OUT, ENDEAVOR! HISTORY'S REPEATING ITSELF!
SHDDR
SHDDR
ANOTHER KID WITH A BRIGHT FUTURE ALL BURNED UP!

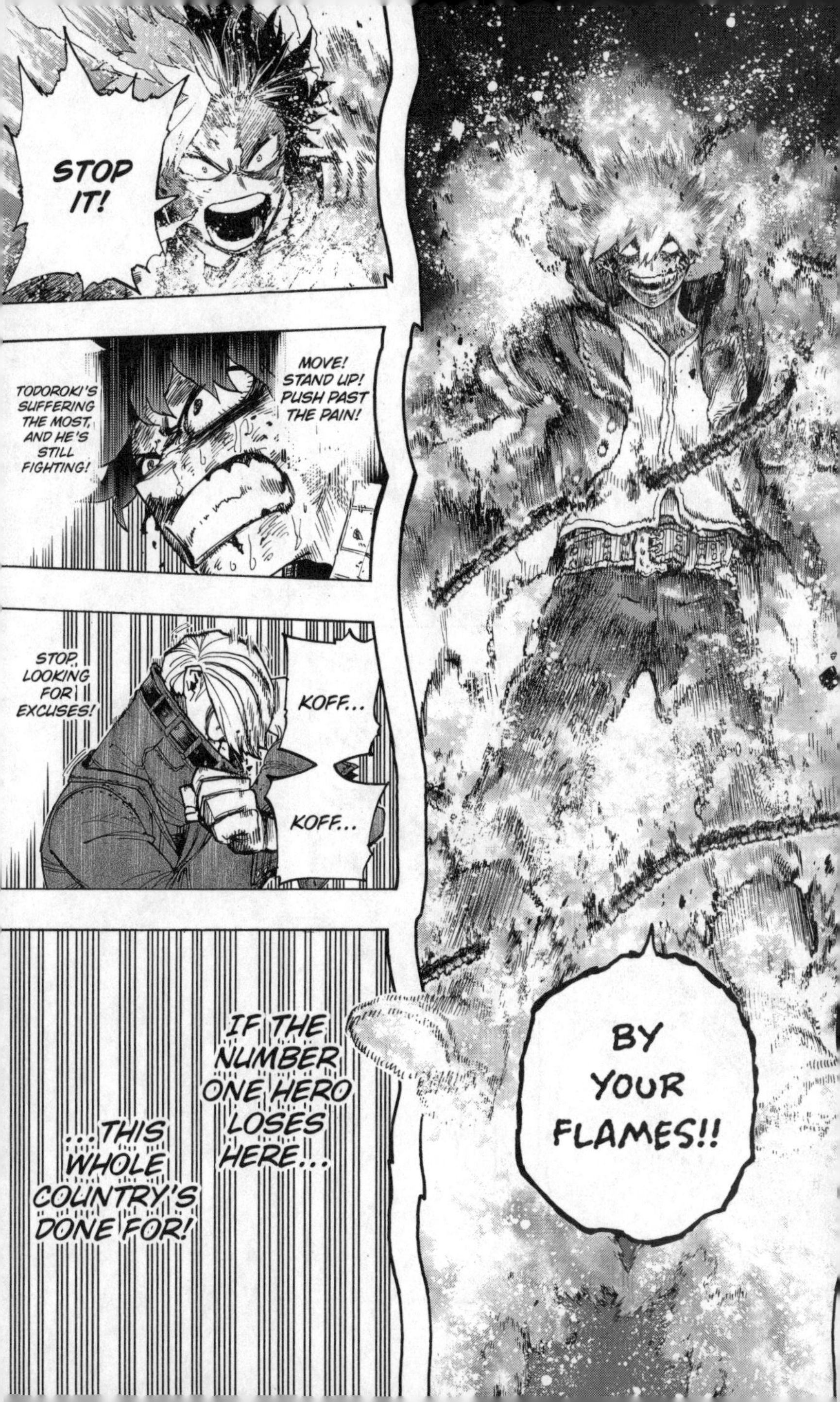
BY YOUR FLAMES!!
STOP IT!
MOVE! STAND UP! PUSH PAST THE PAIN!
TODOROKI'S SUFFERING THE MOST, AND HE'S STILL FIGHTING!
KOFF...
KOFF...
STOP LOOKING FOR EXCUSES!
IF THE NUMBER ONE HERO LOSES HERE...
...THIS WHOLE COUNTRY'S DONE FOR!

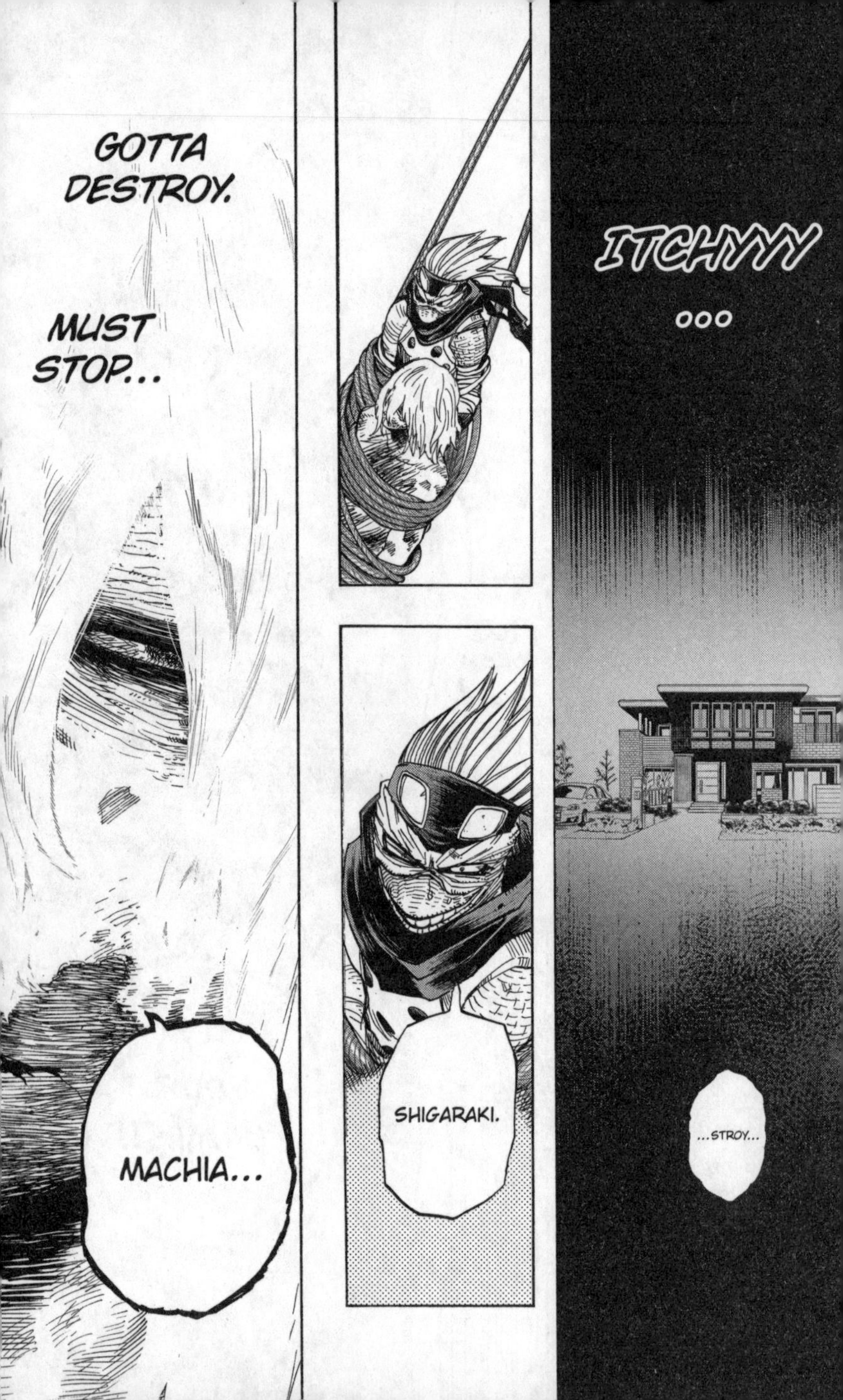
ITCHYYY
...
...STROY...
SHIGARAKI.
GOTTA DESTROY.
MUST STOP...
MACHIA...

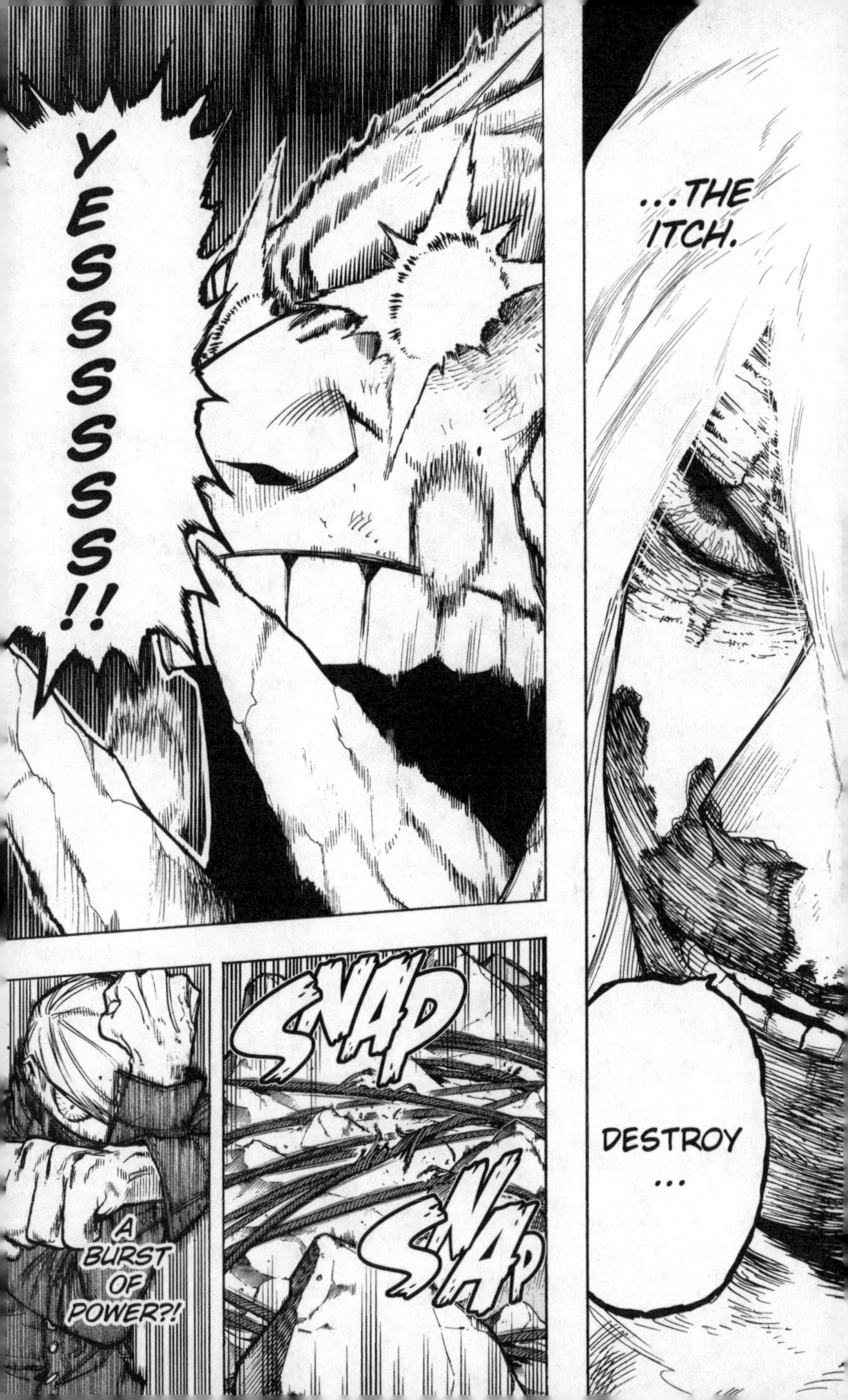
...THE ITCH.
DESTROY ...
YESSSSSS!!
SNAP
SNAP
A BURST OF POWER?!

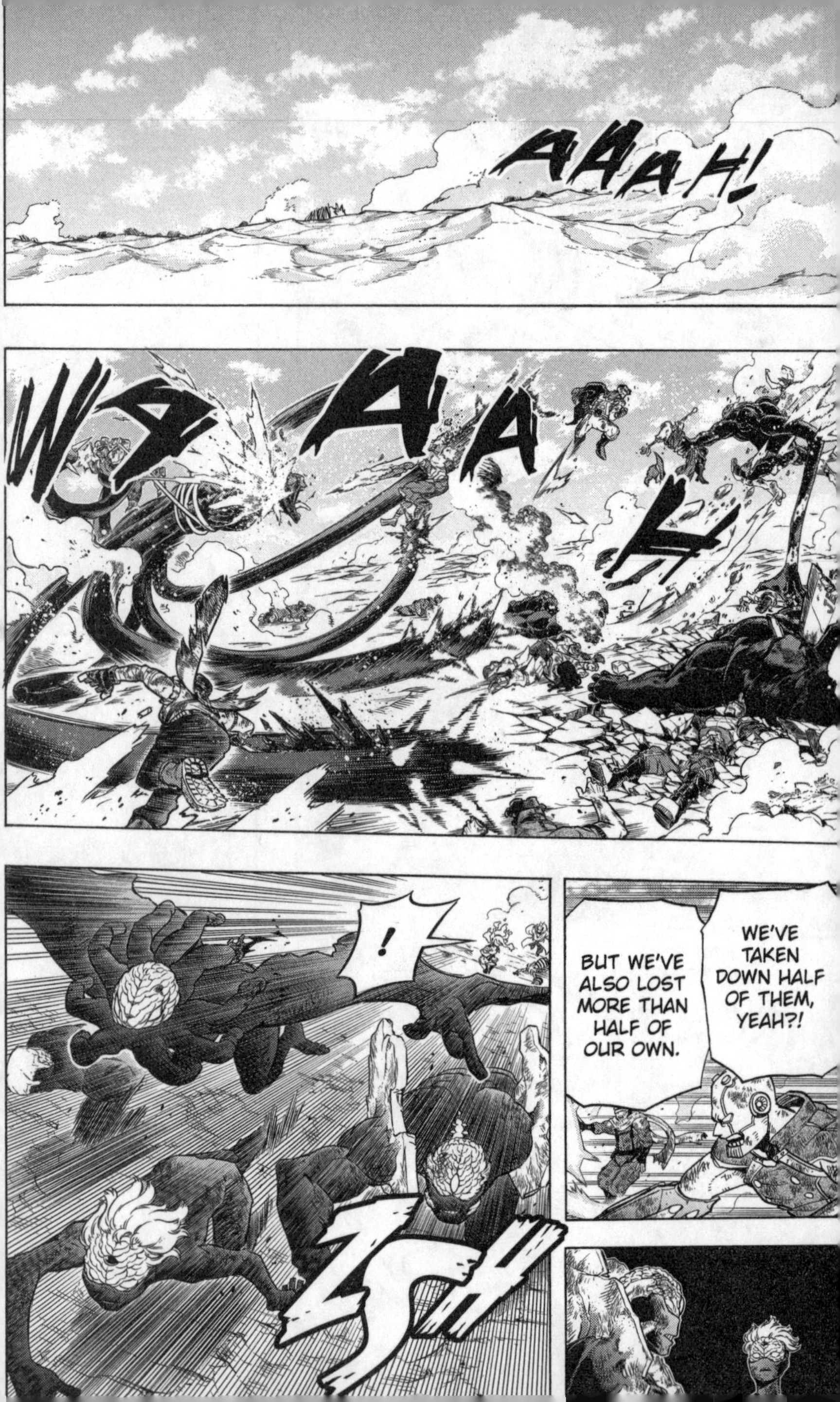
AAAH!
WAAAAH
WE'VE TAKEN DOWN HALF OF THEM, YEAH?!
BUT WE'VE ALSO LOST MORE THAN HALF OF OUR OWN.
!
ZSH

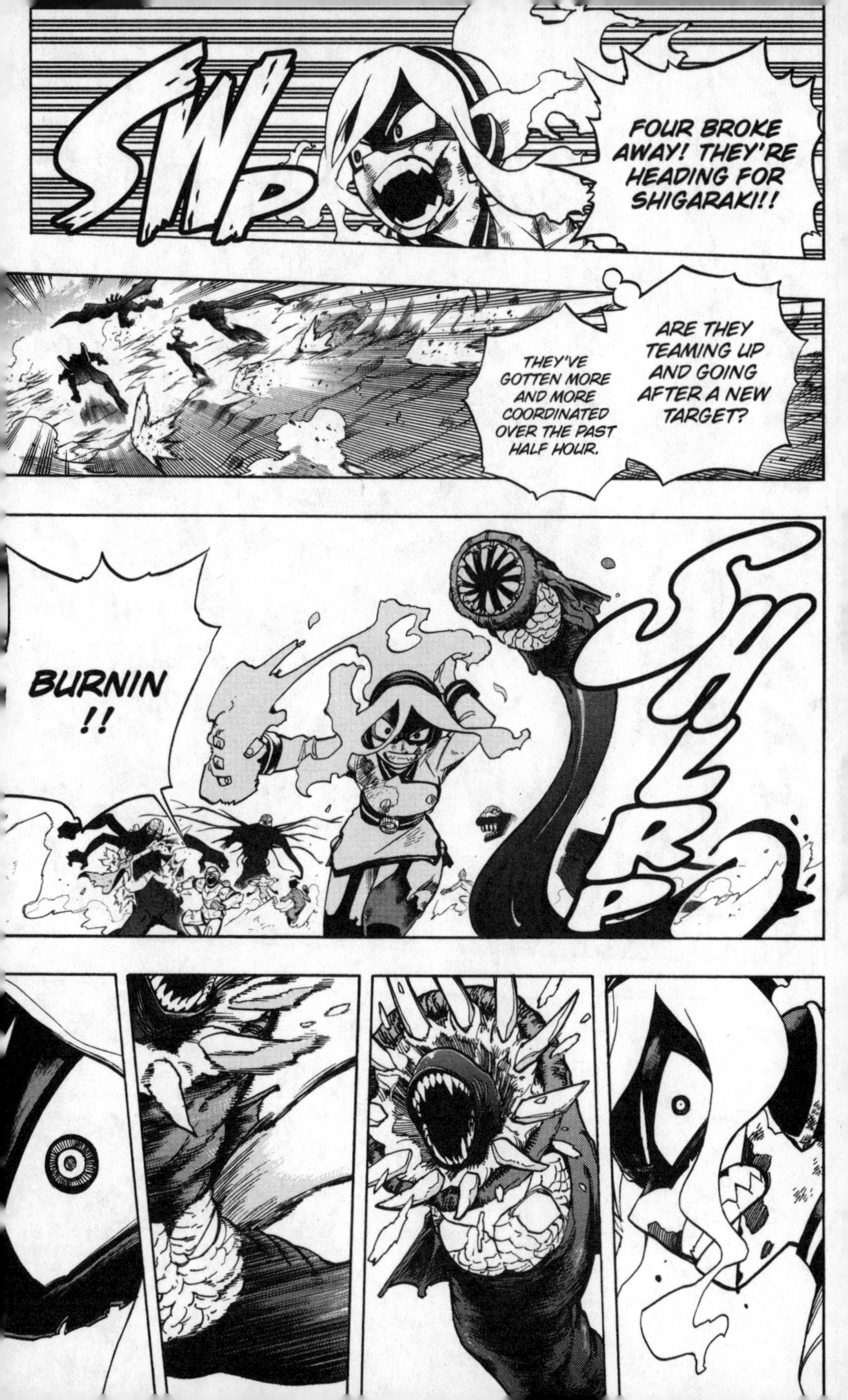
FOUR BROKE AWAY! THEY'RE HEADING FOR SHIGARAKI!!
SWP
ARE THEY TEAMING UP AND GOING AFTER A NEW TARGET?
THEY'VE GOTTEN MORE AND MORE COORDINATED OVER THE PAST HALF HOUR.
CHLRP
BURNIN !!

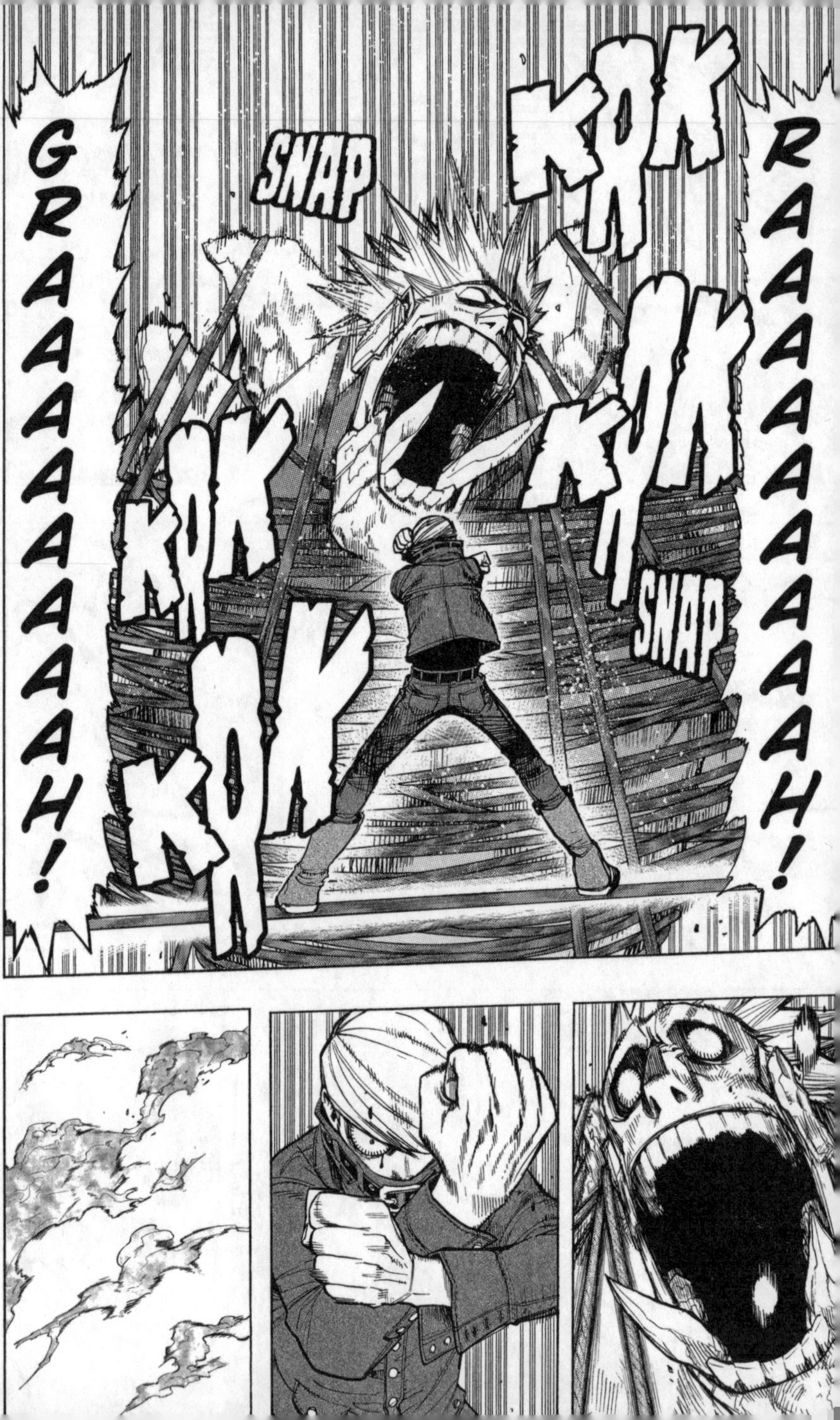
RAAAAAAAAAH!
KOK
KOK
SNAP
SNAP
KOK
KOK
GRAAAAAAAAH!

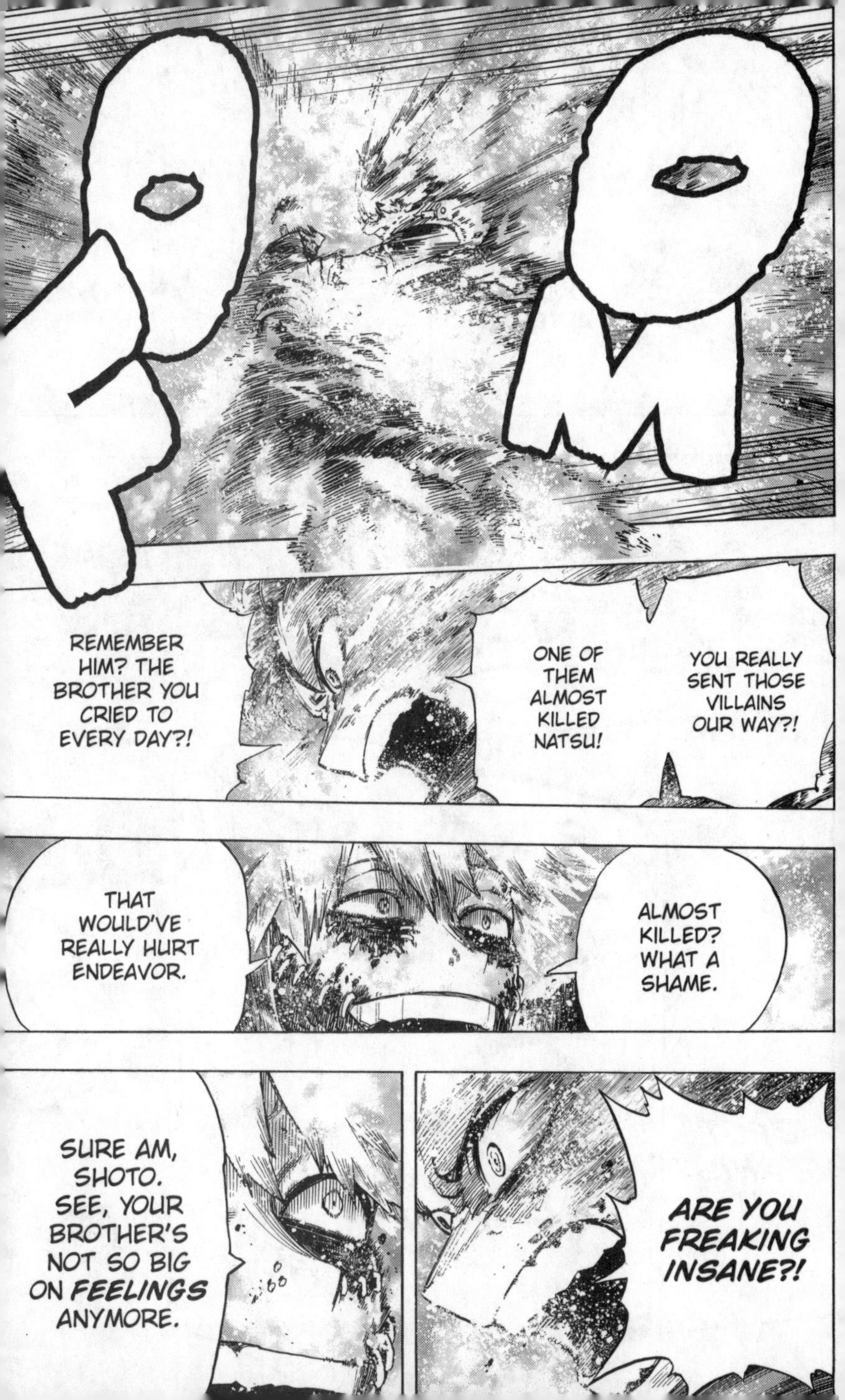
YOU REALLY SENT THOSE VILLAINS OUR WAY?!
ONE OF THEM ALMOST KILLED NATSU!
REMEMBER HIM? THE BROTHER YOU CRIED TO EVERY DAY?!
ALMOST KILLED? WHAT A SHAME.
THAT WOULD'VE REALLY HURT ENDEAVOR.
ARE YOU FREAKING INSANE?!
SURE AM, SHOTO. SEE, YOUR BROTHER'S NOT SO BIG ON FEELINGS ANYMORE.

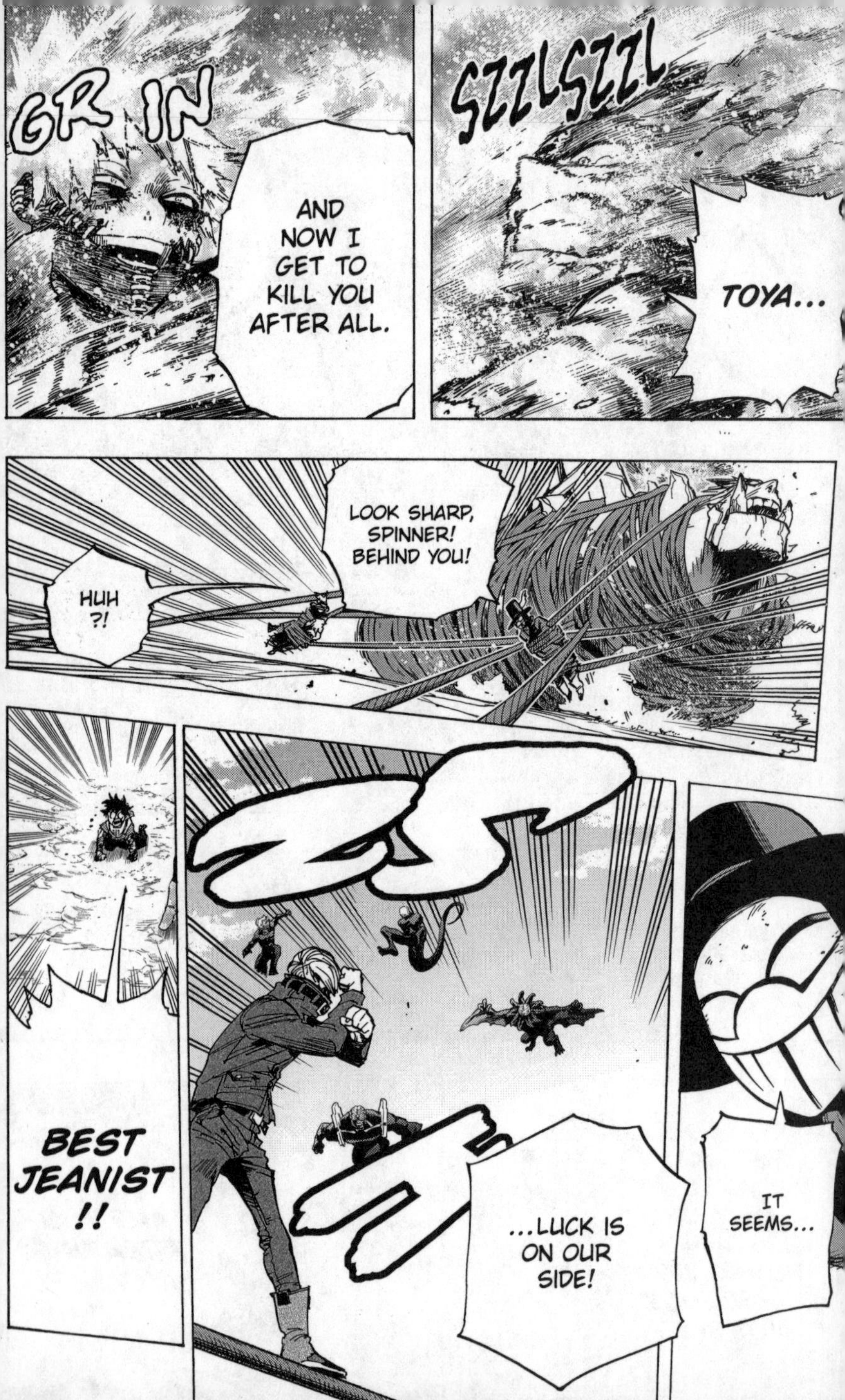
SZZLSZZL
TOYA...
GR IN
AND NOW I GET TO KILL YOU AFTER ALL.
LOOK SHARP, SPINNER! BEHIND YOU!
HUH ?!
IT SEEMS...
...LUCK IS ON OUR SIDE!
BEST JEANIST !!

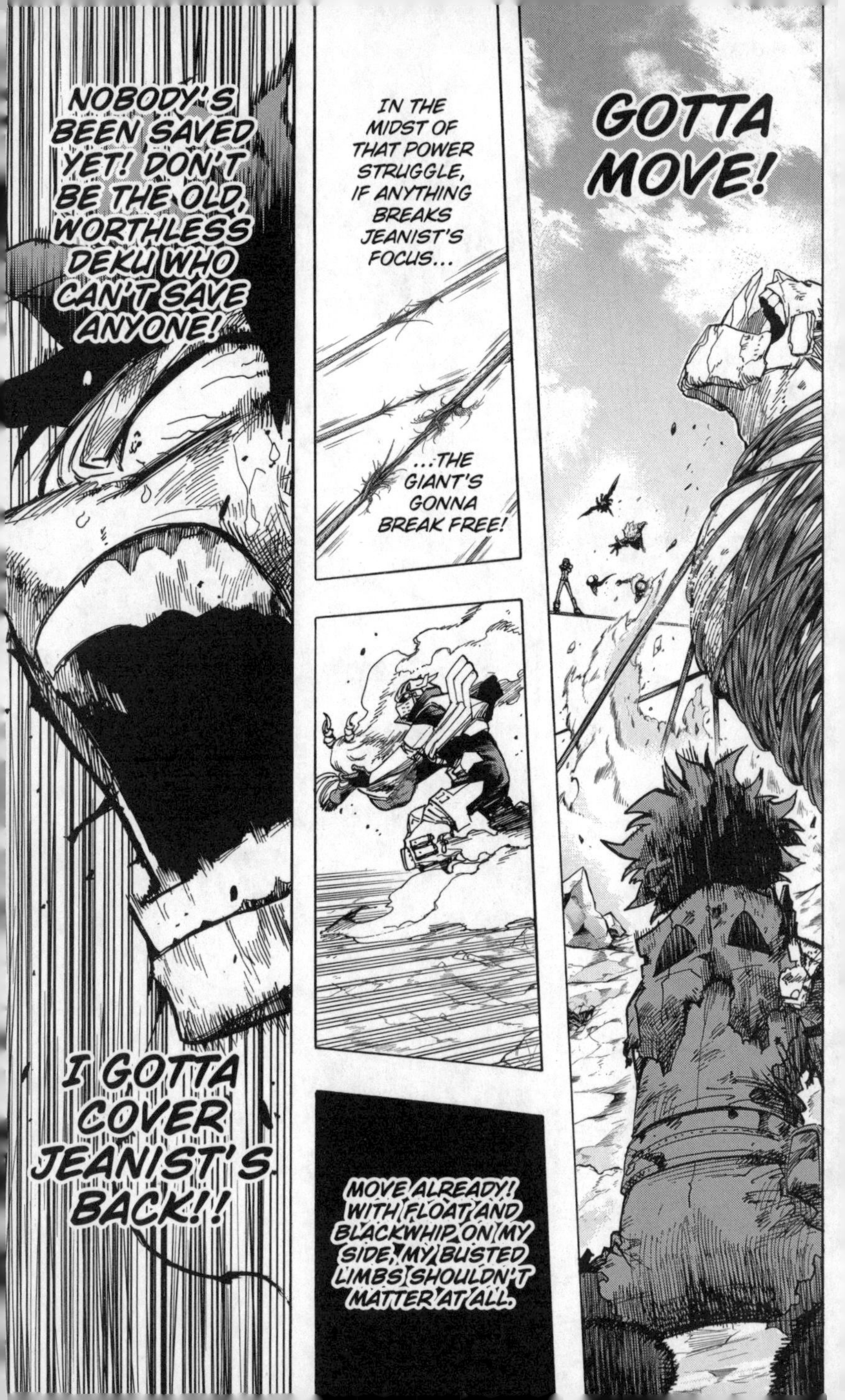
GOTTA MOVE!
IN THE MIDST OF THAT POWER STRUGGLE, IF ANYTHING BREAKS JEANIST'S FOCUS...
...THE GIANT'S GONNA BREAK FREE!
MOVE ALREADY! WITH FLOAT AND BLACKWHIP ON MY SIDE, MY BUSTED LIMBS SHOULDN'T MATTER AT ALL.
NOBODY'S BEEN SAVED YET! DON'T BE THE OLD, WORTHLESS DEKU WHO CAN'T SAVE ANYONE!
I GOTTA COVER JEANIST'S BACK!!

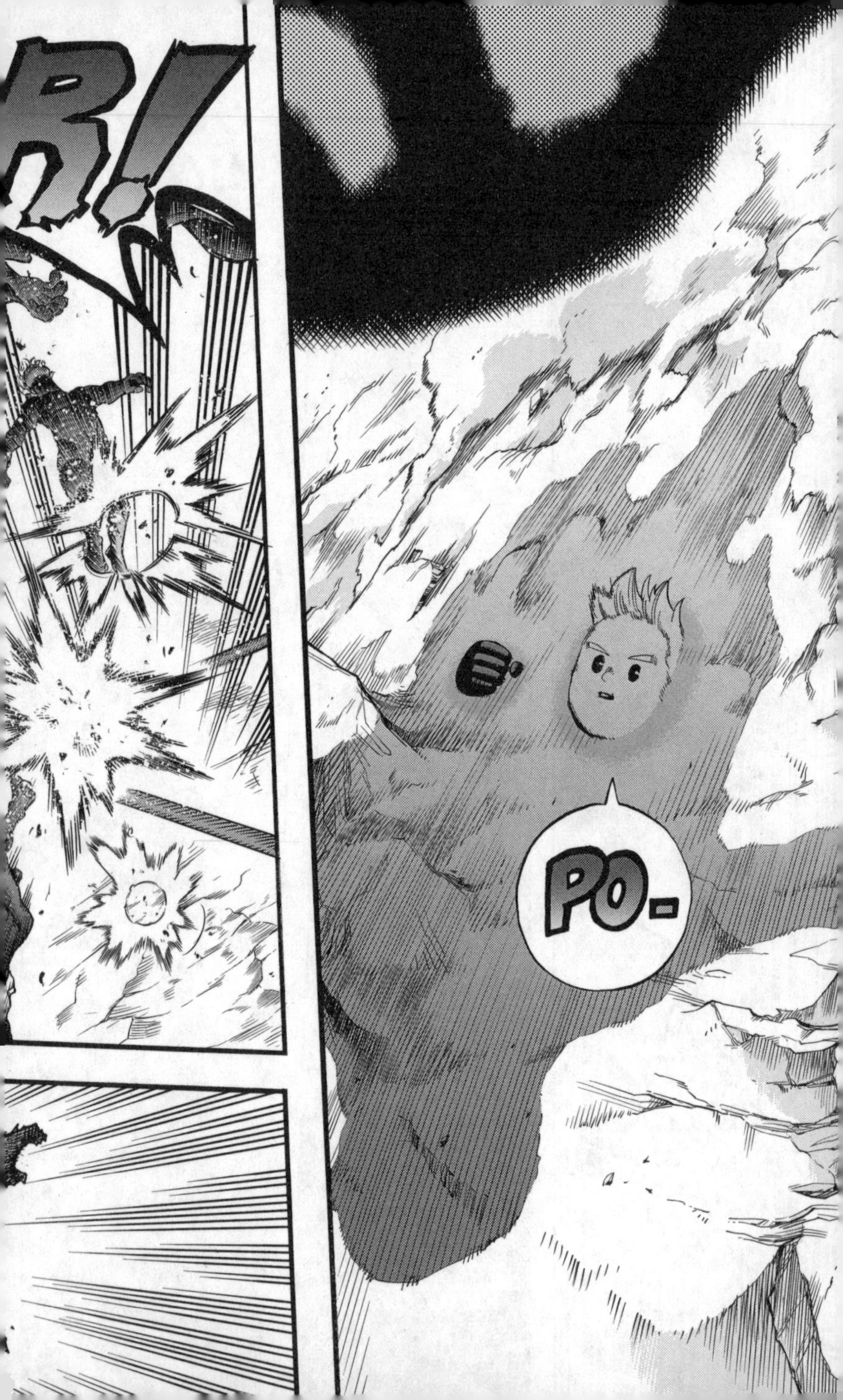
PO-
R!

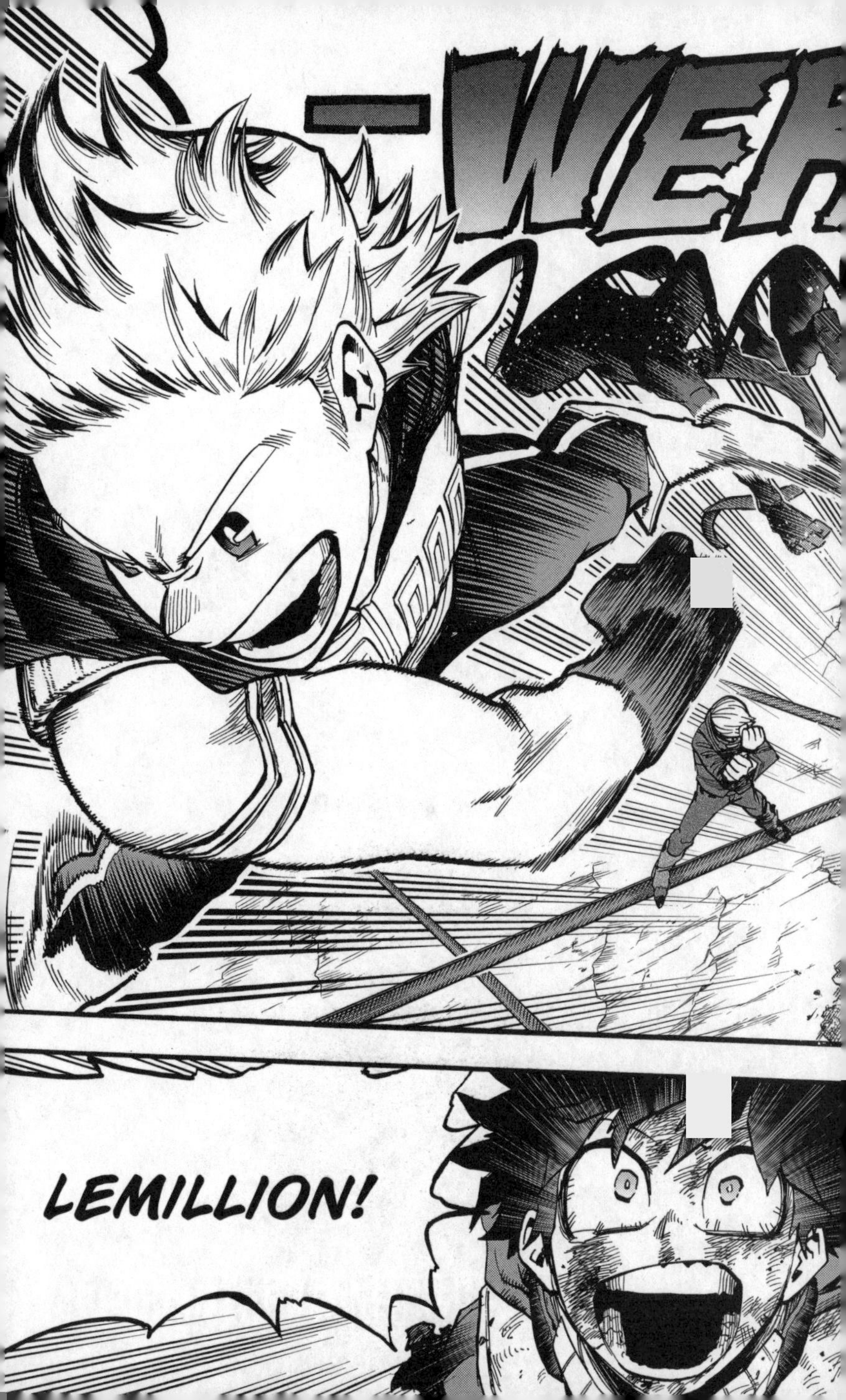
-WER
LEMILLION!

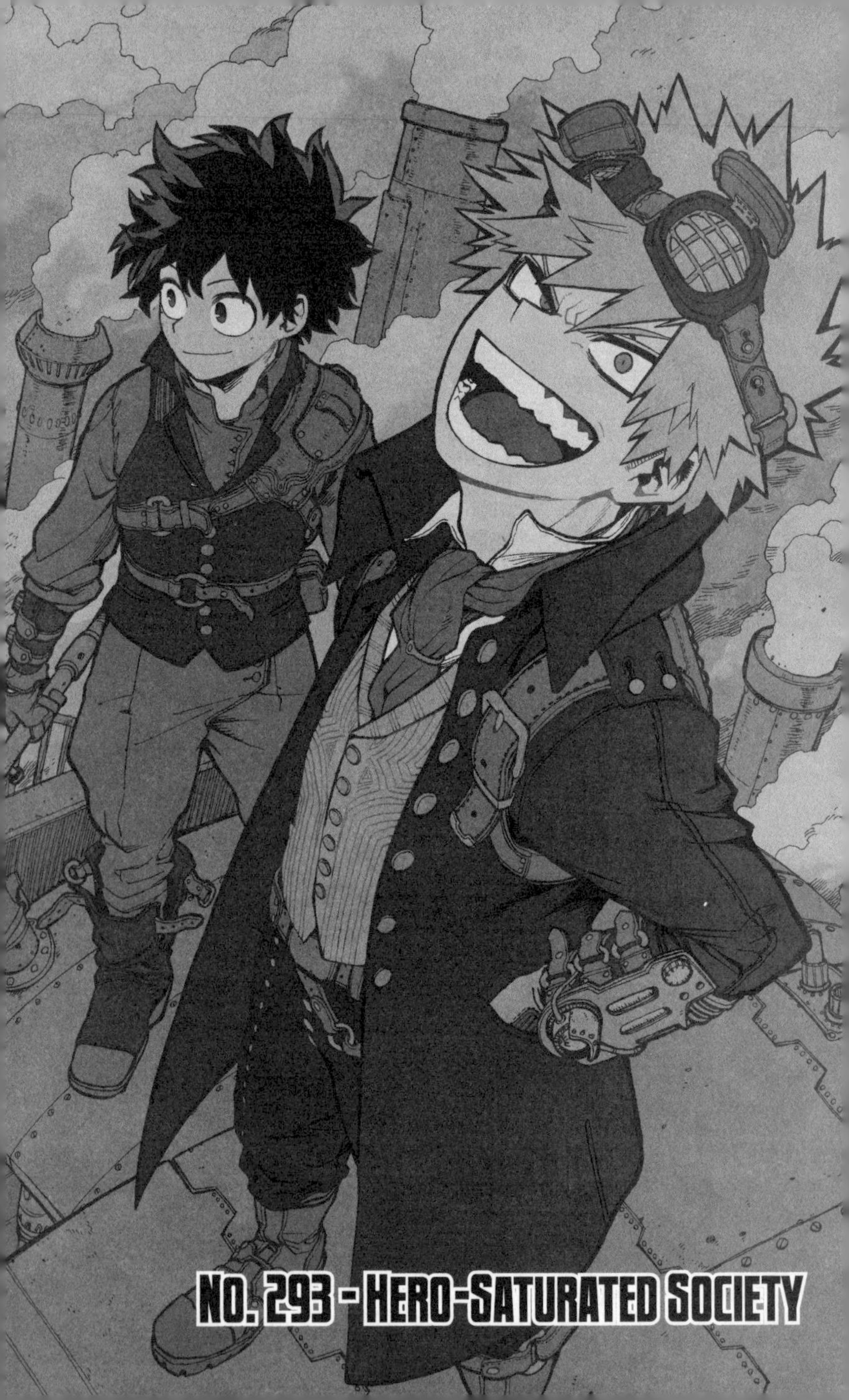
No. 293 - Hero-Saturated Society

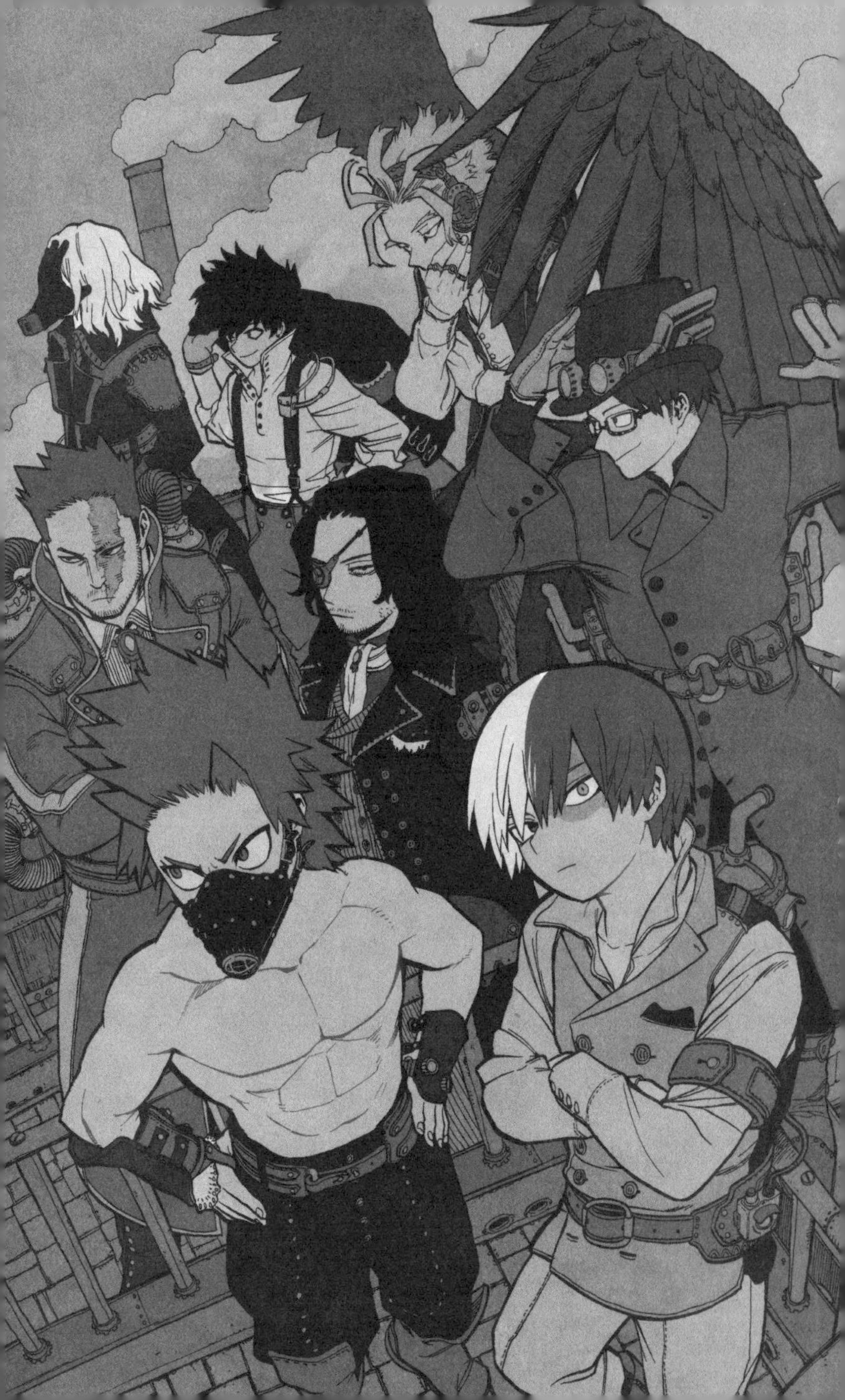

MY HERO ACADEMIA

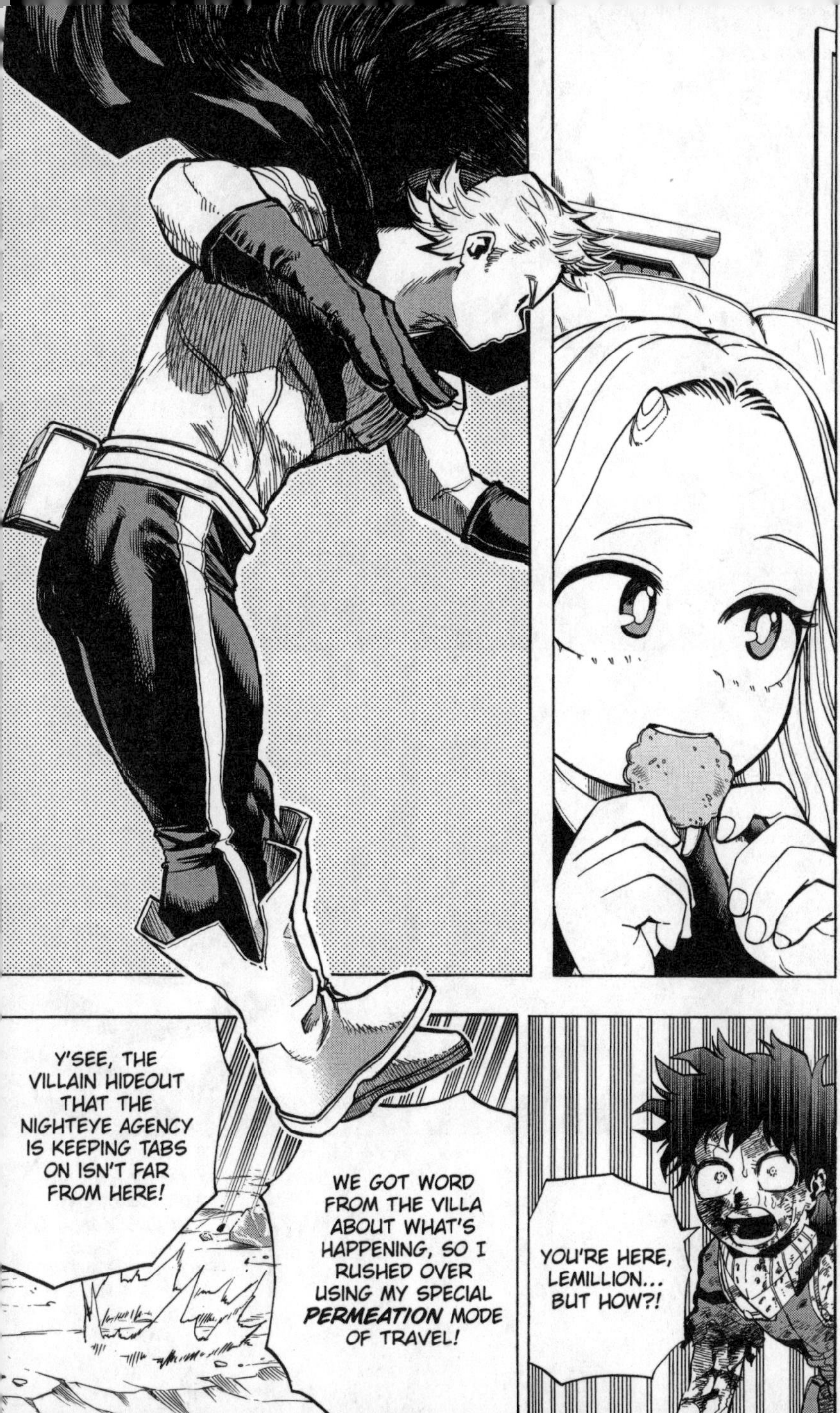
YOU'RE HERE, LEMILLION... BUT HOW?!
WE GOT WORD FROM THE VILLA ABOUT WHAT'S HAPPENING, SO I RUSHED OVER USING MY SPECIAL *PERMEATION* MODE OF TRAVEL!
Y'SEE, THE VILLAIN HIDEOUT THAT THE NIGHTEYE AGENCY IS KEEPING TABS ON ISN'T FAR FROM HERE!

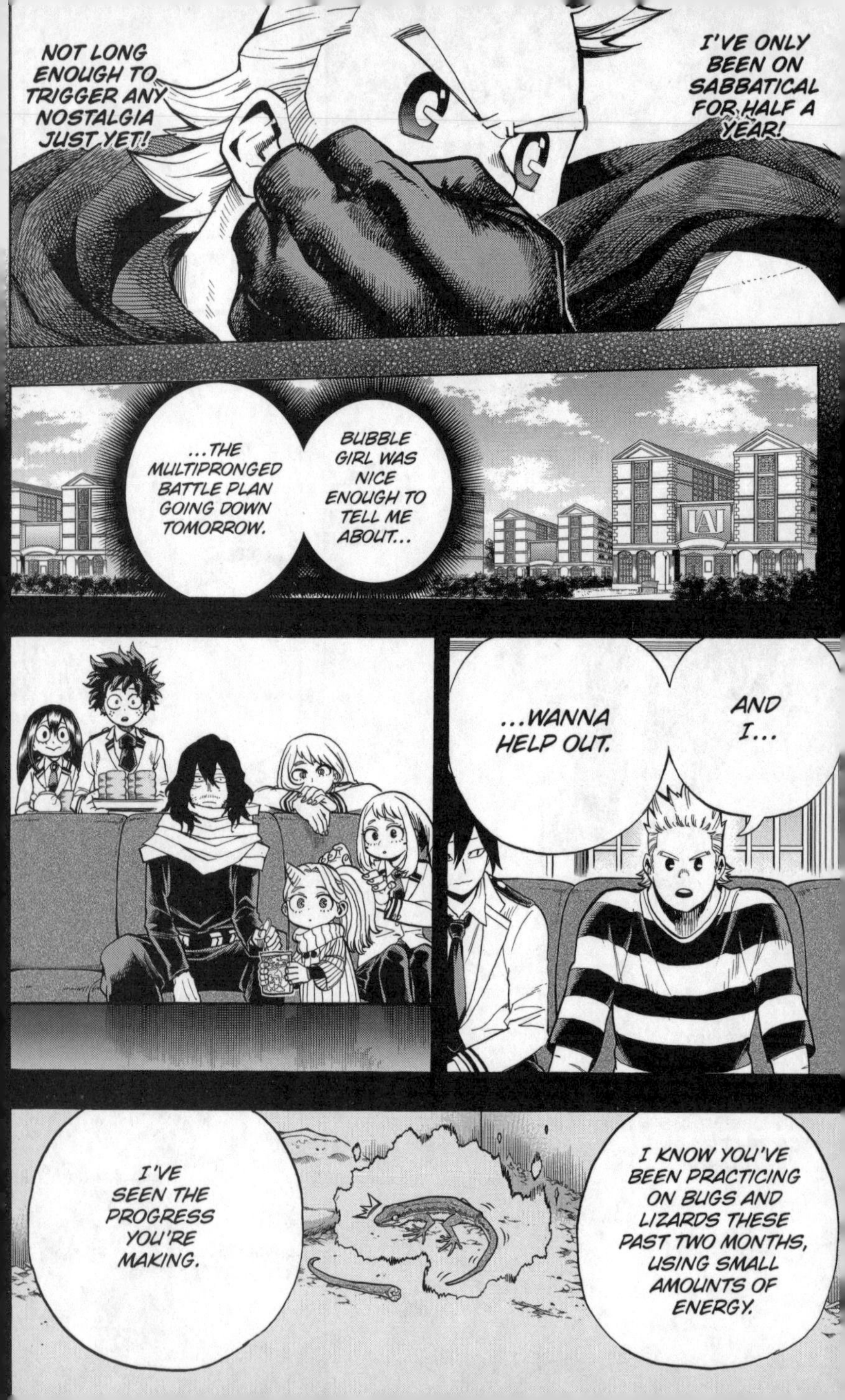
I'VE ONLY BEEN ON SABBATICAL FOR HALF A YEAR!
NOT LONG ENOUGH TO TRIGGER ANY NOSTALGIA JUST YET!
BUBBLE GIRL WAS NICE ENOUGH TO TELL ME ABOUT...
...THE MULTIPRONGED BATTLE PLAN GOING DOWN TOMORROW.
AND I...
...WANNA HELP OUT.
I KNOW YOU'VE BEEN PRACTICING ON BUGS AND LIZARDS THESE PAST TWO MONTHS, USING SMALL AMOUNTS OF ENERGY.
I'VE SEEN THE PROGRESS YOU'RE MAKING.

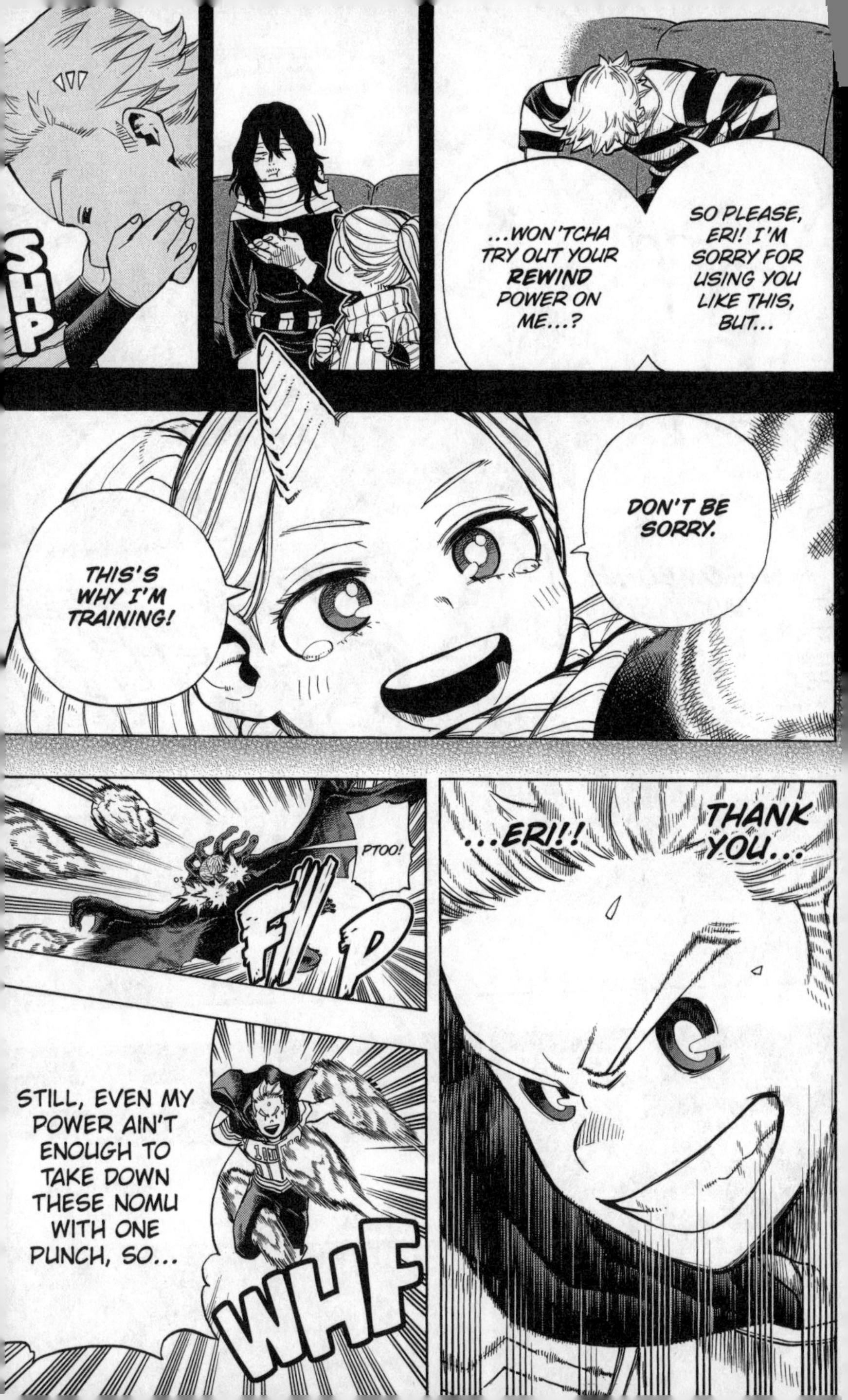
SO PLEASE, ERI! I'M SORRY FOR USING YOU LIKE THIS, BUT...
...WON'TCHA TRY OUT YOUR REWIND POWER ON ME...?
SHP
DON'T BE SORRY.
THIS'S WHY I'M TRAINING!
THANK YOU...
...ERI!!
PTOO!
STILL, EVEN MY POWER AIN'T ENOUGH TO TAKE DOWN THESE NOMU WITH ONE PUNCH, SO...
WHF

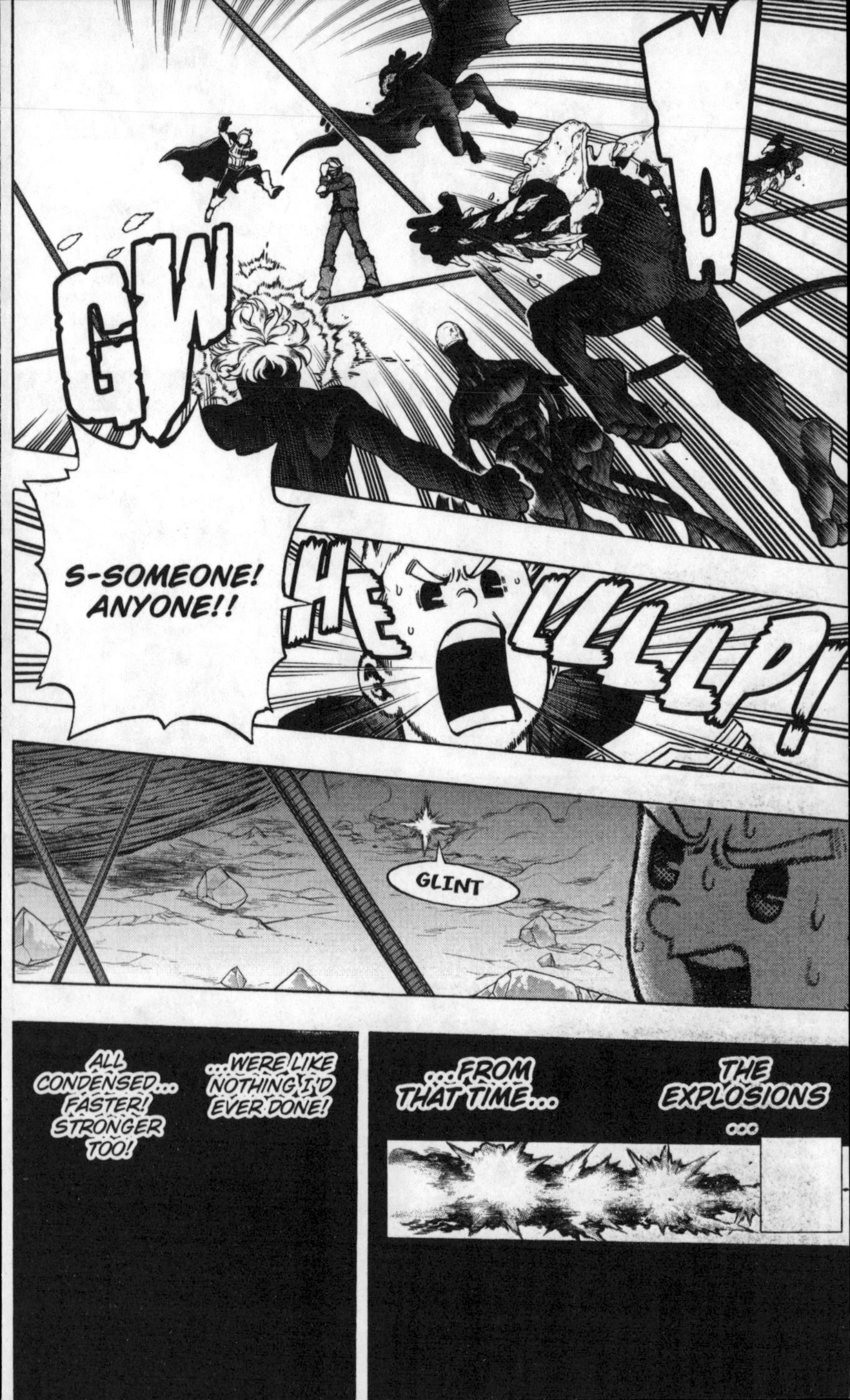
A
GW
S-SOMEONE! ANYONE!!
HELLLP!
GLINT
THE EXPLOSIONS...
...FROM THAT TIME...
...WERE LIKE NOTHING I'D EVER DONE!
ALL CONDENSED... FASTER! STRONGER TOO!

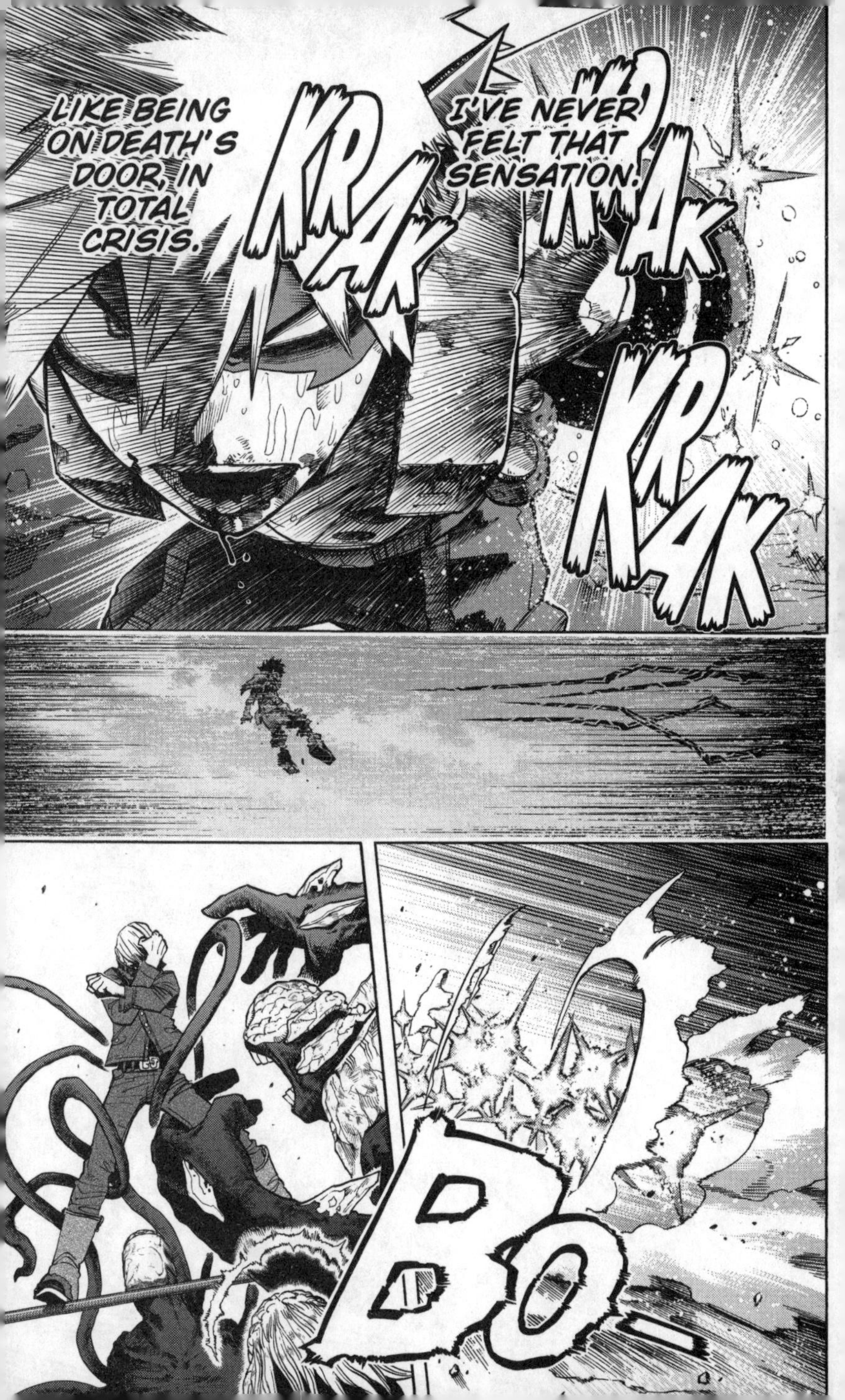
I'VE NEVER FELT THAT SENSATION.
LIKE BEING ON DEATH'S DOOR, IN TOTAL CRISIS.
KRAK
KRAK

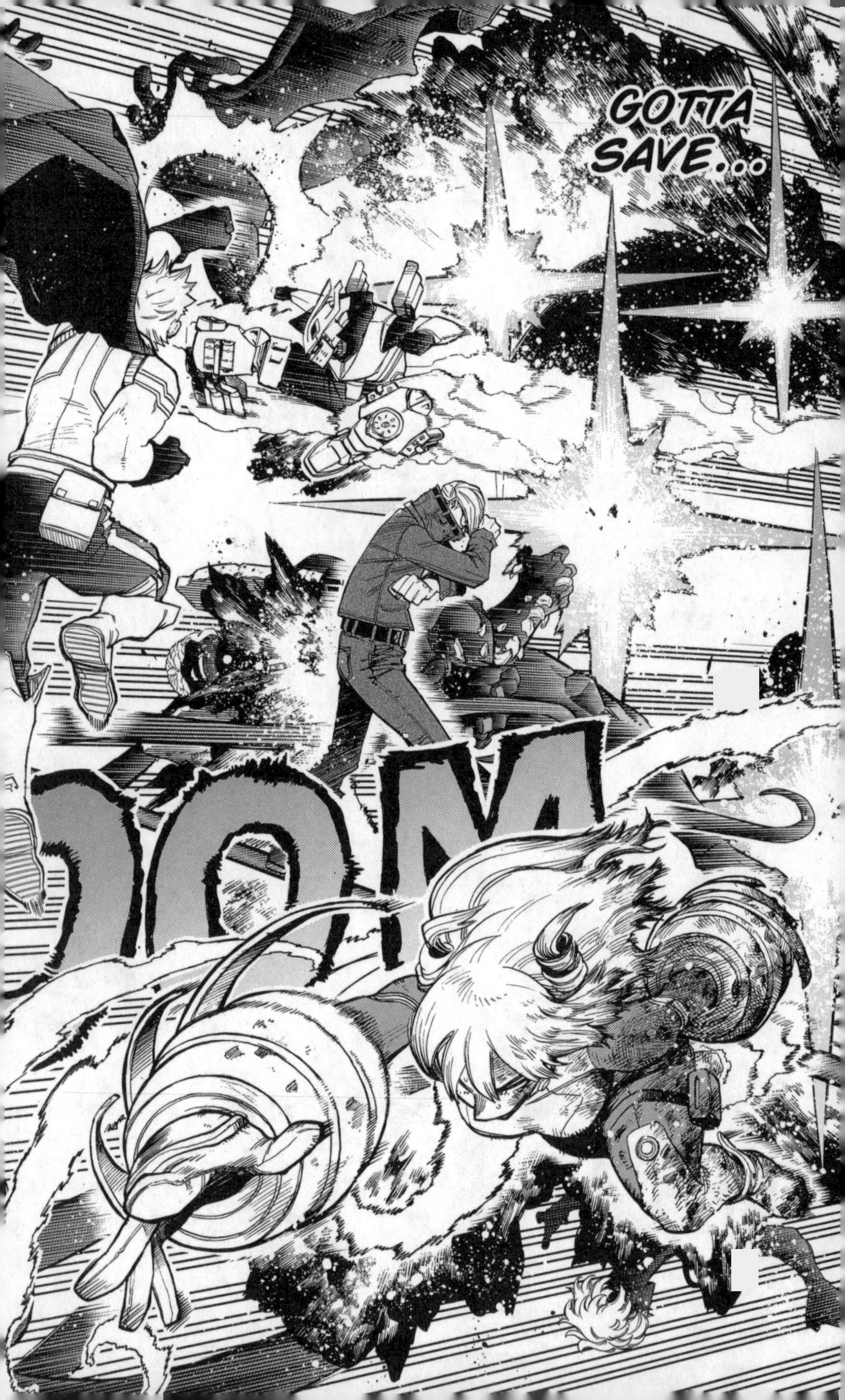
GOTTA SAVE...
OOM

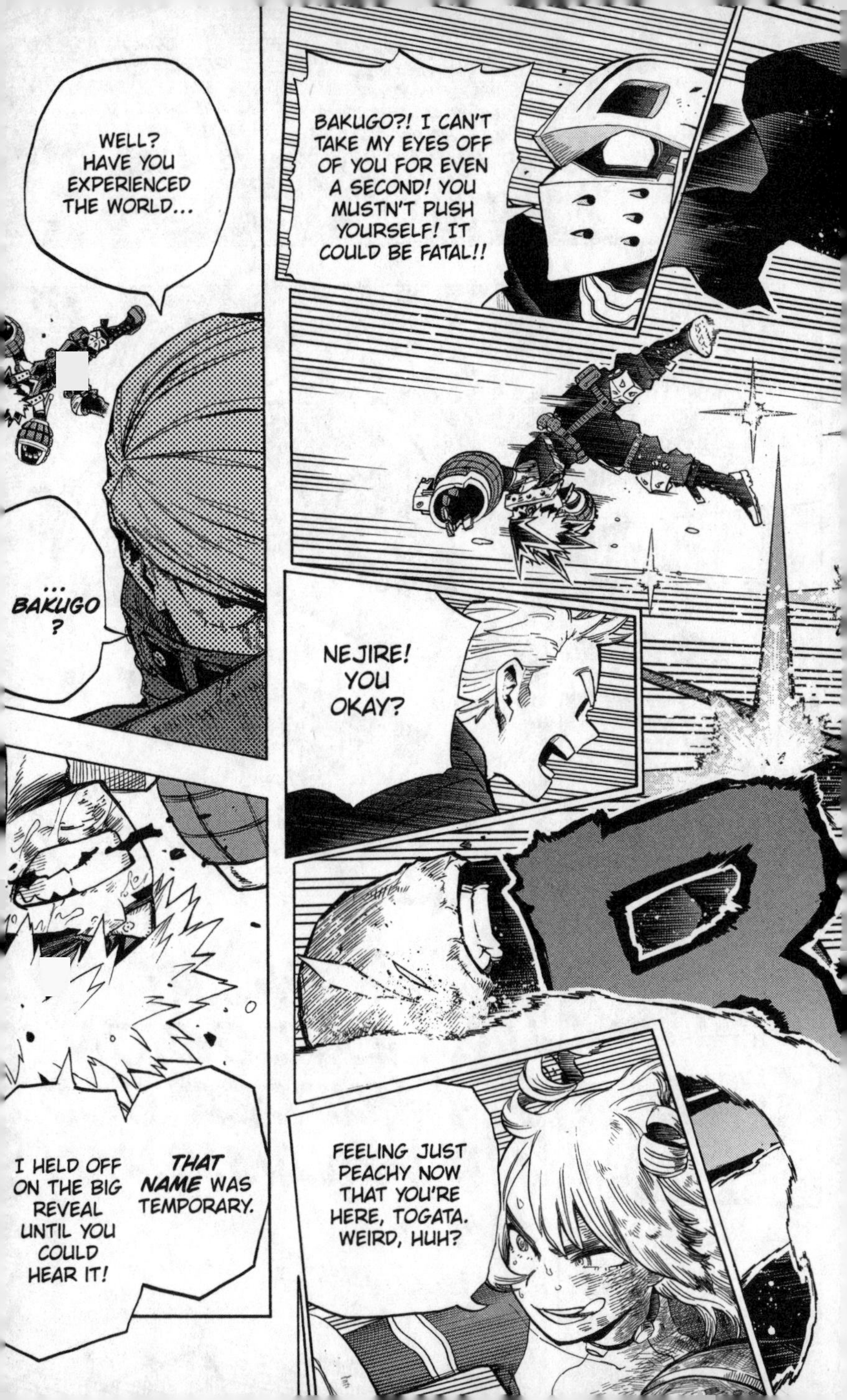
BAKUGO?! I CAN'T TAKE MY EYES OFF OF YOU FOR EVEN A SECOND! YOU MUSTN'T PUSH YOURSELF! IT COULD BE FATAL!!
NEJIRE! YOU OKAY?
FEELING JUST PEACHY NOW THAT YOU'RE HERE, TOGATA. WEIRD, HUH?
WELL? HAVE YOU EXPERIENCED THE WORLD...
...BAKUGO?
THAT NAME WAS TEMPORARY.
I HELD OFF ON THE BIG REVEAL UNTIL YOU COULD HEAR IT!

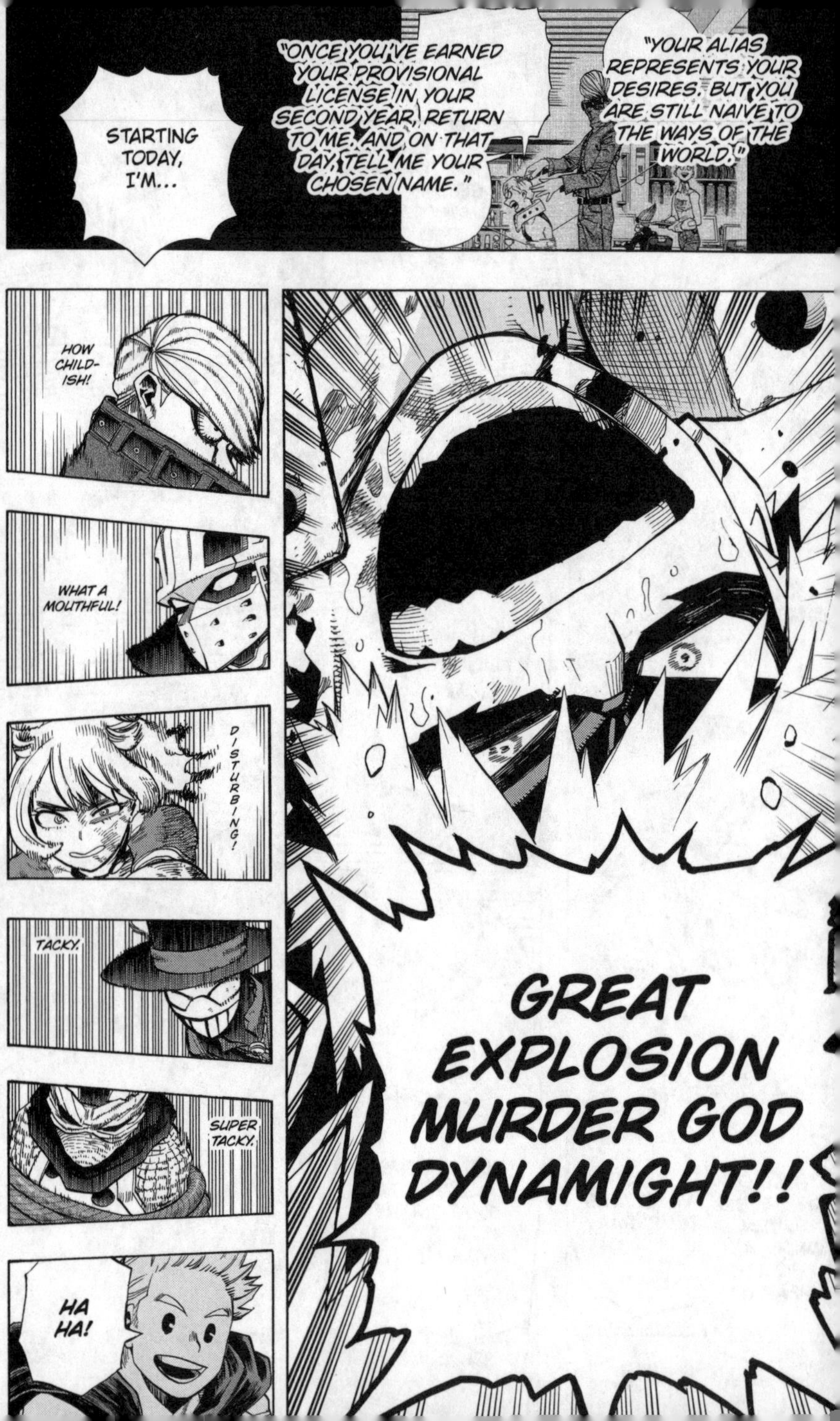
"YOUR ALIAS REPRESENTS YOUR DESIRES. BUT YOU ARE STILL NAIVE TO THE WAYS OF THE WORLD."
"ONCE YOU'VE EARNED YOUR PROVISIONAL LICENSE IN YOUR SECOND YEAR, RETURN TO ME. AND ON THAT DAY, TELL ME YOUR CHOSEN NAME."
STARTING TODAY, I'M...
GREAT EXPLOSION MURDER GOD DYNAMIGHT!!
HOW CHILD-ISH!
WHAT A MOUTHFUL!
DISTURBING!
TACKY.
SUPER TACKY.
HA HA!

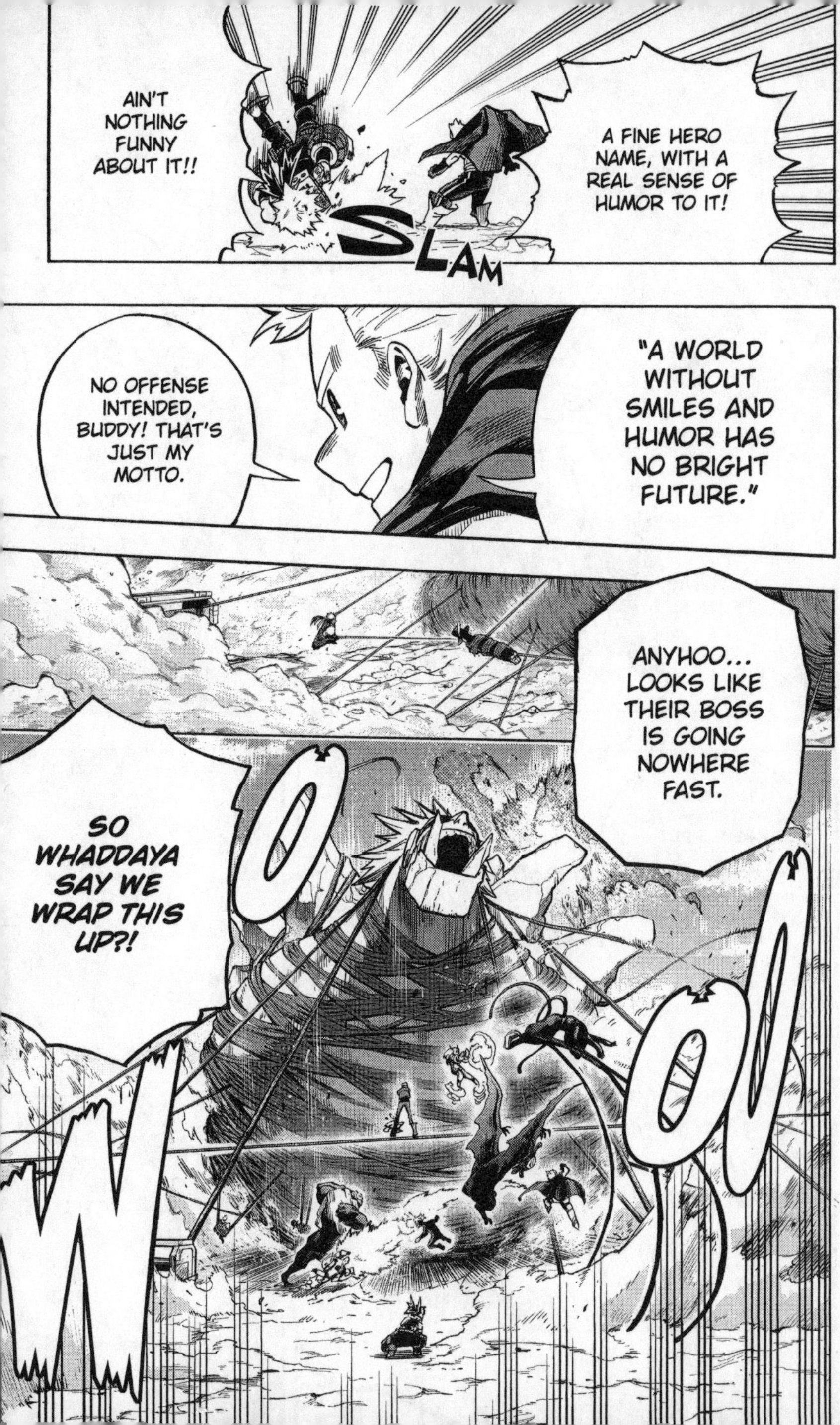
A FINE HERO NAME, WITH A REAL SENSE OF HUMOR TO IT!
AIN'T NOTHING FUNNY ABOUT IT!!
SLAM
"A WORLD WITHOUT SMILES AND HUMOR HAS NO BRIGHT FUTURE."
NO OFFENSE INTENDED, BUDDY! THAT'S JUST MY MOTTO.
ANYHOO... LOOKS LIKE THEIR BOSS IS GOING NOWHERE FAST.
SO WHADDAYA SAY WE WRAP THIS UP?!
WOOO

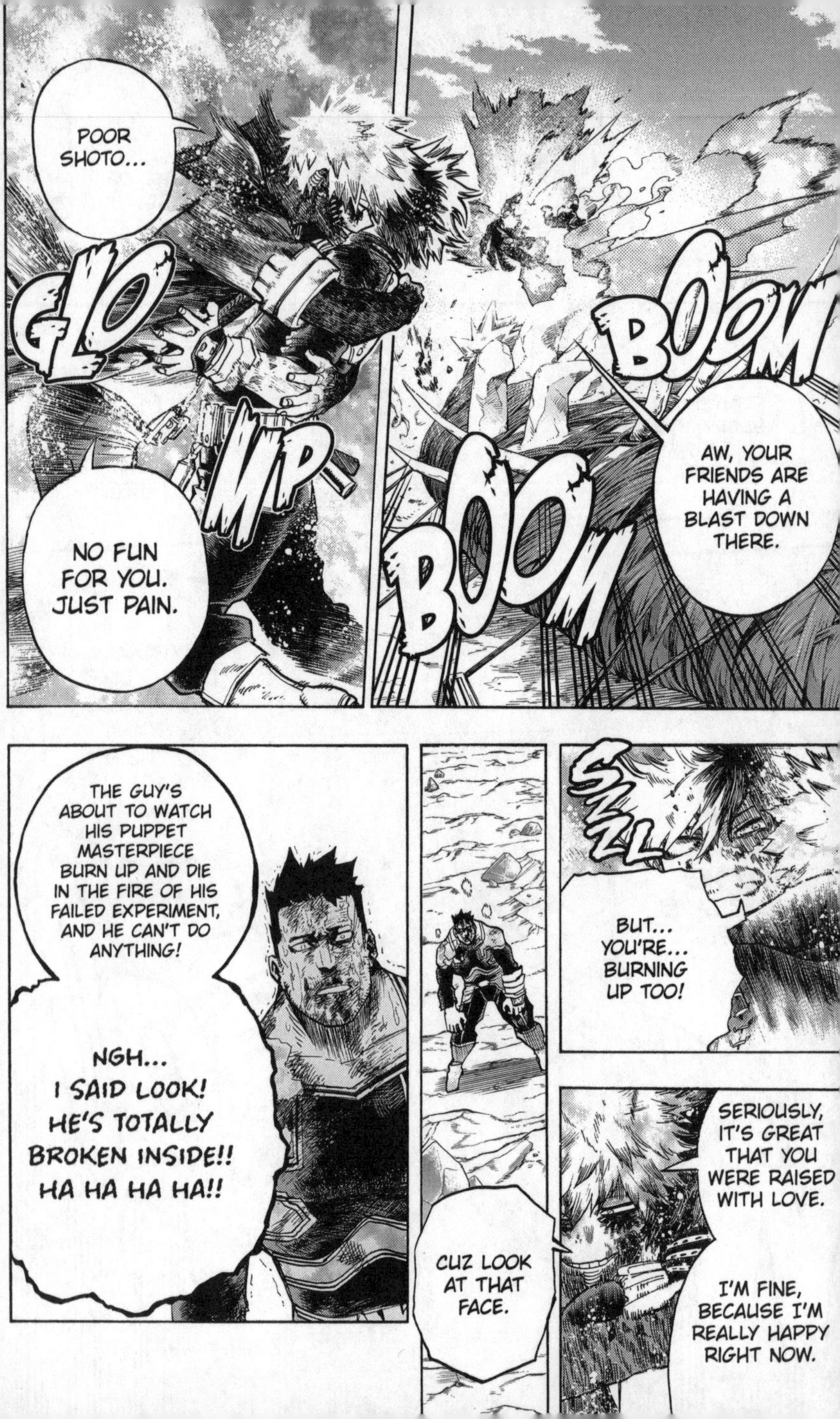
BOOM
BOOM
AW, YOUR FRIENDS ARE HAVING A BLAST DOWN THERE.
POOR SHOTO...
GLOMP
NO FUN FOR YOU. JUST PAIN.
SNZZL
BUT... YOU'RE... BURNING UP TOO!
SERIOUSLY, IT'S GREAT THAT YOU WERE RAISED WITH LOVE.
I'M FINE, BECAUSE I'M REALLY HAPPY RIGHT NOW.
CUZ LOOK AT THAT FACE.
THE GUY'S ABOUT TO WATCH HIS PUPPET MASTERPIECE BURN UP AND DIE IN THE FIRE OF HIS FAILED EXPERIMENT, AND HE CAN'T DO ANYTHING!
NGH... I SAID LOOK! HE'S TOTALLY BROKEN INSIDE!! HA HA HA HA!!

HA
SHOTO!! ONCE MY FIRE BURNS YOU TO ASH...
...I WONDER...
HA
...WHAT KINDA FACE DAD'LL MAKE?!
HA
HA
HA

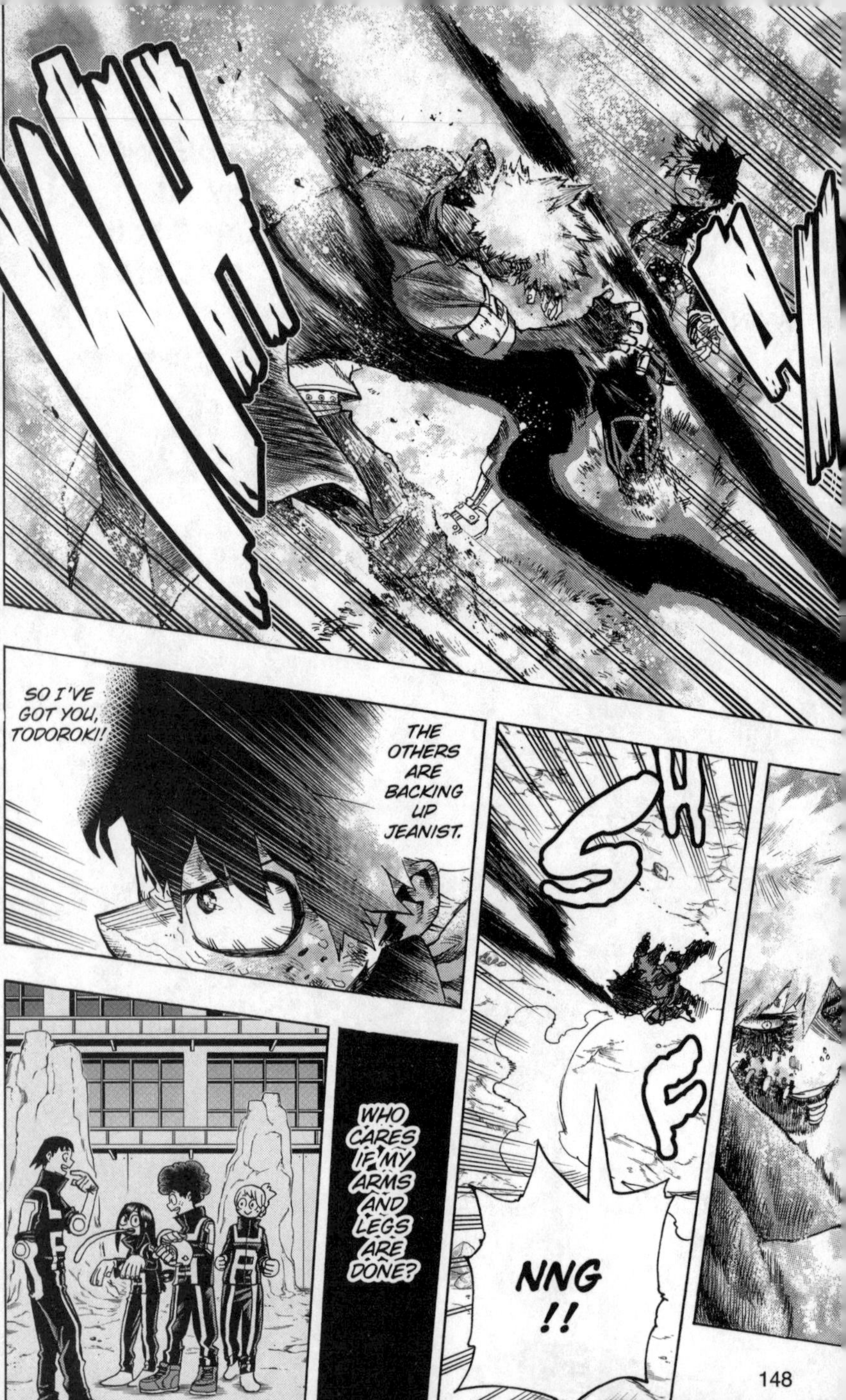
NNG !!
THE OTHERS ARE BACKING UP JEANIST.
SO I'VE GOT YOU, TODOROKI!
WHO CARES IF MY ARMS AND LEGS ARE DONE?

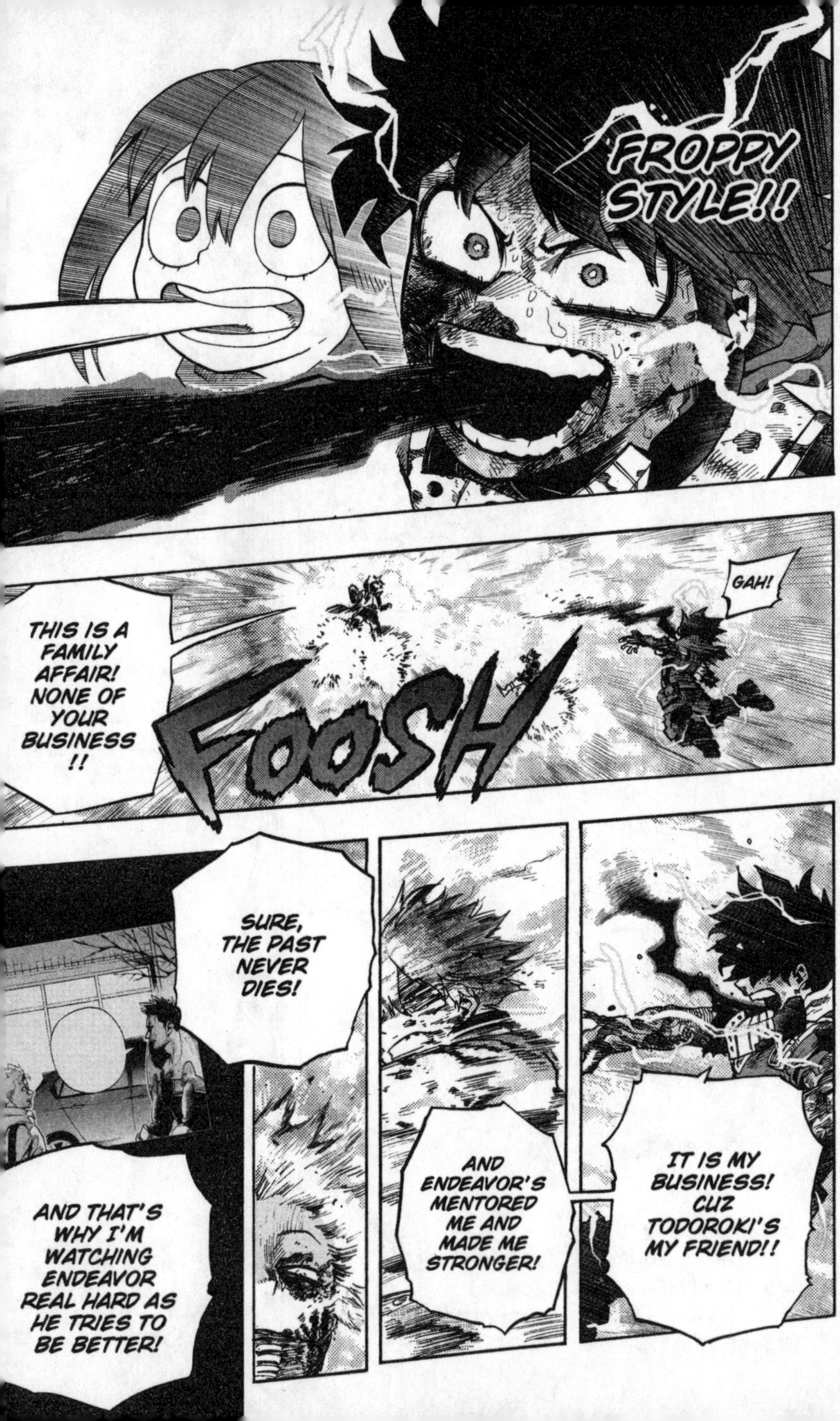
FROPPY STYLE!!
GAH!
FOOSH
THIS IS A FAMILY AFFAIR! NONE OF YOUR BUSINESS!!
IT IS MY BUSINESS! CUZ TODOROKI'S MY FRIEND!!
AND ENDEAVOR'S MENTORED ME AND MADE ME STRONGER!
SURE, THE PAST NEVER DIES!
AND THAT'S WHY I'M WATCHING ENDEAVOR REAL HARD AS HE TRIES TO BE BETTER!

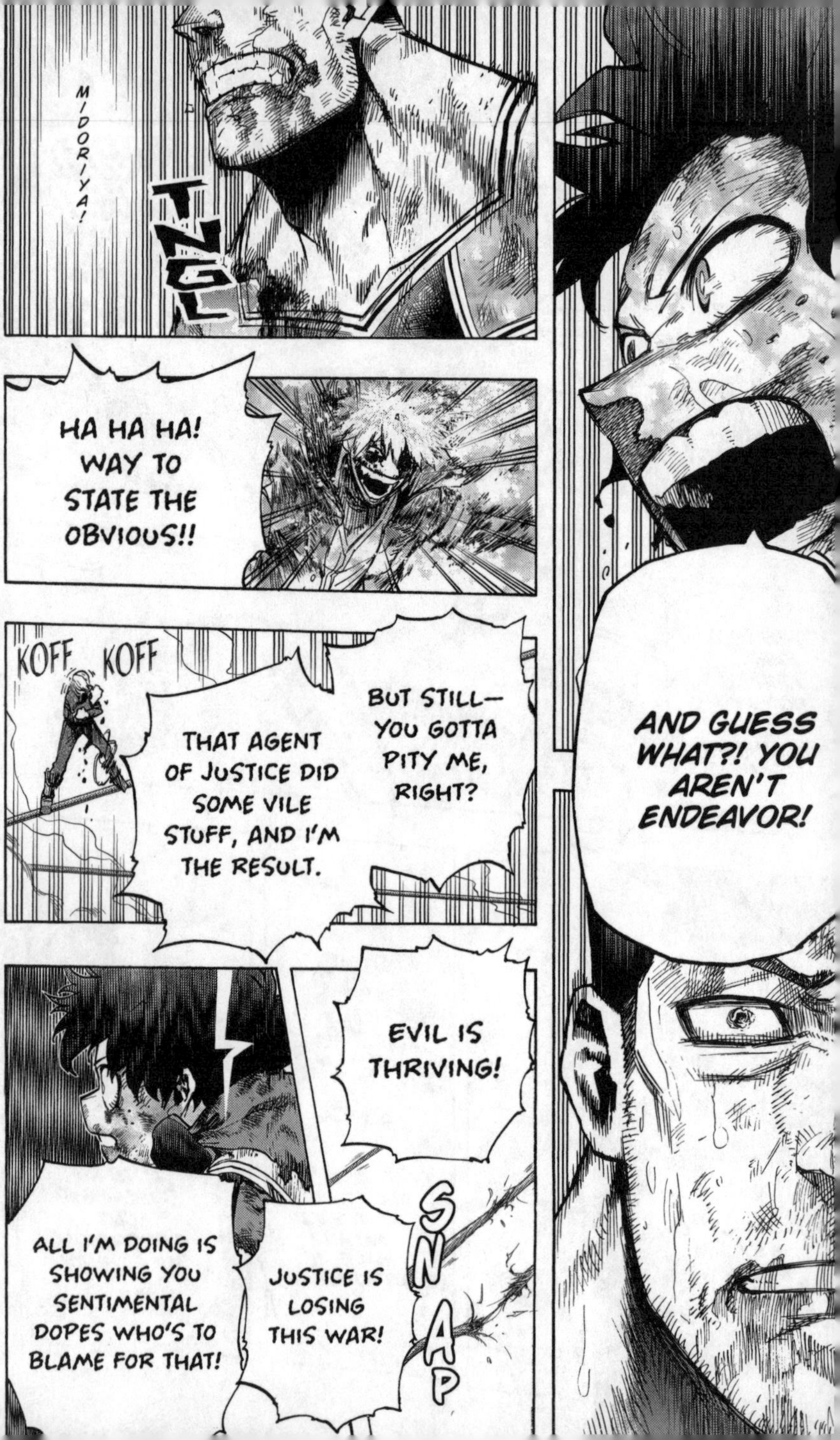

AND GUESS WHAT?! YOU AREN'T ENDEAVOR!
MIDORIYA!
TNGL
HA HA HA! WAY TO STATE THE OBVIOUS!!
BUT STILL— YOU GOTTA PITY ME, RIGHT?
THAT AGENT OF JUSTICE DID SOME VILE STUFF, AND I'M THE RESULT.
KOFF KOFF
EVIL IS THRIVING!
SNAP
JUSTICE IS LOSING THIS WAR!
ALL I'M DOING IS SHOWING YOU SENTIMENTAL DOPES WHO'S TO BLAME FOR THAT!

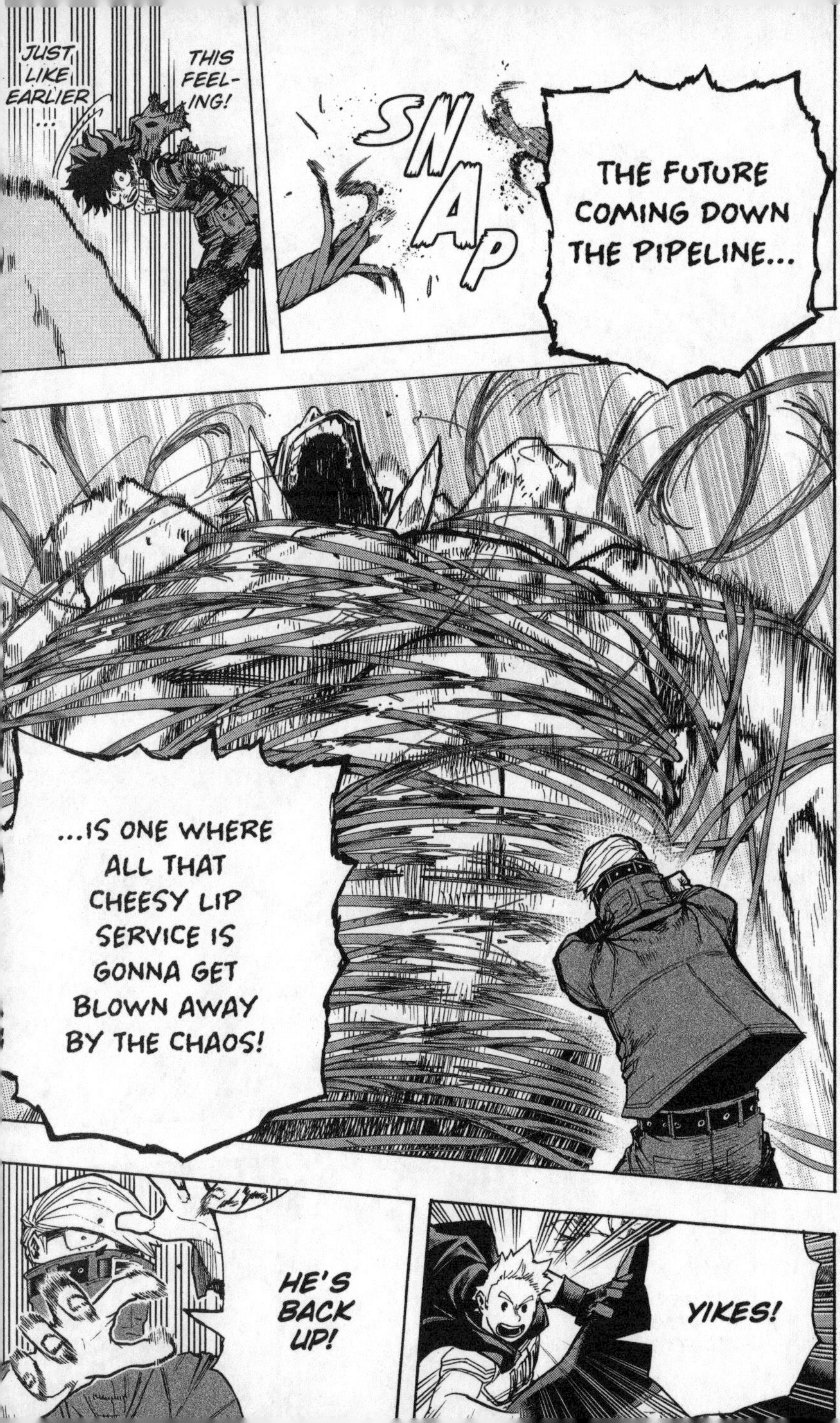
THE FUTURE COMING DOWN THE PIPELINE...
SNAP
THIS FEEL-ING!
JUST LIKE EARLIER...
...IS ONE WHERE ALL THAT CHEESY LIP SERVICE IS GONNA GET BLOWN AWAY BY THE CHAOS!
YIKES!
HE'S BACK UP!

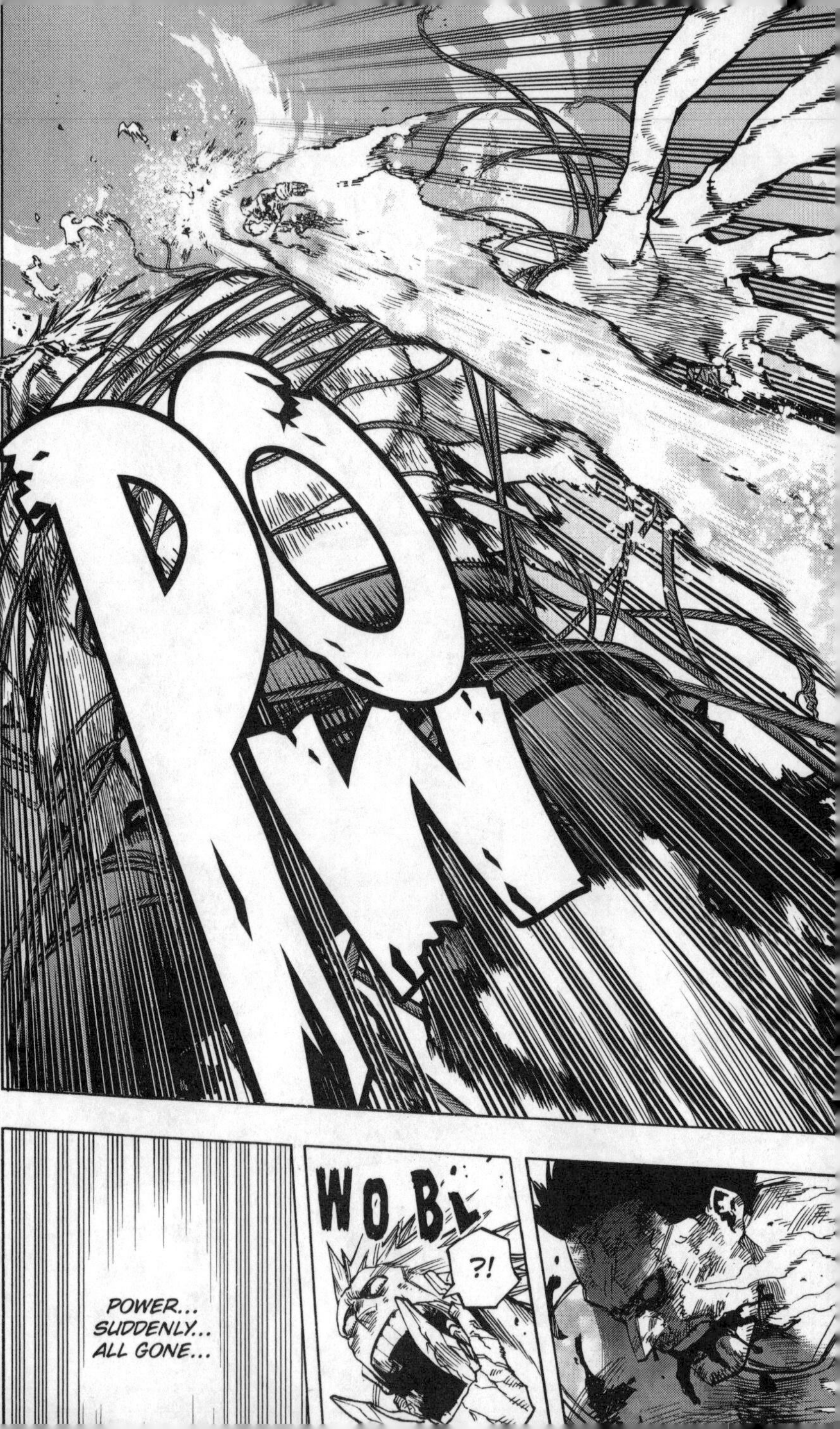
DOM
WOBL
?!
POWER... SUDDENLY... ALL GONE...

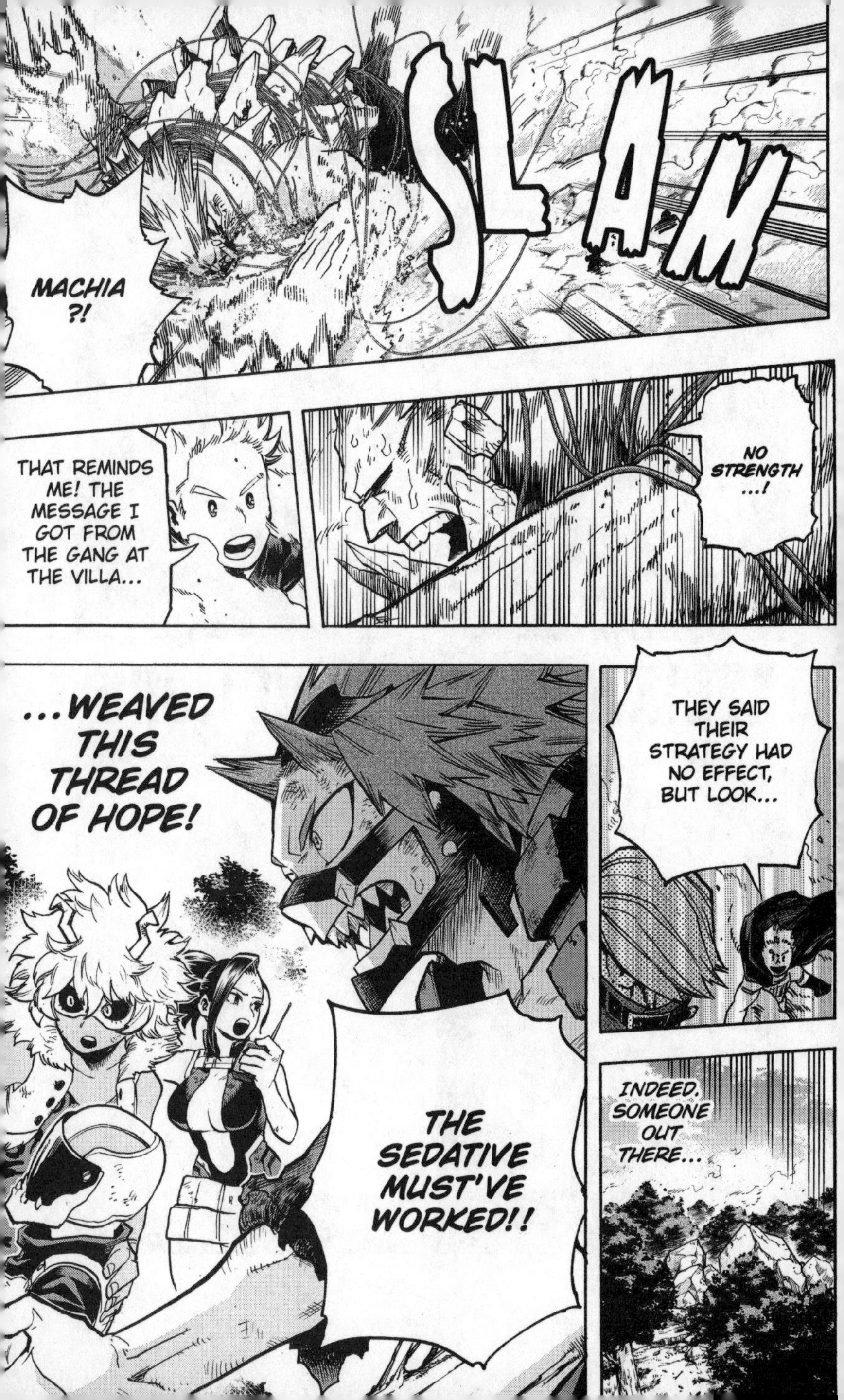
SLAM
MACHIA?!
NO STRENGTH...!
THAT REMINDS ME! THE MESSAGE I GOT FROM THE GANG AT THE VILLA...
THEY SAID THEIR STRATEGY HAD NO EFFECT, BUT LOOK...
INDEED. SOMEONE OUT THERE...
...WEAVED THIS THREAD OF HOPE!
THE SEDATIVE MUST'VE WORKED!!

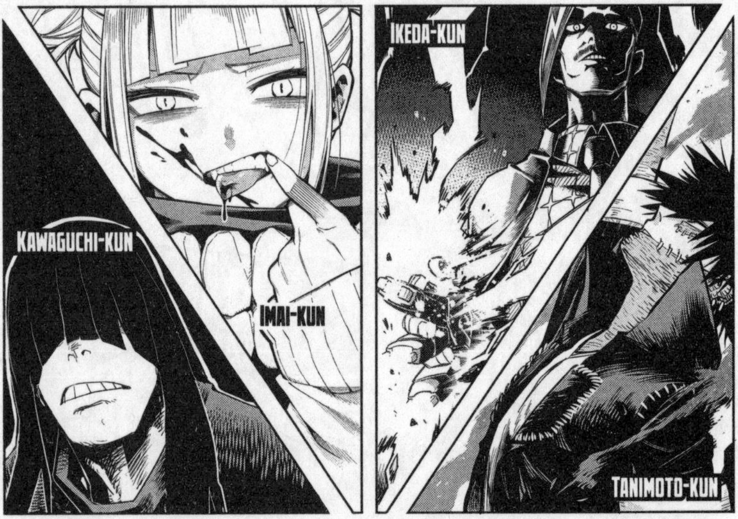
IKEDA-KUN
TANIMOTO-KUN
IMAI-KUN
KAWAGUCHI-KUN

ASSISTANT INTRODUCTIONS

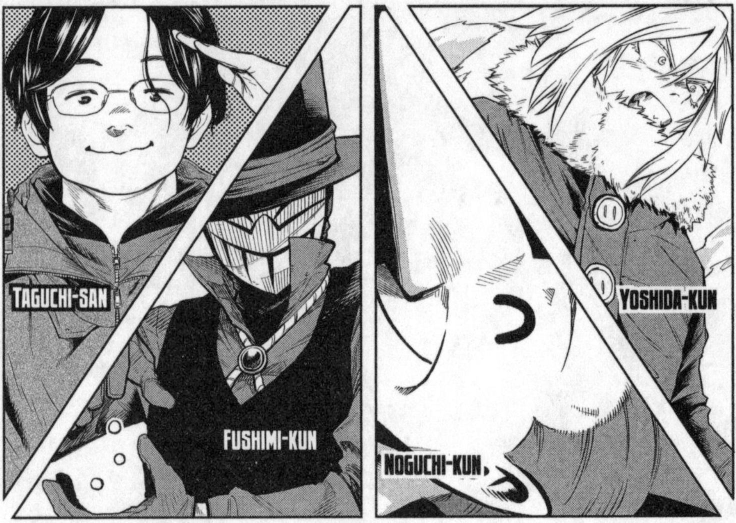
YOSHIDA-KUN
NOGUCHI-KUN
TAGUCHI-SAN
FUSHIMI-KUN

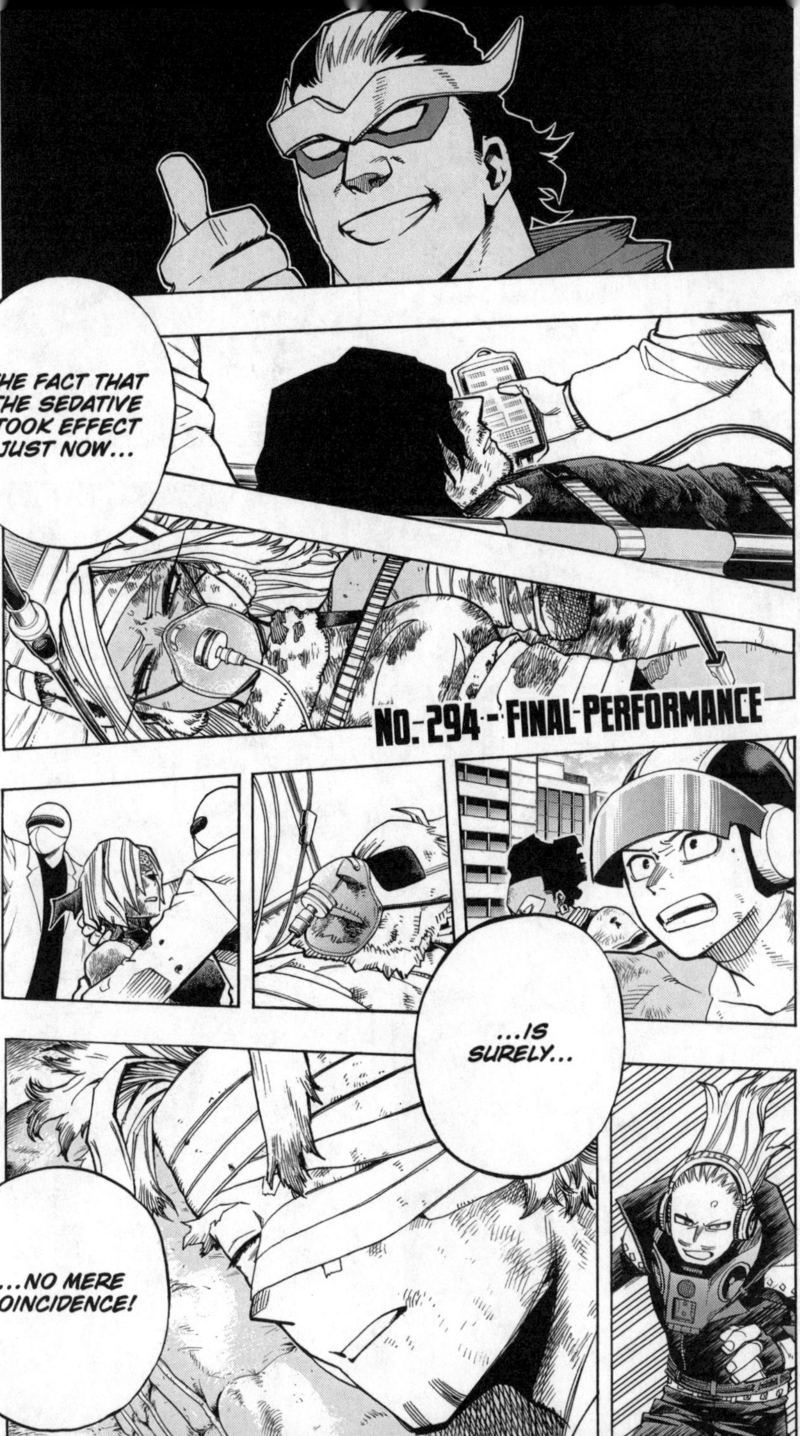
THE FACT THAT THE SEDATIVE TOOK EFFECT JUST NOW...
NO. 294 - FINAL PERFORMANCE
...IS SURELY...
...NO MERE COINCIDENCE!

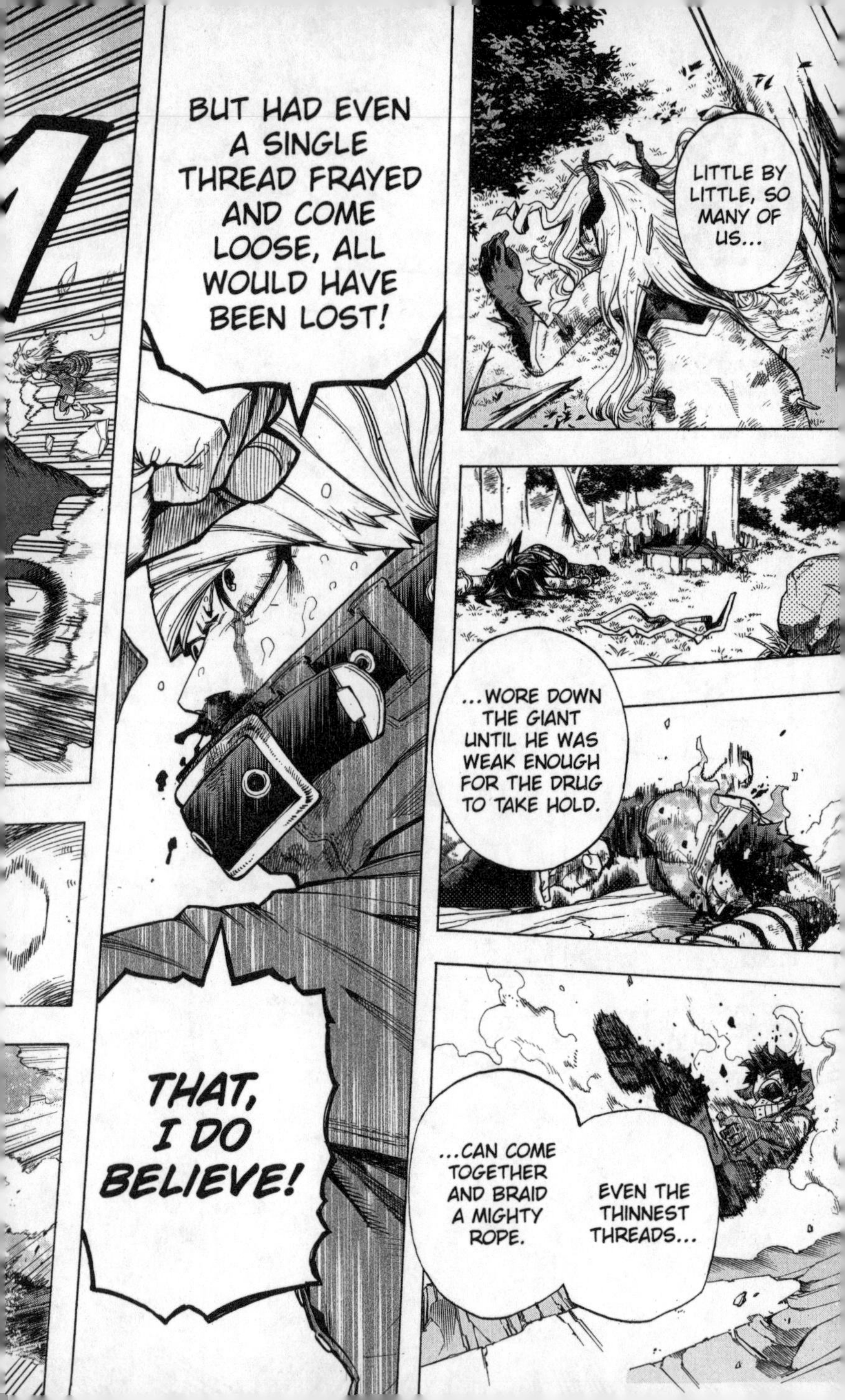
LITTLE BY LITTLE, SO MANY OF US...
...WORE DOWN THE GIANT UNTIL HE WAS WEAK ENOUGH FOR THE DRUG TO TAKE HOLD.
EVEN THE THINNEST THREADS...
...CAN COME TOGETHER AND BRAID A MIGHTY ROPE.
BUT HAD EVEN A SINGLE THREAD FRAYED AND COME LOOSE, ALL WOULD HAVE BEEN LOST!
THAT, I DO BELIEVE!

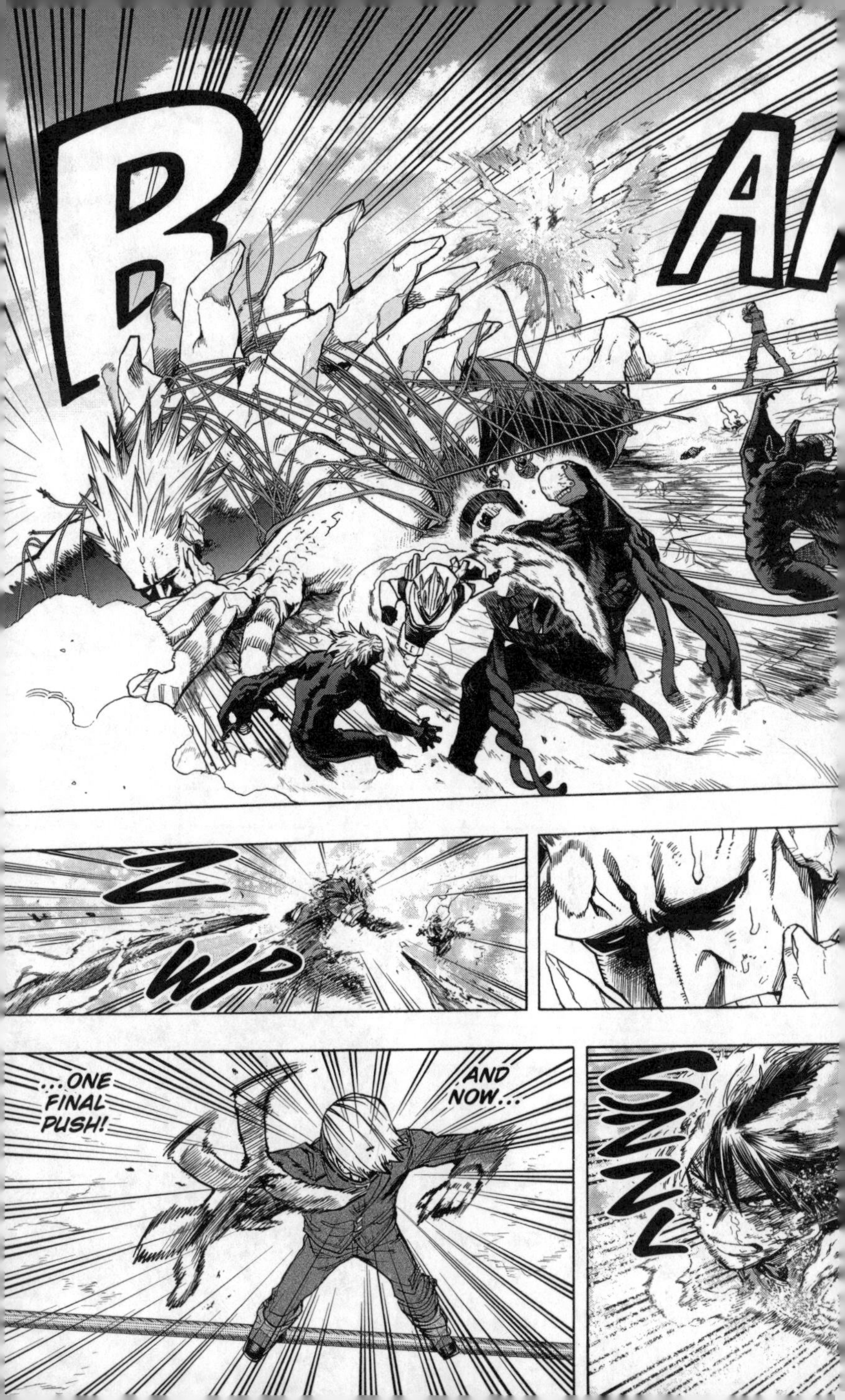
ZWP
AND NOW...
...ONE FINAL PUSH!

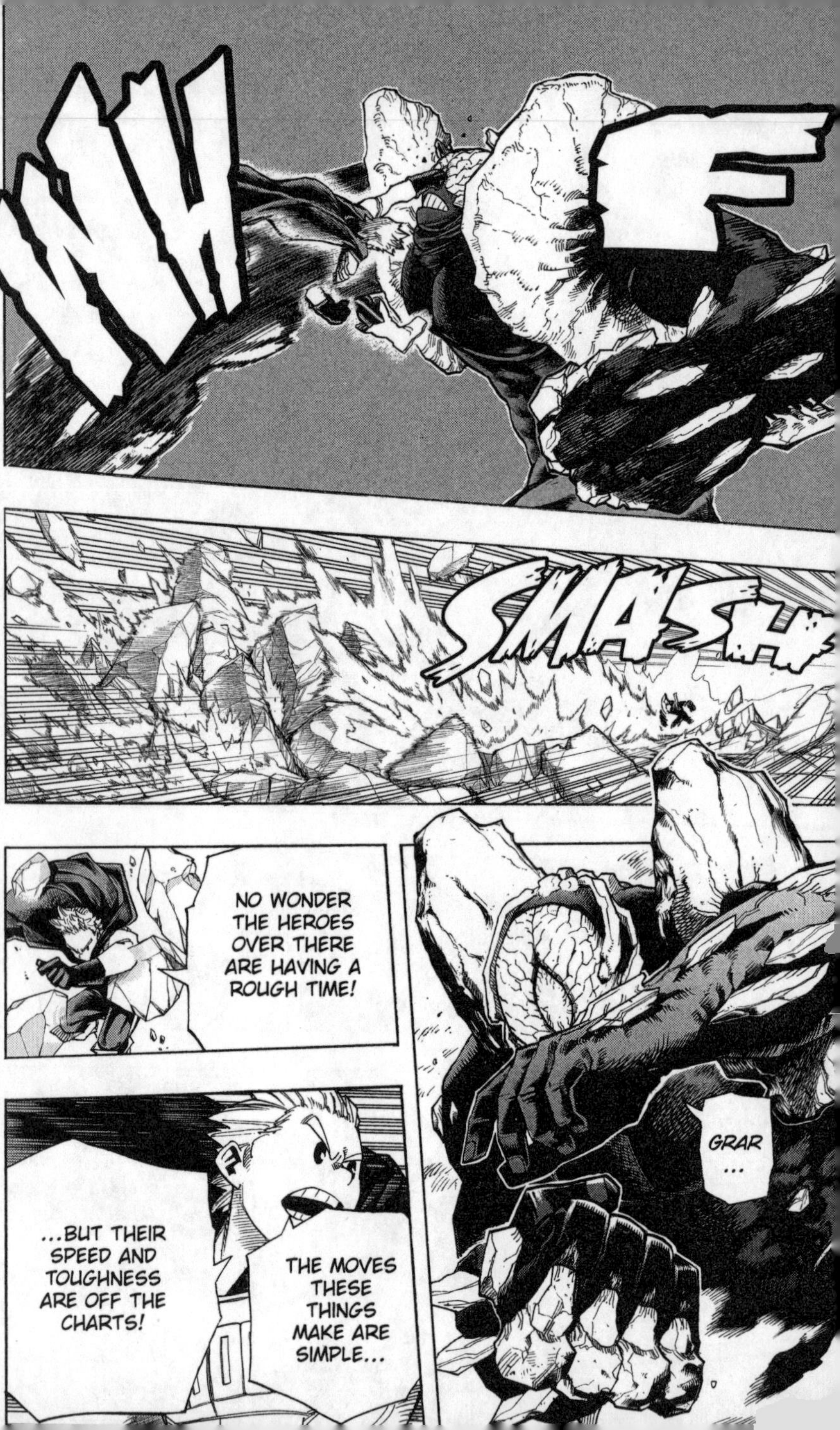
SMASH
GRAR ...
NO WONDER THE HEROES OVER THERE ARE HAVING A ROUGH TIME!
THE MOVES THESE THINGS MAKE ARE SIMPLE...
...BUT THEIR SPEED AND TOUGHNESS ARE OFF THE CHARTS!

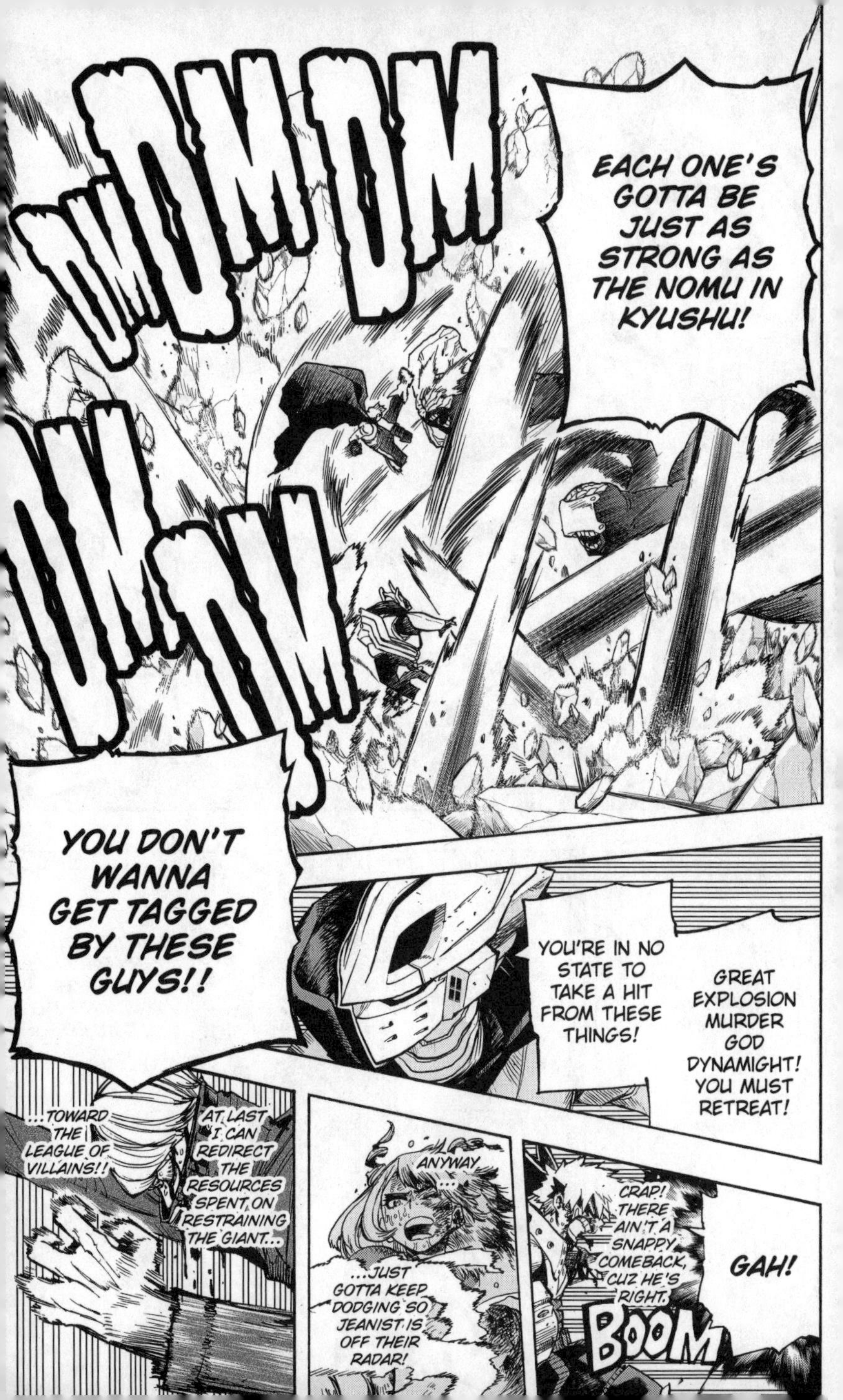
EACH ONE'S GOTTA BE JUST AS STRONG AS THE NOMU IN KYUSHU!
YOU DON'T WANNA GET TAGGED BY THESE GUYS!!
GREAT EXPLOSION MURDER GOD DYNAMIGHT! YOU MUST RETREAT!
YOU'RE IN NO STATE TO TAKE A HIT FROM THESE THINGS!
CRAP! THERE AIN'T A SNAPPY COMEBACK, CUZ HE'S RIGHT.
GAH!
BOOM
ANYWAY...
...JUST GOTTA KEEP DODGING SO JEANIST IS OFF THEIR RADAR!
AT LAST I CAN REDIRECT THE RESOURCES SPENT ON RESTRAINING THE GIANT...
...TOWARD THE LEAGUE OF VILLAINS!!

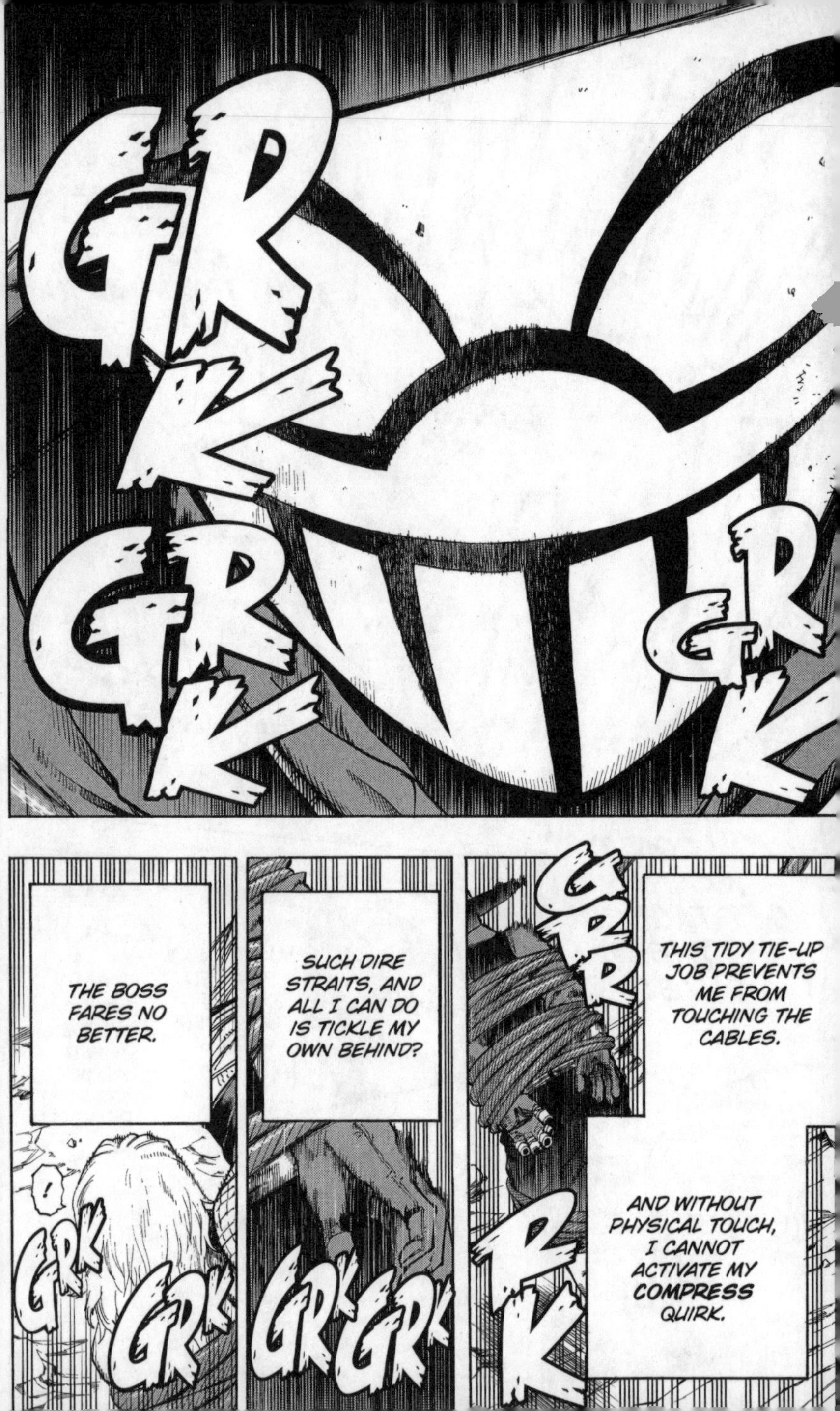
GRK
GRK
GRK
THIS TIDY TIE-UP JOB PREVENTS ME FROM TOUCHING THE CABLES.
GRRK
AND WITHOUT PHYSICAL TOUCH, I CANNOT ACTIVATE MY COMPRESS QUIRK.
SUCH DIRE STRAITS, AND ALL I CAN DO IS TICKLE MY OWN BEHIND?
GRK GRK
THE BOSS FARES NO BETTER.
!
GRK GRK

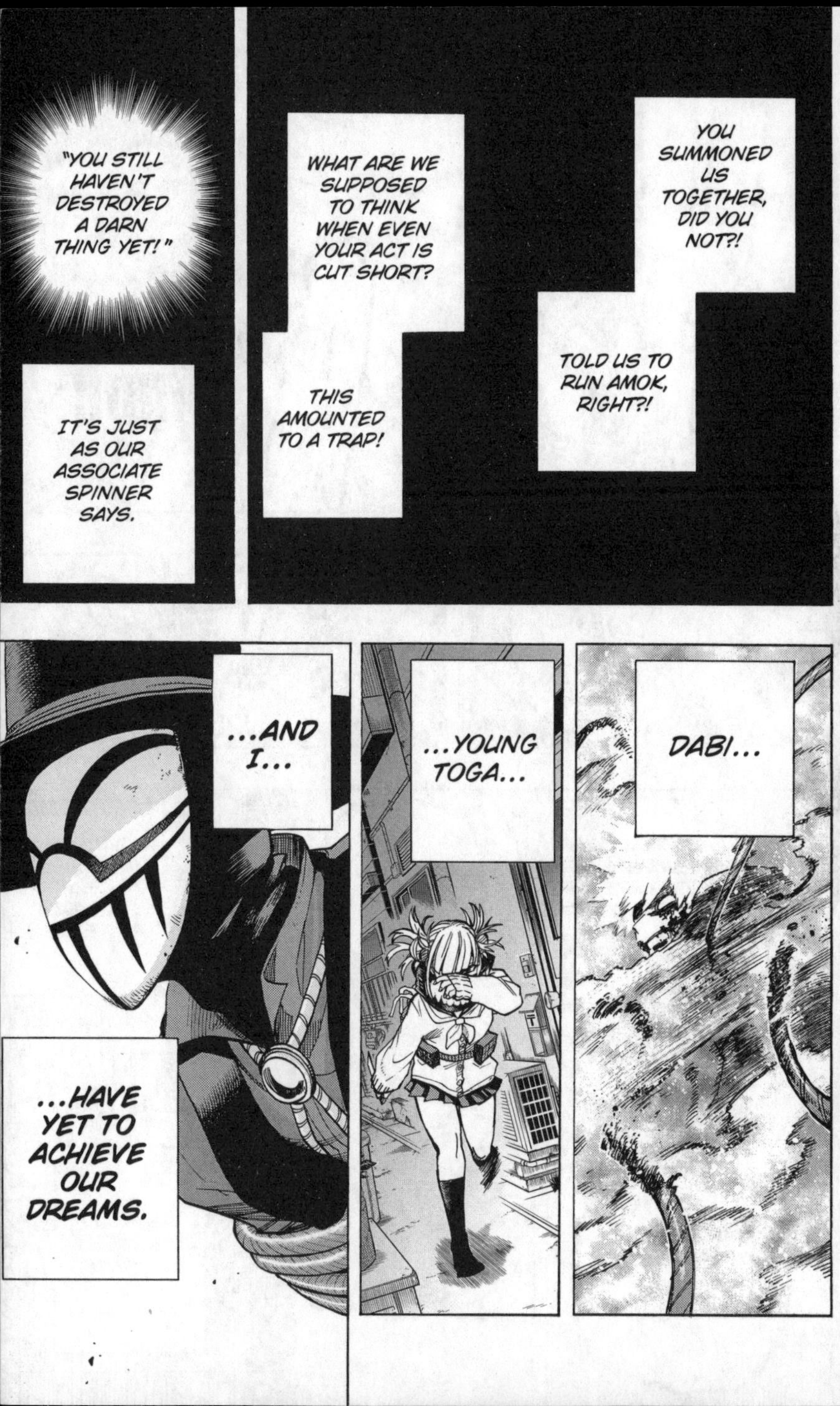
YOU SUMMONED US TOGETHER, DID YOU NOT?!
TOLD US TO RUN AMOK, RIGHT?!
WHAT ARE WE SUPPOSED TO THINK WHEN EVEN YOUR ACT IS CUT SHORT?
THIS AMOUNTED TO A TRAP!
"YOU STILL HAVEN'T DESTROYED A DARN THING YET!"
IT'S JUST AS OUR ASSOCIATE SPINNER SAYS.
DABI...
...YOUNG TOGA...
...AND I...
...HAVE YET TO ACHIEVE OUR DREAMS.

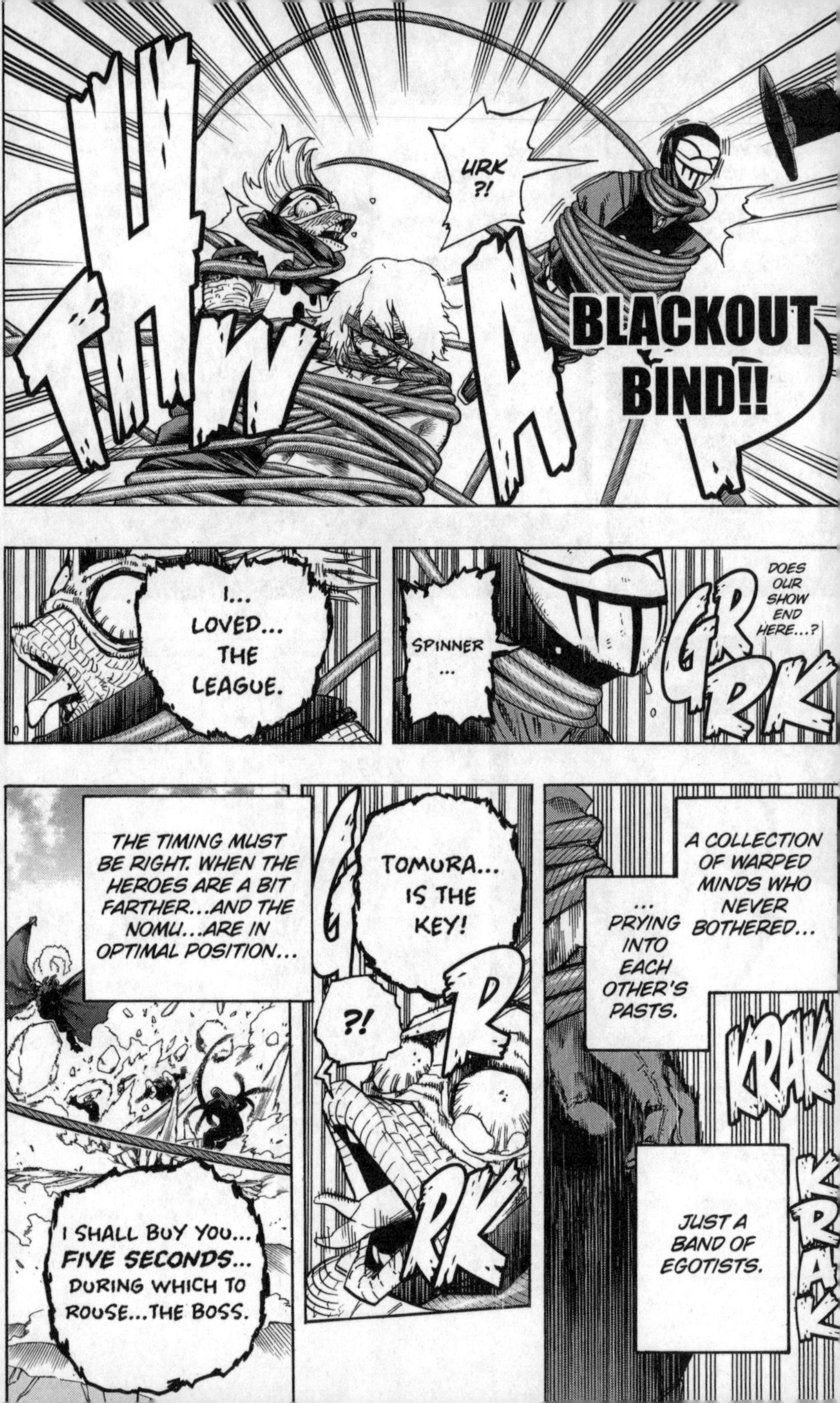
URK ?!
BLACKOUT BIND!!
DOES OUR SHOW END HERE...?
SPINNER ...
GRRK
I... LOVED... THE LEAGUE.
A COLLECTION OF WARPED MINDS WHO NEVER BOTHERED...
... PRYING INTO EACH OTHER'S PASTS.
KRAK
JUST A BAND OF EGOTISTS.
KRAK
TOMURA... IS THE KEY!
?!
THE TIMING MUST BE RIGHT. WHEN THE HEROES ARE A BIT FARTHER...AND THE NOMU...ARE IN OPTIMAL POSITION...
I SHALL BUY YOU... **FIVE SECONDS...** DURING WHICH TO ROUSE...THE BOSS.

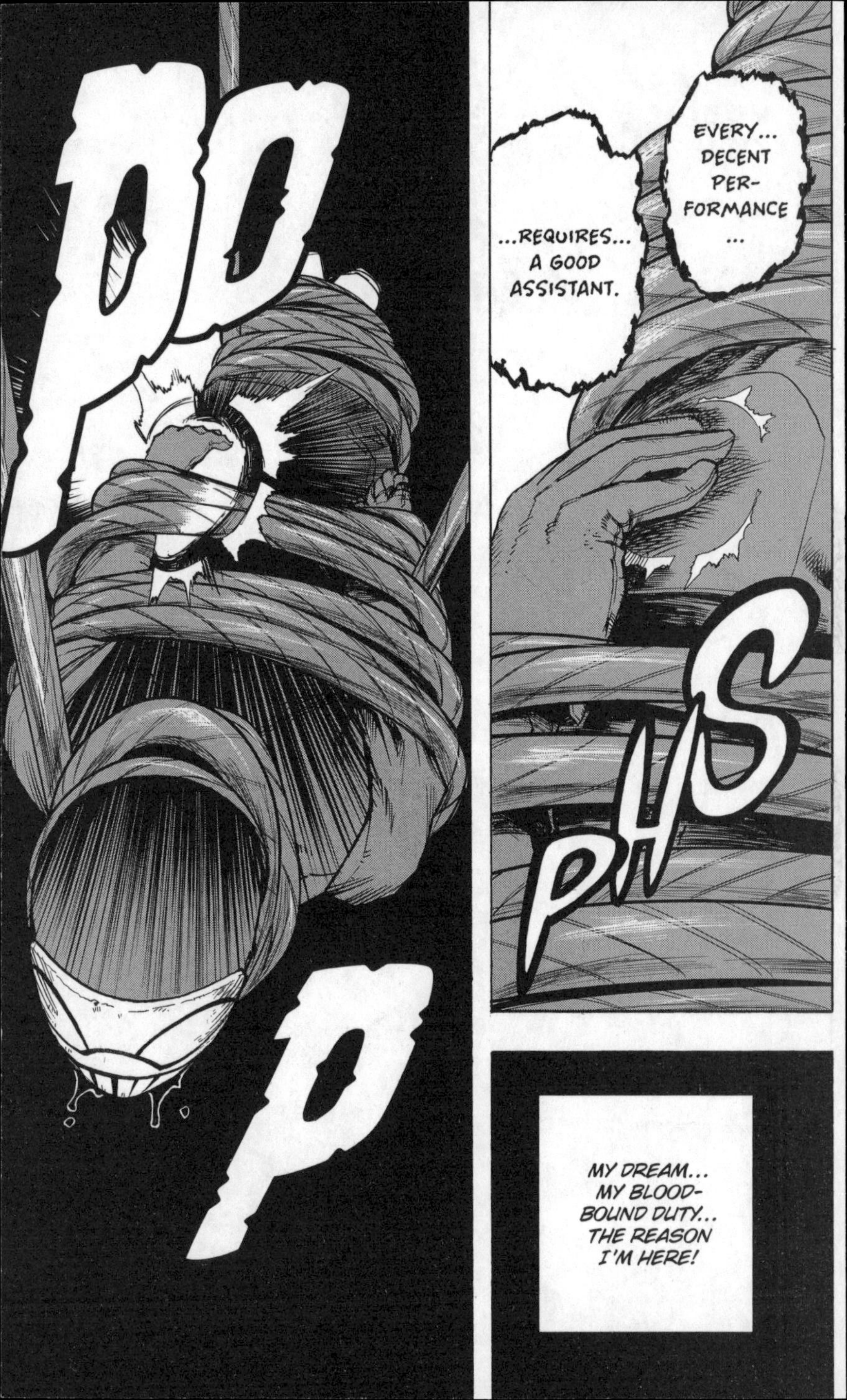
EVERY... DECENT PER-FORMANCE ...
...REQUIRES... A GOOD ASSISTANT.
PHS
MY DREAM... MY BLOOD-BOUND DUTY... THE REASON I'M HERE!
PO
P

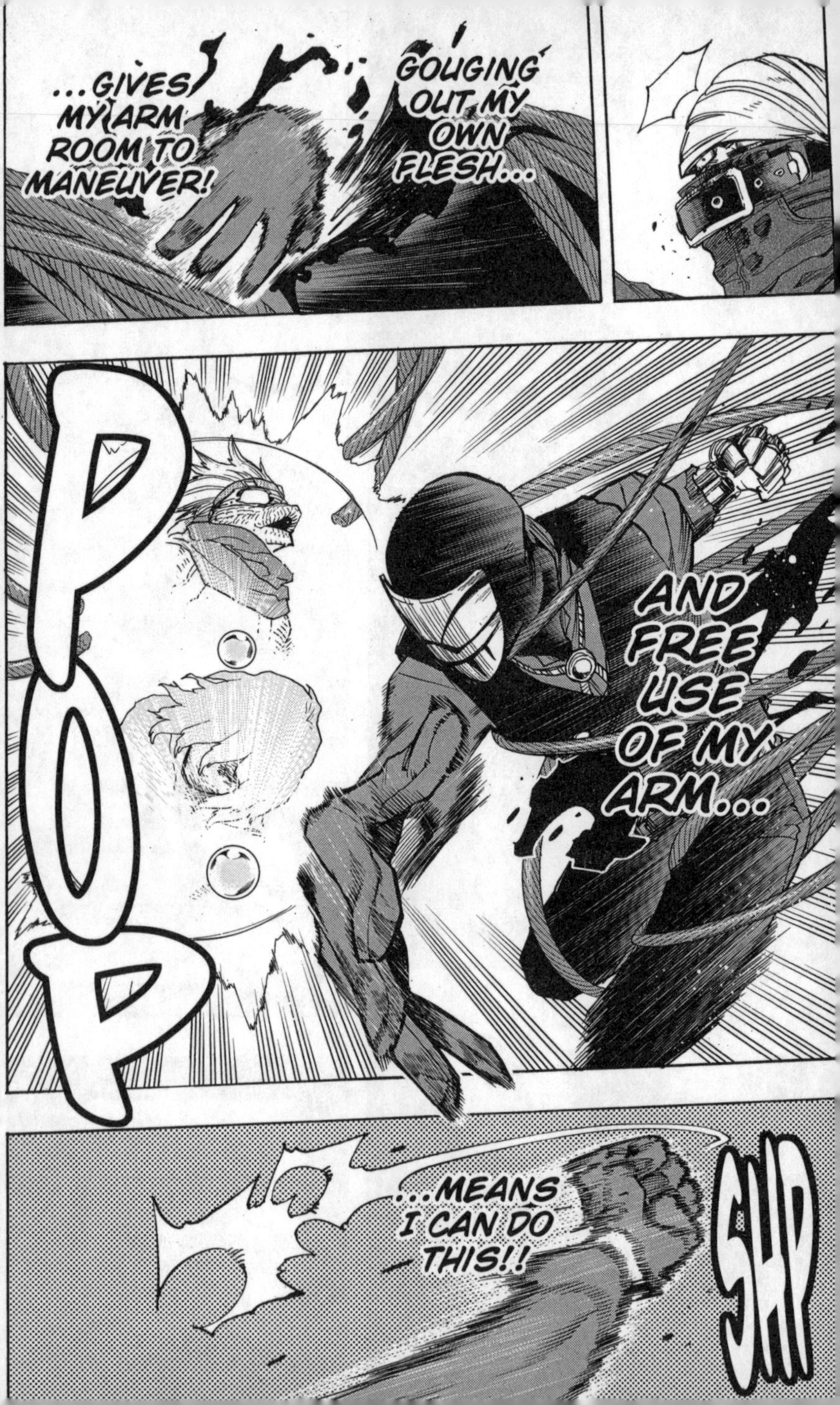
GOUGING OUT MY OWN FLESH...
...GIVES MY ARM ROOM TO MANEUVER!
AND FREE USE OF MY ARM...
POP
SHP
...MEANS I CAN DO THIS!!

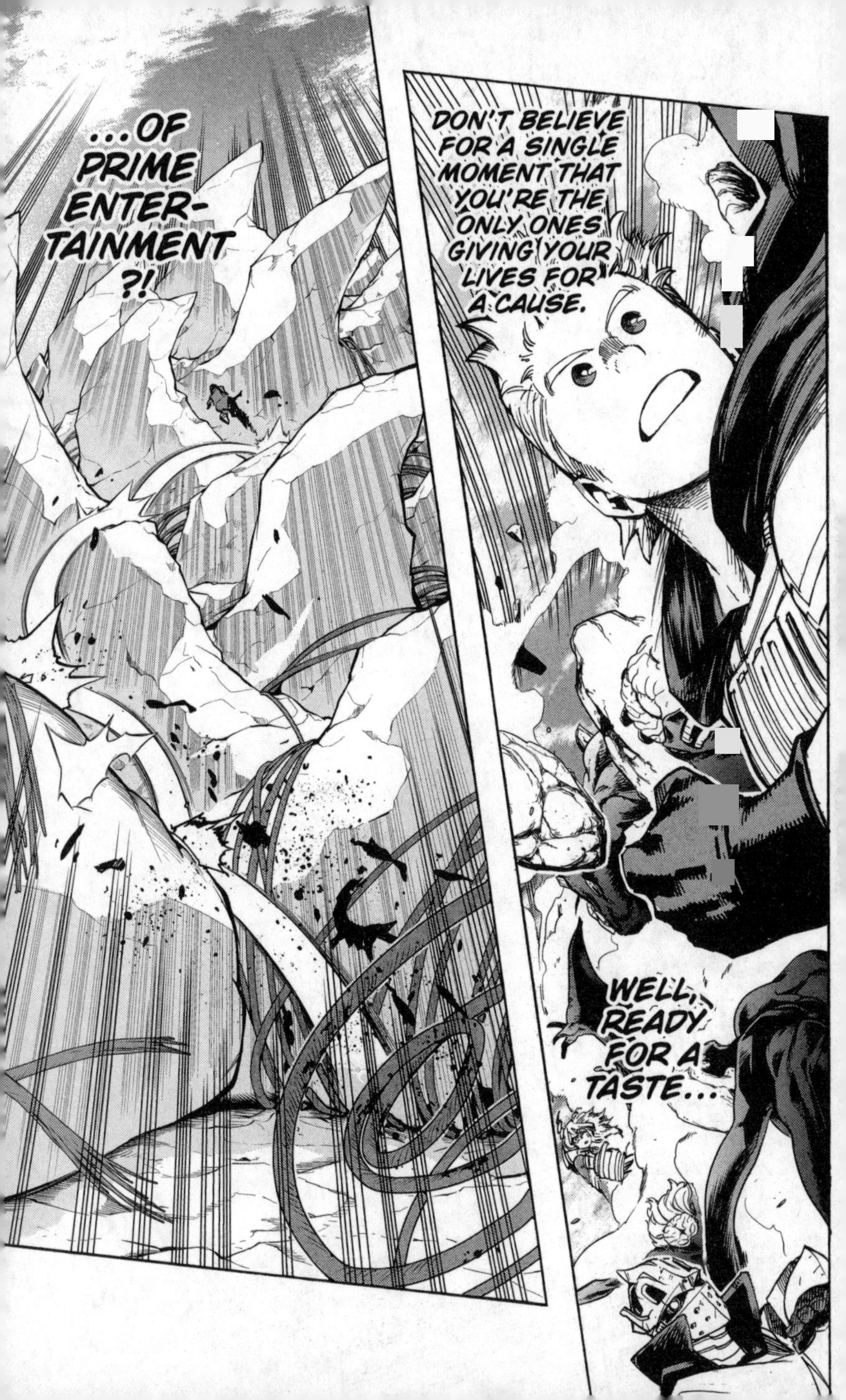
DON'T BELIEVE FOR A SINGLE MOMENT THAT YOU'RE THE ONLY ONES GIVING YOUR LIVES FOR A CAUSE.
WELL, READY FOR A TASTE...
...OF PRIME ENTERTAINMENT ?!

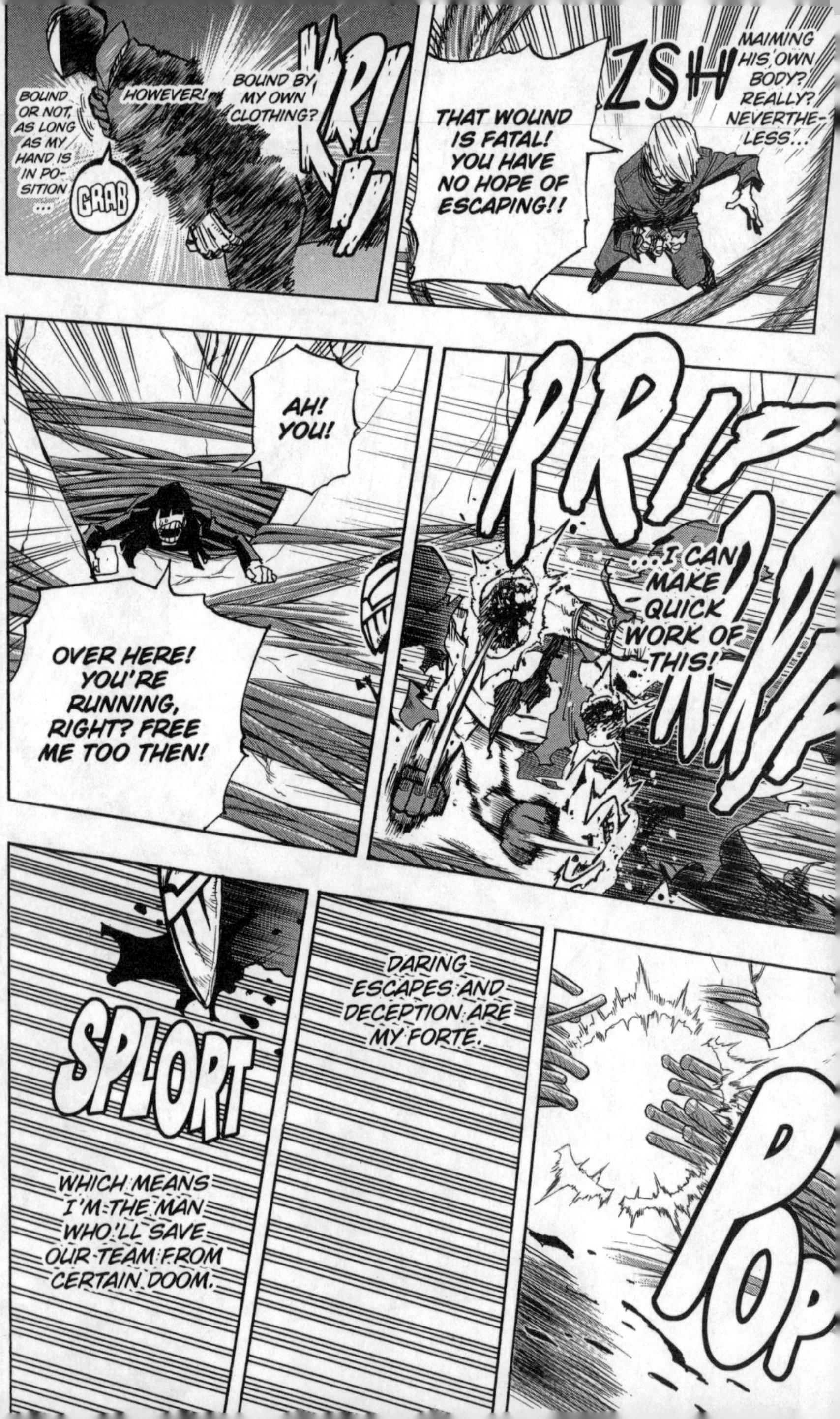
ZSH
MAIMING HIS OWN BODY? REALLY? NEVERTHELESS...
THAT WOUND IS FATAL! YOU HAVE NO HOPE OF ESCAPING!!
KRI
BOUND BY MY OWN CLOTHING?
HOWEVER!
BOUND OR NOT, AS LONG AS MY HAND IS IN POSITION...
GRAB
RRIP
...I CAN MAKE QUICK WORK OF THIS!
AH! YOU!
OVER HERE! YOU'RE RUNNING, RIGHT? FREE ME TOO THEN!
POP
DARING ESCAPES AND DECEPTION ARE MY FORTE.
SPLORT
WHICH MEANS I'M THE MAN WHO'LL SAVE OUR TEAM FROM CERTAIN DOOM.

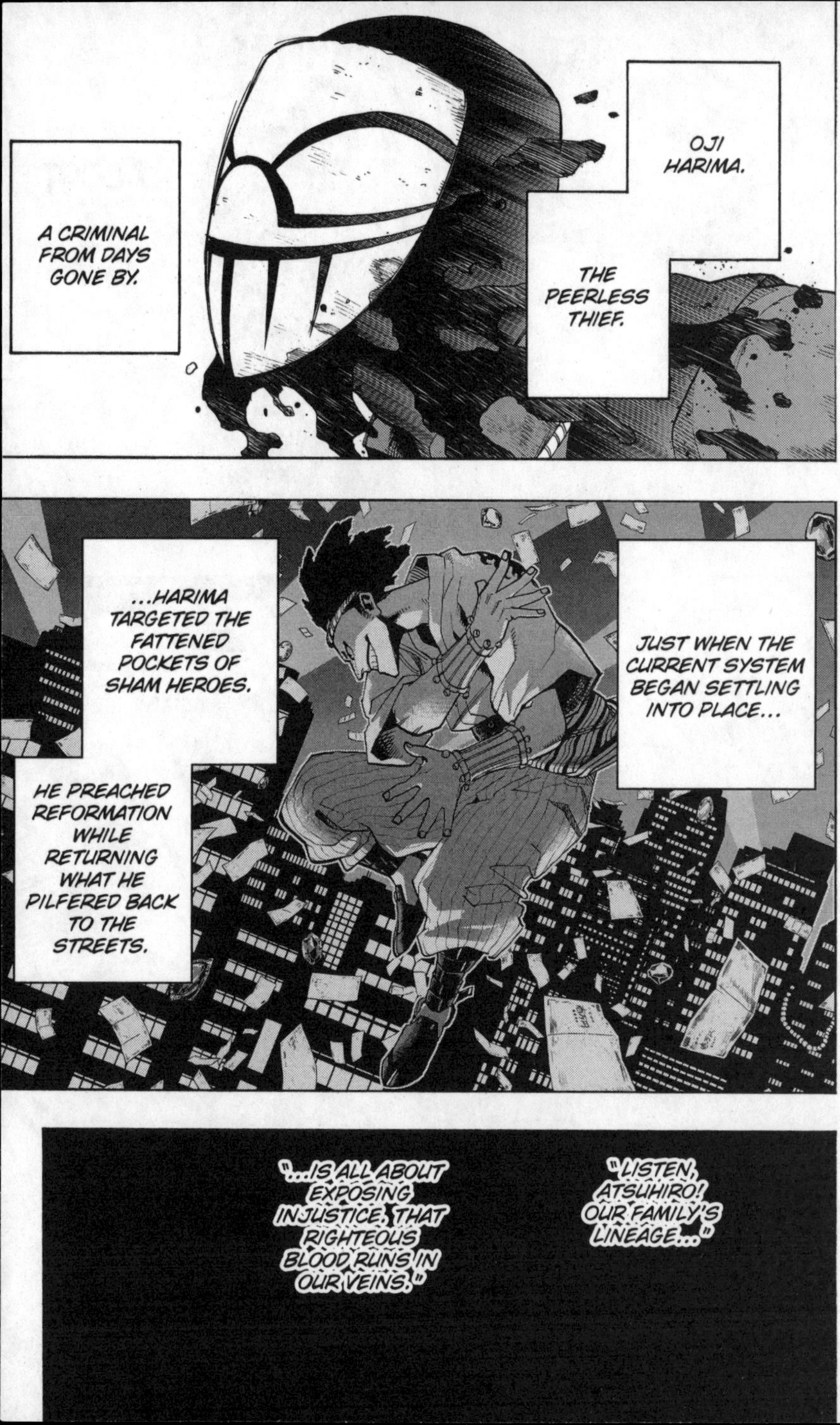
OJI HARIMA.
THE PEERLESS THIEF.
A CRIMINAL FROM DAYS GONE BY.
JUST WHEN THE CURRENT SYSTEM BEGAN SETTLING INTO PLACE...
...HARIMA TARGETED THE FATTENED POCKETS OF SHAM HEROES.
HE PREACHED REFORMATION WHILE RETURNING WHAT HE PILFERED BACK TO THE STREETS.
"LISTEN, ATSUHIRO! OUR FAMILY'S LINEAGE..."
"...IS ALL ABOUT EXPOSING INJUSTICE. THAT RIGHTEOUS BLOOD RUNS IN OUR VEINS."

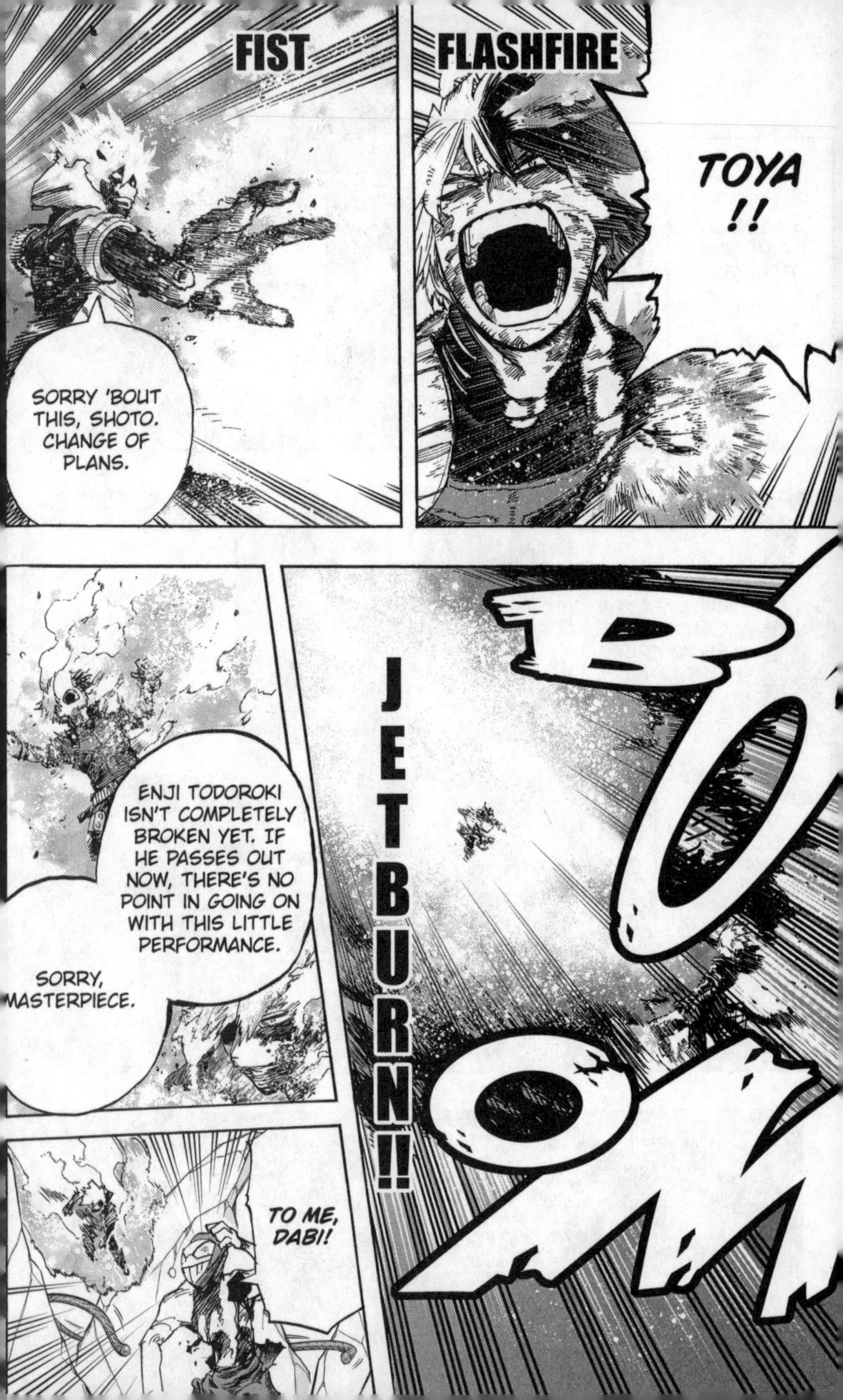
FLASHFIRE
TOYA!!
FIST
SORRY 'BOUT THIS, SHOTO. CHANGE OF PLANS.
BOOM
JET BURN!!
ENJI TODOROKI ISN'T COMPLETELY BROKEN YET. IF HE PASSES OUT NOW, THERE'S NO POINT IN GOING ON WITH THIS LITTLE PERFORMANCE.
SORRY, MASTERPIECE.
TO ME, DABI!

HARIMA...
POP
THE REFORMATION THAT YOU COULD NOT ACHIEVE...
...I NOW HAND OFF TO MY BOSS.
I AM HARIMA'S GREAT-GREAT-GRANDSON!
THE PARANORMAL LIBERATION FRONT'S... NO, THE LEAGUE OF VILLAINS' SHIGARAKI...
THE BANDIT KING'S BLOOD FLOWS THROUGH ME!
...WILL CHANGE THE WORLD IN MY STEAD.
WHAT'S THAT, YOU SAY? YOU BARELY NOTICED ME?!
ALL PART OF THE ACT! IT'S ALL FOR THAT TA-DA MOMENT...

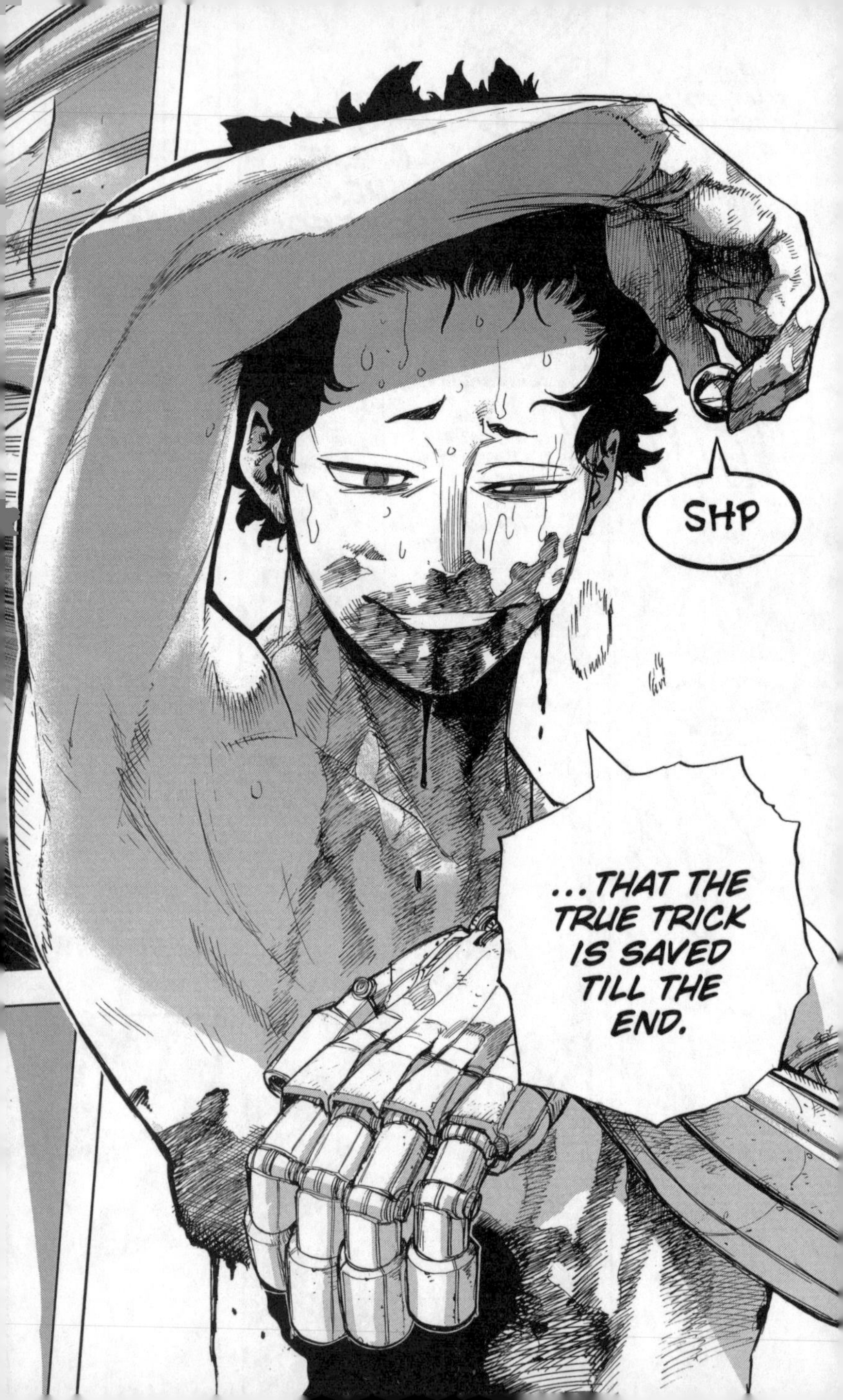
SHP
...THAT THE TRUE TRICK IS SAVED TILL THE END.

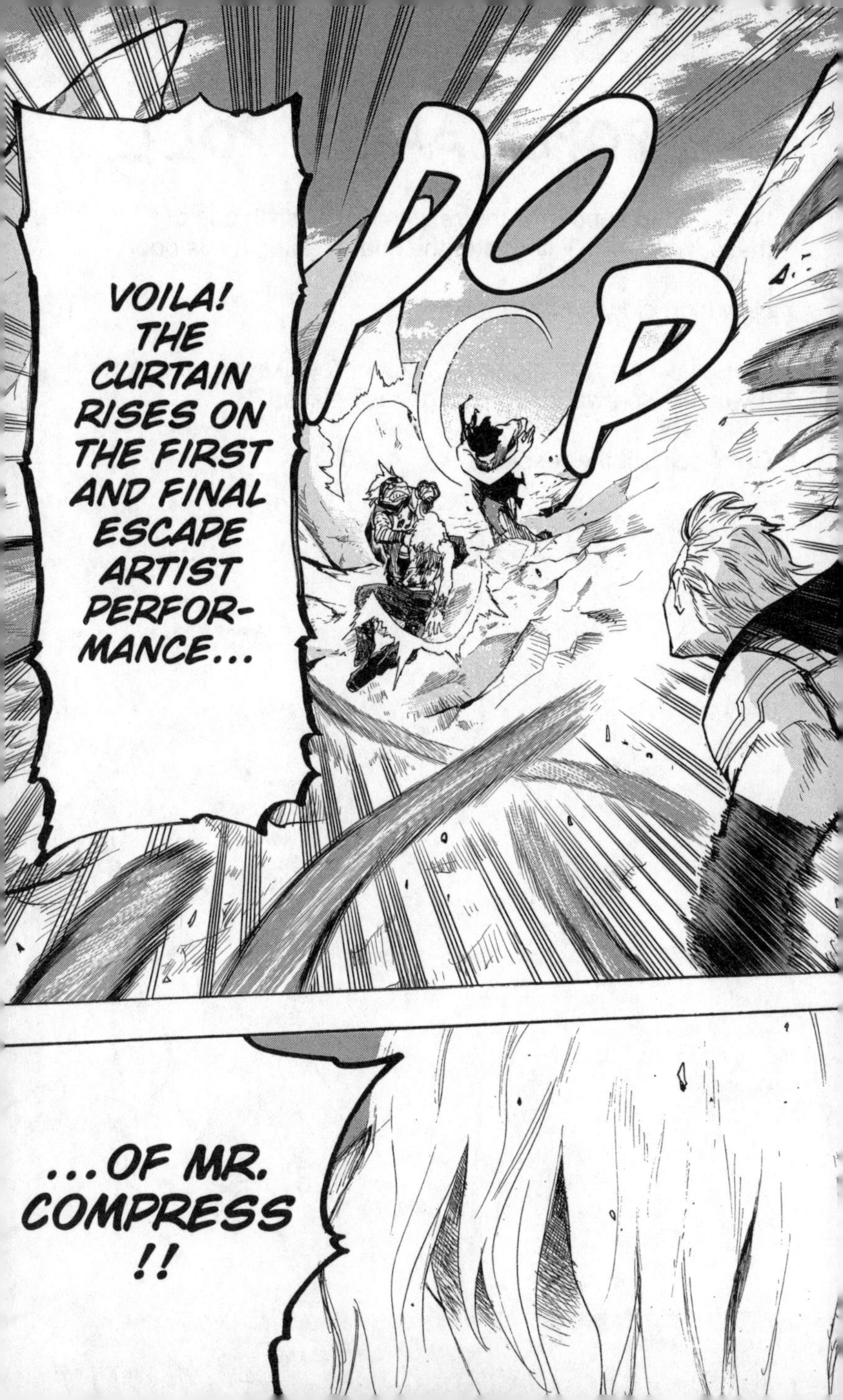
POP
VOILA! THE CURTAIN RISES ON THE FIRST AND FINAL ESCAPE ARTIST PERFORMANCE...
...OF MR. COMPRESS !!

THE POPULARITY POLL

I'm proud to announce the results for the sixth one of these, which you'll find after the final chapter in this book.

How high did your faves place?

Tsutsutaka Agoyamato and Chikuchi Togeike are some of my faves, so I wonder how high they placed?*

Go check out the results!

*Agoyamato came in 152nd place with two votes, and Togeike did not receive any votes.

You all sent in lots of votes!
Thanks for that!

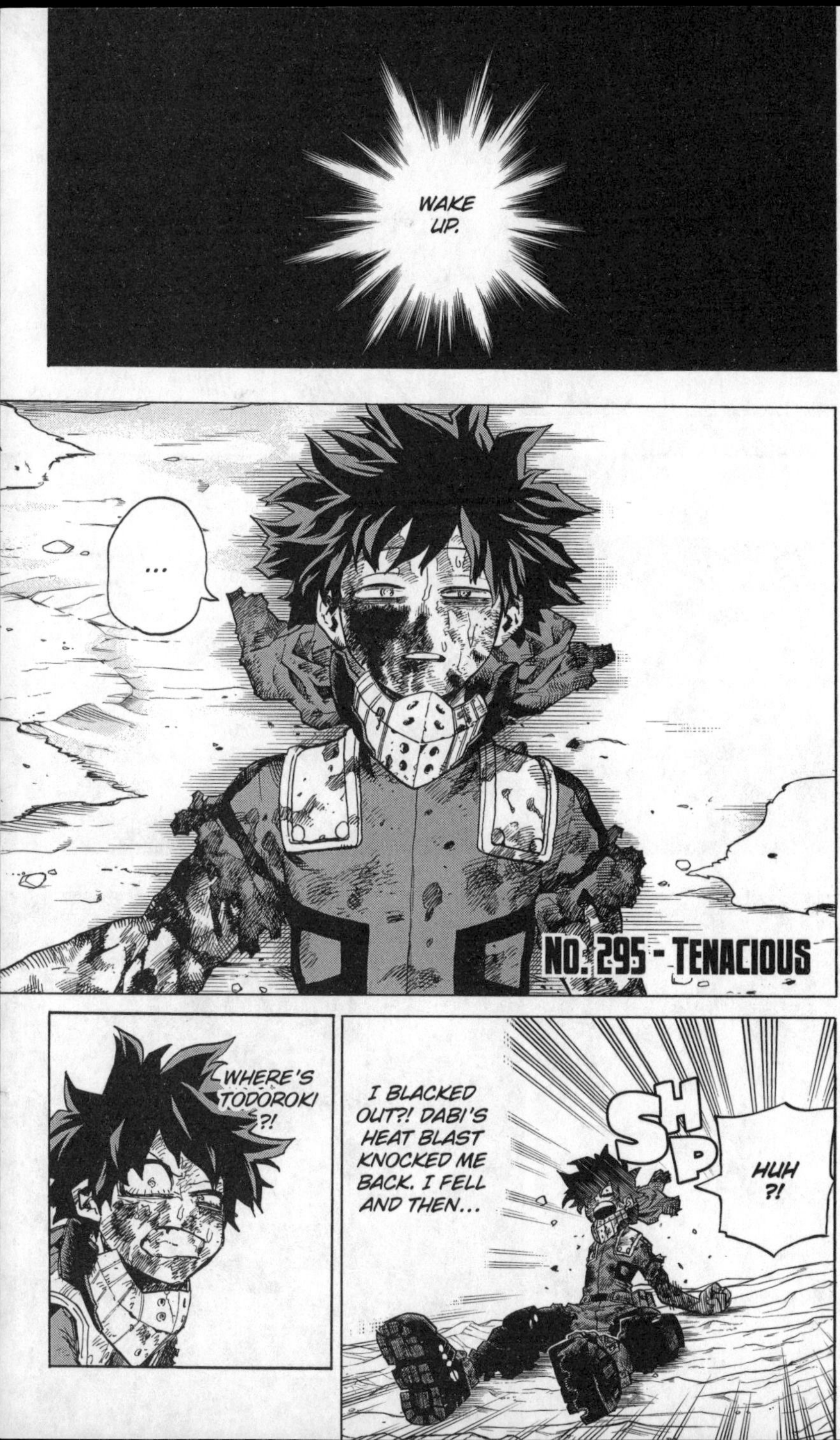
WAKE UP.
...
NO. 295 - TENACIOUS
HUH ?!
SHP
I BLACKED OUT?! DABI'S HEAT BLAST KNOCKED ME BACK. I FELL AND THEN...
WHERE'S TODOROKI ?!

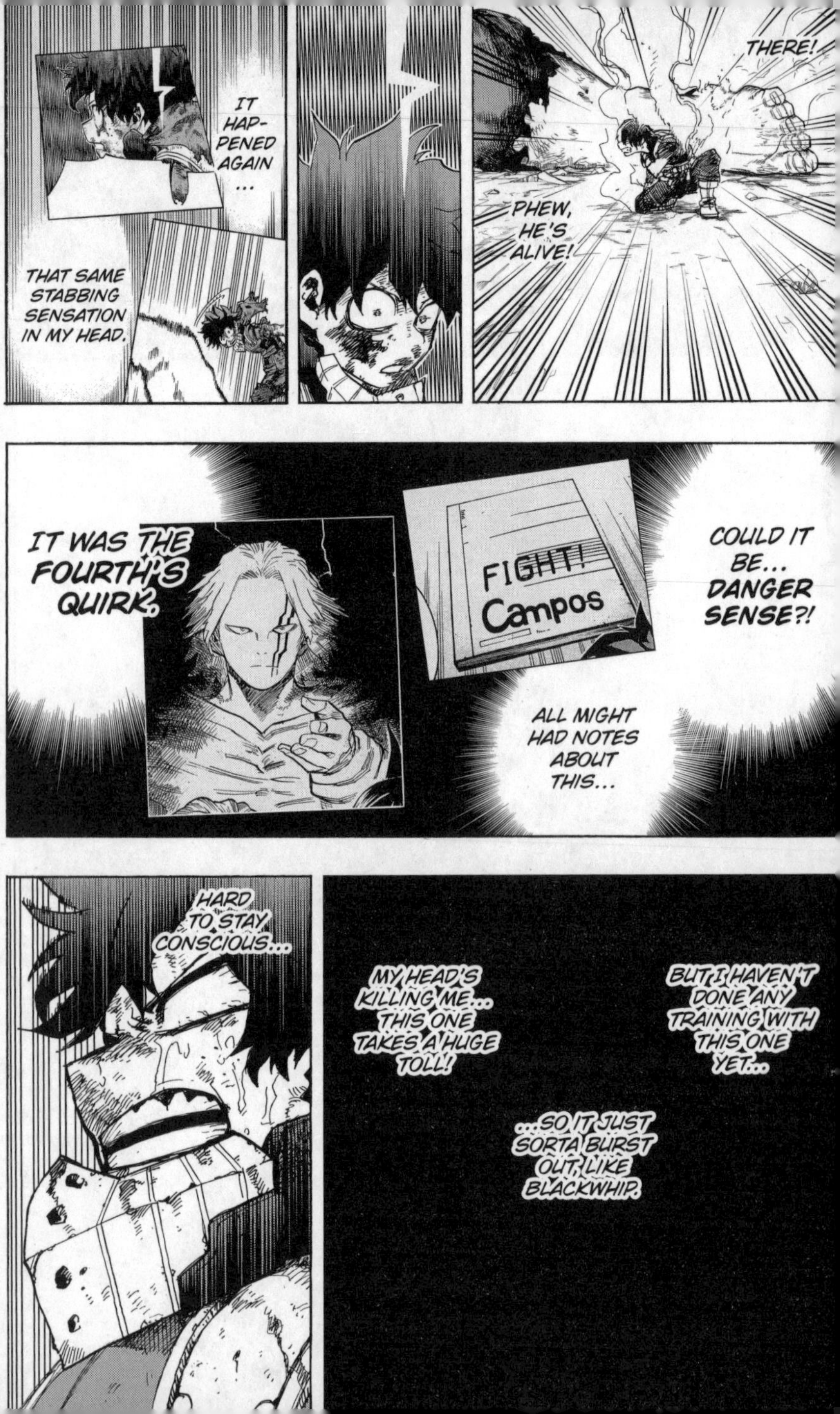
THERE!
PHEW, HE'S ALIVE!
IT HAPPENED AGAIN...
THAT SAME STABBING SENSATION IN MY HEAD.
COULD IT BE... DANGER SENSE?!
ALL MIGHT HAD NOTES ABOUT THIS...
FIGHT! Campos
IT WAS THE FOURTH'S QUIRK.
BUT I HAVEN'T DONE ANY TRAINING WITH THIS ONE YET...
MY HEAD'S KILLING ME... THIS ONE TAKES A HUGE TOLL!
...SO IT JUST SORTA BURST OUT, LIKE BLACKWHIP.
HARD TO STAY CONSCIOUS...

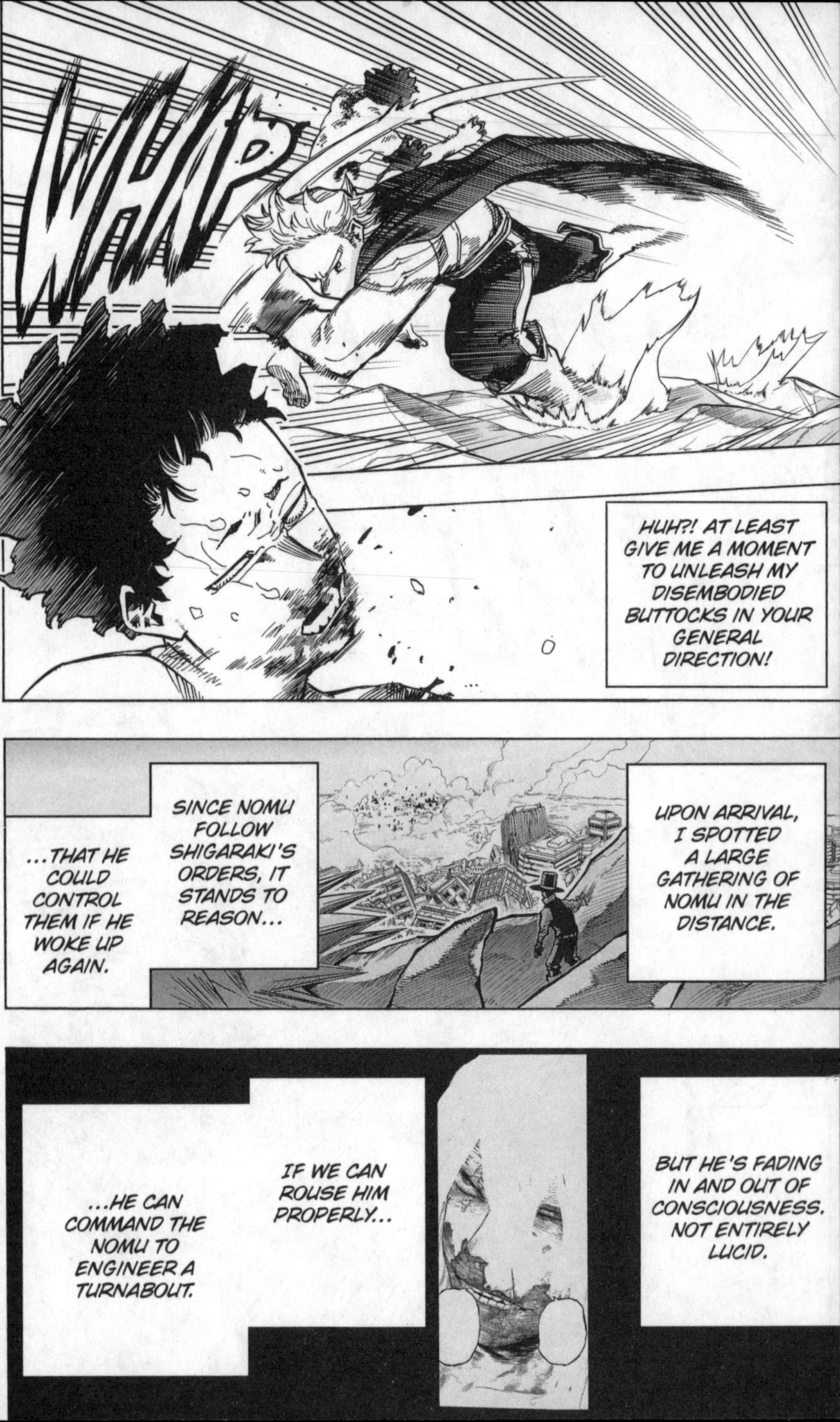
WHAP
HUH?! AT LEAST GIVE ME A MOMENT TO UNLEASH MY DISEMBODIED BUTTOCKS IN YOUR GENERAL DIRECTION!
UPON ARRIVAL, I SPOTTED A LARGE GATHERING OF NOMU IN THE DISTANCE.
SINCE NOMU FOLLOW SHIGARAKI'S ORDERS, IT STANDS TO REASON...
...THAT HE COULD CONTROL THEM IF HE WOKE UP AGAIN.
BUT HE'S FADING IN AND OUT OF CONSCIOUSNESS. NOT ENTIRELY LUCID.
IF WE CAN ROUSE HIM PROPERLY...
...HE CAN COMMAND THE NOMU TO ENGINEER A TURNABOUT.

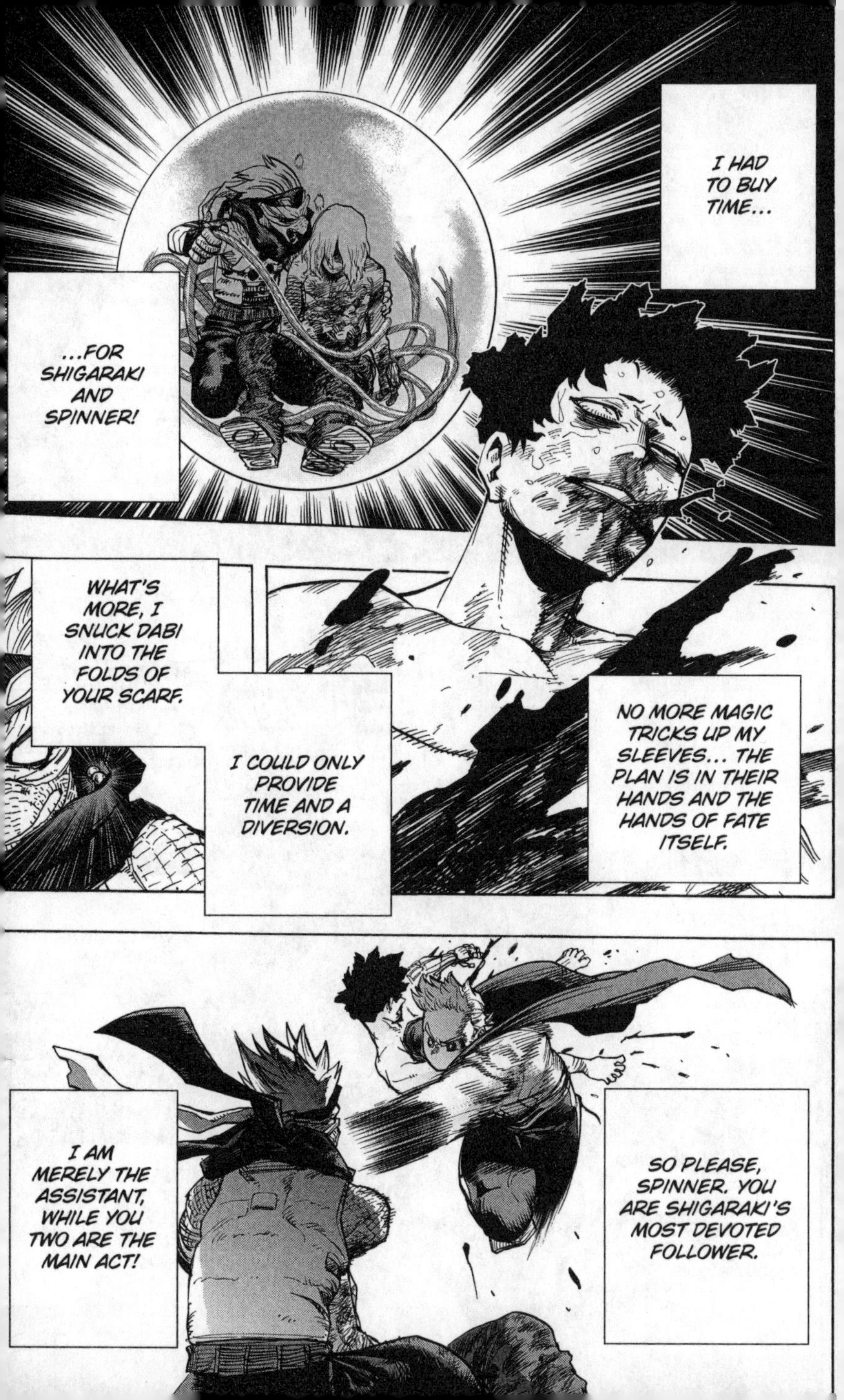
I HAD TO BUY TIME...
...FOR SHIGARAKI AND SPINNER!
NO MORE MAGIC TRICKS UP MY SLEEVES... THE PLAN IS IN THEIR HANDS AND THE HANDS OF FATE ITSELF.
WHAT'S MORE, I SNUCK DABI INTO THE FOLDS OF YOUR SCARF.
I COULD ONLY PROVIDE TIME AND A DIVERSION.
SO PLEASE, SPINNER. YOU ARE SHIGARAKI'S MOST DEVOTED FOLLOWER.
I AM MERELY THE ASSISTANT, WHILE YOU TWO ARE THE MAIN ACT!

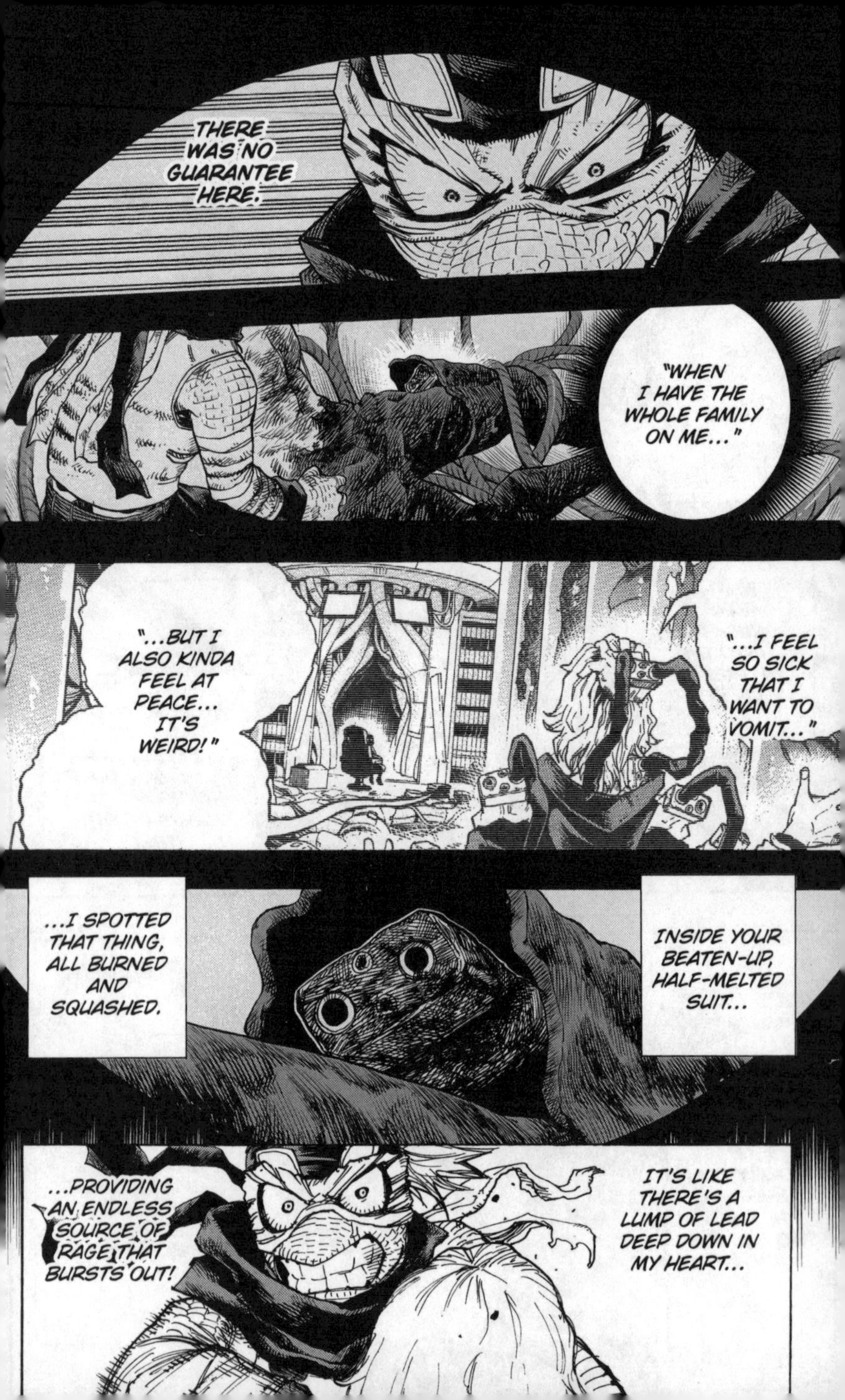
THERE WAS NO GUARANTEE HERE.
"WHEN I HAVE THE WHOLE FAMILY ON ME..."
"...I FEEL SO SICK THAT I WANT TO VOMIT..."
"...BUT I ALSO KINDA FEEL AT PEACE... IT'S WEIRD!"
INSIDE YOUR BEATEN-UP, HALF-MELTED SUIT...
...I SPOTTED THAT THING, ALL BURNED AND SQUASHED.
IT'S LIKE THERE'S A LUMP OF LEAD DEEP DOWN IN MY HEART...
...PROVIDING AN ENDLESS SOURCE OF RAGE THAT BURSTS OUT!

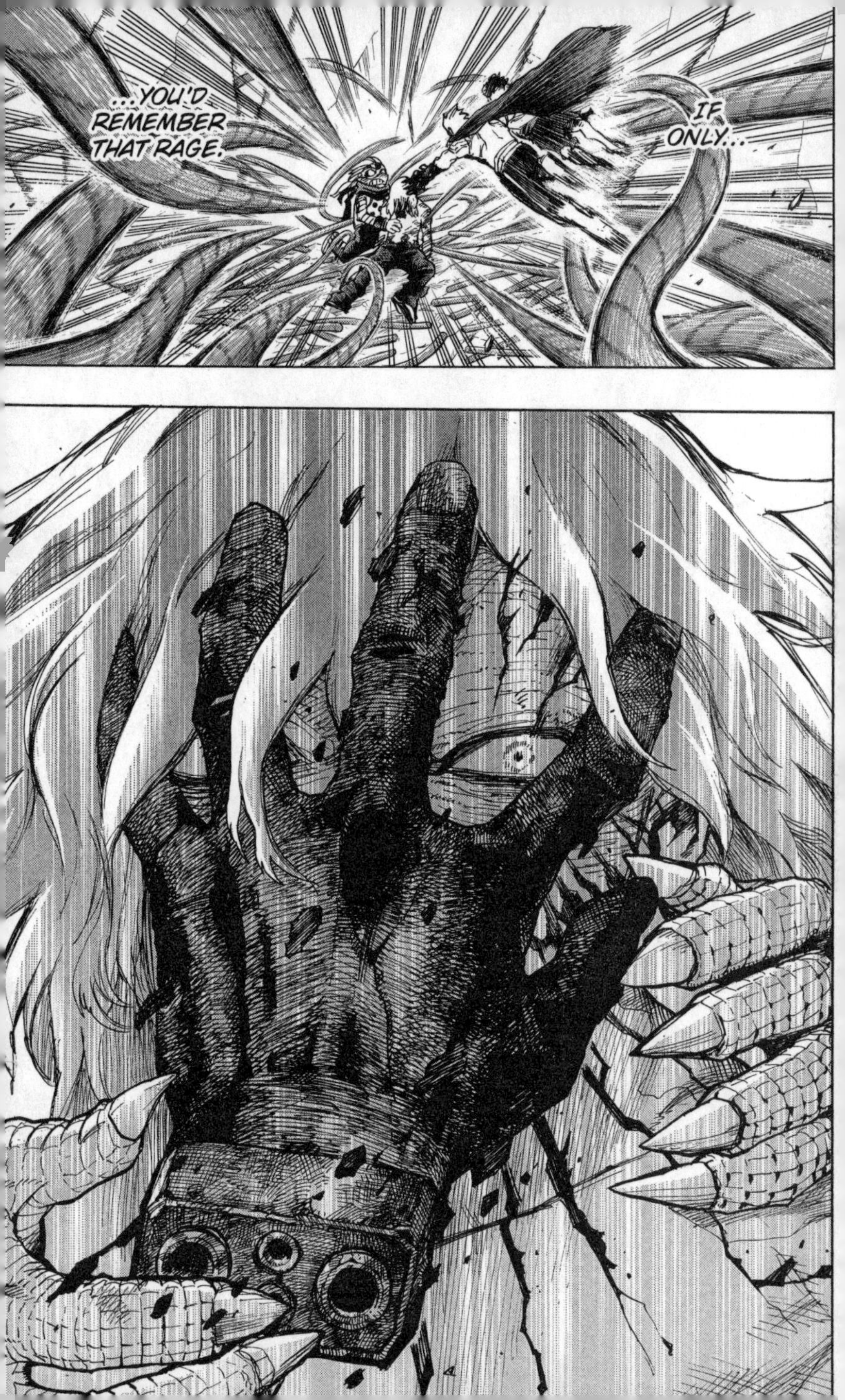
IF ONLY...
...YOU'D REMEMBER THAT RAGE.

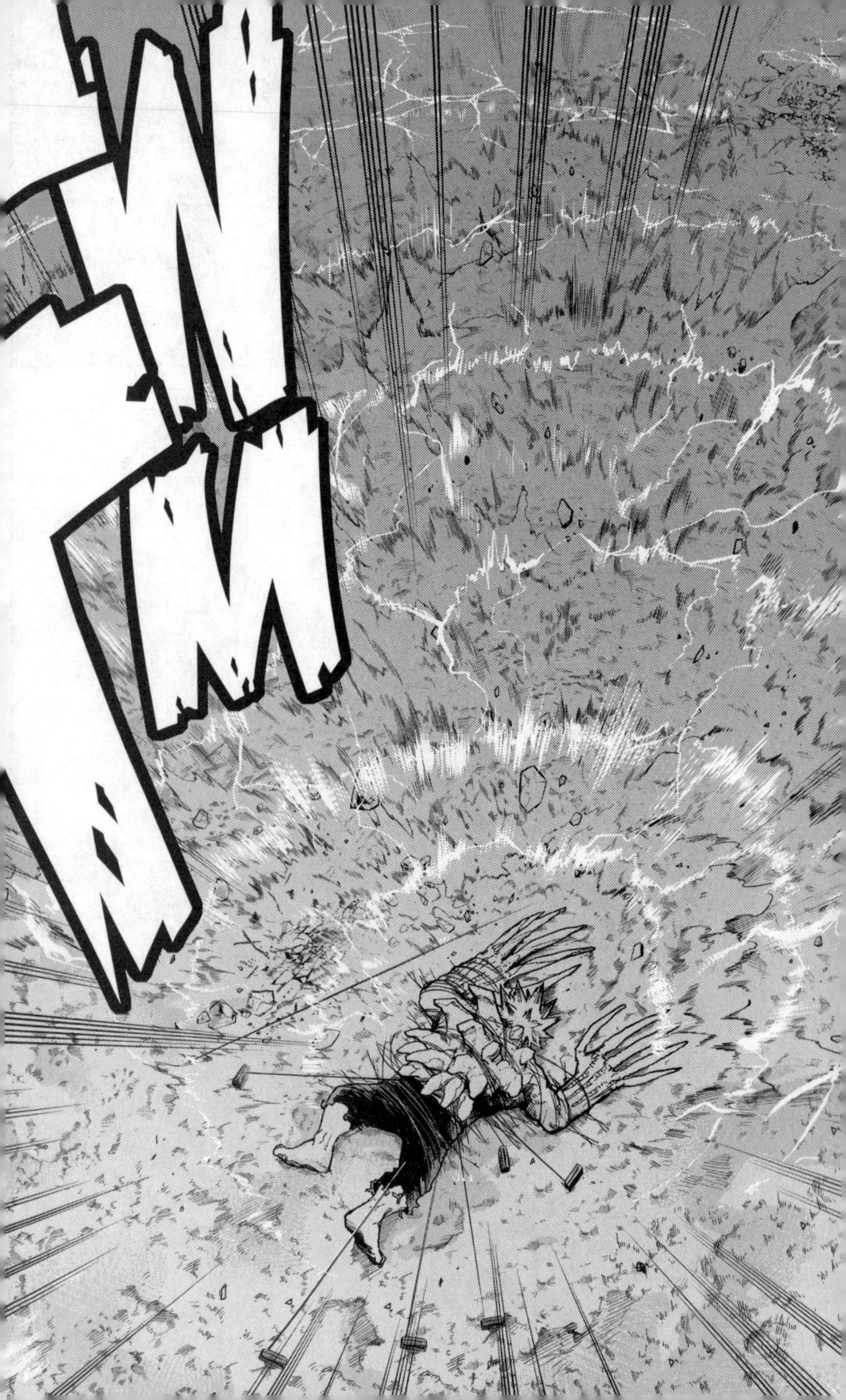

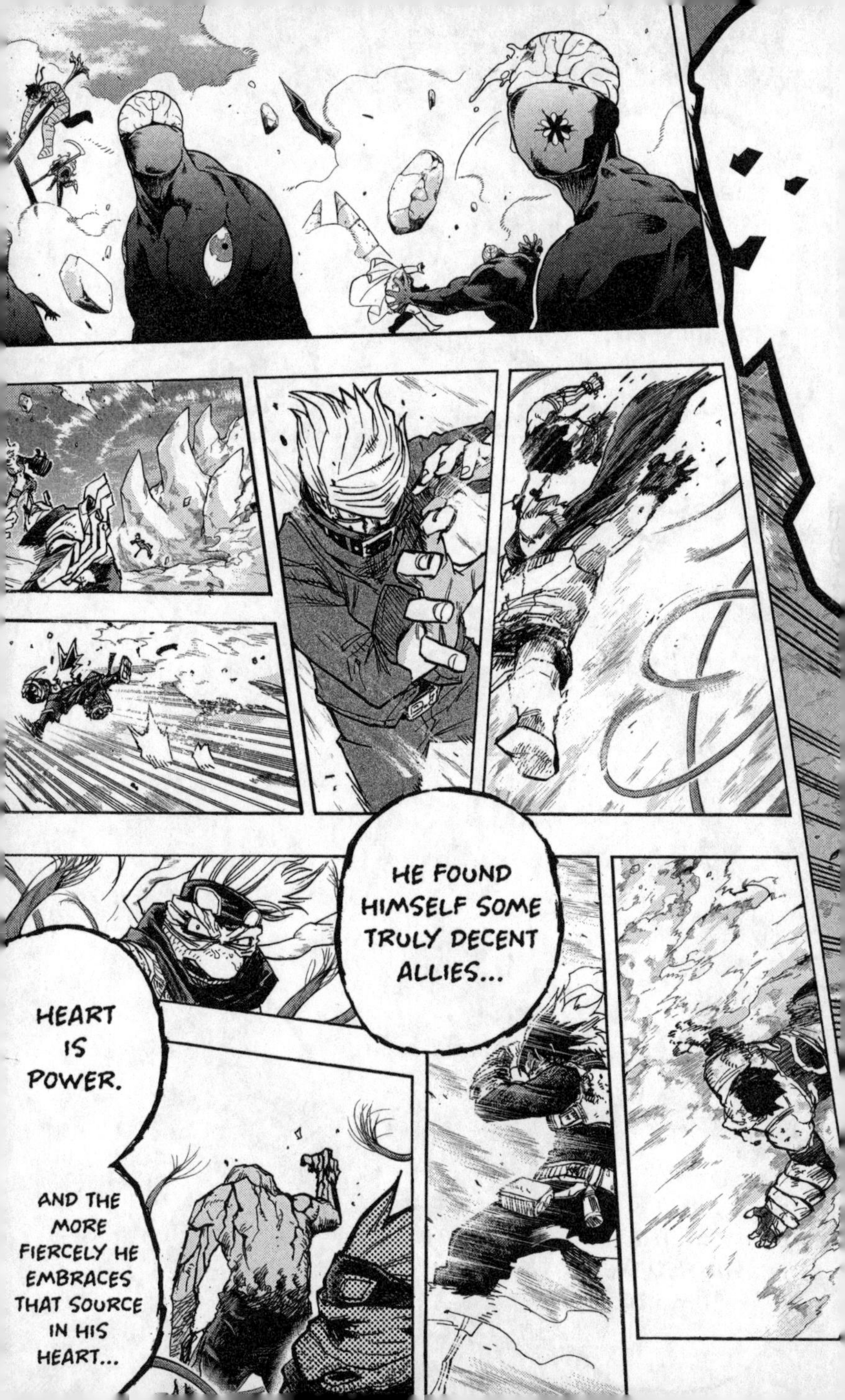
HE FOUND HIMSELF SOME TRULY DECENT ALLIES...
HEART IS POWER.
AND THE MORE FIERCELY HE EMBRACES THAT SOURCE IN HIS HEART...

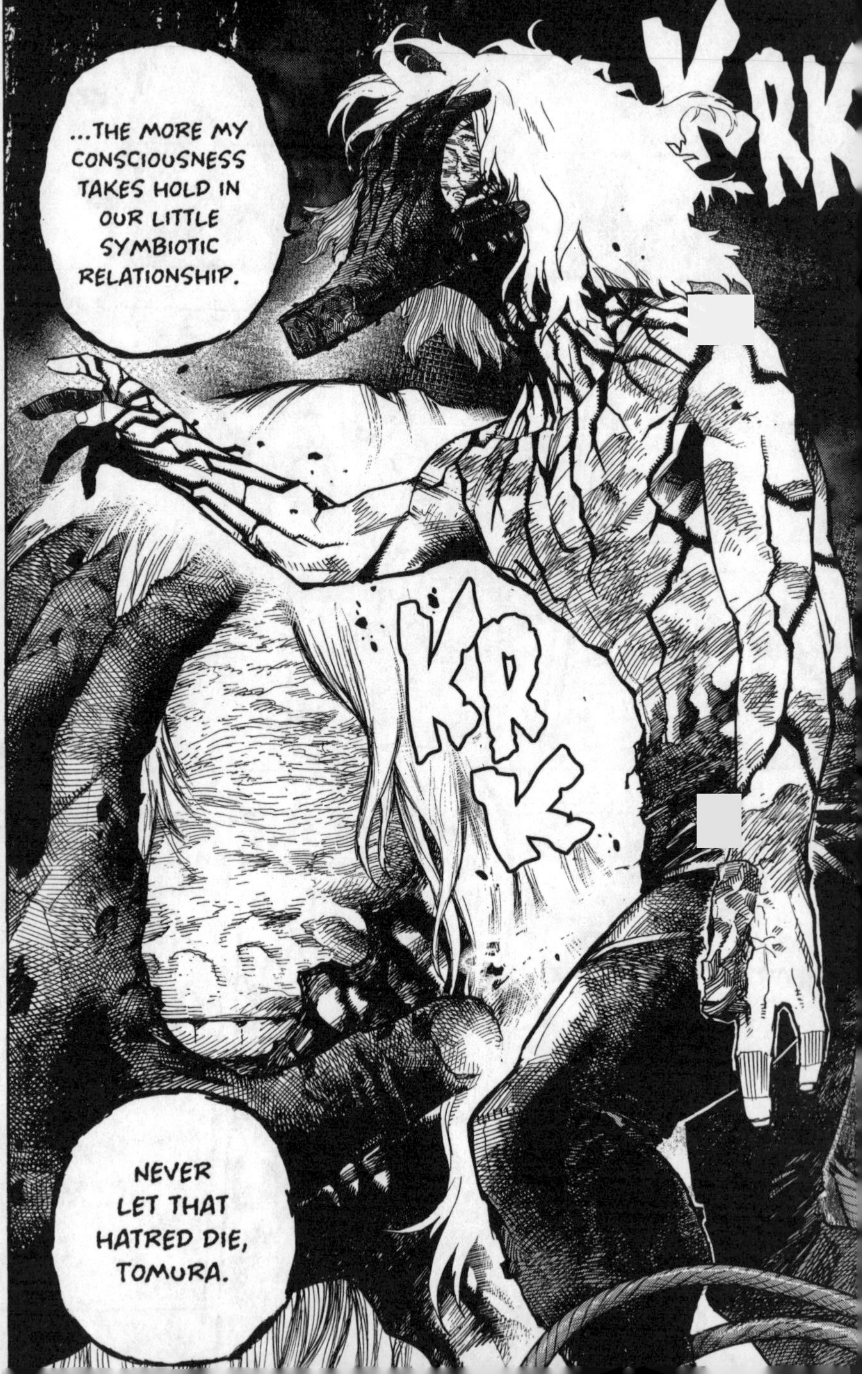
KRK
...THE MORE MY CONSCIOUSNESS TAKES HOLD IN OUR LITTLE SYMBIOTIC RELATIONSHIP.
KRK
NEVER LET THAT HATRED DIE, TOMURA.

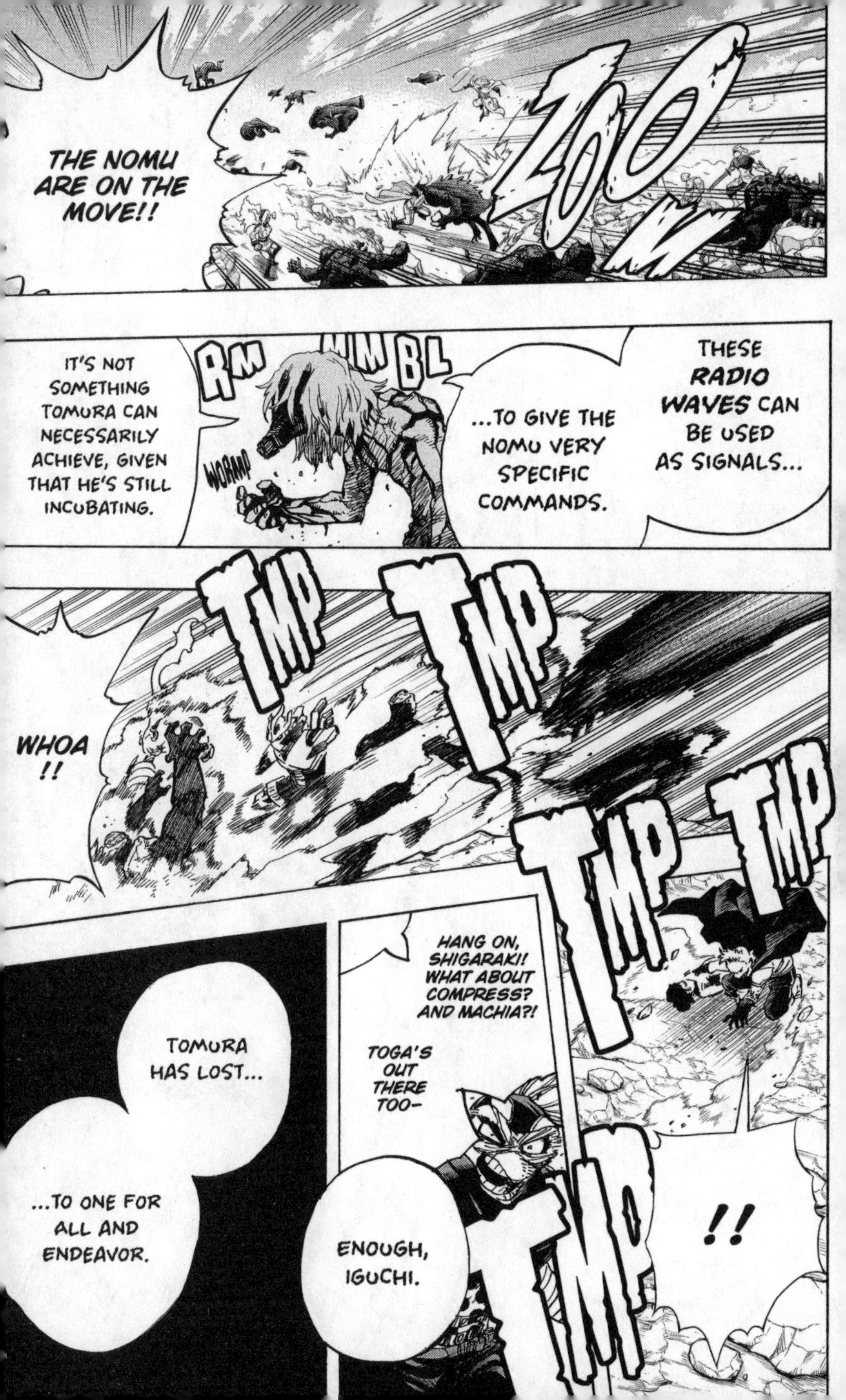
ZOOO
THE NOMU ARE ON THE MOVE!!
THESE RADIO WAVES CAN BE USED AS SIGNALS...
...TO GIVE THE NOMU VERY SPECIFIC COMMANDS.
RMMMBL
WORMP
IT'S NOT SOMETHING TOMURA CAN NECESSARILY ACHIEVE, GIVEN THAT HE'S STILL INCUBATING.
TMP
TMP
WHOA!!
TMP
TMP
HANG ON, SHIGARAKI! WHAT ABOUT COMPRESS? AND MACHIA?!
TOGA'S OUT THERE TOO-
!!
TMP
ENOUGH, IGUCHI.
TOMURA HAS LOST...
...TO ONE FOR ALL AND ENDEAVOR.

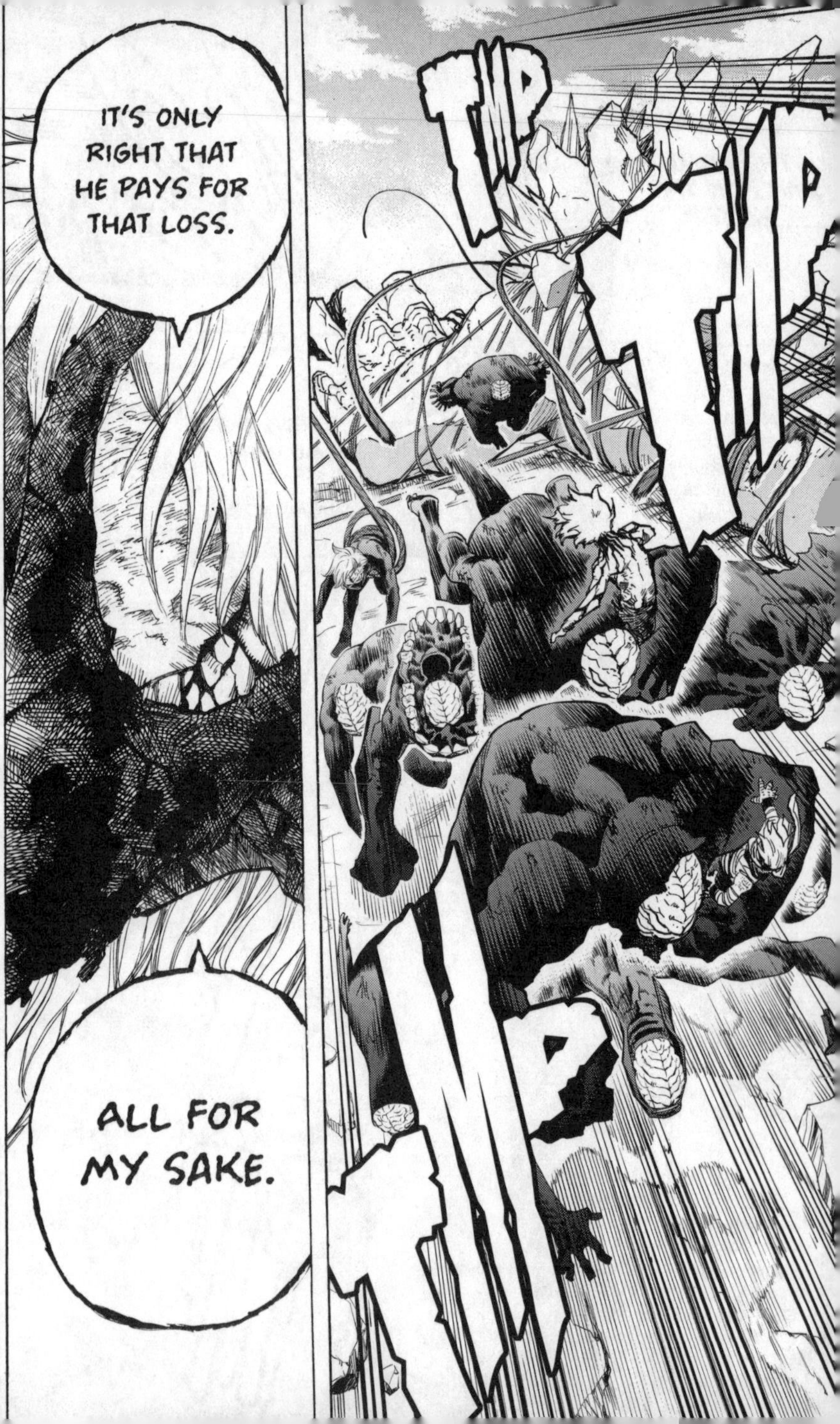
TMP
TMP
TMP
IT'S ONLY RIGHT THAT HE PAYS FOR THAT LOSS.
ALL FOR MY SAKE.

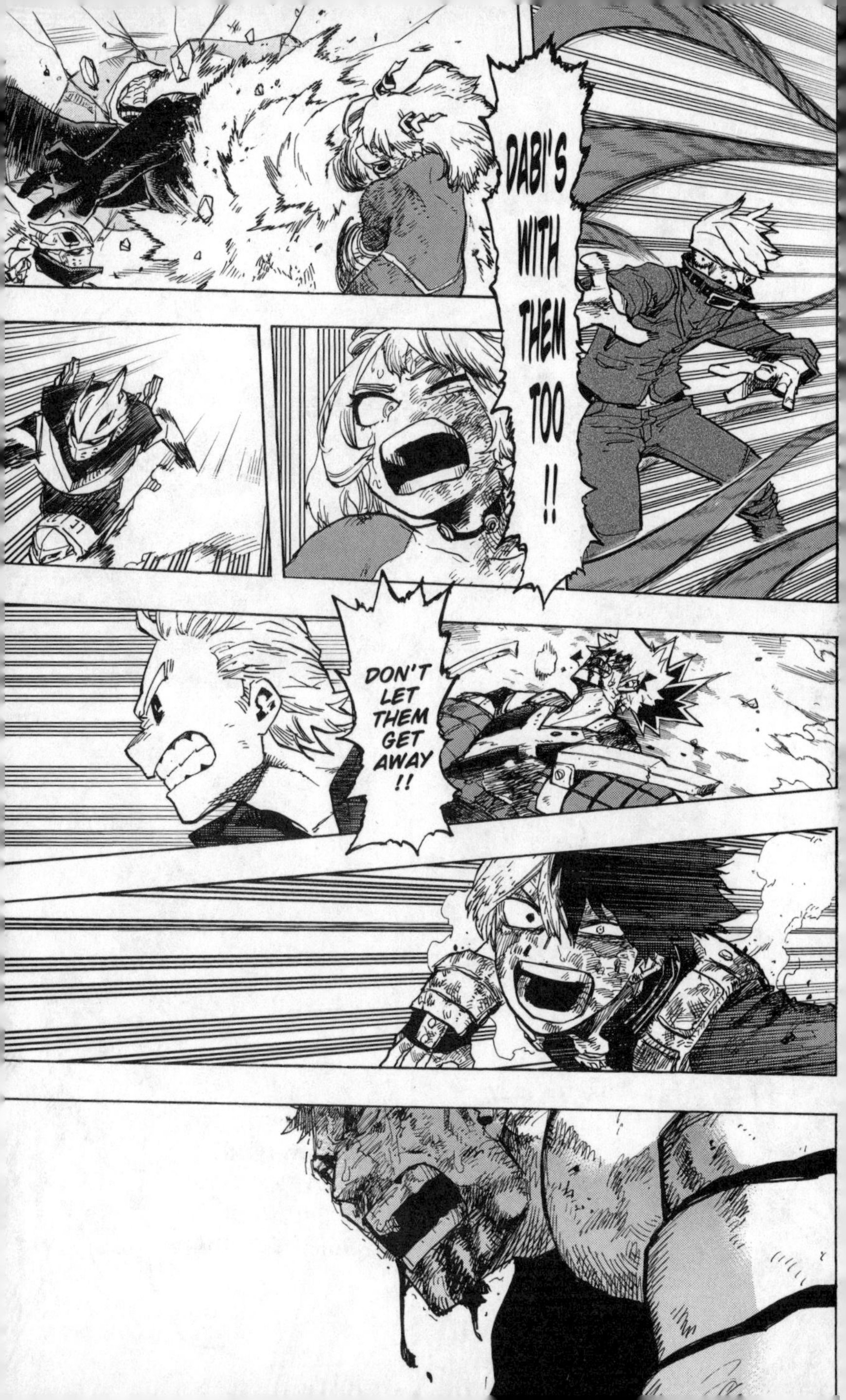
DABI'S WITH THEM TOO !!
DON'T LET THEM GET AWAY !!

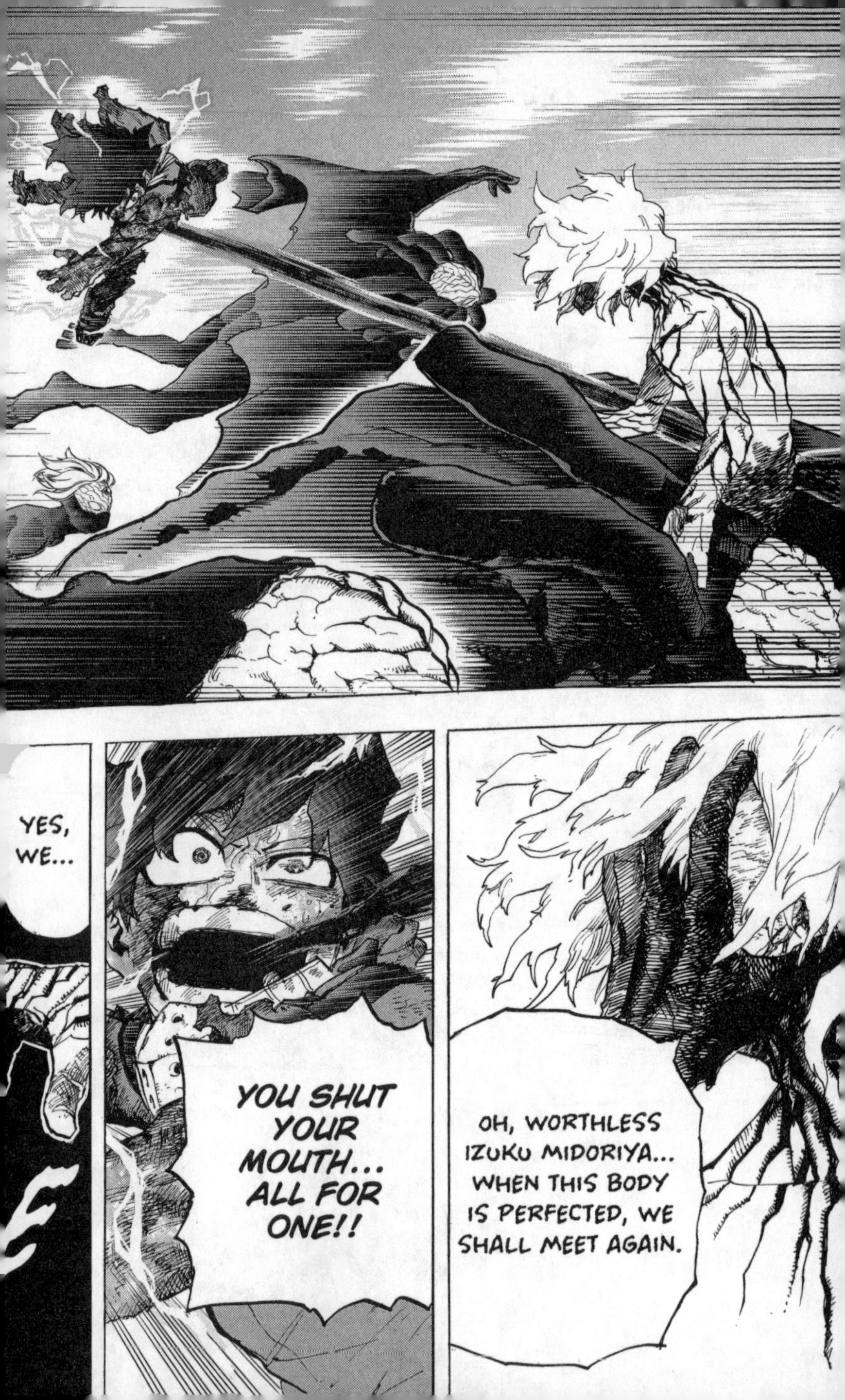
OH, WORTHLESS IZUKU MIDORIYA... WHEN THIS BODY IS PERFECTED, WE SHALL MEET AGAIN.
YOU SHUT YOUR MOUTH... ALL FOR ONE!!
YES, WE...

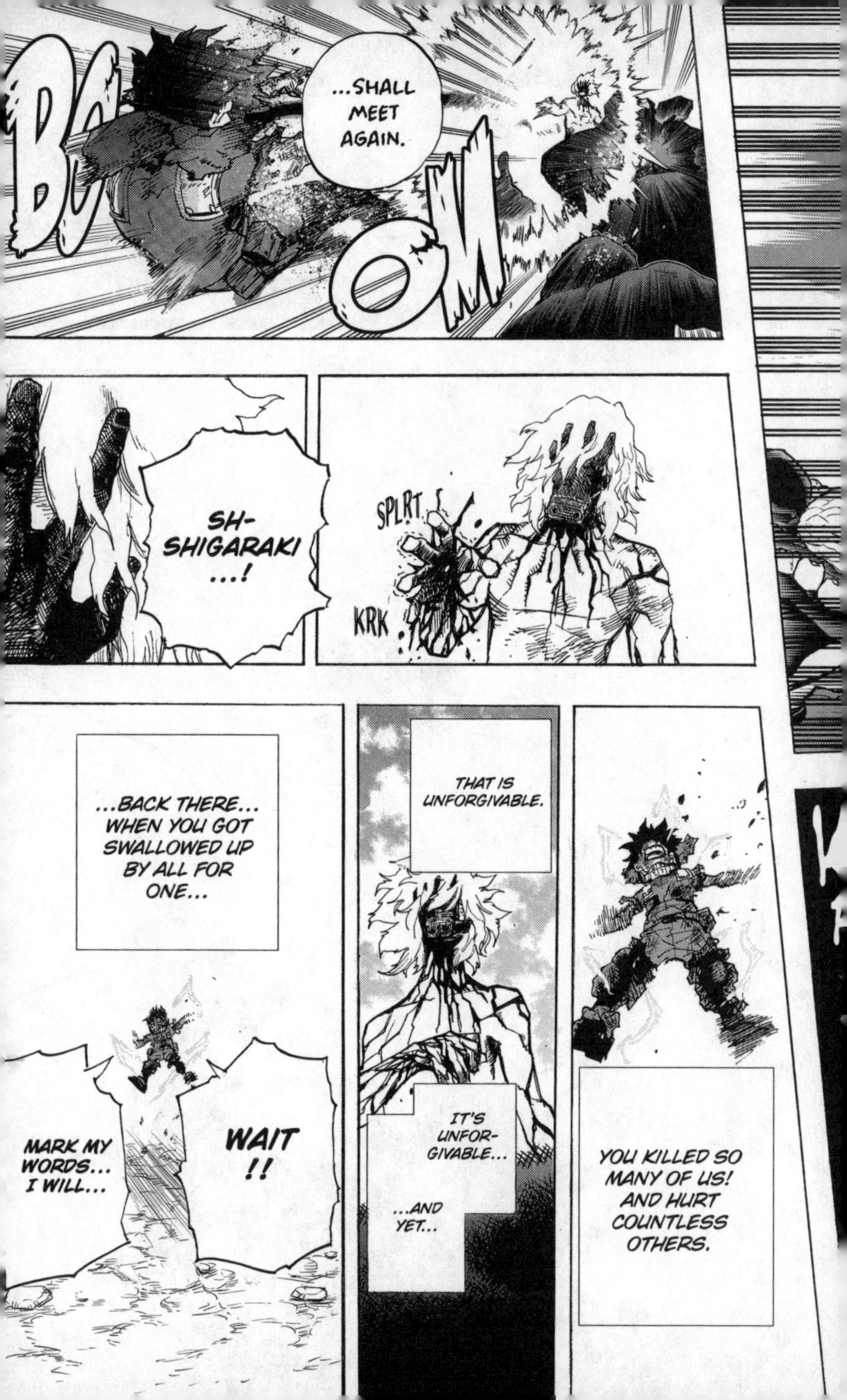
...SHALL MEET AGAIN.
BOOM
SPLRT
KRK
SH-SHIGARAKI ...!
YOU KILLED SO MANY OF US! AND HURT COUNTLESS OTHERS.
THAT IS UNFORGIVABLE.
IT'S UNFORGIVABLE...
...AND YET...
...BACK THERE... WHEN YOU GOT SWALLOWED UP BY ALL FOR ONE...
WAIT !!
MARK MY WORDS... I WILL...

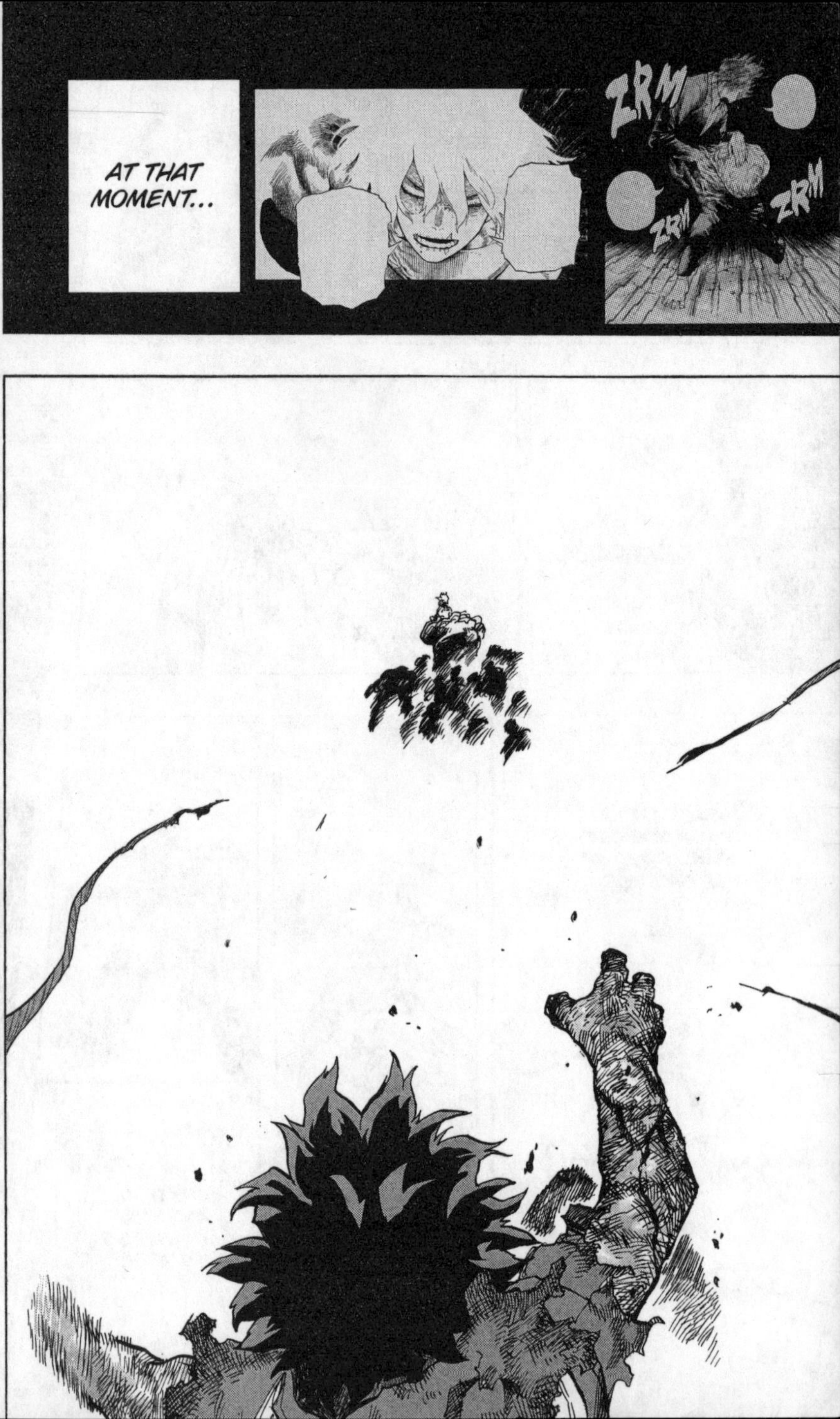
ZRM
ZRM
ZRM
AT THAT MOMENT...

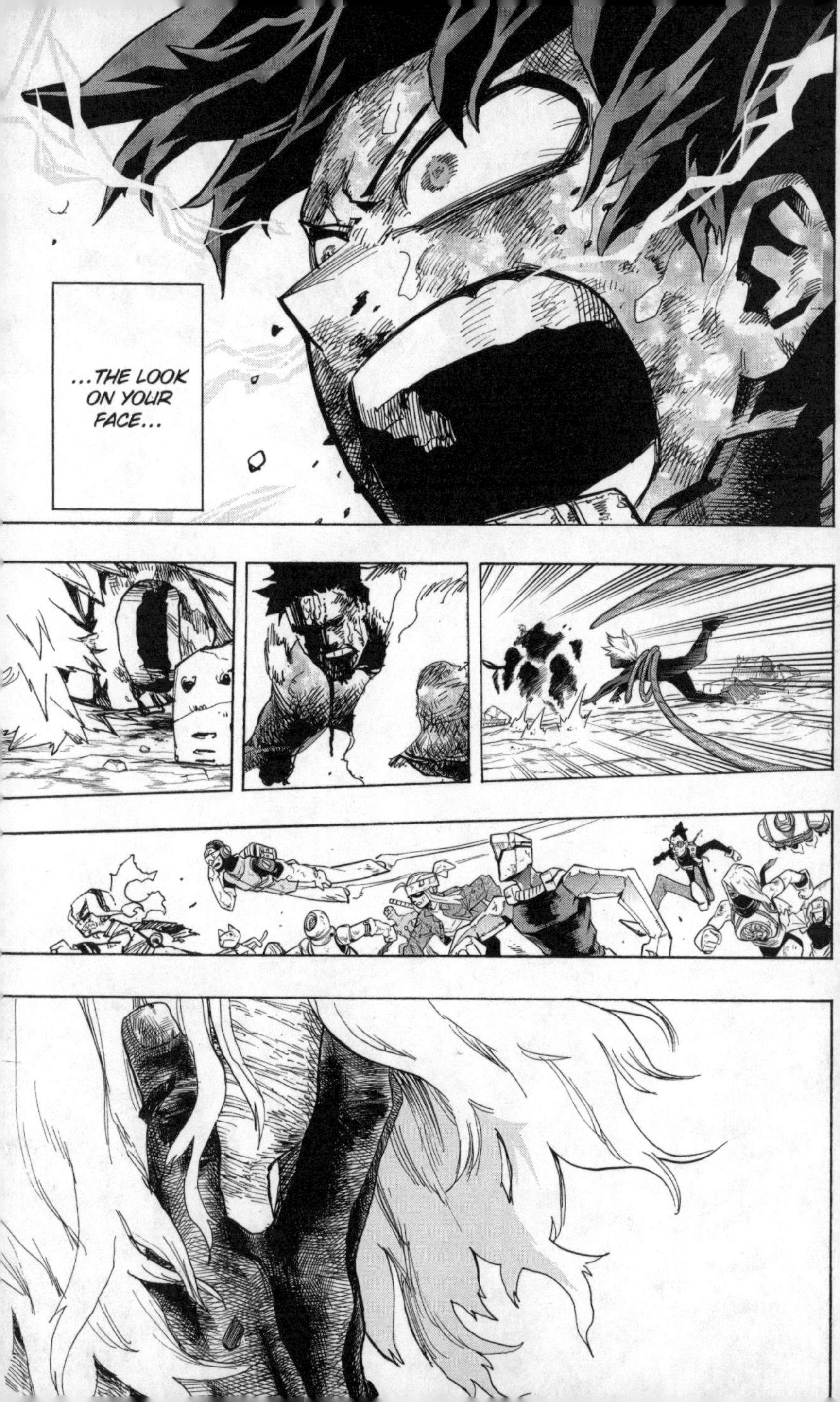
...THE LOOK ON YOUR FACE...

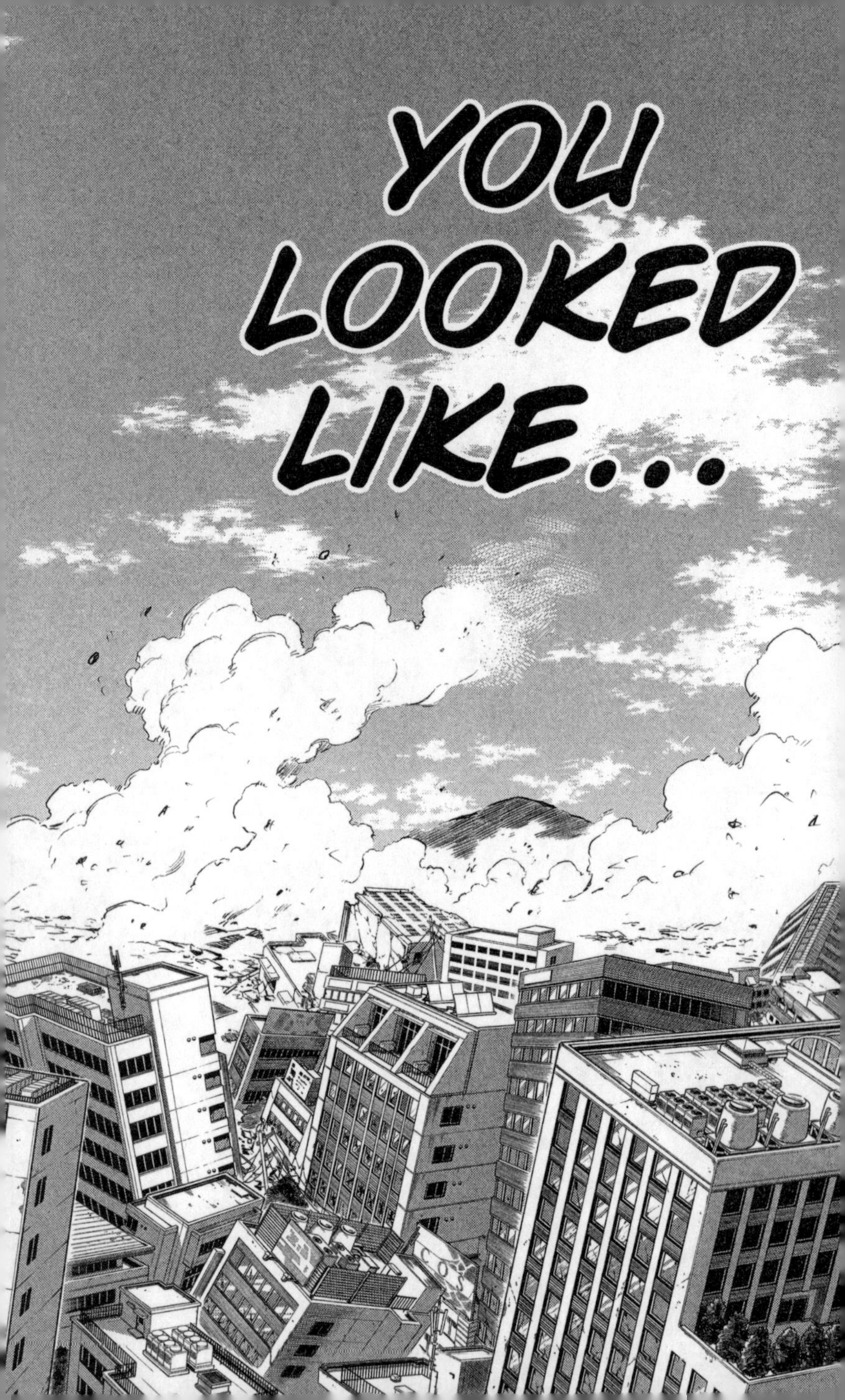
YOU LOOKED LIKE...

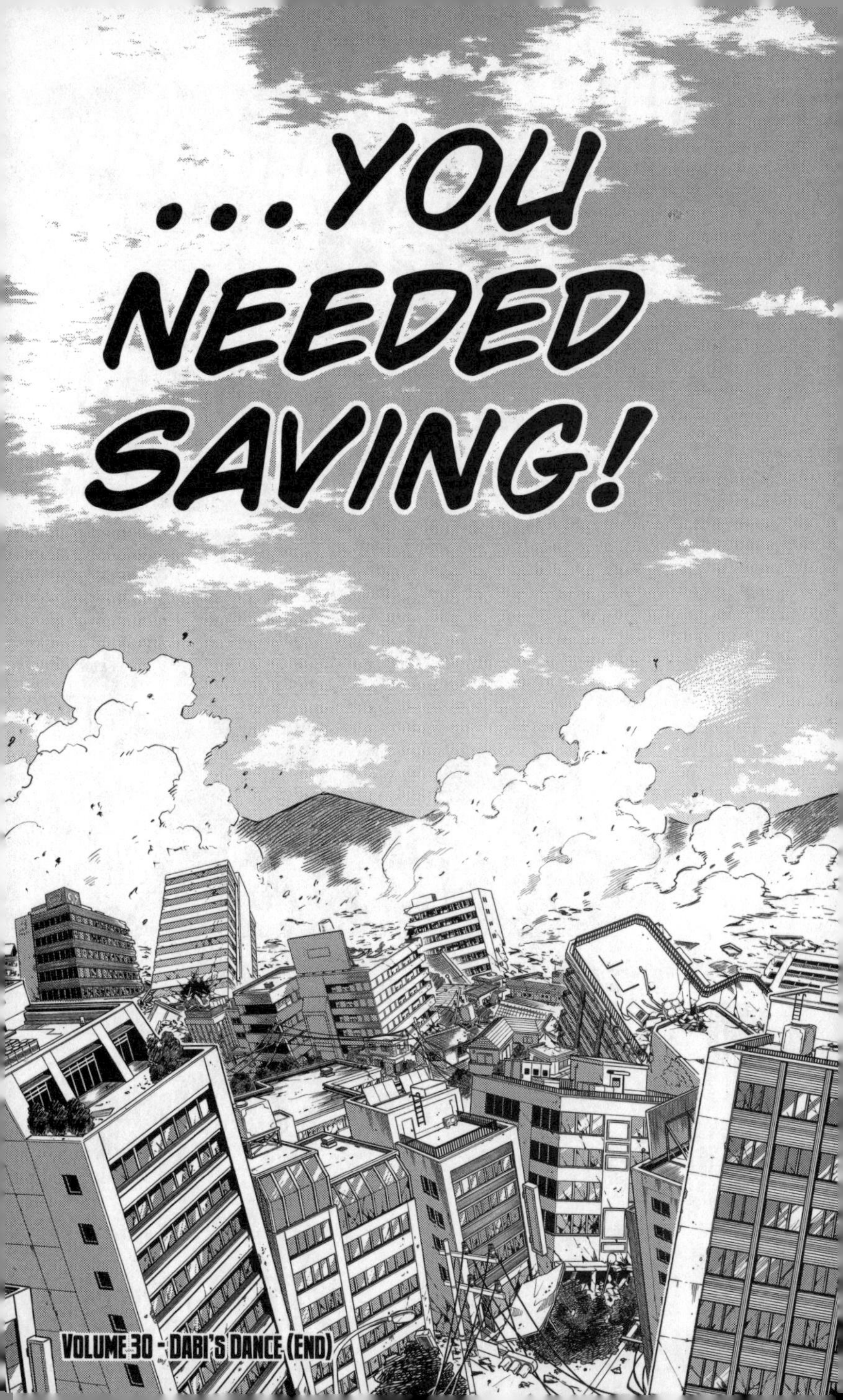
...YOU NEEDED SAVING!
VOLUME 30 - DABI'S DANCE (END)

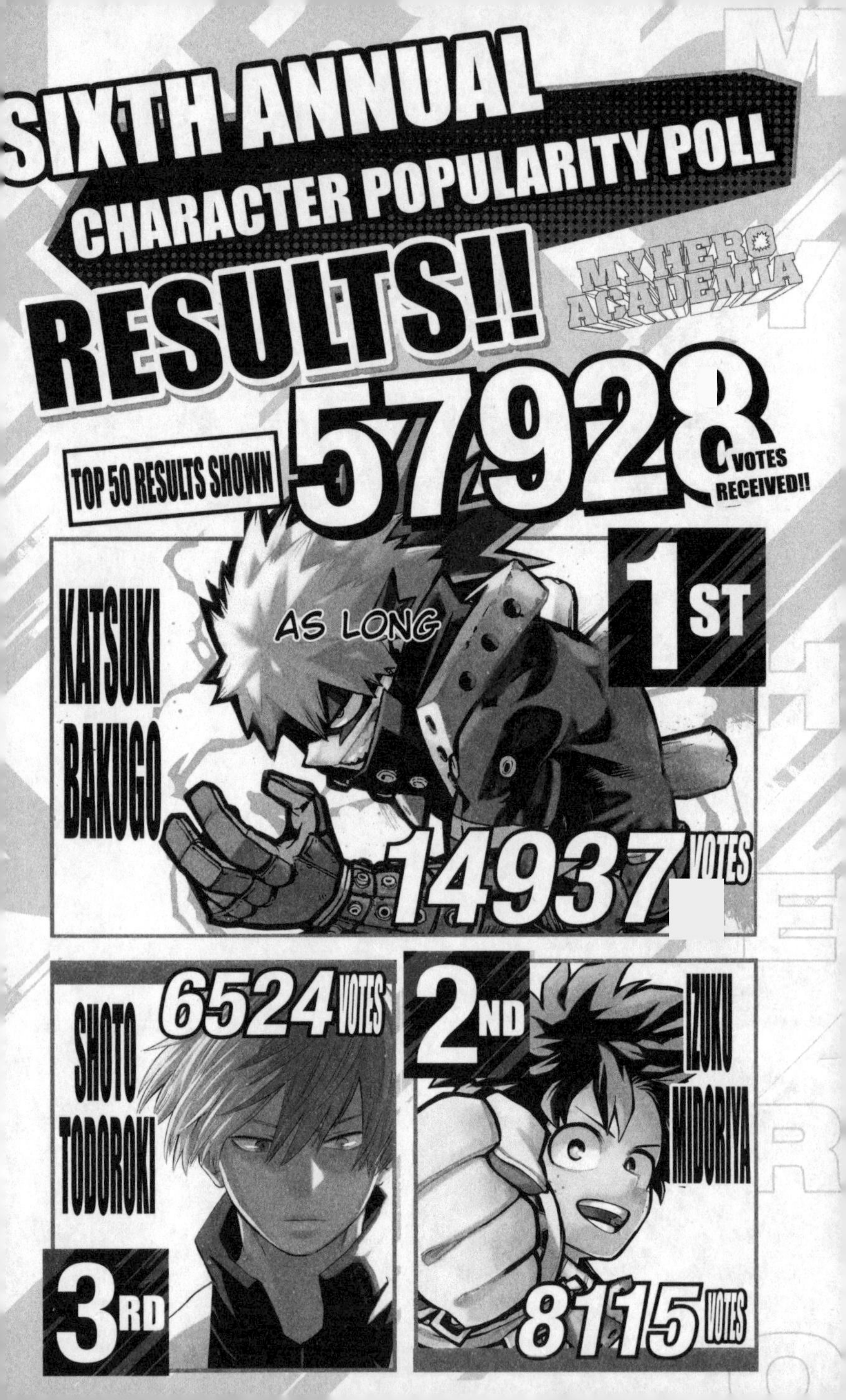
SIXTH ANNUAL
CHARACTER POPULARITY POLL
RESULTS!!
MY HERO ACADEMIA
TOP 50 RESULTS SHOWN
57928 VOTES RECEIVED!!
1ST
KATSUKI BAKUGO
AS LONG
14937 VOTES
2ND
IZUKU MIDORIYA
8115 VOTES
3RD
SHOTO TODOROKI
6524 VOTES

EIJIRO KIRISHIMA

6TH *1999* VOTES

ERASER HEAD

5TH *2708* VOTES

TENYA IDA

4TH *3722* VOTES

TOMURA SHIGARAKI

10TH *1170* VOTES

YO SHINDO

9TH *1244* VOTES

ENDEAVOR

8TH *1344* VOTES

HAWKS

7TH *1962* VOTES

11th:	Present Mic		(1167 votes)
12th:	Momo Yaoyorozu		(1047 votes)
13th:	Denki Kaminari		(905 votes)
14th:	All Might (Symbol of Peace)		(746 votes)
15th:	Kyoka Jiro		(629 votes)
16th:	Ochaco Uraraka		(616 votes)
17th:	Himiko Toga		(606 votes)
18th:	Fumikage Tokoyami		(502 votes)
19th:	Mirio Togata		(493 votes)
20th:	Mirko		(492 votes)
21st:	Tsuyu Asui		(482 votes)
22nd:	Dabi		(478 votes)
23rd:	Nejire Hado		(376 votes)
24th:	Hitoshi Shinso		(354 votes)
25th:	Tamaki Amajiki		(312 votes)
26th:	Twice		(272 votes)
27th:	Sir Nighteye		(267 votes)
28th:	Mina Ashido		(253 votes)
29th:	Hanta Sero		(229 votes)
30th:	Fat Gum		(214 votes)
31st:	Chronostasis		(206 votes)
32nd:	Overhaul		(196 votes)
33rd:	Mezo Shoji		(188 votes)
34th:	Best Jeanist		(173 votes)
35th:	Mashirao Ojiro		(166 votes)
36th:	Mustard		(146 votes)
37th:	Magne		(140 votes)
38th:	Eri		(125 votes)
39th:	Horikoshi Sensei		(110 votes)
40th:	Minoru Mineta		(84 votes)
41st:	Neito Monoma		(80 votes)
42nd:	Yuga Aoyama		(65 votes)
43rd:	Mei Hatsume		(63 votes)
44th:	Toru Hagakure		(59 votes)
45th:	Seiji Shishikura		(55 votes)
46th:	Toya Setsuno		(54 votes)
47th:	Mt. Lady		(53 votes)
48th:	Oboro Shirakumo		(51 votes)
49th:	All For One		(43 votes)
50th:	Cementoss		(37 votes)

Based on a poll taken in Weekly Shonen Jump in Japan, January 2021.

VILLAINS

THE GROWN-UP

MR. COMPRESS (32) (ATSUHIRO SAKO)

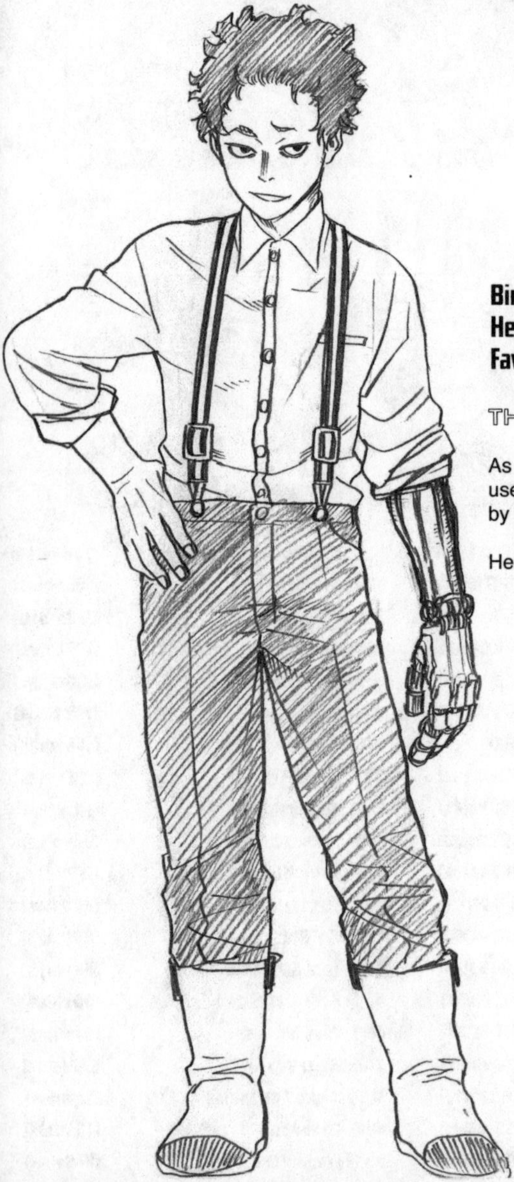

Birthday: 10/8
Height: 181 cm
Favorite Thing: Magic

THE SUPPLEMENT

As a former magician, he's used to just barely scraping by in life.

He'll be back.

THE CONTRIBUTIONS

This old standby!! We've got more art contributions from the spin-off artists!!

Vigilantes' Betten Sensei!!

And **Team-Up Missions' Akiyama Sensei!!**

Both are way bigger experts than me when it comes to art, so every time I receive these gifts, I'm like, "Whoaaaa, dude!"

Turn the page, and you'll get to see that art! Thrilling, right?

Also, *Vigilantes* volume 12 and *Team-Up Missions* volume 2 are on sale now (in Japan)!! Don't forget to read those too!

THE AFTERWORD
(LET'S ABBREVIATE AS T.A.W.)

We've made it to volume 30. At some point, I wrote about how 30 volumes was my original estimate for the series' total length. So I'm just as surprised as anyone that the story is taking so long to tell.

In the last volume, I said that this one would represent a big turning point, which was referring to the end of the giant battle. But the story goes on! Thanks for your continued support, as always!

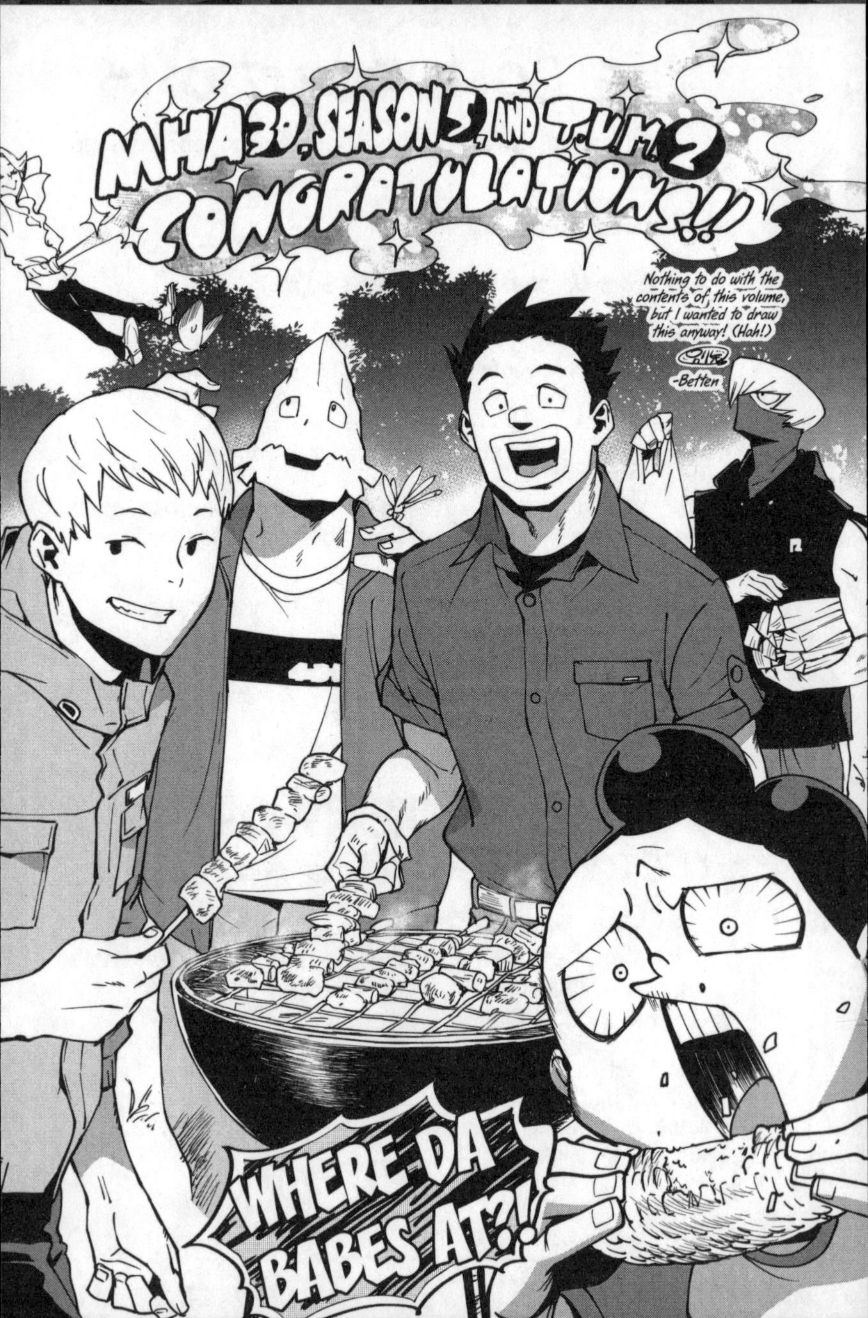
MHA 30, SEASON 5, AND T.U.M. 2
CONGRATULATIONS!!
Nothing to do with the contents of this volume, but I wanted to draw this anyway! (Hah!)
-Betten
WHERE DA BABES AT?!

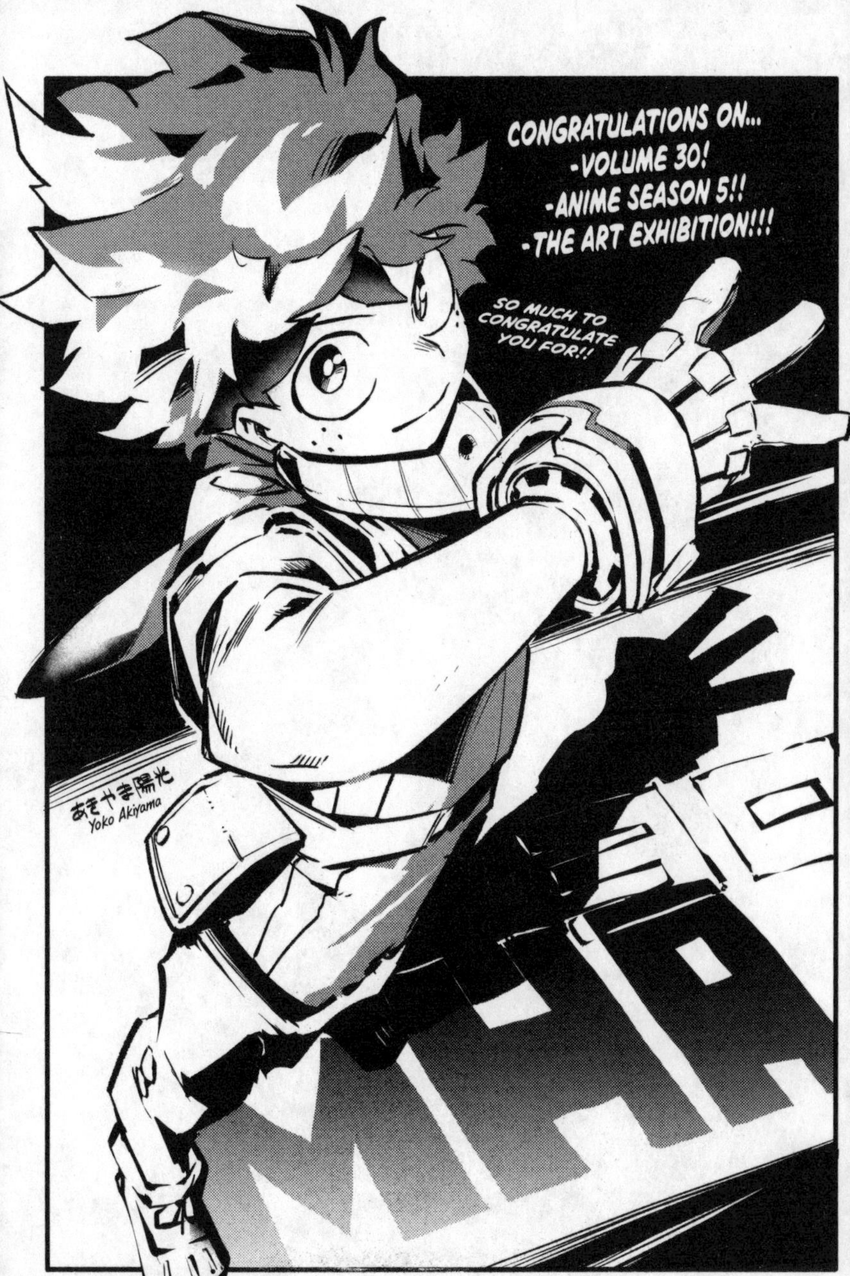
CONGRATULATIONS ON...
-VOLUME 30!
-ANIME SEASON 5!!
-THE ART EXHIBITION!!!
SO MUCH TO CONGRATULATE YOU FOR!!
あきやま陽光
Yoko Akiyama

CAN MUSCLES CRUSH MAGIC?!

MAGIC AND MUSCLES

STORY AND ART BY
HAJIME KOMOTO

I n the magic realm, magic is everything—everyone can use it, and one's skill determines their social status. Deep in the forest, oblivious to the ways of the world, lives Mash. Thanks to his daily training, he's become a fitness god. When Mash is discovered, he has no choice but to enroll in magic school where he must beat the competition without revealing his secret—he can't use magic!

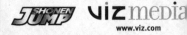

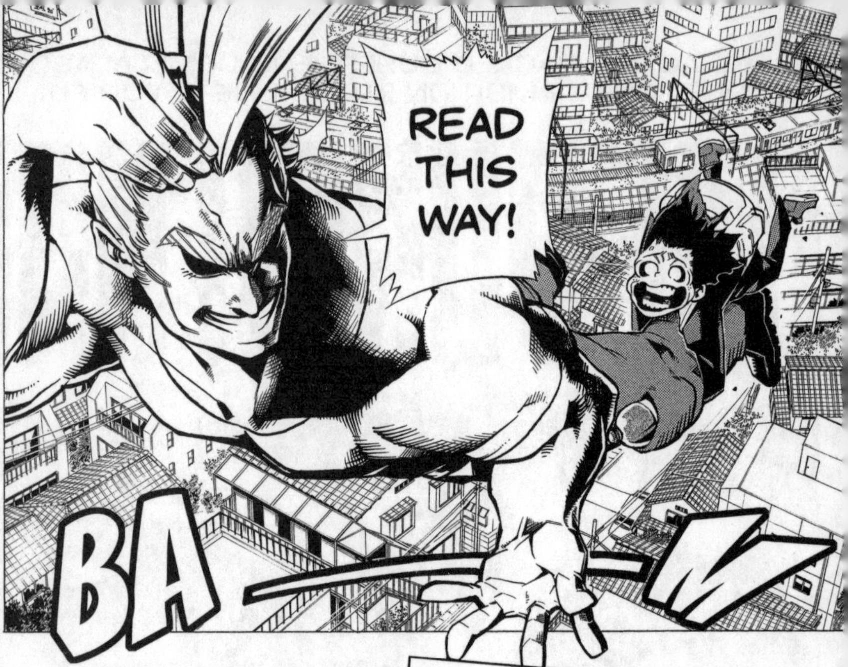
READ THIS WAY!
BA-M

MY HERO ACADEMIA

reads from right to left, starting in the upper-right corner. Japanese is read from right to left, meaning that action, sound effects, and word-balloon order are completely reversed from English order.

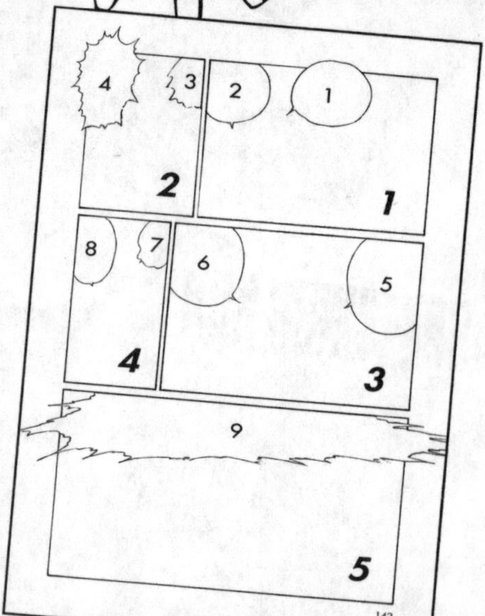
1
2
1
3
4
2
5
6
3
7
8
4
9
5
142